MAIL AND TELEPHONE SURVEYS

Mail and Telephone Surveys

THE TOTAL DESIGN METHOD

DON A. DILLMAN

Washington State University
Pullman, Washington

A WILEY-INTERSCIENCE PUBLICATION

JOHN WILEY & SONS, New York • Chichester • Brisbane • Toronto • Singapore

Library of Congress Cataloging in Publication Data:

Dillman, Don A   1941-
  Mail and telephone surveys.

  "A Wiley-Interscience publication."
  Bibliography: p.
  Includes index.
  1. Social surveys.   2.   Questionnaires.   I.   Title.
HN29.D54   301.15'4   78-581
ISBN 0-471-21555-4

Printed in the United States of America

20 19 18 17 16

To

WALTER L. SLOCUM

PREFACE

This book describes the step-by-step details of how to conduct successful mail and telephone surveys. It is written for the person who has at least a rudimentary knowledge of the purposes and procedures of survey research and wants specific guidance on how to mount a mail or telephone survey. I hope this book enables researchers to conduct their own surveys and to conduct them well.

Students and professional researchers alike are frequently thwarted in their attempts to do survey research because the costly face-to-face interview has heretofore been considered the only viable means of conducting surveys. Recent improvements in procedures for conducting mail and telephone surveys suggest that the inherent limitations that these methods were once thought to have—such as low response rates and dependence on extremely short questionnaires—can be overcome, and that both methods can now compete with face-to-face interviews for many kinds of studies. For certain studies they are superior. The methods reported here provide a potential boon to the researcher with good ideas who lacks the resources to mount a face-to-face interview survey to test those ideas.

The approach to surveying described in this book is called the "total design method" (TDM). This term is a result of the premise on which it is based, namely, to maximize both the quantity and quality of responses, attention must be given to every detail that might affect response behavior. The TDM relies on a theoretically based view of why people do and do not respond to questionnaires and a well-confirmed belief that attention to administrative details is essential to conducting successful surveys.

The development of the TDM was hardly premeditated. Work on it was initiated as a result of the frustration I once experienced in an ill-fated attempt to mount a statewide face-to-face interview survey of the general public in Washington. Several barriers, the common denominator of which was cost, loomed in my way. Unable to locate any others with plans to implement a statewide survey who might allow me to piggyback questions onto their questionnaire and faced with the difficult problem of establishing a sampling frame (it was the year prior to the decennial census in a state that had been experiencing uncommon growth), the effort would have cost far more than my research budget allowed. When I was on the verge of abandoning the project, a colleague suggested that I consider a mail survey. Despite the problems I "thought" mail surveys had, such a survey seemed a better alternative than the others before me—limiting myself to face-to-face interviews in only one county of the state or switching to an entirely different population, such as students or members of a voluntary association. I hesitantly took my colleague's advice and tried a mail questionnaire. It was this survey in which the details of the TDM for mail surveys were first worked out. Since then the TDM procedures have been refined through the course of nearly 50 other surveys. This extensive use convincingly demonstrates that a response rate of nearly 75 percent can be attained consistently in mail surveys of the general public and that even higher response rates are probable in surveys of more specialized populations, such as employees of a single organization or members of a profession. The step-by-step details reported here for TDM mail surveys are based on the results of extensive tests by the author and other researchers.

The work on the TDM for telephone surveys commenced a short time after that first mail survey, when I was asked to establish and direct a telephone laboratory for the Washington State University Social Research Center. The telephone, which I had always thought to be more of a novelty than a serious method for conducting surveys, soon proved to be far more capable of obtaining social science data than most social scientists had thought. Repeated surveys demonstrated that response rates of 80–90 percent can consistently be attained for general public surveys. Even higher response rates are routine for surveys of more specialized populations. In the course of conducting these studies, it became apparent that the principles already successfully applied to mail surveys were similarly applicable to collecting data by telephone. Some 30 surveys have provided the opportunity to develop the TDM for telephone surveys to the level described in this book.

Viable mail and telephone survey methods open new opportunities for survey research and create new challenges. Certain kinds of surveys, heretofore thought impossible, can now be undertaken successfully. In addition, the TDMs for mail and telephone make it unnecessary to accept the inevitable compromises that must usually be accepted because of the high costs of face-to-face interviews (e.g., limited sample size and geographical distribution). Thus a portion of this book is devoted to the implications of mail and telephone survey methods for when and how survey research is accomplished.

Finally, I wish to emphasize at the outset that the TDM procedures I describe for mail and telephone surveys are not finished products—both can probably be improved further. This book lays a foundation that will help stimulate research that may lead to the full realization of the potential of mail and telephone surveys. Consequently, I attempt to go further than simply describing how to conduct mail and telephone surveys and look toward their acceptance as standard components of the survey researcher's arsenal of data collection techniques.

I am indebted to Washington State University for the institutional support that made possible the research on which this book is based. Its Agricultural Research Center supported much of the development of the TDM for mail and telephone surveys under projects 0031 and 0106. Its Social Research Center supported development of the telephone TDM from 1971 to 1973, during which time I directed its Public Opinion Laboratory. Much of the actual writing was done while I was on professional leave granted to me by the university.

So many individuals have contributed to this book that it is difficult to acknowledge their help adequately. I am especially indebted to the several dozen individuals whose names appear in the footnotes to Tables 1.1 and 1.2 for allowing me to have a hand, either directly or indirectly, in the design of their surveys.

I also want to acknowledge the specific actions of F. Ivan Nye, who first recommended that I "try" the mail questionnaire and later directed me to exchange theory as a means of interpreting respondent behavior; James F. Short and Melvin DeFleur, who were responsible for establishing the Social Research Center's telephone laboratory; Max von Broembsen, Pat Brandimore, and Joe Neil, who made directing the laboratory a pleasure; Howard M. Bahr, who persuaded me to begin work on this book; John Finney, who contributed to development of the TDM and commented on portions of the manuscript; James A. Christenson, who worked closely with me in development of the TDM for mail surveys and provided a thorough review of the manuscript; Riley Dunlap, whose detailed reading of the complete manuscript and expert editorial hand produced substantial improvements in the manuscript; Jean Gorton Gallegos, whose excellent research skills contributed to development of the TDM for telephone surveys; Kenneth R. Tremblay, Jr., who read and reread all the chapters, contributing substantively and editorially to each of them; Bernard Babbitt who saw to it that computer services were available when needed, and made "same-night" reporting of telephone interview results a routine accomplishment; and Sherry C. Brummel, Patricia Richards, and Katharine Lewis, who provided skilled operational support for numerous surveys and occasional reminders of how long it has taken for this enterprise to be completed.

James H. Frey made numerous substantive contributions to this book in earlier phases of the writing. At one time it was planned that he would be an author. Other commitments made that impossible, but his influence on various portions of the book is considerable.

Walter L. Slocum was the first to convince me that a viable mail survey method could be developed. Based on his own research, he provided specific recommendations of how to accomplish it. Many of his recommendations (some of which were reported in the *American Sociological Review* in 1956) are at the core of the TDM for both the mail and telephone surveys. When I sought his advice, he inevitably responded with pointed constructive criticism. This book is dedicated to him in appreciation for his generous help, and for other reasons. His career at Washington State University (1951–1975) was a conscious combination of concern over the production of sociological knowledge and its application to solving practical problems. He also contributed generously and substantially to the career development of his many junior colleagues. My debt to him is both personal and professional.

Finally, I want to acknowledge some individuals whose contributions are less direct, but personally quite significant: George Beal, Joe Bohlen, Gerald Klonglan, and Richard Warren, whose "shop" at Iowa State University provided the training opportunities that prepared me for the research on which this book is based; Joye Dillman, spouse and colleague, and our children, Andrew and Melody, each of whom understands in a unique way why and how this book was written.

DON A. DILLMAN

Pullman, Washington
November 1977

CONTENTS

MAIL AND TELEPHONE SURVEYS

Chapter One

THE TOTAL DESIGN METHOD (TDM):

··

A New Approach to Mail and Telephone Surveys

For too long mail and telephone questionnaires have been considered the stepchildren of survey research. Social scientists have viewed them as having little worth.[1] Data collected by these two methods have always been considered suspect unless proven otherwise, the opposite of the view held toward the accepted survey method, face-to-face interviews. When occasionally one or the other of the methods turned in an outstanding performance, it was usually explained away by the existence of easy survey conditions, and praise was limited to a commendation for having performed beyond the method's inherent potential. Neither the mail nor telephone has been considered anything more than a poor substitute for the much heralded face-to-face interview.

Perhaps this view was justified, because the two methods had many deficiencies and problems. Surveys by mail typically elicited extremely low response rates, even with short questionnaires, and high response to relatively long questionnaires was very rare indeed, especially in surveys of the general public. Further, it was not possible to reach many people by mail questionnaires; among those to whom questionnaires could be delivered, the best educated were far more likely to respond. Even completed questionnaires left much to be desired. They were often of low quality, containing many unans-

1

wered questions and responses that were either too skimpy to be meaningful or too illegible to be understood. It is not surprising, then, that users of the mail questionnaire treated response rates well below 50 percent as "acceptable" and explained away problems of data quality with disclaimers such as, "this is the best we can expect from a mail questionnaire."

Objections to telephone surveys were at least as severe; until the last few years data collection by phone was rare. The biggest problem was that many people did not have telephones; those who did tended to have higher than average incomes and education. It was believed that interviews that could be terminated by simply hanging up the phone (rather than having to remove the interviewer from one's home) would produce unacceptably low response rates and make it necessary to keep interviews far shorter than needed for most research. Finally, complete dependence on vocal communication, made difficult by the hum of static and disconnection-prone wires, led to the telephone being viewed as possibly an interesting idea for tomorrow, but not at all useful today.

That day has arrived for the mail as well as the telephone survey. Recent developments, described in detail in this book, have brought both methods to the point of being competitive with face-to-face interviews for many kinds of studies. Both are now used in ways thought impossible only a few years ago. They have been brought to this level of effectiveness through research, conducted by the author and other researchers, that has introduced new perspectives to the matter of how such surveys can and should be conducted.

This book describes in step-by-step detail methods for conducting mail and telephone surveys using questionnaires of a length and complexity adequate for social science research. The problems of response quantity and quality are solved in part by a procedure called the "total design method." This is nothing more than the identification of each aspect of the survey process (even the minute ones) that may affect response quantity or quality and shaping them in a way that will encourage good response. These efforts are guided by a view about why people do and do not respond to interviews and questionnaires, and a concern that the weakest link in surveying is often the researcher's inability to mount and carry through a precisely ordered and timed implementation process so necessary for maximizing response. Thus the total design method (TDM), described in detail later in this chapter, rests on both a theory of response behavior and an administrative plan to direct its implementation.

THE NEED FOR ALTERNATIVES TO FACE-TO-FACE INTERVIEWS

The need for this book stems only in part from improvements in mail and telephone surveys. There is also a growing concern that face-to-face interviews may not be as successful as they once were and are becoming prohibitively expensive. For example, recent evidence suggests that response rates to face-to-face interviews are on the decline.[2] A committee convened by the American Statistical Association in 1973 noted that, although hard data on response rates are difficult to come by, it appears that survey firms face increased difficulty in getting cooperation from respondents:

> Spokesmen from a number of private survey organizations, large and small, who were queried . . . all report that their completion rates on general population samples now average about 60 to 65 percent, in spite of three or four call backs. This recent experience is in contrast to a completion figure of 80 to 85 percent for the same firms in the decade of the 60's. The remaining 35 to 40 percent non-response divides about equally between refusals and not-at-homes.[3]

The conference also concluded that some (but not all) survey research organizations operating from university settings faced higher refusal rates and increasing resistance to their interviewers.[4]

Most disturbing is the difficulty interviewers face in locating respondents. An increasing number of call-backs are now required to reach the occupants of sampled households.[5] Members of the conference concluded that the existence of more households in which both spouses are employed has contributed to no one at home when the interviewer stops by, a trend that is likely to increase. Another reason for "not-at-home's" is the continuing urbanization of life styles that results in people being away from their homes more of the time, either at work or in pursuit of leisure activities. Still another reason is increased geographical mobility; nearly one-fifth of the United States' population moves each year. Because of problems in locating prospective respondents, the costs for conducting face-to-face interviews have skyrocketed. This dilemma was summarized by a participant in the American Statistical Association Conference, who noted that response rates that had in recent months dropped to 60 or 65 percent could be raised to the former 80 to 85 percent, but to do so "would be at the prohibitive cost of seven times the original survey."[6]

Even before these recent developments, very few researchers were able to obtain the resources that would allow them to commission large-scale face-to-face interviews devoted solely to their research problems. A common technique for lowering expenses is to share costs among researchers, each buying as many minutes of a face-to-face interview as needed for his or her particular questions. Although this offers a solution to the financial problems faced by some researchers, it does not help researchers interested in a population that no other researchers are willing to pay to have surveyed at that time. Examples of such populations are the general public in some (but not all) states and their various regions, and persons in particular occupational roles (e.g., architects or city engineers).

Another problem facing users of face-to-face interviews is finding competent interviewers. Interviewing is an arduous and highly skilled activity in which experience plays a very important role. Interviewers must be able to operate comfortably in a climate in which strangers are viewed with distrust and must successfully counter respondents' objections to being interviewed. Increasingly, interviewers must be willing to work at night to contact residents in many households. In some cases this necessitates providing protection for interviewers working in areas of a city in which a definite threat to the safety of individuals exists. Thus the securing, training, and supervision of interviewers, if done well, is demanding and costly.

Faced with these difficulties, compromises are increasingly likely in the design and execution of face-to-face interviews. Populations of less scope and significance are often studied. Instead of interviewing school teachers of an entire state, those in one city are studied. Instead of interviewing the population of a city whose characteristics closely match those of the state's population, the handy "university city" is chosen, in which characteristics such as education and income are dramatically skewed by the presence of the sponsoring university. In other cases a switch in population type may be made from the general public to university students, or perhaps to an even more captive audience such as students in a single classroom. Still another compromise is to decrease the size of the sample to a number so small that confident generalization of results to the sampled population cannot be made. Changes in survey procedures, such as reducing the number of call-backs and thereby increasing potential bias, may also be made. Occasionally a researcher makes fundamental changes in the study design. For example, instead of collecting the information required for a sophisticated multiple variable analysis of the determinants of marital conflict among a large number of couples, the researcher may switch to in-depth case studies. Finally, there may be abandonment of the face-to-face interview altogether in favor of other data collection methods. In the past, switching to other data collection methods, usually mail questionnaires, was considered just another undesirable compromise.

In light of the increasing difficulties of face-to-face interviewing, it seems likely that alternative data collection methods will experience increased use, regardless of their projected adequacy. However, by using the total design method (TDM) researchers can now expect to get good results that will in some cases be comparable to those which could be obtained through face-to-face interviews and at a much lower cost. The development of viable mail and telephone methods has the potential for encouraging research projects that until now were deemed unfeasible. For example, some populations are so geographically dispersed that face-to-face interviews are usually too costly. Examples are dentists, ministers, stockbrokers, county planners, and university alumni. Another type of study generally viewed as prohibitively costly is a panel study of the general public, which requires relocating respondents even though many have left the county or state in which they were previously surveyed.

The lower cost of doing surveys by mail or telephone makes it possible to base sample size decisions on what is needed to accomplish research objectives. In face-to-face interview studies, sample size is more often determined by how many cases one can afford than by the number that is, in some sense, ideal for the study. Sample sizes are seldom sufficient to allow confident generalization to subcategories of the population, for example, 18–24-year-olds in a survey of voters. Although quota sampling or oversampling is frequently done to get adequate representation for subcategories of special interest, it is only a limited solution. More frequently, researchers would like to generalize results to many more subcategories than interviewing costs allow. Further, in some cases knowledge of potential respondent characteristics is insufficient to allow foresight for effective stratification. The most general solution is to substantially increase the sample size, a solution that is more likely to be possible for mail and telephone surveys than for face-to-face interviews.

Thus the efforts to develop workable alternatives to the face-to-face interview have been influenced by two quite different sets of factors. One factor is the increasingly high cost and difficulty of locating respondents, requiring concessions to be made by those who use face-to-face interviews. The other influence is the attractiveness of adding mail and telephone methods to the survey researcher's arsenal of techniques, enabling him or her to do kinds of surveys not previously done. These developments are a boon to the researcher with good ideas but without the means for doing face-to-face interviews.

WHY MAIL AND TELEPHONE METHODS HAVE BEEN INADEQUATE

One of the most compelling reasons for writing this book is the inadequacy of current literature as a source of specific directions for conducting mail and telephone surveys. Despite an expanding literature, treatment of both techniques is limited, and many crucial issues are completely ignored. To conduct successful surveys, the would-be user needs a methodological "recipe" that includes all the ingredients and directions for combining them. The existing literature provides little more than fragmented commentary on how this or that technique might contribute to a survey's success.[7] Nevertheless, it provides the basis for several crucial assumptions of the total design method (TDM) and must be discussed. Since past research has tended to focus either on the mail or telephone survey (each poses rather different problems), we discuss them separately, beginning with past research on mail questionnaires.

Past Research on Mail Surveys

Despite its generally bad reputation, there is no shortage of research using mail questionnaires. In fact, social scientists have generally ignored admonitions not to use mail questionnaires and have depended on them a large proportion of the time. For example, a review of major sociology journals showed that in a recent 8-year period one article using mail questionnaires was published for every two articles based on face-to-face interviews.[8]

This research has spawned a very large number of methodological articles—well over 200—that deal in some way with how to improve response, and a score or more are added each year. Among the incredible number of topics that have been studied in an effort to improve response rates are:

1. Advance notification by letter[9] or telephone[10] that a questionnaire is being sent.
2. White or off-white stationery.[11]
3. More expensive methods of delivering mail, i.e., airmail and certified delivery.[12]
4. Denomination of stamps.[13]
5. Inclusion of stamped return envelopes.[14]
6. Shorter questionnaires.[15]
7. Attractive questionnaire layout.[16]
8. Official sponsorship of survey.[17]
9. Personalization of correspondence.[18]
10. Addition of title under sender's name.[19]
11. Anonymity and confidentiality.[20]
12. Cover letter's composition: permissive (versus firm),[21] long and reasoned (versus short and punchy),[22] a plea for help (versus offer of reward),[23] a request for favor,[24] stress on social usefulness of study,[25] and importance of respondent to study success.[26]
13. Offers of incentives, including money,[27] trading stamps,[28] lottery tickets,[29] survey results,[30] instant coffee,[31] pencil,[32] tie clip,[33] and note pad.[34]
14. Enclosure of incentive (versus promise).[35]
15. Use of repeated follow-ups by mail and/or telephone.[36]
16. Timing of follow-ups.[37]

What can we conclude from these studies? Very little has been decided by them. The results of research on some techniques are far from consistent, as the following examples attest. Advance notice of questionnaires has both stimulated and depressed response rates.[38] Personalization has been reported to increase response in some instances, to have no effect in others, and to decrease it in still others.[39] Although short questionnaires seem, on an intuitive level, to be far better than long ones, some researchers have achieved better results with long ones, and sometimes no difference has been reported.[40] Some researchers have reported better success with white or off-white stationery, and others have reported more favorable results when it is brightly colored.[41] Although few researchers, the author included, doubt the effectiveness of follow-ups, at least one study reported a negligible increase in response.[42]

Attempts to clarify the techniques that actually work by reviewing and analyzing the research have not been particularly revealing. The general inconclusiveness of these efforts was clearly stated at the end of a recent review by Kanuk and Berenson:

> Despite the large number of research studies reporting techniques designed to improve response rates, there is no strong empirical evidence favoring any techniques other than the followup and the use of monetary incentives.[43]

The difficulty of arriving at definitive conclusions stems primarily from the way past research has been conducted. Most studies focused on only one or two techniques at a time. Thus when we find that the effects of a particular technique (for example, personalization) are reported to be quite different in two surveys, our efforts to reconcile the differences are generally thwarted by such facts as the experiments were applied to different populations, the questionnaires dealt with very different topics, and different numbers of follow-ups were employed. Further confounding our ability to explain reported differences is the usual void of information concerning many other aspects of the study design that might influence response rates—for example, questionnaire layout and design, length of the questionnaire, and the basic appeal of the cover letters. For these reasons, exhaustive reviews of the available literature, of which there have been several, seemed destined to be unhelpful.[44] In fact, it would be surprising if these exercises in subjective assessments produce results that are either consistent or definitive, as demonstrated by an examination of these reviews.

Past research on mail questionnaires also suffered from a more fundamental problem. Implicitly, although probably not intentionally, researchers assumed that respondent behavior is primarily a reaction to particular aspects of mail questionnaire studies, rather than a reaction to the whole. It is more correct to assume that the decision to respond is based on an overall, subjective evaluation of all the study elements visible to the prospective respondent. The nature of any survey is communicated to respondents in diverse ways: the shape, size, and color of the envelope; the way the address is affixed to the envelope; the postage; content of the cover letter; whether and how inside addresses and salutation are affixed; the color and size of the stationery; the content and appearance of the questionnaire; and so on. Each element contributes to the overall image of the study. This suggests that to maximize response rate all aspects of a study should be designed to create the most positive image.

It also suggests that the manipulation of one or two techniques independently of all others may do little to stimulate response. Indeed, we are faced with the possibility that certain features that are incorporated into a study because they reportedly increase response rates may not do so because of their relation to the other aspects of the study. For example, telling a respondent that it will only take a few minutes to complete a questionnaire sounds like a good practice; however, that message is probably received negatively if offered in reference to a 20-page questionnaire. Likewise it sounds like a good practice to suggest in a cover letter that the respondent is asked to contribute to the solution of an important social problem. However, if the questionnaire consists of only five brief items on one page, it seems unlikely that the recipient will believe that such a short questionnaire could possibly help with the major problems described in the cover letter. As a result, the questionnaire will probably be dispatched to the garbage can instead of the post office.

The tendency of past research to focus on reactions to individual techniques has had the unfortunate effect of directing attention in the wrong way. Instead of focusing on the prospective respondent, it focused on the technique. As a result, this research ignored the important question of how to *maximize* the probability of response. Instead it asked to what extent does personalization, follow-ups, stamped return envelopes, or whatever, make a difference in the response. The former is a far more important question, because the answer determines whether the mail questionnaire is a satisfactory data collection method. Answers to the latter can do little more than identify specific techniques, each of which may affect response a little bit.

The criticism that mail questionnaire research lacks a theory,[45] although true, seems more a criticism of the fact that techniques rather than people were the organizing focus. It reflects the inevitable shortcoming of the way articles have been written: first a straightforward description of a particular technique, the reporting of an experiment, and on the basis of that unique experiment involving a particular population, topic, and number of questions, speculation about whether researchers should use it. Until the respondent's behavior and the reasons for it become the focus of research, we seem destined to conduct experiment after experiment and still not contribute to our knowledge of how to maximize response rates.

Past research exhibits still other shortcomings that limit its usefulness for finding ways to maximize response in the studies normally done by social scientists. One of these is that most studies used questionnaires far shorter than those needed for most social science research. Another is the fact that the topics for research were quite different from those likely to be pursued by social scientists, as evidenced by a large number of articles based on topics likely to be pursued only by market researchers. Finally, a substantial portion of the research focused on very specialized populations (e.g., users of a particular product or directors of a particular agency), where it was possible to take advantage of that homogeneity by using group-specific appeals. Only rarely were techniques reported for improving response for heterogeneous populations such as the general public—perhaps the most difficult population from which to consistently elicit high response rates. The effect of a particular technique, such as a stamped return envelope, may be quite different for a long questionnaire on family relationships sent to a statewide sample of families by a university than when a stamped return envelope is used on a four-item product identification survey sent to corporation executives by a market research company.

Thus past research on mail questionnaires provides very little information about how response might be maximized for the types of studies likely to be of interest to social scientists. Further, it does not provide us with a concept of respondent behavior that can guide efforts to construct an effective methodology. Nonetheless, it provides a rich source of ideas about techniques that might in some way be woven together to form an effective method. This is how we used it to develop the total design method (TDM) for mail questionnaires.

Past Research on Telephone Surveys

The research literature on telephone surveys is as thin as that for the mail questionnaire is thick. Its research potential has long been darkened by the shadow cast by the famous *Literary Digest* debacle of 1936. In that year pollsters for the Digest predicted a landslide victory for Landon over Roosevelt in the presidential race. Their downfall was traced in part to the use of telephone listings as a sampling frame and the clear social class bias associated with having a telephone.[46] At the time of the survey, only about 35 percent of households in the United States had telephones.[47] As Aronson has pointed out, having a telephone served to define and enhance the social status of individuals.[48] The class bias of telephone access continues, albeit to an ever lessening degree.

In this context, it is perhaps not surprising that social researchers used the telephone primarily as a complement to other survey methods. Several researchers found the telephone to be an effective means of prodding the return of mail questionnaires.[49] Some found that a prior telephone call to arrange for personal interviews increased the probability of completion and the efficiency of doing so.[50] The telephone was also effectively used to provide advance notice of mail questionnaires.[51] In addition, the telephone served as a means of reinterviewing respondents previously surveyed by face-to-face methods, especially in cases in which geographical mobility made follow-ups difficult. The use of the telephone as a reinterviewing technique produced high response rates ranging from 84 to 100 percent.[52]

Market researchers were the first to make extensive use of the telephone as a sole means of securing data from respondents. The reluctance of social scientists, sociologists in particular, to adopt the telephone as a means of collecting data can be illustrated by a review of the articles published in major sociology journals over an 8-year period.[53] Only one article reporting data obtained by means of telephone interviews was published for every 20 articles using face-to-face interviews. This lack of use is reinforced by a near void of experiments and other research aimed at improving the quantity and quality of response to telephone surveys. Further, there is an absence of reliable information on how long respondents can be kept on the line, the nature of topics that can be discussed, and the type of question construction procedures that are most appropriate. Also, procedures for adapting questionnaires to the peculiar requirements of telephone interviewing and training telephone interviewers were not reported. In sum, the telephone was treated as little more than a novelty, occasionally viewed with interest, but not of sufficient importance to warrant sustained research.

Since work on this book began, just a few short years ago, the use of the telephone has mushroomed. This is not too surprising now that the percentage of United States' residences with telephones has reached an all-time high of 94 percent.[54] Indeed, in 23 states, at least 95 percent of households have telephones.[55] Thus the probability of social class bias stemming from the availability of phones has greatly diminished. For many specialized populations, for example, agency directors, architects, and ministers, nearly 100 percent coverage by telephone is possible, eliminating altogether the bias stemming from the absence of telephones. Further, the greater difficulty of overcoming problems of new listings, recent changes in numbers, and unlisted numbers has been reduced with the development of random digit dialing techniques.[56] Also, improvements in telephone technology make dialing someone thousands of miles away easier than it used to be to reach someone across town, and decrease the likelihood of difficulty in communication. Finally, the glamour of doing surveys almost overnight to report opinions on events that are undergoing dramatic change (such as Watergate and presidential campaigns) has given the telephone an irresistable appeal. Thus it is not surprising that most major survey organizations are now doing some research by telephone.

The rapid emergence of the telephone as a survey research tool has meant that most researchers have proceeded on their own, without the benefit of published work. To the extent that an exchange of information has occurred, it has been primarily by word of mouth. Perhaps a reason for so rapid an emergence of the capability to do telephone surveys without the stimulus of published information is that surveyors simply adapted their normal interviewing procedures to the telpehone; thus their methods might very appropriately be termed face-to-face interviews by telephone!

Most of the social science community has little information on telephone surveys and continues to be plagued by not knowing what response rates to expect for various populations, how long different types of people will stay on the telephone, and the unique requirements of telephone interviews. The available knowledge comes primarily from verbal reports of survey directors at conferences[57] and published comments based on private discussions,[58] rather than the publication and systematic analysis of empirical results. This leaves us with many unanswered questions. For example, the observation that surveys up to an hour can be made without any problems[59] is not specific about whether that is feasible with all populations, whether it can be expected only in call-back telephone interviews, and whether the quality of data remains good throughout the interview.

The total design method (TDM) for telephone surveys represents the author's trial and error efforts to develop satisfactory methods of telephone interviewing, guided in part by the sharing of information with other researchers and, to a lesser extent, by published work. The basic assumptions are the same as those for the mail survey method. Fundamentally, it is assumed that the best results in terms of quantity and quality occur when as little as possible is left to chance. Each aspect of conceptualizing and implementing telephone questionnaires was considered open to design considerations. The same theory of respondent behavior and concern over the development of a satisfactory administrative plan provided basic guidance.

The results are increasingly convincing that telephone interviewing is unique and that simply adopting normal procedures for face-to-face interviews is not sufficient. In the long run, the development of satisfactory methods depends on an understanding of the differences between the two methods and appropriate differences in design.

THE TOTAL DESIGN METHOD

The TDM consists of two parts. The first is to identify each aspect of the survey process that may affect either the quality or quantity of response and to shape each of them in such a way that the best possible responses are obtained. The second is to organize the survey efforts so that the design intentions are carried out in complete detail. The first step is guided by a theoretical view about why people respond to questionnaires. It provides the rationale for deciding how each aspect, even the seemingly minute ones, should be shaped. The second step is guided by an administrative plan, the purpose of which is to ensure implementation of the survey in accordance with design intentions. The failure of surveys to produce satisfactory results occurs as often from poor administration as from poor design. First, let us consider why people respond to surveys.

Why People Respond:
The Theoretical Basis of the Total Design Method

The process of sending a questionnaire to prospective respondents, getting them to complete the questionnaire in an honest manner and return it can be viewed as a special case of "social exchange." The effort to call people on the telephone and complete an interview may also be considered as a special, albeit somewhat different, case of social exchange. The theory of social exchange, the tenants of which have been most notably developed by Homans, Blau, and Thibaut and Kelley,[60] asserts that the actions of individuals are motivated by the return these actions are expected to bring and, in fact, usually do bring from others. Social exchange is different from the more familiar economic exchange in which money serves as a precise measure of the worth of one's actions. It is a broader concept and can be distinguished from economic exchange as follows: under it, future obligations are created that are diffuse and unspecified; the nature of the return cannot be bargained about but must be left to the discretion of the one who owes it; the range of goods, services, and experiences exchanged is quite broad. It is assumed that people engage in any activity because of the rewards they hope to reap, that all activities they perform incur certain costs, and that people attempt to keep their costs below the rewards they expect to receive. Fundamentally then, whether a given behavior occurs is a function of the ratio between the perceived costs of doing that activity and the rewards one expects the other party to provide at a later time. Thus there are three things that must be done to maximize survey response: minimize the costs for responding, maximize the rewards for doing so, and establish trust that those rewards will be delivered.

There are numerous ways that each can be achieved; this is the topic to which we now turn.

Rewards.   The rewards most researchers can offer to respondents are few. This fact in itself may go far in accounting for the low response rates typically obtained with mail questionnaires. Those rewards which the researcher does have at his or her disposal are mostly intangible, but the power to reward should not be underestimated. For example, Thibaut and Kelley point out that being regarded positively by another person has a reward value for many individuals.[61] Explaining to someone that they are part of a carefully selected sample and that their response is needed if the study is to be successful represents a way of expressing positive regard for respondents. Personalization techniques of real signatures, individual salutations, and individually typed letters are also methods of showing positive regard. Telephone interviewers can communicate positive regard by statements to that effect and with their tone of voice.

Blau states that a time-consuming service of great material benefit might be properly repaid by mere verbal appreciation.[62] This can be accomplished by liberally sprinkling all forms of communication with "our grateful appreciation," or "our sincere thanks in advance." It is perhaps for this reason that a follow-up postcard designed as a thank you for the prompt return of "the questionnaire sent to you last week" has been found to be followed by a response burst equal to that which follows the original mailing.[63]

Being "consulted" has been pointed to by both Blau and Homans as a means of providing a reward to people while getting needed information.[64] Telling people that "It's not known what people like yourself think on these important issues, so we are attempting to find out," and posing such open-ended questions as, "Is there anything else you would like to tell us which might help in our future efforts to understand how people feel on this issue?" suggest a consulting type of approach.

Blau also suggests that supporting one's values can be rewarding to the person.[65] One difficulty of employing this approach is determining that which is valued by all or most respondents in a sample. A study on attitudes toward community living and population redistribution illustrates one way this problem was solved. The study was done at a time at which state and federal lawmakers were considering possibilities for population redistribution efforts. It was assumed that a widely shared value among citizens was that their preferences be heard in the policy formation process, and second, the specific issue of what kind of community settlement patterns should dominate the American landscape was of sufficient importance that citizens would want their voices heard. Thus the cover letter to respondents honestly explained:

Bills have been introduced in Congress and our State Legislature aimed at encouraging the growth of rural and small town areas and slowing down that of large cities. These bills could greatly affect the quality of life provided in both rural and urban places. However, no one really knows in what kinds of communities people like yourself want to live or what is thought about these proposed programs. To find out, our research unit is conducting this study . . . results will be made available to officials and representatives in our state's government, members of Congress . . .

This principle of supporting one's values is similar to one proposed by Slocum et al. of appealing to respondents on the basis of the study's "social usefulness."[66]

Of course, tangible rewards may also be offered to respondents. Among the rewards that have been offered are various denominations of coins, note pads, a chance of winning a turkey, a packet of instant coffee, a pencil, and war savings stamps. Not every incentive of this type, as typically used, should be considered as a reward. As discussed later, they may also perform an important role in the creation of trust.

When the researcher has so few rewards to offer a potential respondent, and these rewards tend to be of a token nature, how can high response rates be obtained? Rewards can be obtained without obligation when, according to Blau, the actions are experienced not as a net cost, but as a net gain.[67] If completing a questionnaire or responding to the interviewer's questions can be made to be a rewarding act, the process itself may provide the motivation to complete and return the mail questionnaire or finish the telephone interview. Thus it becomes important to make the questionnaire as interesting as possible. The fact that some people enjoy answering questionnaires regardless of content may explain why a certain percentage of response can be obtained on almost any topic.

Costs.   The costs respondents incur may be reduced in a number of ways. Time is perhaps the major cost experienced by respondents. It follows that greater cost would be incurred in completing long questionnaires or interviews than short ones. However, the time cost to respondents cannot be measured simply in terms of the number of questions or even the minutes required to complete it. A respondent acts on the basis of anticipated costs as well as those already incurred. A questionnaire that looks formidable may be rejected simply because it looks like it will take a long time to complete. Similarly, indicating that an interview will be short seems likely to encourage a respondent to continue. Efforts to make questionnaires clear and concise and to give them a less formidable appearance (e.g., by reducing size and using an attractive layout) may do a great deal to decrease respondents' expectations that a questionnaire will be too time consuming for them to consider doing. The critical issue is finding the delicate balance between the researcher getting the amount of information he or she wants without respondents finding the questionnaire too costly in terms of time and effort.

Thibaut and Kelley have pointed out that cost is high when great physical or mental effort is required and when embarrassment or anxiety accompany the action.[68] Complex questions, directions that are difficult to understand, and related aspects that confuse the respondent seem likely to produce feelings of inadequacy or even anxiety and therefore incur cost. The frequently offered observation that persons with low education or those who are less experienced in expressing themselves in writing are less likely to return completed questionnaires is perhaps due to the costly effort, both physical and mental, required of such respondents.

In addition, to give personal information about themselves represents potential risk for respondents. Questions of a very personal nature imply greater costs. Thus overly direct questions about such things as sexual behavior, methods of disciplining children, and religious beliefs may produce anxiety or even embarrassment in persons who would otherwise be quite willing to complete and return a questionnaire. Efforts to soften such questions, and perhaps eliminate the most objectionable, might well be expected to decrease costs incurred by respondents. Respondents probably experience a continual debate within themselves about how much of their lives they will expose. This cost, that is, exposure, is weighed against perceived benefits.

Another possible cost to respondents is that they subordinate themselves to the researcher and therefore must admit that the researcher has power over them. Power is described by Blau as an outcome of an exchange process in which an individual needs a service from another, but has nothing of equal value with which to reciprocate.[69] When that which the respondent has to offer (the completed questionnaire) is of less value to the researcher than what the researcher can and will reciprocate with, subordination to the researcher is necessary to equalize the exchange. Subordination is suggested in a statement of appeal such as this: "For us to help you solve your community problems it is necessary for you to complete this questionnaire." Such appeals should not be used. In contrast, a statement like "would you please do me a favor," which has frequently been suggested as effective in cover letters, may derive its effectiveness from the implication that the researcher is in some way subordinate to the respondent. Thus what might have been incurred as a cost to the respondent cannot only be avoided, but can perhaps be turned into a reward of implied power.

Finally, direct monetary costs may also be an important factor. Having to furnish an envelope and place their own stamp or stamps on it may not seem to be a significant cost to respondents until one considers the low reward situation. Although the cost in dollars (or more appropriately, cents) is small, it represents a very tangible cost and may therefore be resented.

Trust. An essential characteristic of social exchange is that there is no way to ensure an appropriate return for a favor. One must "trust" that the other will discharge his or her obligation to return the favor with another. If trust cannot be established by the researcher for "sending you a copy of results," or "supplying results to decisionmakers who will be determining future policies," the rewards that can be offered to the respondent are limited to those which are included with the appeal, for example, a small gift, expression of appreciation, or appeals for consultation.

The reason that token financial incentives have been found so effective in mail questionnaire research may lie not in their monetary value, but rather in the fact that they are a symbol of trust. They represent the researcher's trust that the respondent will accept an offer made in good faith. Second, incentives may stimulate the belief on the part of the respondent that future promises (e.g., a copy of results or putting the results to good use) will be carried out. Support for the notion that monetary incentives are effective for these reasons comes from the finding that increasing the size of an incentive does not always increase response, and in fact may tend to decrease it, and that including it in the appeal is more effective than promising to send it on return of the questionnaire.[70] The closer the monetary incentive comes to the value of the service performed, the more the transaction tends to move into the realm of economic exchange and the easier it becomes for many people to refuse it.

The financial incentives frequently used do not represent the only means of promoting trust. A stamped return envelope may be effective for the same reasons. In addition, an unknown researcher presenting him or herself only by name to potential respondents seems less likely to generate trust than one who can be identified with a known established organization, especially if that organization symbolizes legitimacy.

Other exchange relationships in which the respondent is involved may be utilized to increase the probability of a returned questionnaire. Communication from an employee's supervisor that a study has been approved and that he or she expects a questionnaire to be returned to the researcher is such an example. A less obvious example may be the case of some complex organizations such as universities. Respondents may return their questionnaires to the researcher, not so much because of any feelings of obligation to the researcher, but because they feel that they have received past benefits from the college or university (e.g., research results that have benefited their business or education provided to them or a relative).

How Reasons for Response Differ for Mail and Telephone Surveys. There are certain key differences between mail questionnaires and telephone interviews with respect to the application of social exchange theory. Typically, contact by telephone is concentrated into a few short minutes, with the potential respondent usually receiving no prior warning. The decision to respond must be made quickly, without knowledge of the information sought. The result is that there is little opportunity to weigh the pros and cons of being interviewed. In contrast, the recipient of the mail questionnaire receives written materials that may be examined at his or her leisure. The decision to respond may be delayed until after the contents have been thoroughly examined. Further, if a response is not forthcoming, contact with the respondent may be renewed one or more times with folllow-ups.

For these reasons, social exchange considerations do not usually affect the decision to complete a telephone interview to the extent that they do for the mail questionnaire. For example, a statement such as, "This study is sponsored by Washington State University," which is aimed at creating trust, seems less likely to accomplish that objective when heard over the telephone than when seen on university letterhead stationery. The authenticity of the letterhead is less likely to be questioned than is the unexpected voice of a stranger. Furthermore, it seems likely that many respondents whose reactions are dominated by the emotion associated with surprise do not comprehend the words read to them by the interviewer. Under these conditions it is likely that many respondents act according to conventional norms of behavior for dealing with strange callers rather than a quick evaluation of what they expect the interaction to provide. For some respondents this means hanging up. For others, it means continuing the conversation even though they would really prefer not to and expecting that it will be an awkward or unpleasant experience.

This does not mean that consideration of costs, rewards, and establishment of trust should be regarded as unimportant in telephone interviews. Quite the opposite is true. For some respondents the importance of exchange considerations may be greater. They are the ones who quickly recover from their surprise, clearly comprehend the message, and ask questions, giving the interviewer the chance to respond with statements about the study's usefulness and importance. A skillful interviewer may be able to transform a respondent's initial lack of enthusiasm to an attitude of concern and helpfulness by convincing him or her that the benefits of participation outweigh the costs. A prior letter to respondents, found to increase response in surveys, may be effective because it removes the element of surprise and enhances the importance of exchange considerations in telephone interviews.[71]

In light of the limited opportunity (unless a prior letter is used) for invoking social exchange considerations with some respondents, the question might be raised as to why telephone surveys typically produce higher response rates than mail surveys. A possible explanation is that telephone interviews take advantage of widely shared norms of telephone behavior. These norms inhibit people from unilaterally terminating telephone conversations. The social exchange considerations take over where the norms leave off, acting to push an already high response even higher. In contrast, there are no conventional norms for completing mail questionnaires in our society, in part because doing so is defined as a distinctly individual activity, whereas telephone interviews involve direct interaction with another person.

Implications for the TDM.   The view that respondents' behavior is motivated by whether they expect the rewards to outweigh the costs of participating in a survey holds several important implications for our work. It underscores the importance of researchers being concerned with all aspects of the study. The fact that researchers usually have few rewards to offer and that questionnaires are often of considerable length emphasize the importance of giving attention to *all* the details of the study.

Our brief excursion into exchange theory suggests several things a researcher might do to encourage response:

1. Reward the respondent by
   showing positive regard
   giving verbal appreciation
   using a consulting approach
   supporting his or her values
   offering tangible rewards
   making the questionnaire interesting
2. Reduce costs to the respondent by
   making the task appear brief
   reducing the physical and mental effort that is required
   eliminating chances for embarrassment
   eliminating any implication of subordination
   eliminating any direct monetary cost
3. Establish trust by
   providing a token of appreciation in advance
   identifying with a known organization that has legitimacy
   building on other exchange relationships

However, it must be acknowledged that the guidance offered by exchange theory is only general. Although examples have been offered of how to provide rewards, lower costs, and establish trust in accordance with the general principles just stated, we cannot speak definitively about the proportion of respondents to whom each will appeal strongly. Other ways of realizing the same principles may also exist. Also, strong declarations cannot be made about how the use of one specific reward is likely to affect the use of another. These are questions that can only be answered by future research in the area.

Despite its current incompleteness, the theoretical considerations deriving from social exchange theory have served usefully and continually as the frame of reference against which design efforts on each aspect of the TDM were checked before deciding to include or exclude them from the step-by-step procedures reported in this book. Understanding this frame of reference is important, indeed prerequisite, for comprehending the essence of the TDM. It is the fabric that holds the various parts together, and thus a large portion of this chapter has been devoted to it. This discussion also makes more meaningful a claim that we state and reemphasize many times in this book—that the TDM is as much a theory of response behavior, many parts of which are still to be tested, as it is a proven way of getting good response. The TDM as described here is by no means a final product.

Administration of the Survey: Planning Ahead

The observation of others who have attempted to use exchange theory in implementing their own studies reveals frequent failure to accomplish that objective fully. This failure often stems from a lack of organization concerning crucial details, rather than from the conscious rejection of one or more of the principles discussed here.

For example, one researcher was unable to implement a carefully timed follow-up procedure that required replacement questionnaires, because too few were printed. Another colleague established too large a sample size without carefully considering the costs of the follow-up process. As a result, he did not have sufficient funds to conduct the final phases of the planned follow-up and had to settle for a response rate that was less than adequate. Still another found herself without enough help to process follow-up reminders; thus personalization procedures were dropped, with a corresponding decline in response rate.

The recommendation to develop plans for adminstration probably strikes some researchers or people much like the common admonition to "get organized." No matter how strenuously the point is made, it receives low priority because of the prevalent belief (better described as a myth) that as long as matters of science are at issue, organizational matters will take care of themselves. Just as error can be reduced through sampling or measurement, so it is also possible to reduce error through adequate planning and tight administrative control. The TDM is as much a carefully orchestrated set of sequential events as specific principles of design. Planning, timing, supervision, and control are fundamental requirements for its successful use. Attention to administrative details is as crucial to obtaining high-quality data as the questionnaire or cover letter.

The essence of an administrative plan is (1) identifying all tasks to be accomplished, (2) determining how each task is dependent on others, (3) determining in what order the tasks must be performed, and (4) deciding the means by which each task is to be accomplished. These principles serve to guide the implementation process, which can be viewed as essentially a decision-making enterprise constantly drawing compromises between costs and research objectives. It operates within the limitations imposed by the available responses, organization demands, and characteristics of the population under study.

It would be nice if we could draw up a precise set of procedures, specifying in minute detail what has to be done at each step before continuing on to the next. This would reduce the TDM to a mechanical routine. However, it is not possible. Implementing the TDM for both mail and telephone surveys is less similar to a game of Monopoly, in which moves are made one at a time, than to army maneuvers in which one must move several elements along together, usually choosing from among several options and constantly making adjustments because the anticipated moves of others did not materialize as expected.

Thus information on the nature of the administrative plan for surveys is presented in this fashion: First, the book is organized in terms of the step-by-step sequences to be followed in conducting surveys. Second, cross-referencing is done to reinforce the importance of not making one decision in isolation from others. Finally, parts of several chapters are reserved for discussions of the problems of organizing personnel and resources for the successful completion of a survey.

RESULTS FROM THE TOTAL DESIGN METHOD:
WHAT THE USER CAN EXPECT

The final question to be addressed in this chapter concerns the results that users of the total design method (TDM) can expect. Our focus here cannot be limited simply to response rates. For either the mail or telephone survey to serve the needs of social scientists, it must be demonstrated that adequate response can be achieved to questionnaires that contain the types of questions required for social science research and are long enough to fulfill the study objectives. Further, it is important to know whether the TDM can be successfully implemented under the conditions usually faced by scientists engaged in social research. One must know whether adequate results can be achieved by others who conduct studies in academic institutions and agencies with the resources at their disposal.

Response to TDM Mail Surveys

To date, nearly 50 individual mail surveys have been conducted that have relied wholly or mostly on the TDM. The results and other descriptive information for these studies are summarized in Table 1.1. These surveys were done by a large number of investigators (identified in the footnotes to Table 1.1) under 37 different projects, providing a test of the usability by others. Although most of the surveys were of populations in Washington State, TDM surveys have been conducted in nine different states throughout the nation. Six surveys were national in scope, with data from almost every state. Although most surveys have been conducted from college or university settings, five were done by state or local agencies. The survey topics were quite varied, and only a careful reading of Table 1.1 can do justice to that variety. Suffice it to say that there was a wide range of topics, from perceptions about crime to the characteristics of truckers who hauled agricultural products.

Although the diversity of the TDM mail surveys has been great, it is equally apparent that the method has not been thoroughly tested in some potentially difficult survey situations. For example, none of the TDM surveys in Table 1.1 were conducted in our largest metropolitan areas, such as New York, Chicago, and Los Angeles. Further, nationwide TDM general public surveys have yet to be undertaken. Thus it is with a note of caution that one should generalize the results of the 48 surveys so far completed to certain survey situations.

The average response rates for the 48 surveys was 74 percent. Equally significant is the fact that no survey obtained less than a 50 percent response rate, a level once considered quite acceptable for mail surveys. Some variation in response can be explained by other characteristics presented in the table. For example, those who in our judgment followed the TDM in complete detail averaged 77 percent, and 71 percent for those who used it in part. In fact, all the response rates under 60 percent were obtained by those who only partly used the method. The latter typically omitted various personalization procedures, did not use the complete follow-up sequence, or did not follow the prescribed questionnaire construction procedures. It is interesting to note that some of those using only part of the TDM have reported very high response rates. In two such studies, one of home economics teachers and the other of state employees, that obtained response rates of 80 and 87 percent respectively, part of the last of the TDM-prescribed follow-ups were

Table 1.1 Response Rates for Studies in which the Total Design Mail Method Was Used

TOPIC/SAMPLE[a]	SAMPLE SIZE[b]	ITEMS[c]/ PAGES[d]	TOTAL DESIGN METHOD USED[e]	RESPONSE RATE[f]
1. Preferences for spending public funds: Washington	4500	158/10	Complete	75%
2. Attitudes about community: Washington	4500	109/10	Complete	75%
3. Crime victimization: Seattle Washington	1500	126/14	In Part	60%
4. Crime victimization: Japanese Americans in Seattle, Washington	800	88/ 8	In Part	73%
5. Attitudes about Washington State University:				
Washington	458	88/10	Complete	66%
Students	273	88/10	Complete	82%
Parents of Students	272	88/10	Complete	82%
Alumni	500	63/ 7	In Part	84%
Alumni	500	63/ 7	Complete	92%
6. Recreational needs: Senior citizens, Latah County, Idaho	800	63/ 6	In Part	65%
7. Impact of land use program: All land owner participants Washington State	1736	63/ 9	In Part	65%
8. Occupational aspirations and achievments: Past graduates of selected rural high schools Washington State				
Females	1277	238/14	In Part	56%
Males	1058	238/14	Complete	65%
9. Goals and Needs in North Carolina	5082	165/10	Complete	70%
10. Community size preferences: Arizona	2250	111/10	Complete	71%
11. Community size preferences: Indiana	8000	85/ 7	In Part	71%
12. Family role behavior: Seattle, Washington	3732	161/12	In Part	50%[g]
13. Attitudes about American Indians:				
Seattle, Washington	2000	194/14	Complete	60%
Previously interviewed in person: Seattle, WA	301	177/14	Complete	65%

Table 1.1 Continued

		SAMPLE SIZE[b]	ITEMS[c]/ PAGES[d]	TOTAL DESIGN METHOD USED[e]	RESPONSE RATE[f]
14.	Community participation: Home Economics Teachers in Washington	567	120/11	In Part	80%
15.	Evaluation of education in selected Washington schools:				
	Graduates--one year later	396	25/ 1	In Part	88%
	Graduates--3 years later	226	77/ 3	In Part	57%
	Graduates--5 years later	382	109/ 4	In Part	74%
16.	Attitudes on pesticides: Farmers in Yakima Valley of Washington	520	83/ 6	In Part	65%
17.	Judicial practices: general jurisdiction and appelate judges in 15 western states	956	66/ 5	In Part	69%
18.	Judicial reorganization: Chief Justices of all State Supreme Courts	50	33/ 4	In Part	94%
19.	Energy use: Students, Washington State University	1000	118/10	Complete	89%
20.	Preferences for spending public funds: four year follow-up of respondents in number 1 above	3100	133/10	Complete	68%
21.	Employment views: Non-academically employed member of American Sociological Association	500	90/14	Complete	87%
22.	Opinions on alternative futures for state:				
	Washington	5000	108/10	Complete	74%
	Citizen participants in Governor's State Wide Task Force	169	108/10	Complete	90%
	Citizen participants in Area Wide Conferences	1170	108/10	Complete	84%
23.	Opinions on proposed goals for county: Pierce County, Washington	1500	128/10	Complete	80%
24.	Characteristics of truckers: All truckers in U.S. licensed to haul exempt agricultural commodities	33,400	60/ 6	In Part	58%

Table 1.1 Continued

	TOPIC/SAMPLE	SAMPLE SIZE	ITEMS/ PAGES	TOTAL DESIGN METHOD USED	RESPONSE RATE
25.	Importance of teaching vs. research: Faculty, Washington State University	897	109/10	Complete	93%
26.	Opinions on proposed city goals: Bellingham, Washington	951	153/10	In Part	64%
27.	Opinions on proposed city goals: Participants of Goals for Bellingham Program	97	153/10	In Part	71%
28.	Environmental attitudes and behavior: Washington	1441	180/14	Complete	65%
29.	Environmental attitudes and behavior: Members of state environmental group	558	180/14	In Part	75%
30.	Opinions on prison reform policies: Washington	1700	106/10	Complete	81%
31.	Community attachment and satisfaction: Iowa	5920	148/10	Complete	78%
32.	Needs of elderly: Senior citizens, Washington	874	225/26	Complete	74%
33.	Community and state needs: Michigan	22,000	163/12	In Part	68%
34.	Community and state needs: Kentucky	5500	188/10	Complete	72%
35.	Serious crime: Texas	1000	60/ 7	Complete	85%
36.	North Carolina today and tomorrow	15,548	196/10	Complete	68%
37.	Satisfaction with jobs: State of Washington employees	3000	81/11	In Part	87%
38.	National survey of sociologists in extension, research, teaching	248	125/ 8	In Part	93%

Table 1.1 Footnotes

[a]Unless otherwise noted a random (or systematic) sample of the indicated general public was surveyed. For example the notation "Washington" means a systematic state-wide sample of the general public was surveyed.

[b]The final sample size was in some instances less because of the inclusion of ineligible persons.

[c]ITEMS is defined as the average number of responses which the respondent is required to make. For example, if one question asked the respondent to select the three most important reasons from a list, it was counted as three items.

Table 1.1 Footnotes, Continued

If it asked him to indicate agreement or disagreement with each of twenty statements, it counted as twenty items. Questions asked only of some respondents were counted in proportion to the percent expected to respond.

[d]All questionnaires were printed in booklet form in units of four. The number of pages on which questions were printed is reported here.

[e]All studies included in this table relied extensively on the Total Design method. This column distinguishes between those studies using the complete method, and those which omitted one or more aspects of it. The omitted aspects are ones which in the author's view are likely to lower the response rate.

[f]The response rate is the percent of eligible persons in the sample presumed to have received the questionnaire, that completed and returned them.

[g]This study required two questionnaires per household.

[h]Sources for the above information are identified here by the numbers assigned above. If more than one name is listed the principle investigator is identified by an asterisk (*).

1. Dillman, D.A. "Public Values and Concerns of Washington Residents." Washington Agricultural Experiment Station Bull. No. 748. Washington State University, Pullman, Washington, 1971.

2. Dillman, D.A. "Preferences for Community Living." Washington Agricultural Experiment Station Bull. No. 764. Washington State University, Pullman, Washington, 1972.

3. Gould, Stuart. Personal communication. 1973.

4. Iye, Tomoaki. "A Victimological Study of the Japanese Community in Seattle." Unpublished Ph.D. dissertation, Washington State University, 1974.

5. Smith, Linda Kay. "Attitudes Held by Students, Their Parents, and the General Public on the in Loco Parentis Position of the University." Unpublished M.A. thesis, Washington State University, 1973; and Dillman, D.A. and Frey, J.H.* "Contribution of Personalization to Mail Questionnaire Response as an Element of a Previously Tested Method." Journal of Applied Psychology, 59 (1974), 297-301.

6. Johnson, Vicki Lynn. "Recreational Pursuits and Needs of Senior Citizens in Rural Areas of Latah County, Idaho." Unpublished M.A. thesis, Washington State University, 1972.

7. Barron J.* and J. Thompson. "Impact of Open Space Taxation in Washington." Washington Agricultural Experiment Station Bull. No. 772. Washington State University, Pullman, Washington, 1973.

8. Price, Dorothy. Personal communication. 1973; and West, Donald. Personal communication. 1973.

9-11 Dillman, D.A., J.A. Christenson , E.H. Carpenter, and R.M Brooks. "Increasing Mail Questionnaire Response: A Four State Comparison." American Sociological Review, (October) 1974.

12. Nye, F. Ivan* and Viktor Gecas. Personal communication. 1973.

Table 1.1   Footnotes, Continued

13. Bahr, Howard* and Bruce Chadwick*. Personal communication. 1973.

14. Stuart, Kathleen Hubbard. "Teachers' Perceptions of Community Participation in Vocational Home Economics Programs." Unpublished Ph.D. dissertation, Washington State University, 1973.

15. Schmidt, Roy Lyn. "The Development and Validation of Follow-Up Instruments for Secondary Schools and Vocational-Technical Institutes in the State of Washington." Unpublished Ph.D. dissertation, Washington State University, 1974.

16. Holscher, Lou. Personal communication. 1973.

17. Berry, Marvin P. "A Study of Judicial Role Orientations in Fifteen Western States." Unpublished Ph.D. dissertation, Washington State University, 1974.

18. McConkie, Stanford S. "Environmental, Institutional, and Procedural Influences in Collegial Decision-Making: A Comparative Analysis of State Supreme Courts." Unpublished Ph.D. dissertation, Washington State University, 1974.

19. Finney, John. Personal communication. 1974.

20. Dunlap, Riley E. and Robert Bruce Heffernan. "Changing Priorities for Spending Public Funds, 1970-1974: A Panel Study of Washington Residents." Washington State University College of Agriculture Research Center, Circular 590, 1976.

21. Panian, Sharon. Personal communication. 1974.

22. Wardwell, John M. and Don A. Dillman. "The Alternatives for Washington Surveys: The Final Report." Prepared for the Washington State Office of Program Planning and Fiscal Management, 1975.

23. Hagood, Richard, Don A. Dillman, and Deanna Rankos. "The Future of Pierce County: A Summary of Results." Unpublished Report, 1974.

24. Cassavant, Kenneth. Personal communication. 1975.

25. Panian, Sharon. Personal communication. 1976.

26. Tremblay, Kenneth R., Jr. "Goals for Bellingham: The Citizens Choose." Prepared for the Washington State Office of Community Development, Olympia, Washington, 1976.

27. Ibid.

28. Dunlap, Riley. Personal communication. 1976.

29. Ibid.

30. Riley, Pam. Personal communication. 1975.

31. Goudy, Willis J. "Interim Nonresponse to a Mail Questionnaire: Impacts on Variable Relationships." Iowa Agriculture and Home Economics Experiment Station, Journal Paper No. J.8456, Iowa State University, 1976.

32. Finney, J. M., G. R. Lee, and M. Zeglen. "Survey Research on the Elderly." Paper presented at Pacific Sociological Meetings, San Diego, California, 1976.

33. Kimball, William. Personal communication. 1976.

Table 1.1   Footnotes, Continued

34. Warner, P. D., R. J. Burdge, S. D. Hoffman, and G. R. Hammonds. "Issues Facing Kentucky." Department of Sociology, University of Kentucky, Lexington, Kentucky, 1976.

35. St. Louis, Alfred. "The Texas Crime Trend Survey." Statistical Analysis Center, Texas Department of Public Safety, 1976.

36. Christenson, James A. "North Carolina Today and Tomorrow." Agricultural Experiment Station, publication numbers 141 to 150, North Carolina State University, Raleigh, North Carolina, 1975-1976.

37. Cadoo, John. Personal communication. 1976.

38. Christenson, James A., Maurice Voland, and Frank Santopalo. "Evaluating the Comparative Productivity of Sociologists in Extension, Research and Teaching." Rural Sociology, Vol. 42, Spring, 1977.

omitted because the investigators felt their response was "high enough." If the TDM had been used fully, response rates for these and all others who used the method in part would have almost certainly improved. Results from these and other studies reported in Table 1.1 suggest that response rates near 90 percent are not unusual for some specialized groups.

Another factor influencing response rate is the type of population surveyed. It is convenient to divide the studies that survey the general public from the remainder, which can be described as specialized populations. This comparison is of special interest inasmuch as the former has traditionally been a difficult population from which to get good response. The results confirm that reputation, with the average response rates for the general public surveys being 70 percent, compared to 77 percent for the specialized ones. If we limit our comparison to only those which have used the complete TDM, the rates are, as we would expect, higher—73 percent and 81 percent, respectively.

Still another factor that influences response rates is the length of the questionnaire. A detailed treatment of length is reserved for Chapter 2; here we note only the two most important findings. First, there is almost no difference in response rates for various lengths below 12 pages, or about 125 items. The response to these questionnaires averaged 76 percent. However, beyond that length the response rates decline to an average of 65 percent. The 10–12-page questionnaire, which is the one most typically used, appears to be an optimal length that cannot be exceeded without endangering response.

Another concern that bears on the viability of results obtained by the TDM is the quality of the completed questionnaires, one indicator of which is the item nonresponse. In virtually all the studies listed in Table 1.1 information was obtained on attitudes, behavior, and demographic (personal) characteristics. Many included such reputedly hard to get answered items as political party, religious affiliation, and income. Overall, item nonresponse was remarkably low, usually not exceeding 3−4 percent of the returned questionnaires. Nonresponse was generally less for personal items than the average for all items, with the exception of income, which was only slightly higher. We conclude that, in spite of considerable length, overall item nonresponse, in particular that on certain crucial items, does not represent a significant problem.

Response to TDM Telephone Surveys

Turning to the telephone TDM results of Table 1.2, it is important to note first the ways these surveys have differed from the mail studies just discussed and the reasons for this difference. First, most are much shorter and have smaller sample sizes. This can be explained by the tendency to use the mail and telephone methods as alternatives to one another and the fact that mail TDM studies are less costly when questionnaires are shorter and the samples larger, facts that are discussed in more detail in Chapter 2. Because respondents seldom cut off an interview once they start, interviews of much greater length than those we report can be conducted without a great effect on response rates.

The table is limited to surveys conducted at Washington State University through the Social Research Center's Public Opinion Laboratory. Thirty-one surveys were conducted under 16 different projects. Relatively few surveys conducted elsewhere followed the procedures we outline, partly because the precise step-by-step method has not been disseminated heretofore in the detail of the mail procedures.

However, the surveys do represent a variety of populations and topics, from ministers to veterinarians and election issues to attitudes on prison reform, and they were conducted by a number of different investigators. Together, these help provide a good assessment of the telephone TDM's versatility when used in a variety of situations.

The average response for the 31 surveys is 91 percent, a full 17 percentage points higher than the average for the mail surveys. The difference persists for both the specialized and general public populations: 96 percent (versus 77 percent for the mail) and 87 percent (versus 70 percent for the mail), respectively.

The single lowest response rate recorded for any of these telephone surveys was 73 percent. This was on a survey of the general public that was devoted entirely to issues of religious commitment. In our opinion that is an extremely difficult topic on which to obtain response and therefore represents a most severe test of the telephone TDM. In light of that difficulty, it is interesting to note that this response is just 1 percentage point under the average response for all the mail surveys reported in Table 1.1.

Although we lack data on how the telephone TDM will perform in other areas of the country, neither do we have information that would lead us to expect great differences from those reported here. The results do not differ greatly from those obtained in other regions of the country by other procedures.

Whether the results shown here for both the mail and telephone TDMs make them adequate for use by others in their particular survey situations is a question that can only be answered individually. It cannot be answered in isolation from a consideration of numerous other ways in which the mail and telephone methods differ from one another and face-to-face interviews. Response rate is only one of a large number of considerations that go into selecting the most satisfactory method for one's study. For this reason, Chapter 2 presents a detailed comparison of all three methods. Its purpose is to help the would-be user of the TDM decide whether mail or telephone surveys are suited to his or her purpose.

For purposes of this chapter, the evidence is sufficient to suggest that the TDM is capable of producing quite satisfactory results for many studies. Certainly the results exceed the expectations ascribed to the two methods only a few short years ago.

CONCLUSION

This book was both pushed and pulled into existence. The "push" came from the emerging concern that face to face interviews, once the only acceptable method for conducting surveys, no longer satisfies the needs of social scientists. Skyrocketing costs have made them unavailable to many researchers with good ideas and have inevitably demanded compromises in study design from those able to use them. Now it even seems questionable whether face-to-face interviews can elicit the expected high response rates, the quality that once distinguished them from other methods. Clearly the need for viable alternatives has never been greater, suggesting that the mail and telephone methods will see greater use regardless of the quality of results they produce. At the same time, past research on mail methods has contributed very little to our knowledge of how to maximize response, a state of affairs brought about by the fact that research has focused almost exclusively on techniques and not respondent behavior. Past research on the telephone was almost nonexistent.

The "pull" was provided by our own research and that of others showing that both the mail and telephone are capable of much more than their poor reputations suggest. This research was guided by a conception of respondent

Table 1.2 Response Rates for Telephone Studies in Which Total Design Telephone Method Was Used

TOPIC/SAMPLE[b]	SAMPLE SIZE[c]	ITEMS[d]/ MINUTES[e]	RESPONSE RATE[f]
1. Opinions on 2-day racism workshop: Washington State University			
Students	198	16/5	99%
Staff	121	16/5	95%
Faculty	112	16/5	93%
Washington State	98	16/5	93%
2. Attitudes on use of drugs I:			
Washington State University: Students	193	16/5	97%
Pullman, Washington	97	16/5	96%
Whitman County, Washington	101	16/5	95%
3. Attitudes on use of drugs II:			
Washington State University: Students	146	20/7	95%
Pullman, Washington	110	20/7	95%
Whitman County, Washington	101	20/7	93%
4. Opinions on second racism workshop: Washington State University			
Students	214	19/6	99%
Staff	109	19/6	94%
Faculty	112	19/6	98%
Pullman, Washington	127	19/6	80%
5. Attitudes toward use of drugs III:			
Washington State University: Students	157	16/5	85%
Pullman, Washington	120	16/5	93%
Whitman County, Washington	118	16/5	89%
6. Kinds of clothing worn by veterinarians: All licensed veterinarians, Washington	200	30/9	98%
7. Candidates and issues in statewide general election: Washington	1040	30/11	78%
8. Opinions on tax reform: Washington	643	10/5	86%
9. Opinions on policies and activities of Washington State University			
Students	279	12/4	100%
Parents of Students	250	12/4	97%
Washington	250	12/4	79%

Table 1.2 *Continued*

TOPIC/SAMPLE[b]	SAMPLE SIZE[c]	ITEMS[d]/ MINUTES[e]	RESPONSE RATE[f]
10. Opinions on rights and responsibilities of men and women: Washington	1143	28/8	82%
11. Opinions on rights and responsibilities of men and women: Ministers of all churches in Washington	647	32/10	96%
12. Opinions on air pollution: Spokane, Washington-- General Public	534	31/8	85%
13. Community size preference and satisfaction: Washington	1354	47/20	90%
14. Religious commitment: Washington	495	52/25	73%
15. Opinions on alternative futures for Washington State	1000	61/25	90%
16. Prison reform: Washington	1300	85/28	85%

Table 1.2   Footnotes

[a]The extent to which the TDM was used is omitted from this table, in contrast to its inclusion in the table on mail studies. It is omitted for two reasons. first, as noted in Chapters 6 and 7 the telephone method has many more implementation options than the mail method, thus making it difficult to provide a meaningful evaluation. Secondly, all of the studies listed here were conducted through the Washington State University Public Opinion Laboratory so that few differences existed with respect to how the studies were implemented.

[b]Unless otherwise noted, a sample of the indicated general public was surveyed. For example, the notation "Washington" means a statewide sample of the general public was surveyed.

[c]The final sample size was in some instances less because of the inclusion of ineligible persons.

[d]Number of items was defined as each time a respondent was expected to provide an answer.

[e]The estimated average time required to complete the interview.

[f]Response rates are calculated as percent of actual contacts ending with completed interviews, and not as percent of original sample size. This procedure is used because (1) in some instances people included in the sample did not have telephones, (2) the proportion of not-at-homes varied considerably among the various surveys, due to differences in call back procedures, and (3) in

Table 1.2   Footnotes, Continued

some surveys mail follow-ups were used to reach not-at-homes. By excluding the effects of these factors from calculation of the response rates meaningful comparisons can be made among the various studies we have reported.

[9]Sources for the above information are identified here by the numbers assigned above. If more than one name is listed the principle investigator is identified by an asterisk (*).

1. Dillman, D. A. Unpublished data. Archives, Washington State University Social Research Center, Pullman, Washington.

2. Hadden, Stuart C. "The Social Creation of a Social Problem." Unpublished Ph.D. dissertation, Washington State University, 1973.

3. Hadden, Stuart C. Op. cit.

4. Dillman, D.A. Unpublished data. Archives, Washington State University Social Research Center, Pullman, Washington.

5. Hadden, Stuart C. Op. cit.

6. Tollefsen, Christine Larsen. "Occupational Dress of Veterinarians." Unpublished M.A. thesis, Washington State University, 1973.

7. Dillman, D.A.*, Jean G. Gallegos, and James H. Frey. "Reducing Refusal Rates to telephone Interviews." Forthcoming Public Opinion Quarterly.

8. Dillman, D.A*, W. Willmans*, and D. Stadelman. Preliminary Report on WSU/UW Tax Surveys. Social Research Center, Washington State University, 1972.

9. Smith, Linda Kay. "Attitudes Held by Students, Their Parents, and the General Public on the in Loco Parentis Position of the University." Unpublished M.A. thesis, Washington State University, 1973.

10. Nye, F. Ivan*, V. Gecas*, and D.A. Dillman. "Sexism: A Test of the Oppression Hypothesis." Unpublished paper. 1973.

11. Finney, John. Personal communication. 1973.

12. Dunlap, Riley E. "Air Pollution in the Spokane Area: A Survey of Public Opinion." Report 6, Environmental Research Center, Washington State University, Pullman, Washington, 1973.

13. Dillman, D.A.*, Jean G. Gallegos, and James H. Frey. "Reducing Refusal Rates to Telephone Interviews." Public Opinion Quarterly, Vol. 40, 1976, pp. 66-78.

14. Finney, John. Personal communication. 1974.

15. Wardwell, John M.* and Don A. Dillman. "The Alternatives for Washington Surveys: The Final Report." Prepared for the Washington State Office of Program Planning and Fiscal Management. 1975.

16. Riley, Pam   Personal communication. 1975.

behavior as a holistic response to survey stimuli. To maximize response, principles of social exchange were used in deciding how to design surveys, and emphasis was placed on the development of an administrative plan to ensure adequate organization for carrying out the intentions of the design. Results from various mail and telephone surveys in which the TDM was used are promising and suggest that both are competitive with face-to-face interviews for many kinds of studies.

To ensure that the methods described in the remainder of this book are understood in the appropriate context, it seems important to comment on our use of the word "total." The term should not be taken as connoting anything approaching finality. The TDM is as much a theory of response behavior as it is a method shown to produce good results. There has not been sufficient use of the TDM or experimentation to determine whether the results obtained are the best possible. Indeed, we have only begun inquiry into the quality of results obtained with the TDM. Thus a final purpose in writing this book is to stimulate others to take up the search for ways to improve these mail and telephone methods further.

The chapters that follow serve distinct objectives. Chapter 2 provides detailed comparisons of the capabilities of the mail and telephone TDMs with those of face-to-face interviews, with a view to fully evaluating the comparative advantages of each. Hopefully this will prevent would-be users from selecting one method or the other only to discover that it cannot possibly produce the desired results. Chapter 3 presents some general principles on how to write survey questions. Its inclusion was deemed essential inasmuch as our experience in working with others suggested that fundamental problems of question construction are a formidable barrier to getting adequate results. Chapters 4 and 5 describe the mail TDM. The first of these focuses on matters of questionnaire construction. Chapter 5 covers the implementation process. Chapters 6 and 7 give similar treatment to TDM telephone studies, with the first again dealing only with questionnaire construction. Chapter 7 handles all details of the implementation process. Chapter 8 discusses the implications of viable mail and telephone methods for survey research and attempts to lay the groundwork for further research aimed at realizing the maximum potential of these methods.

NOTES

1. M. Parten, *Surveys, Polls, and Samples* (New York: Harper and Row, 1950); Claire Sellitz, Marie Jahoda, Morton Deutsch, and Stuart W. Cook, *Research Methods in Social Relations* (Chicago: Holt, Rinehart, and Winston, 1959); Fred N. Kerlinger, *Foundations of Behavioral Research* (New York: Holt, Rinehart, and Winston, 1965).
2. Anonymous, "The Public Clams Up on Surveys Taken," *Business Week,* September 15, 1973, pp. 216–220; American Statistical Association Conference on Surveys of Human Populations, "Report on the ASA Conference on Surveys of Human Populations," *The American Statistician, 28,* February 1974, p. 31.
3. American Statistical Association, *Ibid.,* p. 31.
4. *Ibid.*

5. *Ibid.*

6. *Ibid.*

7. An exception is Paul L. Erdos, *Professional Mail Surveys* (New York: McGraw-Hill, 1970), which focuses only on mail surveys and is oriented to market researchers.

8. The period covered was 1965–1972. The journals included *The American Sociological Review, Social Forces, Sociological Inquiry, Social Problems, Sociometry, Journal of Educational Sociology, Rural Sociology, Journal of Social Psychology, Pacific Sociological Review,* and *Sociological Quarterly.*

9. R. C. Buse, "Increasing Response Rates in Mailed Questionnaires," *American Journal of Agricultural Economics,* August 1973, pp. 503–508; Edward M. Smith and Wendell Hewett, "The Value of a Preliminary Letter in Postal Survey Response," *Journal of the Market Research Society, 14,* 1972, pp. 145–151; David J. Purcel, Howard F. Nelson, and David N. Wheeler, "Questionnaire Follow-Up Returns as a Function of Incentives and Responder Characteristics," *Vocational Guidance Quarterly,* March 1971, pp. 188–193; G. Allen Brunner and Stephen J. Carroll, Jr., "The Effect of Prior Telephone Notification on the Refusal Rate in Fixed Address Surveys," *Journal of Advertising Research, 9,* 1969, pp. 42–44; James H. Myers and Arne F. Haug, "How a Preliminary Letter Affects Mail Survey Returns and Costs," *Journal of Advertising Research, 9,* 1969, pp. 37–39; Neil M. Ford, "The Advance Letter in Mail Surveys," *Journal of Marketing Research, 4,* 1967, pp. 202–204; James E. Stafford, "Influence of Preliminary Contact on Mail Returns," *Journal of Marketing Research, 3,* 1966, pp. 410–411; Eugene E. Heaton, Jr., "Increasing Mail Questionnaire Returns with a Preliminary Letter," *Journal of Advertising Research, 5,* 1965, pp. 36–39; Stanley S. Robin, "A Procedure for Securing Returns to Mail Questionnaires," *Sociology and Social Research, 49,* October 1965, pp. 24–35; Sol Levine and Gerald Gordon, "Maximizing Returns on Mail Questionnaires," *Public Opinion Quarterly, 22,* 1958, pp. 568–575.

10. Stafford, *Ibid.;* F. B. Waisanen, "A Note on the Response to a Mailed Questionnaire," *Public Opinion Quarterly, 18,* 1954, pp. 210–212.

11. Paul L. Erdos, 1970, *op. cit.*

12. R. C. Buse, *op. cit.;* David B. Orr and Clinton A. Neyman, Jr., "Considerations, Costs, and Returns in a Large-Scale Follow-Up Study," *Journal of Educational Research, 58,* 1965, pp. 373–378; Monroe G. Sirken, James W. Pifer, and Morton L. Brown, "Survey Procedures for Supplementing Mortality Statistics," *American Journal of Public Health, 50,* 1960, pp. 1753–1764; Jeanne E. Gullahorn and John T. Gullahorn, "Increasing Returns From Non-Respondents," *Public Opinion Quarterly, 23,* 1959, pp. 119–121; Levine and Gordon, *op. cit.;* William M. Kephart and Marvin Bressler, "Increasing the Response to Mail Questionnaires: A Research Study," *Public Opinion Quarterly, 22,* 1958, pp. 123–132; Hyman Goldstein and Bernard H. Kroll, "Methods of Increasing Mail Response," *Journal of Marketing, 22,* 1957, pp. 55–57; W. M. Phillips, "Weakness of the Mail Questionnaire," *Sociology and Social Research, 35,* 1951, pp. 260–267; John A. Clausen and Robert N. Ford, "Controlling Bias in Mail Questionnaires," *Journal of the American Statistical Association, 42,* 1947, pp. 497–511.

13. Wayne E. Hensley, "Increasing Response Rate by Choice of Postage Stamps," *Public Opinion Quarterly 38,* 1974, pp. 280–283; Donald S. Longworth, "Use of a Mail Questionnaire," *American Sociological Review, 18,* 1953, pp. 310–313.

14. Hensley, *Ibid.;* Dorothy L. Barlett, Pamela B. Drew, Eleanor G. Fahle, and William A. Watts, "Selective Exposure to a Presidential Campaign Appeal," *Public Opinion Quarterly, 38,* 1974, pp. 264–270; John F. Veiga, "Getting the Mail Questionnaire Returned: Some Practical Research Considerations," *Journal of Applied Psychology, 59,* 1974, pp.

217—218; Buse, *op. cit.*; Frederick Wiseman, "Methodological Bias in Public Opinion Surveys," *Public Opinion Quarterly, 36,* 1972, pp. 105–108; Bruce K. Eckland, "Effects of Prodding to Increase Mail-Back Returns," *Journal of Applied Psychology, 49,* 1965, pp. 165–169; Orr and Neyman, *op. cit.*; Robin, *op. cit.*; John J. Watson, "Improving the Response Rate in Mail Research," *Journal of Advertising Research, 5,* 1965, pp. 48–50; Jeanne E. Gullahorn and John T. Gullahorn, "An Investigation of the Effects of Three Factors on Response to Mail Questionnaires," *Public Opinion Quarterly, 27,* 1963, pp. 294–296; Andrew E. Kimball, "Increasing the Rate of Return in Mail Surveys," *Journal of Marketing, 25,* 1961, pp. 63–64; Christopher Scott, "Research in Mail Surveys," *Journal of the Royal Statistical Society,* Series A., 124, 1961, pp. 143–205; E. C. Hammond, "Inhalation in Relation to Type and Amount of Smoking," *Journal of the American Statistical Association, 54,* 1959, pp. 35–51; Levine and Gordon, *op. cit.*; D. O. Price, "On the Use of Stamped Return Envelopes with Mail Questionnaires," *American Sociological Review, 15,* 1950, pp. 672–673; R. M. Seitz, "How Mail Surveys May Be Made to Pay," *Printers Ink,* December 1, 1944, pp. 17–19ff.

15. E. G. Francel, "Mail Administered Questionnaires: A Success Story," *Journal of Marketing Research, 3,* 1966, pp. 89–91; Goldstein and Kroll, *op. cit.*; National Education Association, "The Questionnaire," *National Education Association Research Bulletin,* 8, 1930, pp. 1–51.

16. Scott, 1961, *op. cit.*; Levine and Gordon, *op. cit.*; R. A. Robinson, "How to Boost Returns From Mail Surveys," *Printers Ink,* June 6, 1952, pp. 35–37.

17. Scott, *Ibid.*; F. Filipello, H. W. Berg, and A. D. Webb, "A Sampling Method for Household Surveys," *Food Technology, 12,* 1958, pp. 387–390; K. E. Clark, "A Vocational Interest Test at the Skilled Test Level," *Journal of Applied Psychology, 33,* 1949, pp. 291–303; R. Watson, "Investigations by Mail," *Market Research, 7,* 1937, pp. 11–16.

18. Buse, *op. cit.*; Smith and Hewett, *op. cit.*; Francel, *op. cit.*; Arnold Linskey, "Experiment in Inducing Response to Mail Questionnaires," *Sociology and Social Research, 49,* 1965, p. 183; Leo G. Reeder, "Mailed Questionnaires in Longitudinal Health Studies: The Problem of Maintaining and Maximizing Response," *Journal of Health and Human Behavior, 1,* 1960, pp. 123–129; Norman Tallent and William J. Reiss, "A Note on an Unusually High Rate of Returns for a Mail Questionnaire," *Public Opinion Quarterly, 23,* 1959, pp. 579–581; G. Frazier and K. Bird, "Increasing the Response to a Mail Questionnaire," *Journal of Marketing, 23,* 1958, pp. 186–187; Levine and Gordon, *op. cit.*; D. A. Hoppe, "Certain Factors Found to Improve Mail Survey Returns," *Proceedings of the Iowa Academy of Science, 59,* 1952, pp. 374–376; Phillips, *op. cit.*; Seitz, *op. cit.*

19. G. Allan Roeher, "Effective Techniques in Increasing Response to Mailed Questionnaires," *Public Opinion Quarterly, 27,* 1963, pp. 299–302; Herbert H. Blumberg, Carolyn Fuller, and A. Paul Hare, "Response Rates in Postal Surveys," *Public Opinion Quarterly, 38,* 1974, pp. 113–123.

20. Buse, *op. cit.*; Bruce Bunning and Don Cahalan, "By-Mail vs. Field Self-Administered Questionnaires: An Armed Forces Survey," *Public Opinion Quarterly, 37,* 1973–1974, pp. 618–624; Walter E. Boek and James H. Lade, "A Test of the Usefulness of the Postcard Technique in a Mail Questionnaire Study," *Public Opinion Quarterly, 27,* 1963, pp. 303–306; Scott, 1961, *op. cit.*; Reeder, *op. cit.*; Kenneth Brandt, "The Use of a Postcard Technique in a Mail Questionnaire Study," *Public Opinion Quarterly, 19,* 1955, pp. 218–222; Don Cahalan, "Effectiveness of a Mail Questionnaire Technique in the Army," *Public Opinion Quarterly, 15,* 1951, pp. 575–580; Walter Mitchell, Jr., "Factors Affecting the Rate of Return on Mailed Questionnaires," *Journal of the American Statistical Association, 34,* 1939, pp. 683–692.

21. Sirken, Pifer, and Brown, *op. cit.*

22. Clausen and Ford, *op. cit.*

23. Watson, *op. cit.*

24. Francel, *op. cit.*

25. Buse, *op. cit.;* Robin, *op. cit.;* Reeder, *op. cit.;* Levine and Gordon, *op. cit.;* W. L. Slocum, L. T. Empey, and H. S. Swanson, "Increasing Response to Questionnaires and Structured Interviews," *American Sociological Review, 21,* 1956, pp. 221–225; Raymond F. Sletto, "Pretesting of Questionnaires," *American Sociological Review, 5,* 1940, pp. 193–200.

26. Linskey, *op. cit.*

27. James C. Hackler and Patricia Bourgette, "Dollars, Dissonance, and Survey Returns," *Public Opinion Quarterly, 37,* 1973, pp. 276—281; Frederick Wiseman, *op. cit.;* Watson, *op. cit.;* Kimball, *op. cit.;* Kephart and Bressler, *op. cit.;* Paul L. Erdos, "How to Get Higher Returns From Your Mail Surveys," *Printers Ink,* February 22, 1957, pp. 30–31; Paul L. Erdos, "Successful Mail Surveys: High Returns and How to Get Them," *Printers Ink,* March 1, 1957, pp. 56–60; R. A. Robinson and Phillip Agisim, "Making Mail Surveys More Reliable," *Journal of Marketing, 15,* 1951, pp. 415–424; Joseph C. Bevis, "Economical Incentive Used for Mail Questionnaires," *Public Opinion Quarterly, 12,* 1948, pp. 492–493; R. A. Robinson, "Five Features Helped This Questionnaire Pull From 60% to 70%", *Printers Ink,* February 22, 1946, pp. 25—26; J. W. Hancock, "An Experimental Study of Four Methods of Measuring Unit Costs of Obtaining Attitude Toward the Retail Store," *Journal of Applied Psychology,* 24, 1940, pp. 213–230; F. K. Shuttleworth, "A Study of Questionnaire Technique," *Journal of Educational Psychology, 22,* 1931, pp. 652–658.

28. R. D. Brennan, "Trading Stamps as an Incentive in Mail Surveys," *Journal of Marketing,* 22, 1958, pp. 306–307.

29. John B. Knox, "Maximizing Responses to Mail Questionnaires: A New Technique," *Public Opinion Quarterly, 15,* 1951, pp. 366–367.

30. Erdos, 1957, "Successful Mail Surveys," *op cit.;* B. E. Etcheverry, "Want Confidential Purchase Data? It's All in How You Ask," *Sales Management,* March 1, 1954, pp. 48ff.

31. Purcel, Nelson, and Wheeler, *op. cit.*

32. *Ibid.*

33. Robinson and Agisim, *op. cit.*

34. Purcel, Nelson, and Wheeler, *op. cit.*

35. Thomas R. Wotruba, "Monetary Inducements and Mail Questionnaire Response," *Journal of Marketing Research, 3,* 1966, pp. 398–399; Hancock, *op. cit.*

36. Darrel Montero, "A Study of Social Desirability Response Bias: the Mail Questionnaire, the Face-to-Face Interview, and the Telephone Interview Compared," 1974 (Preliminary Draft, Department of Sociology, University of California at Los Angeles); Buse, *op. cit.;* Don A. Dillman, "Increasing Mail Questionnaire Response in Large Samples of the General Public," *Public Opinion Quarterly, 36,* 1972, pp. 254–257; Hackler and Bourgette, *op. cit.;* Peter Ognibene, "Correction of Nonresponse Bias in Mail Questionnaires," *Journal of Marketing Research, 8,* 1971, pp. 233–235; Peter Ognibene, "Traits Affecting Questionnaire Response," *Journal of Advertising Research, 10,* 1970, pp. 18–20; William H. Sewell and Vimal P. Shah, "Socioeconomic Status, Intelligence, and the Attainment of Higher Education," *Sociology of Education, 40,* 1967, pp. 1–23; Charles S. Mayer and Robert W. Pratt, Jr., " Note on Nonresponses in a Mail Survey," *Public Opinion Quarterly, 30,* 1966–1967, pp. 637–646; Eckland, *op. cit.;* Orr and Neyman, *op. cit.;* Robin, *op. cit.;* Clark E. Vincent, "Socioeconomic Status and Familial Variables in Mail Questionnaire Responses," *American*

Journal of Sociology, 69, 1964, pp. 647–653; Joseph R. Hochstim, "Alternatives to Personal Interviewing," *Public Opinion Quarterly, 27,* 1963, pp. 629—630; W. K. Kirchner and N. B. Mousley, "A Note on Job Performance," *Journal of Advertising Psychology, 47,* 1963, pp. 223–233; Monroe G. Sirken and Morton L. Brown, "Quality of Data Elicited by Successive Mailings in Mail Surveys," *American Statistical Association,* Proceedings of the Social Statistics Section, 1962, pp. 118–125; Scott, 1961, *op. cit.;* Marjorie N. Donald, "Implications of Nonresponse for the Interpretation of Mail Questionnaire Data," *Public Opinion Quarterly, 24,* 1960, pp. 99–114; Sirken, Pifer, and Brown, *op. cit.;* Tallent and Reiss, *op. cit.;* Filipello, Berg, and Webb, *op. cit.;* Levine and Gordon, *op. cit.;* Slocum, Empey, and Swanson, *op. cit.;* Phillips, *op. cit.;* Albert Ellis, "Questionnaire Versus Interview Methods in the Study of Human Love Relationships," *American Sociological Review, 12,* 1947, pp. 541–553; Seerley Reid, "Respondents and Non-Respondents to Mail Questionnaires," *Educational Research Bulletin, 21,* 1942, pp. 87–96; Sletto, *op. cit.;* Edward A. Suchman and Boyd McCandless, "Who Answers Questionnaires?" *Journal of Applied Psychology, 24,* 1940, pp. 758–769; H. A. Toops, "The Returns From Follow-up Letters to Questionnaires," *Journal of Applied Psychology, 10,* 1926, pp. 92–101.

37. Buse, *Ibid.;* Wiseman, *op. cit.;* Dillman, *Ibid.;* S. Stephen Kegeles, Clinton F. Fink, and John P. Kirscht, "Interviewing a National Sample by Long-Distance Telephone," *Public Opinion Quarterly, 33,* 1969–1970, pp. 412–419; W. E. Cox, Jr., "Response Patterns to Mail Surveys," *Journal of Marketing Research, 3,* 1966, pp. 392–397; Francel, *op. cit.;* Robert C. Nichols and Mary Alice Meyer, "Timing Postcard Follow-ups in Mail Questionnaire Surveys," *Public Opinion Quarterly, 30,* 1966–1967, pp. 306–307; Eckland, *Ibid.;* Robin, *Ibid.;* Sirken and Brown, *op. cit.;* Scott, *Ibid.;* Sirken, Pifer, and Brown, *Ibid.;* Levine and Gordon, *Ibid.;* H. Zimmer, "Validity of Extrapolating Nonresponse Bias From Mail Questionnaire Follow-ups," *Journal of Applied Psychology, 40,* 1956, pp. 117–121; Longworth, *op. cit.*

38. G. Allen Brunner and Stephen J. Carroll, Jr., "The Effect of Prior Telephone Appointments on Completion Rates and Response Content," *Public Opinion Quarterly, 31,* 1967–1968, pp. 652–654; Kephart and Bressler, *op. cit.;* F. G. Scott, "Mail Questionnaires Used in a Study of Older Women," *Sociology and Social Research, 41,* 1957, pp. 281–284.

39. The conflicting findings are summarized by Don A. Dillman and James H. Frey, "Contribution of Personalization to Mail Questionnaire Response as an Element of a Previously Tested Method," *Journal of Applied Psychology, 59,* 1974, pp. 297–301.

40. Scott, 1961, *op. cit.;* Ward S. Mason, Robert J. Dressel, and Robert K. Bain, "An Experimental Study of Factors Affecting Response to a Mail Survey of Beginning Teachers," *Public Opinion Quarterly, 25,* 1961, pp. 296–299; Sirken, Pifer, and Brown, *op. cit.;* H. Durant and I. Mass, "Who Doesn't Answer?" *Bulletin of the British Psychological Society, 29,* 1956, pp. 33—34; Clausen and Ford, *op. cit.;* Sletto, *op. cit.*

41. Purcel, Nelson, and Wheeler, *op. cit.;* Gullahorn and Gullahorn, 1963, "Three Factors in Response to Mail Questionnaires," *op. cit.*

42. Scott, 1961, *op. cit.;* W. S. Miller and E. J. Engquist, Jr., "On the Effectiveness of 'Follow-ups' in Mail Canvasses," *Bulletin of the American Statistical Association, 2,* 1942, pp. 189–190.

43. Leslie Kanuk and Conrad Berenson, "Mail Surveys and Response Rates: A Literature Review," *Journal of Marketing Research, 12.* November 1975. p. 451.

44. Attempts to do such reviews have been undertaken elsewhere. A comprehensive and especially well done review of the literature prior to 1960 was reported by Scott, 1961, *op. cit.* Blumberg attempted to update that review in a very recent but far less ambitious effort, Blumberg, Fuller, and Hare, *op. cit.*

45. Kanuck and Berenson, *op. cit.;* Arnold S. Linsky, "Stimulating Responses to Mailed Quesionnaires: A Review," *Public Opinion Quarterly, 39,* 1975, pp. 82–101.

46. Daniel Katz and Hadley Cantril, "Public Opinion Polls," *Sociometry,* 1, 1937, pp. 155–179.

47. Statistical Abstract of the United States: 1937 (Washington, D.C.: U. S. Department of Commerce, 1937).

48. Sidney H. Aronson, "The Sociology of the Telephone," *International Journal of Comparative Sociology, 12,* 1971, pp. 163–167.

49. Donald, *op. cit.;* Suchman and McCandless, *op. cit;* Reid, *op. cit.;* Seymour Sudman, "New Uses of Telephone Methods in Survey Research," *Journal of Marketing Research,* 3, 1966, pp. 163–167.

50. Slocum, Empey, and Swanson, *op. cit.;* Sudman, *Ibid.;* Brunner and Carroll, 1967–1968, *op. cit.*

51. Wiseman, *op. cit.*

52. Kegeles, Fink, and Kirscht, *op. cit.;* Lolagene Coombs and Ronald Freedman, "Use of Telephone Interviews in a Longitudinal Fertility Study," *Public Opinion Quarterly,* 28, 1964, pp. 112–117; David Goldberg, Harry Sharp, and Ronald Freedman, "The Stability and Reliability of Expected Family Size Data," *Milbank Memorial Fund Quarterly, 37,* 1959, pp. 369–385; Slocum, Empey, and Swanson, *op. cit.*

53. See Note 8 for journals reviewed.

54. U. S. Bureau of the Census, *Statistical Abstract of the United States: 1975,* 96th edition (Washington, D. C.: U. S. Department of Commerce, 1975), p. 516.

55. *Ibid.*

56. See Sudman, *op. cit.* for an explanation of random digit dialing.

57. National Center for Health Services Research, *Advances in Health Survey Research Methods: Proceedings of a National Invitational Conference.* May 1–2, 1975, DHEW Publication No. (HRA) 77–3154.

58. Seymour Sudman, "Sample Surveys," in *Annual Review of Sociology,* Vol. 2, (Palo Alto; Annual Reviews, 1976), pp. 107–120.

59. Reeder, *op. cit.;* Sudman, *Ibid.*

60. Peter M. Blau, *Exchange and Power in Social Life* (New York: John Wiley and Sons, 1964); George C. Homans, *Social Behavior: Its Elementary Forms* (New York: Harcourt, Brace and World, 1961); J. W. Thibaut and H. H. Kelley, *The Social Psychology of Groups* (New York: John Wiley and Sons, 1959).

61. Thibaut and Kelley, *Ibid.*

62. Blau, *op. cit.*

63. Dillman, *op. cit.*

64. Blau, *op. cit.;* Homans, *op. cit.*

65. Blau, *op. cit.*

66. Slocum, Empey, and Swanson, *op. cit.*

67. Blau, *op. cit.*

68. Thibaut and Kelley, *op. cit.*

69. Blau, *op. cit.*

70. J. W. Hancock, *op. cit.;* F. G. Scott, *op. cit.*

71. Dillman, Gallegos, and Frey, *op. cit.*

Chapter Two

WHICH IS BEST:

....

The Advantages and Disadvantages of Mail, Telephone, and Face-to-Face Surveys

Recently, as I concluded a presentation on the relative merits of the mail, telephone, and face-to-face survey methods, a student asked me which was best. I responded in some detail, noting that each had certain advantages and disadvantages, and ended by saying that there was no simple answer to the question. This did not satisfy the questioner, who then asked, "Yes, but on balance which do you prefer?" At this I was tempted to reply the way I had once heard a harried colleague answer a similarly difficult question by simply declaring, "Well, it all depends, and that's final!" Even though such an answer could hardly be considered satisfactory, it does make clear the dilemma one faces in choosing among the three methods. The most important message of this chapter is that the question of which method is best cannot be answered in abstract terms. Although each method has certain strengths and weaknesses, they do not apply equally, or sometimes at all, to every survey situation. Thus, until the attributes of each method are considered in relation to the study topic, the population to be surveyed, and the precise survey objectives, the question of which is best cannot be answered.

The researcher who wants to survey alumni of a major university who are likely to be scattered among the 50 states and several foreign countries probably only has one choice—the mail questionnaire. Similarly, a researcher who finds it necessary to complete a survey in a 2-week period will probably find that the telephone is the only method that can do the job. If one is faced with surveying a low-income, low-education, minority population, chances are good that the face-to-face interview is the only acceptable method. However, most survey decisions are not as clear-cut. They involve finding the most desirable, or as some would put it, the "least objectionable," balance among sampling methods, survey costs, allowable complexity of questions, and a host of other factors.

Certainly, we do not wish to make answering what may seem a simple question unduly complex, only to conclude by saying that in the end it all depends on the survey situation and what the researcher is willing to sacrifice. Yet the use of any of the three methods requires accepting less of certain qualities to achieve others, the desirability of which cannot be isolated from a consideration of the survey topic and the population to be studied. The purpose of this chapter is to prepare the reader to make a more informed choice of methods, discussing the criteria usually important to choosing among them. The fact that the question of relative superiority no longer has a simple answer is indicative of the improvement that has taken place in mail and telephone survey methods. As long as mail questionnaires obtained low response and large segments of the population did not have telephones, face-to-face interviews were simply beyond challenge. Although this is still true for some survey situations, for others—the number of which continues to increase—it is not the case.

Developments such as those fostered by the TDM reveal an attribute of face-to-face interview surveys that is often overlooked. Compromises in survey design are almost always made, for example, sample sizes that are smaller than desirable, inadequate respondent selection methods, and restrictions in the coverage of the survey. Such deficiencies were usually accepted because there was no reasonable alternative. Any thought of switching methods was invariably repressed by the realization that, although some deficiencies might be eliminated, this could only be accomplished by accepting the overwhelmingly glaring ones of other methods.

This chapter is organized around a set of surveying problems with which each survey method must contend. Each method is evaluated in terms of how well it handles each problem. The conclusion to the chapter is a checklist that explicitly compares the performance of each method for solving each problem, providing a form for handy reference when making the crucial decision of which method to employ. Although the process of evaluating pros and cons associated with the use of each method remains partly subjective, this chapter suggests that steps toward its objectification can and are being made.

OBTAINING COMPLETED QUESTIONNAIRES FROM A
REPRESENTATIVE SAMPLE

It is impressive to hear someone announce that he or she has achieved a response rate of 95 percent, or, as has been known to happen, 100 percent. However, the glamour that comes from such an achievement fades quickly when it is learned that the sample was biased, and we are left to wrestle with the perplexing question, "95 percent of what?" Response rate is only one indicator of representativeness. In many surveys it is not a very good indicator and is certainly far less important than others. The prevailing obsession with response rate often leads to overlooking other barriers to representativeness, five of which are considered here. Each concerns a critical event in the process of identifying, locating, and questioning potential respondents.

The first is the actual *sampling* and whether each unit of the population has an equal (or at least known) opportunity of being included, the probability of which depends on whether one is knocking on doors or sampling from a prepared list, as is frequently the case with telephone and mail surveys. A problem that logically follows is whether *selection criteria* can be adequately applied for purposes of determining which member of the sampled unit (e.g., household) is to be surveyed. Another distinct question, and usually the next step in the survey process, is whether the selected respondent can be *located* for purposes of completing the questionnaire. The fact that they sometimes cannot be found is evidenced by the prevalent use of *substitution procedures,* the next topic. Although not a recommended practice, substitution is often deemed necessary, and the varying implications for each survey method must be considered. These four barriers to accessing a representative sample, each of which holds somewhat different implications for the three methods, set the stage for consideration of the *response rates* each method is likely to achieve. The discussion of this most common indicator of survey success is put into fuller context by evaluating the probable *bias from refusals,* which also differs by method.

Is There a Known Opportunity for All Members of the Population To Be Included in the Sample?

A sample cannot be considered representative of a population unless all members of that population have a known chance of being included in the sample. If a complete list of the members of a population is available, which is rarely the case, a representative sample can be drawn regardless of the data collection method used. Populations in which complete enumeration is occasionally possible include doctors, lawyers, agency directors, and ministers.

Representativeness becomes a problem only when one deals with populations not completely enumerated, such as the general public, the unemployed, and the disabled.

In face-to-face interviews of the general public, area probability sampling methods are normally used. To draw such a sample, blocks or other geographic units are first randomly drawn. Then, dwelling units within each of these areas are similarly selected. This procedure ensures that all households have an equal chance of being included.[1] Published lists, from which samples are often drawn for mail and telephone surveys, do not approach this level of completeness. Lists of television owners, telephone subscribers, utility users, or car owners inevitably provide incomplete enumerations. These listings typically fall short of being completely adequate in one or more of the ways described below.

First, certain members of the general population do not possess the attribute(s) necessary for them to be placed on the relevant list. Many households do not have cars, telephones, or even utility service. For example, although households with telephones have reached an all-time national high of 94 percent, that percentage varies by state and by region within each state. According to the U.S. Statistical Abstract, only about 76 percent of the households in Alaska and 77 percent in Mississippi had phones in 1973, compared to nearly 100 percent in Connecticut, New Hampshire, New Jersey, and Vermont. Thirty-nine states now have at least 90 percent of their households with telephones.[2]

The U.S. Census collects information on whether members of households have a telephone "available." The enumeration question used by the Census tends to be somewhat ambiguous; thus people may interpret the word "available" in quite different ways. Consequently, people in several different households may list the same telephone (e.g., a telephone in the hallway of an apartment building) as the one available to them. Using this rough indicator of telephone availability, Census reports show substantial problems in using telephones to reach some segments of the general public. For example, less than half of households composed of either Spanish or Black families headed by a male and residing in nonmetropolitan areas have a telephone available.[3] In contrast, slightly over 95 percent of the white families above the poverty level report having a telephone available. Although the extent to which telephones are unavailable is much less today than in former years, it still represents a substantial problem in some areas of the country and for some segments of the population. The same holds true for automobile registrations and utility listings.

A second shortcoming of general public listings is that people are sometimes able to keep their names off them. The telephone directory is an excel-

lent example. Although precise information on the distribution of these numbers is difficult to obtain, the proportion of households with unlisted telephone numbers appears to be quite high in certain areas of the country, that
is, large cities. In contrast, it approaches zero in many rural areas. In addition,
the social characteristics of those people with unlisted telephone numbers
may make them a distinctive group. For example, it was reported in one study
that people with unlisted numbers were less educated, younger, more mobile,
more likely to.be divorced, poorer, belonged to fewer organizations, more
likely to rent their homes, and to have more and younger children than those
people with listed numbers.[4] The extent to which this represents a potential
problem for those doing surveys by telephone has been lessened, however,
by the development of random digit dialing procedures. Under this method
(described in Chapter 7) telephone numbers are randomly generated based
on all possible numbers thought to be in use. Consequently, unlisted telephones are just as likely to be sampled as listed ones.[5] This may reduce the
problems associated with unlisted numbers, but it does not solve the problem
of reaching those without telephone service, nor does it solve the problem for
the mail questionnaire researcher who wants to use the telephone directory as
a sampling source, since unlisted telephone numbers also mean unlisted
addresses.

The third and perhaps most perplexing problem in using available lists is
that inevitably they are somewhat out of date. This problem varies depending
on the nature of the list. Advances in computer technology have made it
possible in some cases, at least theoretically, to obtain up-to-date listings.
Information on utility users is kept up to date at least monthly in some cities.
On the other hand, voluntary organization lists may only be updated every
year or two. Telephone directories are a prime example of the problem of
dated listings. Directories are published at various intervals, but the most
usual interval is annually. The newly published directory is itself from 1 to
perhaps 3 or 4 months old because of printing and publication time. In
addition, mobility patterns of Americans cause most directories to become
outdated quickly. Approximately one out of five Americans moves each year,
with one out of 15 moving across county lines.[6] The result is that those who
recently moved into an area are not included in the directory. Even those
moving from one house to another within a city or who for some other reason
have their phone numbers changed may be missed.

The number of people not listed in the telephone directory varies considerably depending on the mobility rate in the study area. One study reported
that the percentage of people who can be reached at the end of the directory
year with the conventional method of sampling is 82 percent, compared to 91
percent at the beginning of the year.[7] A method for maximizing the chances of

drawing a representative sample from directories is to plan a study to coincide with the new directory's release. However, this does not present a solution to those interested in surveying areas covered by more than one directory. In general, the release of directories within a geographic region or state is staggered throughout the year; regardless of the time of the year one chooses, some directories will be outdated. A more effective solution may therefore be the random digit dialing method already described.

A fourth problem in the use of listings is that many include someone other than the desired respondent. For example, utility listings often include only the owner or manager of rental units to whom bills are sent, and not the occupants. Likewise, automobile registrations are often involved in legal entanglements; those who rely for transportation on a particular automobile are not always the ones whose names are on the registration lists.

A fifth problem with lists is that duplication of individuals is frequent; it is impossible to know the chance of each person being included in the sample. One reason for duplication is that individuals obtain, for business and social reasons, listings in more than one directory. This is especially true in metropolitan regions covered by several directories. Another example of duplication consists of households in which both spouses, and even children, have separate listings. The obvious result is that some people or households have a greater chance of being selected than others. Duplication also occurs in utility lists in which one person may be listed as the utility payee for a number of housing units. This is especially true when the geographic area being sampled contains numerous multiple-dwelling units.

A final difficulty associated with the use of available listings is gaining access to them. Many lists are confidential and cannot be obtained under any circumstances, for example, recipients of social services and unlisted phone numbers. Some lists, such as automobile registrations or utility customers, may be available only under certain negotiated circumstances. Today it is more difficult to obtain some listings because of the concern for the maintenance of individual privacy and the apparent rising distrust of political institutions.[8]

Given these problems of listings of the general public, it seems almost impossible to gain access to a completely representative sample of the general public by using available records. Some segments of the population are overrepresented; others are underrepresented. Knowing this, the researcher must be concerned that those omitted do not differ significantly from those actually selected, or that the overrepresented portion does not skew the sample data. Clearly, on the basis of the potential for sample representativeness, face-to-face surveys that can use area probability sampling methods have a significant advantage over mail and telephone survey methods that usually depend on some form of listing.

Can the Selection of Respondents Within Sample Units Be Controlled?

Some surveys require that members of a sampling unit, such as the household, be listed and that preestablished criteria be used to select respondents. In household surveys this is necessary to obtain an accurate sample of the general public. If selection criteria are not employed, the researcher is likely to end up with information from only those persons most likely to be at home at the time interviews were taken. Thus unemployed homemakers and retired people are likely to be disproportionately represented. Prescribed selection procedures are available for both telephone and face-to-face interviews and can be easily utilized to ensure proportional representation.[9] However, such procedures are more difficult to use in a mail survey, unless the household composition is known ahead of time; this is rarely the case. Even where composition is known and the mailing envelope is addressed to the selected respondent, the researcher still cannot be certain of the identity of the person completing the questionnaire. Once it is received, any member of the household could conceivably fill out the questionnaire, and the researcher's lack of awareness makes him or her powerless to do anything about it.

The mail questionnaire is also at a disadvantage when the sampling unit is an organization or agency. This applies particularly to surveys in which the researcher is unsure of the appropriate respondent. For example, the desired respondent may be "the person in charge of hiring" or the "Dean of Students" whose name is unknown. To identify the right person, one or more contacts with the organization may be required. Such contacts can be made by telephone or in person with relative ease.

A method frequently employed in mail studies to overcome this problem is to send the questionnaire to a high official and ask for it to be "passed on" to the employee who best fits the description of the person wanted. Besides losing the power of direct appeal, this procedure results in the questionnaire being placed in a kind of double jeopardy. The official to whom it is sent may simply decide to discard it, rather than forward it. Even if it is passed on to the appropriate person, the possibility remains that this person will not complete it. Frequently researchers attempt to avoid the loss of a questionnaire through hierarchical shuffling by sending an advance letter explaining the study and asking to whom the questionnaire should be sent. This technique also faces a dual problem of nonresponse, first from the person initially contacted and later from the identified respondent. Perhaps the main difficulty of attempting to select respondents by mail is that, to be successful, the process itself requires feedback that must be evaluated before deciding who is the appropriate person. This is a complex alternative requiring a fairly intricate set of instructions that the recipients may not be able or willing to follow.

Thus it seems clear that the telephone and face-to-face interviews provide clear-cut advantages regarding the problem of selecting respondents within households or other sampling units. However, it must be remembered that if people lack telephones, as is the case for some household samples, the application of selection criteria becomes a meaningless consideration.

Can Selected Respondents Be Located?

A respondent who cannot be located cannot be surveyed. Although all three methods exhibit certain drawbacks in the ease with which potential respondents can be contacted, the most severe ones are associated with face-to-face interviews.

As noted in Chapter 1, locating respondents has become an increasingly difficult problem for face-to-face interviewers. The geographical dispersion of households plus the inability to locate a respondent on the first attempt presents a difficult and costly dilemma. Returning some distance to an area of a city or to another city to pick up a single interview entails considerable time and cost. Even if a meeting can be scheduled for the respondent by another member of the household, diminishing the risk of getting no data at all, travel time makes the process quite inefficient. The cost and difficulty of interviewing persons who work or are otherwise occupied during daytime hours are further increased by the limited hours, usually in the early evening, during which contact must be made. In addition, concern over interviewer safety at night in large cities or very rural areas may mean that interviewers must be escorted, resulting in still higher costs. Finally, people are less willing to let strangers into their homes during the evening hours. Thus locating and interviewing respondents must often be concentrated into the very narrow period of early evening hours.

An occasional difficulty in locating respondents for face-to-face interviews is overcoming "gatekeepers" and "gatekeeping" devices. In certain cities, for example, entire housing areas are closed off to all but those who can prove they are invited visitors. The same is true for many apartment buildings, which have outer doors that are always locked. The interviewer who must contend with a guard or doorman seems less likely to gain entry. The same can be said for the interviewer who must talk to a potential respondent through an intercom device, a situation often made more difficult by street noises that force one to raise one's voice above a normal conversational level and prevents the use of the friendly smile and neat appearance to help gain entry.

The mail method offers certain clear-cut advantages over the telephone and face-to-face methods. Respondents who are not at home when interviewers call, either in person or by phone, usually pick up their mail. If they are away for an extended period of time, arrangements are usually made for forwarding their mail. Failing that, the mail will be there when the prospective respondent returns. Thus the mail questionnaire has a high probability of reaching the respondent where other methods fail. For example, we are frequently successful in eliciting the return of a mail questionnaire from persons we were unable to contact after a minimum of 10 attempts by telephone scattered over more than a week. In one study, 20 percent of the respondents who could not be contacted for a telephone interview returned a mail version of the interview schedule without any follow-up efforts. Further, if prospective respondents to a mail questionnaire have moved to an entirely different geographic location, for example, to another state and have left a forwarding address, they can be contacted without additional cost. In telephone and face-to-face interview surveys, they would probably have to be dropped from the sample.

However, there are two important drawbacks to using mail questionnaires to locate respondents. One is the lack of immediate feedback from respondents or those who know their whereabouts. Whereas contact with other family members, which is likely in telephone or face-to-face interview surveys, may produce information about the selected respondents' temporary unavailability, or perhaps ineligibility, a letter may simply lie unanswered. The second difficulty is that spouses or secretaries may prevent the questionnaire from reaching selected respondents. As another type of gatekeeper, they may sometimes keep potential respondents from being aware that a survey is in process.

The telephone's main advantage is that call-backs can be made repeatedly until the respondent is located with very little cost. Calls to homes and offices alike, widely separated by distance, can be precisely timed to catch respondents who are there only a short period each day, with no thought to the geographical distance that separates them. This possibility places the telephone on an equal basis with the mail questionnaire in ability to reach respondents. Although each method has its disadvantages, both fare better than face-to-face interviews.

Is Substitution of Respondents Detrimental?

The substitution of an available person or household for one that cannot be contacted is not a good survey practice, and we do not recommend it. As asserted by one noted statistician: "Substitution does not help; it is only equivalent to building up the size of the initial sample, leaving the bias of nonresponse undiminished."[10] Despite these words of caution, substitution is commonplace. It is accomplished either by increasing the size of the sample to guarantee a certain number of respondents or by explicitly substituting people who are available for those who are not. There are two basic forms of substitution; each has different implications for survey results.

One form of substitution occurs most frequently in household surveys when the selected respondent is not at home, and another person, usually the spouse, is interviewed in his or her place. The seriousness of this form of substitution greatly depends on the nature of the survey. If the primary interest is in household characteristics and family behavior, likely to be known equally well by both spouses, the consequences may not be serious. Although it is improbable that spouses would provide the same answers to attitudinal questions, the degree of similarity seems likely to be greater than would be obtained by the alternative of substituting a different household. However, in some studies such switches may have dramatic consequences. For example, substituting the husband for his wife in a study of family nutrition patterns, or substituting the wife for her husband in a study of time devoted to watching sports events on television may dramatically increase response errors. Although the consequences for making this type of substitution do not differ by method, the temptation that the researcher will ask for a substitution is much greater in the face-to-face interview, for which call-back costs are so high.

In the second form of substitution, sample units may be switched when a unit in the original sample cannot be contacted. The undesirable consequences of this substitution are greater in mail and telephone surveys. In face-to-face interviews of the general public, a common method of substitution is to move a certain number of houses down the block. The fact that housing within neighborhoods tends to be somewhat homogeneous means that the substituted household is likely to contain people with similar characteristics (e.g., education, occupation, income, and perhaps stage in family life cycle).[11]

The substitution of households in telephone surveys has more serious consequences than in face-to-face interviewing; households substituted in telephone surveys are not as likely to be similar to the original household as those in face-to-face surveys. This is true regardless of whether directory sampling or random digit dialing methods are used. The nature of the implementation process in telephone studies provides other reasons to be concerned with substitution. Typically, a considerable number of telephone calls are conducted in a very short period of time. Considerable bias may result when substitution is used freely after making only one or two attempts to contact the respondent and if these calls are made during specific hours, for example, 6–9 p.m. each evening, when certain types of respondents are less likely to be home. It seems likely that households with several persons (as opposed to single-person households) are more likely to have someone at home most of the time. In addition, households containing older people and women are more likely to be reached regardless of the time of telephone calls.

Finally, on certain nights of the week it might be more difficult to find certain types of people at home. For example, in some states high school athletic events are held on specific nights of the week(e.g., Friday night football) and tend to draw families of school-age children. These various sources of bias can be neutralized by making numerous calls back at different times of the day, whereas free substitution would encourage it.

As a general rule, substitution is not freely used in mail questionnaire research, at least explicitly. The researcher who sets a sample size far larger than the number of returns desired and thus substitutes large sample size for follow-ups and other response-inducing methods is in effect substituting respondents. This type of implicit substitutability is more serious than that used for not-at-homes in other types of surveys. In effect, substitutes are used for those who refuse to return the questionnaire. Those who refuse are likely to differ from respondents in quite a number of characteristics, such as education, interest in the topic, and so on. Fortunately, the nature of the mail method mitigates against explicit substitution to reach a certain number of questionnaires. Although telephone or face-to-face interviews can simply be stopped when a given number is reached, there is a lag time of about 2 months from initial contact to the return of all questionnaires in mail TDM surveys. Thus practical considerations dictate against restarting the process to achieve a specific sample size.

Although substitution is hazardous for all three methods, the danger is least for face-to-face interviews, because of presumably homogeneous neighborhoods. In some respects this is fortunate, because the pressures for doing it are also greatest in face-to-face surveys. In any case, substitution should be strenuously avoided.

Can Adequate Response Rules Be Attained?

Despite the great importance given to response rate comparisons, they are very difficult to make because various methods are used to compute them. One way of calculating response rates is to determine the percentage of people in the original sample from whom completed questionnaires are obtained. Thus if 50 of 100 persons in the original sample return their questionnaires, the response rate is 50 percent, calculated as

$$\text{Response rate} = \frac{\text{number returned}}{\text{number in sample}} \times 100$$

This method shows how well one has done in reaching *all* potential respondents. However, it cannot be used if substitution procedures are a part of the study design. When used in a study without substitution procedures, it tends to reflect the financial situation of the researcher (i.e., the extent to which intensive follow-up efforts to contact respondents can be afforded) as much or more than it reflects the inherent capability of the method to elicit complete interviews.

Another procedure frequently used for determining response rates provides a more direct indicator of a method's response-inducing capabilities. The response rate is calculated as the percentage of contacts with eligible respondents that result in completed interviews or questionnaires. The essential difference between this method and the former is that unmade contacts are excluded from consideration. The formula for this calculation would be

$$\text{Response rate} = \frac{\text{number returned}}{\text{number in sample} - (\text{noneligible} + \text{nonreachable})} \times 100$$

For example, if in a sample of 100 people, 10 were shown to be ineligible (e.g., not registered voters), and 10 could not be located after repeated efforts, the original sample of potential respondents would be adjusted to 80. Then, if 50 questionnaires were returned, the response rate would be 62.5 percent.

The definition of response rates in this manner tends to underestimate response for mail questionnaires. In face-to-face and telephone interviews a refusal is not considered such until a contact is made. In mail studies, the opposite is assumed, that is, a nonresponse is a refusal until proven otherwise. Usually hidden within this category is a certain number of questionnaires that for one reason or another failed to reach the respondent. This may occur because the questionnaire is sent by bulk-rate mail that is not forwarded or returned when a respondent's address changes. It may be that intermediaries simply fail to bring the survey to the desired respondent's attention. In addition, persons occasionally receive questionnaires when they are not eligible for the survey. For example, it was discovered in a survey of university alumni that a number of "boosters" who had never attended the university were on the mailing list from which the sample was drawn. We were not cognizant of this fact until several such people wrote in response to follow-up mailings. It would have been inappropriate to include these ineligible alumni in the calculation of the response rate for that study.

Researchers who use the latter technique for deciding what constitutes a legitimate contact often do not use the same methods. For example, in some studies, death, senility, poor health, inability to communicate in English, and temporary absence are considered acceptable reasons for not counting a contact in the response rate calculation. In others, one or more of them are not considered legitimate. This uneven use of criteria for excluding potential respondents from response rate calculations adds to the confusion of comparing response rates reported in the literature. Another source of difficulty is the fact that researchers often fail to report the way their response rates are calculated. There is no way of knowing, for example, how ineligible contacts were handled, who was designated a "refusal" and on what basis. In some cases, particularly in face-to-face interviews, response rates are not reported at all!

Recognizing these difficulties, what can be concluded about the probable response rates that each method can achieve? The users of face-to-face interviews have been taught to expect that completions (as a percentage of contacts) will comfortably exceed 80 or 90 percent. Although the evidence, reported in Chapter 1, suggests that lower response rates are becoming more common, there is insufficient empirical information available to claim that response rates below 80 percent are becoming the norm except perhaps in large metropolitan areas. It is unclear to what extent overt refusals (as opposed to not-at-homes) contribute to the lower response rates that are reported. Further, we have not seen evidence to suggest that the response rates for samples other than the general public are on the decline.

The results of our TDM studies lead us to conclude that response rates to mail questionnaires are usually lower than those obtained by either of the interview methods, assuming that intensive call-back efforts are made for the latter. When put to its most difficult test, that is, surveys of the general public using lengthy questionnaires, response rates from 60 to 75 percent are achieved. The highest response rate obtained was 84 percent for a crime victimization survey in Texas.[12] Although high by some standards, these rates are somewhat below what would probably have been obtained by face-to-face interviews from the same populations. For homogenous samples, the difference between mail surveys and the others diminishes. Response rates for such groups as home economics teachers, state employees, and State Supreme Court judges can be expected to exceed 85 percent, a rate that is very close to that obtained by other methods.

The response rates of our TDM telephone surveys of the general public average about 85 percent (computed on the basis of contacts), somewhat higher than for the mail TDM, and from a low of 73 percent to a high of 92 percent. The highest response rates, those over 90 percent, have only been obtained when respondents received a prior letter informing them that they would be called at a later time. This requires names and addresses and therefore cannot be used with random digit dialing.[13] In those few instances in which different general public samples have been surveyed on the same topic by both the mail and telephone methods, response rates for the latter ranged from 11 to 15 percentage points higher. On homogenous samples, that is, students, students' parents, university faculty and staff, veterinarians, and ministers, the response always exceeds 90 percent and is sometimes very close to 100 percent. The response rates of these groups equal and perhaps surpass those which would probably have been obtained by face-to-face interviews.

In concluding this section it is important to reemphasize the difficulty of making explicit comparisons and the methodological hazards of doing so. Our concern here is response-inducing capabilities, independent of other considerations such as cost and length, which are considered elsewhere in this chapter. Thus we ask, what is the likelihood that someone will agree to be surveyed when actually confronted with the request, regardless of the effort necessary to reach them. In this context, we conclude that the face-to-face interview is best, the telephone a close second, and the mail survey a somewhat more distant third, with the performance of mail questionnaires being much improved by the use of the TDM.

Can Unknown Bias from Refusals Be Avoided?

If a significant number of contacts end in refusals, it is important to know whether those who did not respond differ greatly from those who responded. Relatively few refusals provide the theoretical potential for introducing considerable error into estimates of the sample characteristics. At the level of a 50 percent response rate, extreme distributions for refusals are capable of affecting an observed distribution by as many as 50 percentage points. For example, suppose the observed distribution on a dichotomous variable is 75 percent "yes" and 25 percent "no." However, if all answered "no," the distribution would be changed to 37.5 percent "yes" and 62.5 percent "no." This potential range of 50 percentage points (from 87.5 to 37.5 percent "yes" and 12.5 to 62.5 percent "no") between the highest and lowest percentages giving one answer or the other is the same regardless of the original distribution of "yes's" and "no's." A little work with pencil and paper should show to the reader's satisfaction that each 10 percent increase in response rate decreases by 10 percentage points the range by which the distribution could be affected by refusals if the actual feelings of nonrespondents are extreme in either direction.

Thus a response rate of 60 percent lowers to 40 percentage points the range of possible effects refusals could ever have on the results; a response rate of 70 percent lowers it to 30 percent, and so on. Fortunately, extreme distributions, or even those in an opposite direction, seldom occur. However, when they do occur and are combined with low response rates, the effect on variable distributions is devastating.

The extent of the differences between respondents and nonrespondents can seldom be determined. However, indirect methods may sometimes be used to make very limited checks for differences. For example, if a sample is drawn from educational or personnel records, the researcher can see if respondents and refusals differ for the information available from those records. If the sample is supposed to be of the general public, comparisons with the U.S. Census records can be made.[14] However, great care must be taken in the interpretation of indirect comparisons, because the characteristics compared frequently have only a slight (or even no) relationship to the dependent variables studied. This leaves the possibility that no matter how close the distributions for the variables being compared, large differences may exist for responses to the questions most central to the objectives of the survey.

Mail questionnaires present a much more serious concern about response selectivity than either of the two interview methods. One reason is that recipients of the mail questionnaire have an opportunity to examine it in its entirety before deciding to respond. Interest in the particular topic, a factor that seems likely to affect one's answers, may be important in determining whether a questionnaire is completed and returned. A second factor that is likely to contribute to respondent selectivity is the ability to provide written answers to a questionnaire. Verbal response to oral questions is usually less difficult than having to read questions, follow special directions, and write answers. People who have less education are thus likely to be underrepresented among those who respond. Older persons also seem likely to be underrepresented, partly because of lower educational attainment, but also because of more difficulties with their seeing and writing capabilities.

One researcher who used the mail TDM followed it with face-to-face interviews and as a result raised the response rate for a sample of the general public in rural communities of northern Iowa from 79 to 93 percent, an increase of 15 percentage points.[15] The additional interviews produced only slight changes in the demographic characteristics of the respondents, but the changes were in the expected direction. For example, the proportion of respondents with less than 11 years of education increased from 31 to 33 percent, and the proportion of people with less than a $6000 income went from 24 to 26 percent. Although these differences confirm that some bias is generated by refusals, the differences were not large enough to be of much concern. However, unless numerous studies on various populations confirm this finding, caution seems in order.

When a refusal occurs in a face-to-face or telephone interview, the interviewer can make limited judgments about the person's attributes. He or she may even get the specific reason for the refusal. The face-to-face interviewer can make judgments on certain demographic characteristics such as age, marital status, family size, socioeconomic status, and so on. Researchers who utilize the mail method have no way of determining nonrespondent characteristics, because they make no personal contact. In sum, the ability to determine nonrespondent characteristics is good for the face-to-face interview, intermediate for the telephone interviewer, and poor for the mail survey.

OBTAINING ANSWERS TO ALL THE QUESTIONS ONE WANTS TO ASK

The importance of choosing a method that will enable one to ask and obtain answers to all the questions necessary to one's study can hardly be overemphasized. If the questions cannot be asked and adequate answers obtained, nothing else really matters. The problems grouped here as questionnaire content issues are many and varied, ranging from the straightforward ones of how many questions can be asked and the allowable types of questions, to whether one can "get by" with sloppy construction procedures. There is a great deal of variation on what can be achieved with each method, making the issues of questionnaire construction critical to decisions on which method to use.

How Long Can the Questionnaire Be?

After response rate, the factor that has contributed most to the poor image of mail and telephone questionnaires is the view that they must be kept short, too short for the study of significant social science questions.[16] In contrast, length has not been viewed as a serious problem in face-to-face interviews. At one time or another most users of the face-to-face method have probably had marathon experiences. I can recall doing a 7-hour interview with an agency director and interviews with several others that required lunch breaks. In a study of farmers, 2- to 3-hour sessions were routine. Although the quality of data obtained in the latter stages of such endurance tests is likely to deteriorate, there is little doubt that the potential exists for the interviews to be accomplished. Even with the general public, face-to-face interviews that run well over 1 hour in length are routinely implemented. Without question, the length capabilities of face-to-face interviews are greater than those of the other methods. However, this does not mean that considerable amounts of information cannot be obtained by mail or telephone surveys.

High response rates have frequently been achieved with lengthy mail questionnaires. For example, Glock and Stark obtained an effective response rate of 75 percent to a 24-page questionnaire on religion.[17] Their questionnaire, sent to members of a sample of church congregations, required approximately 475 separate responses. Erdos has reported a 75 percent response to a 12-page questionnaire sent to members of a specialized population.[18] In addition, there are the results from the application of the TDM present in Chapter 1.

The response rates obtained through the TDM show consistent variation with length (Table 2.1). Although interpretation must be made cautiously because of the relatively small number of studies, not all of which used the TDM in its entirety, an overall trend is apparent. There is not much difference in the response rates for questionnaires of less than 12 pages or those which contain less than 125 items for either the general public or specialized populations. This suggests that increasing length up to these limits does not have an adverse effect on response rates. It further suggests that the maxim of "the shorter the better" may represent an oversimplification or even a myth. However, going beyond 12 pages seems almost certain to affect response. None of the general public TDM mail questionnaires of this length elicited a response rate of more than 65 percent, well below the average for all shorter questionnaires. The two lengthy questionnaires that used the complete TDM and elicited the highest response rates had certain distinct qualities that may have accounted for the very high response. One was a 14-page questionnaire sent to sociologists, who are more accustomed than most people to doing questionnaires. The other, 26 pages long—the longest for which the TDM has been used—was sent to senior citizens who had responded earlier to a single letter of inquiry sent to their households, asking whether any senior citizens lived there. This is the only one of the 48 studies that used such a prior screening procedure that might have encouraged higher response. Thus we tentatively conclude that 11 pages, or 125 items, represent plateaus beyond which response rate reductions can be expected.

In the case of the telephone survey, Colombotos reported no difficulty with hour-long interviews for a sample of physicians.[19] Telephone interviews in a leisure research study averaged 20 minutes, with virtually no termination once the interviews were underway.[20] Warland, in a national survey on consumer behavior with interviews that averaged 30 minutes, found that only 4 percent of the sample terminated after the interview had commenced.[21] Studies using the TDM have shown that respondents terminating in the middle of interviews seldom exceed 2 percent. In one such study of the general public using interviews averaging close to 20 minutes, only 10 out of 1018 persons who started the interview terminated before its completion.[22] The evidence clearly suggests that once people are on the telephone, the length of interview does not appear to be a major problem.

We are not sure how long interviews can be before cut-offs become a major problem. One reason for this is that length is often a key factor in choosing between mail and telephone surveys. The mail method presents considerable cost savings over the telephone method when interviews longer than 10–15 minutes are required. A second reason for preferring mail questionnaires on longer interviews is a concern that among the general public the quality of information may tend to decrease with lengthy telephone inter-

Table 2.1   Response Rates by Length of Questionnaire in 48 Mail TDM Studies

LENGTH	SPECIALIZED POPULATIONS		GENERAL PUBLIC		AVERAGE PERCENT RESPONSE
	(N)	% Response	(N)	% Response	
Pages					
≤ 5	(5)	76	-	-	76
6-7	(5)	73	(2)	78	74
8-9	(3)	77	-	-	77
10-11	(10)	83	(12)	73	77
12-13	-	-	(2)	59	59
14+	(6)	70	(3)	62	67
Items					
≤ 75	(10)	76%	(1)	85%	77
76-100	(5)	78%	(2)	69%	75
101-125	(7)	80%	(4)	75%	82
126-150	(1)	68%	(3)	73%	72
150+	(6)	68%	(9)	66%	67

[a]These data are derived from Table 1.1 of Chapter 1. The Total Design Method was only partly used in some of these studies.

views. The fact that respondents must listen very intently, relying entirely on their sense of hearing for comprehension, often with distractions in the background, suggests to us that they are likely to tire more quickly in telephone interviews than other methods.

Before leaving the question of how much information one can obtain without adversely affecting either response rates or data quality, it is appropriate to raise questions about the necessary length of any questionnaire. The factors that lead researchers to plan lengthy face-to-face interviews are sometimes irrelevant to either mail questionnaires or telephone interviews. The major cost of face-to-face interviews is making contact with respondents. The additional cost of adding another 10–15 minutes of questions to an already planned interview is negligible in comparison. This is the primary reason that many surveys consist of the questions of many researchers that are piggybacked on top of one another to comprise a single survey. When only one researcher's questions are to be asked in a survey, there is still considerable temptation to ask as many questions as respondents seem willing to tolerate. Questions that do not fit into the theoretical framework are often added simply because they seem interesting. The nagging fear that hindsight will reveal that a very critical question was omitted leads to the inclusion of questions that the researcher views as relatively unimportant. The all too frequent result is the production of mounds of data that remain unanalyzed.

The rules for telephone interviewing are quite different. The additional cost (i.e., toll charges and interviewer time) for adding more questions is almost as much as the cost of conducting entirely new interviews at a later date with the same respondents or even a different sample. The piggy-backing of successive series of unrelated questions, so important to reducing face-to-face interview costs, is simply not necessary in telephone interviews. Thus whether an interviewer can hold a respondent on the phone for an hour or more may be relatively unimportant for most researchers. The additional cost of adding questions to mail questionnaires is extremely small until the point at which more postage is required (beyond 10–11 pages with the TDM). However, the generally low cost of conducting mail surveys and the likelihood of low responses to long questionnaires suggest that the piggy-backing of questions is not a good idea. Instead of forcing as many questions as possible into one survey, the researcher would be better advised to do a second mail survey.

We conclude that, although the length capabilities of both mail and telephone surveys must be considered as moderate, they are quite sufficient for many studies of interest to social scientists. In addition, since the necessity of great length is questionable, the importance of this advantage, once an overwhelming one for face-to-face interviews, is lessened.

What Types of Questions Can Be Asked?

Each of the three methods uses a different mode of communication. Consequently, there are differences in the types of questions that can be asked. The face-to-face interview is clearly the most versatile. Researchers can rely on simultaneous or successive use of all the respondent's senses, observe the respondent's reactions with all of their own, and utilize that feedback to keep the interview going smoothly. The full use of visuals (e.g., objects, maps, diagrams, and cards with answer categories) can be made. In contrast, the telephone depends only on what can be communicated vocally. To comprehend questions, the respondent must concentrate on each successive word or phrase and remember it. Although they can probe and clarify questions, interviewers cannot observe reactions for clues as to whether the question is understood; they must depend on the respondent to tell them. The mail questionnaire is different. The respondent is in complete control and can read at his or her own speed. However, the respondent must be able both to follow directions and understand the question in the manner intended. This method does not allow the feedback that provides interviewers the opportunity to clarify misunderstood questions. Thus greater simplicity in question construction and wording are generally required for mail and telephone questionnaires. There are several types of limitations.

How Complex Can the Question Be?   Simplicity is imperative for the telephone interview. The necessity to read both the question and answer categories and to keep the entire question brief enough to be comprehended place very stringent limits on question complexity. Whereas a respondent might reasonably be expected to choose among five or perhaps more lengthy answer categories in surveys done either in person or by mail, that is difficult to accomplish by telephone. Rank-order questions, in which a respondent is asked to read a long series of questions and pick the most important one, are also difficult to transform into a telephone format, as are questions that depend on maps or diagrams. In some cases we found it possible to ask complex questions, including those that depend on maps, over the telephone by certain formulation procedures (discussed in Chapter 6), but the mere fact that special formulation procedures are needed suggests the existence of serious constraints.

The limits on mail questionnaires are for the most part related to respondent motivation. The lack of an interviewer to explain how certain questions are to be answered makes it essential that questions sometimes used in face-to-face interviews be modified or eliminated from mail questionnaires. However, these limitations are not as great as those for the telephone, where memory must try to accomplish what a visual display can accomplish in face-to-face and mail surveys.

Can Open-ended Questions Be Used?   Open-ended questions, that is, those for which no answer choices are provided, present little difficulty for either the telephone or face-to-face interview. However, to get good answers, interviewers must skillfully use probes such as, ''Is there anything else?'' ''Can you think of anything at all?'' and ''Are there any other reasons?'' to elicit more than perfunctory answers. This is because respondents often find it difficult to create and verbalize answers to such questions.

The absence of an interviewer puts the mail questionnaire at a very distinct disadvantage. Not only do some people find it more difficult to express themselves in writing than orally, but the absence of the interviewer's probes frequently results in answers that cannot be interpreted and sometimes in no answer at all. The difficulty of open-ended questions and the near impossibility of solving it represents one of the most severe shortcomings of mail questionnaires.

Can Screen Questions Be Used? A third type of question that creates more problems for some methods than others is the screen question, that is, one that applies to only some respondents. In many studies respondents are eligible to answer less than half the questions. Unless a respondent has performed a certain act or holds a particular view, entire sections of questions may have to be deleted. Such questions are more difficult to handle in mail questionnaires than by either of the other methods. Not only does the mere presence of twice as many questions as any one respondent is expected to answer contribute to a formidable appearance that may discourage the respondent from attempting to answer, but directions for skipping questions must be provided. Construction procedures can overcome this problem only on a limited basis. For example, it is not difficult to direct respondents to skip a few questions or even a few pages. If it is known ahead of time which questions do not apply to certain respondents, different questionnaires can be sent. In contrast, screen questions present no problem to either the face-to-face or telephone interviewer, because interviewers can ask such questions without respondents being aware of them.

Can Question Sequence Be Controlled? A fourth type of question, and one that is especially problematic for mail questionnaires, is that which must be asked either before or after certain others. For example, researchers sometimes ask respondents to rank the importance of several "problem areas" and then proceed to inquire in detail about one of those problems. It is important that the ranking question come prior to the detailed question; the answer to the detailed question must not bias response to the ranking question. Although these types of questions present relatively little problem for the telephone or face-to-face survey methods, the sequence in which questions are completed on a mail questionnaire is beyond the researcher's control. Also beyond control is the possibility that respondents may go back and change answers to conform to a thought generated by more detailed questions that occur later. In surveys for which sequence is important, the mail questionnaire cannot be used with full confidence.

Can Tedious or Boring Questions Be Asked? A fifth type of question for which the capabilities of the methods differ is that which is tedious and boring. Long, abstract, and redundant attitude items are an example. Detailed questions on seemingly insignificant (at least to the respondent) opinions or behavior for each member of the family is another example. Even very dedicated respondents may begin to look anxiously at the clock when asked to give the entire medical history of their fourth child. The motivation required for the completion of the mail questionnaire puts it at a definite disadvantage with regard to this kind of question. Although questionnaire construction procedures may be used to liven up a questionnaire, that may be very difficult to accomplish for certain questions deemed absolutely essential to a study. Even when the respondent can be motivated to complete such questionnaires, it is questionable whether the detail will be as accurate or as complete as that obtained by interview methods. Although mid-interview terminations are usually infrequent for telephone interviews, questions of this nature increase the likelihood of such terminations. The greater ease with which a respondent may terminate leads us to conclude that face-to-face interviews are most successful for tedious or boring questions.

Can Item Nonresponse Be Avoided?   Another dimension on which survey methods may be evaluated is whether answers are obtained for every question. The controlling influence of an interviewer makes it difficult for respondents to skip items. The person interviewed may find it easier to give an answer he or she would just as soon skip than to go through the difficulty of getting the interviewer to pass over it. Interviewers also prevent items from being inadvertently skipped or overlooked. This gives a clear advantage to the telephone and face-to-face interviews.

Although the absence of an interviewer increases the risk of nonresponse for mail questionnaires, it does not appear to be a significant problem when the TDM is used for mail studies. One aspect of the TDM is a construction procedure explicitly aimed at minimizing the chance that questions will be skipped. An analysis of five mail studies conducted on statewide samples of the general public in four different states reveals that item nonresponse is uniformly low, averaging between 3.5 and 4.6 percent.[23] If there had not been some questions with recognized construction defects, the item nonresponse would have been lower. It was noted in these studies that the item nonresponse for personal data, traditionally deemed difficult to get, averaged around 2 percent. When the questionnaire construction procedures of the TDM are used, item nonresponse represents only slightly more of a problem in mail than in interview surveys.

Is Inadequate Attention to Construction Procedures Detrimental?

Few would argue against the importance of giving careful attention to such matters as question order, use of lead-ins and transitions, and other matters of questionnaire construction. Yet in practice these issues are often accorded only minimal attention. The consequences of ignoring these aspects of questionnaire construction not only affect the accuracy of response, but in some cases whether an interview or questionnaire is completed.

The consequences of not giving very careful attention to questionnaire construction are least for face-to-face interviews. The interviewer can frequently compensate for any shortcomings of the questionnaire because of his or her capability for continuously monitoring feedback from the respondent. A blank look or frown may be all that is needed for the interviewer to realize that something is amiss and to cause him or her to either pause expectantly or reread the question. Interviewers can also lessen the impact of abrupt transitions by an impromptu pause and an informative yet neutral declaration that, "Now we are going to talk about something different!" It is perhaps for these reasons that researchers using face-to-face interviews often spend little or no time trying to give continuity or a sense of order to their questionnaire.

The sensitivity of the telephone interview to questionnaire structure is considerably greater. Respondents who miss a single word or phrase may find the remainder of a question totally incomprehensible and feel a bit embarrassed at having to ask the interviewer to reread it. Because the interviewer lacks visual feedback, he or she often does not know when clarification is needed. Under these circumstances, the effort expended in deciding, for example, whether to substitute a pronoun for a noun is frequently well spent. The same is true of effort spent deciding whether one word sounds too much like another. If the reproduction of one's voice is imperfect, as is the case with telephone transmission, the similar sound of certain words is likely to create confusion. This was demonstrated to us very clearly when a mail follow-up survey showed that the person we understood from our telephone interview to be a carpenter turned out to be a copper miner! Explicit transitions such as "Next I am going to ask you four questions about air pollution from automobiles," not generally used in personal interviews, may be especially valuable for telephone surveys, decreasing the risk that specific words and phrases are misunderstood. Question ordering that jumps from one topic to another and back again without warning, as so often happens in face-to-face interviews, must be avoided altogether in telephone interviews, inasmuch as this further confounds the already difficult task of comprehension by the respondent.

The mail questionnaire presents even more problems with regard to questionnaire construction. The absence of an opportunity for immediate interviewer feedback creates an especially great need for clear and unambiguous questions. Still more problematic is an element to which little or no attention is given in telephone and face-to-face interviews—interest-arousing questions and transitions. It may take only one glaring flaw in the construction and design of a mail questionnaire to stimulate rejection. The TDM emphasizes the crucial nature of a well-structured questionnaire in achieving response.

OBTAINING ACCURATE ANSWERS

It is one thing to get answers to questions. It is quite another to be sure they are valid answers, and still another to know whether they come from the right person. The factors that influence whether honest answers are obtained constitute one more general area in which the three methods can be assessed and on which there are marked differences in their performance capabilities.

Can Social Desirability Bias Be Avoided?

One source of inaccuracy is a tendency to offer socially desirable answers, that is, to answer questions in a way that conforms to dominant belief patterns among groups to which the respondent feels some identification or allegiance. An example of a socially desirable response bias arises when people say that they like living in their community, even though on the whole they dislike it a great deal. To answer otherwise would be to express a belief that is unpopular among people whose approval the respondent values.

The face-to-face interview represents an interpersonal situation in which actors affect one another's images and behavior. We would expect that the tendency to omit socially desirable answers would be greater in that situation than when an interviewer is not present. Hyman has noted:

> To the extent that a respondent's reaction derives from social or interpersonal involvement (between himself and the interviewer), we may expect it to result in bias since under such conditions the response will be primarily a function of the relation between the respondent and the interviewer instead of a response to the task. Under what conditions is the social component of the involvement increased? First of all it is obvious that if we remove the interviewer from the physical environment we decrease the possibility of respondent involvement with him as a personality.[24]

It would seem that the transfer of the interviewer from the scene to the telephone decreases the probability of socially desirable responses and that his or her removal (as in the case of the mail questionnaire) decreases it even further. This has been confirmed by research. However, research also shows that the differences may be minor and in some cases nonexistent. For example, Hochstim concluded that in general respondents were most honest in mail surveys, least honest in the face-to-face interview, and intermediate in the telephone interview. For questions on intimate relations and drinking patterns, he reported that although socially desirable responses were given more frequently in the face-to-face situation, there were no differences between mail and telephone surveys.[25]

In a survey of physicians about the reporting of certain physical disabilities and the reading of medical journals, Colombotos found that face-to-face interviews gave more than twice as many socially desirable answers compared to telephone interviews.[26] However, he concluded that, for the entire study, differences between the two methods were relatively small. Although he reported no overall differences in the social desirability of responses from a second study, some were noted for specific questions. On questions concerning the controversial issues of abortion and marijuana, it was found that the largest number of socially desirable answers came from face-to-face interviews, next most from the telephone survey, and fewest from the mail survey.[27] Thus face-to-face interviews have the highest probability for producing socially desirable answers, the telephone survey next, and the mail survey least. The greatest advantage of face-to-face interviews—the physical presence of the interviewer—may at times be its greatest drawback.

Can Interviewer Distortion and Subversion Be Avoided?

In many ways, the interviewing phase of a research study represents a very perilous part of the research enterprise. Events during this stage are those over which the researcher has little control. Thus it is imperative that interviewers be carefully selected, well trained, and have a strong sense of commitment to their tasks.

As a part of their training, interviewers are invariably admonished to read questions exactly as they are worded (and therefore as every other interviewer reads them). Further training is provided in neutral probing, for example, through simply restating the question or deflecting the respondent's questions by such stock phrases as "we would like you to answer in terms of the way the question is stated." Whether these instructions are always followed is questionable. Interviewers sometimes take considerable liberty in interpreting questions to the respondents. Further, specific words may unconsciously be emphasized and others underemphasized. The monotony of repeating the same questions again and again may lead to involuntary omission of key words and phrases without the interviewer's awareness. Also, a sense of boredom and carelreeness may creep into an interviewer's voice and stimulate a respondent to be equally nonchalant in his or her answers.

Deliberate subversion is an even greater concern in interviewing. Most researchers who depend extensively on face-to-face interviews can recount horror stories of interviewers completing the interview forms in their motel rooms rather than tracking down respondents. We can recall one instance in which data were ready for publication when the investigator was informed through the "grapevine" that one of several interviewers had fabricated most of the interviews. A check discovered that this had taken place; not only were those interview forms lost, but so was the representativeness of the sample (because this particular interviewer was the only one conducting interviews in a certain geographic region of the state).

To prevent such occurrences, many researchers regularly conduct mini-reinterviews with respondents to discover whether reported interviews actually took place and to gain evidence as to whether all the questions were asked. The latter is accomplished by selecting certain questions to be asked again in the reinterview. The threat to the interviewer of being caught in this manner is a strong deterent to the complete fabrication of interviews, but it is difficult to catch limited forms of subversion such as not asking open-ended follow-ups or abstract attitudinal questions. Some variation between the original and follow-up interviews is to be expected on such questions. Such "fudging" probably happens far more than we would like to admit. It is done to shorten difficult interviews and because of empathy for bored or tired respondents. It is also caused by a "who cares?" attitude.

Both distortion and subversion are far easier to control in telephone interviewing conducted under the centralized conditions that are a part of the TDM than in face-to-face interviews in the field. The obvious reason is close supervision. The ability to monitor at least one side of an interview provides the opportunity to remedy defects in an interviewer's method of asking questions and to be sure each question is asked. Also, equipment is available that makes it possible to listen to both sides of a conversation and assist interviewers in improving their skills. One slight disadvantage of telephone interviewing is that very little time elapses between actual interviews, with the result that the process soon takes on a considerable degree of monotony that can lead to the inadvertent omission of phrases and sentences. However, an alert supervisor can usually prevent this.

Can Contamination by Others Be Avoided?

The answers to items on questionnaires sometime represent the views of others more than those of the desired respondent. The possibility for such contamination is greater for the mail questionnaire than for either the face-to-face or telephone interview. Respondents can simply turn the mail questionnaire over to someone else and ask them to complete it. A less extreme form of contamination, and one we believe more likely, is for respondents to ask for advice from others while answering the questions. However, it must be recognized that respondents may choose to answer a questionnaire privately and never let anyone else know how they have answered it. Unfortunately, the researcher can never be sure under what conditions the mail questionnaire was completed; thus the possibility of contamination becomes a constant concern.

The presence of an interviewer tends to lessen the possibility of contamination in telephone and face-to-face interviews. However, its occurrence is not eliminated, especially for the face-to-face interview. If other members of a household are present when a respondent is interviewed, these persons may freely offer advice, which is willingly accepted by the respondent, or, their mere presence may constrain respondents so that they answer in ways different from what they would otherwise. For example, if asked a question about satisfaction with family relationships, respondents might reasonably be expected to indicate greater satisfaction than would be indicated if others were not present.

The telephone interview is the best method in terms of the ability to control contamination. In most cases only the respondent hears the questions, making it difficult for others to understand the questions or affect the answers. Even if another person is on an extension telephone, that person has little chance to offer advice inasmuch as extensions are usually located in separate rooms, making direct conversation with the respondent difficult.

Can Consultation Be Obtained When Needed?

What may at first seem like contamination may be an important means of obtaining accurate information. In some surveys the major concern is to get accurate behavioral data (e.g., number of times one has visited the doctor during the past year), rather than perceptions or attitudes (e.g., whether the health services of the community are considered adequate). Thus the individual who provides the data may be considered far less important than the accuracy of the data.

Each method has certain difficulties associated with respondents obtaining needed consultation. The mail questionnaire can be filled out by whichever member of the household possesses the necessary knowledge, and written documents can be consulted at the respondent's convenience. However, whether people will go to the extra effort required is another question. Consultation usually requires interest and motivation, factors that provide great difficulty for users of mail questionnaires.

The difficulty encountered with face-to-face interviews is that the person who has the necessary knowledge to answer certain questions may not be home at the time of the interview. In the case of written records, the interviewee may not know where to find them. The only alternative in some cases is the costly rescheduling of a later interview for a time when the most knowledgeable household member is available.

The situational constraints under which telephone interviews are usually conducted are not generally conducive to getting information from sources other than the respondent. People tend to attach a sense of urgency to completing a telephone interview and are less likely to be willing to check records, consult other persons to find the needed information, and so on. However, if a person with the necessary knowledge is not at home, a return call may be made with relative ease. Thus there is little basis for recommending one method over another with respect to the ability to secure accurate data when consultation is needed.

ADMINISTERING THE SURVEY

Just as the problem of response rate has so frequently led methodologists to advise against the use of mail and telephone surveys, the problem of lack of resources has led to that advice being ignored. If one lacks the financial resources to sponsor a face-to-face interview survey, there is little to be accomplished by touting the method's merits. In addition to money, other resources are necessary for the administration of surveys, two of which are skilled personnel and time. We consider all three in this section.

Can the Personnel Requirements Be Met?

The personnel required for implementing each type of study differs greatly; those for face-to-face interviews are the most difficult to find. The skills needed for conducting field interviews are great. Interviewers must be trained to solve most of their own problems. Often they must understand sampling procedures and how to deal with a multitude of situations that are encountered only infrequently. By its nature, interviewing is highly demanding, requiring people who are not afraid to travel or work alone at night. A high level of commitment to the researcher and the scientific enterprise seems necessary. These requirements generally mean that there is a very limited pool of interviewers on which to draw. Relatively few people are willing and able to be absent from their homes for several days, or even weeks, at a time. Even graduate students, the labor pool of last resort, are tied to class schedules, their own teaching, and other work commitments for much of the year. In addition, an extensive supervision network that also requires highly competent personnel is needed, and the availability of people with interviewing and supervisory skills is as low as the cost is high.

In contrast, the requirements for telephone interviewing are much less. Close supervision means that the variety of skills needed are fewer and the required training less. To a certain extent interviewers may be trained on the job, with a supervisor helping them through especially difficult, but unusual, problems. Interviewing during evening hours may actually be advantageous insofar as the recruitment of personnel is concerned. In college and university settings, students, particularly those who have received training in research methodology, may be used. Their schedules can usually be fit to interviewing needs. Also, parents of small children who find it difficult to be away from home during the day and persons who hold down regular 8 to 5 jobs can sometimes be recruited without difficulty. Another aspect of telephone interviewing is that relatively few interviewers can conduct a large number of interviews in a short period of time, in sharp contrast to the rate of two or three a day often expected for face-to-face interviews. The result is that one can sometimes get by with a smaller staff in a telephone study than when the face-to-face approach is used.

Personnel requirements for a mail questionnaire study are even less difficult to meet. The fact that the workers are not required to deal directly with respondents means that even the modest requirements for telephone interviewing do not have to be met. The skills required are for the most part highly generalized clerical skills—typing, sorting, and processing correspondence. The development of a high division of labor can further simplify the skills required of each worker. Finally, the number of different persons needed for a mail study is far less than that required for either face-to-face or telephone surveys with equal sample sizes.

Can the Survey Be Implemented as Fast as Desired?

In some studies the time required for collecting the data is crucial; for example, one may want to minimize the time that elapses between the first interview and the last. The concern is that some event will occur in the midst of data collection, for example, an international crisis, that will affect the responses of those not yet surveyed. Second, researchers sometimes find themselves facing a deadline, such as fiscal year or contract period, which means that their funds must be used quickly. Further, the sponsors of the research sometimes want their data in the shortest possible time.

As a general rule, telephone surveys are the fastest to complete. The speed with which they can be completed was first demonstrated to the general public in 1973 and 1974, when telephone surveys provided virtually overnight assessments of the dramatic unfolding of Watergate-related events. Analyses of citizen reaction to certain events, for example, the President's resignation, were reported on television from 1 to 3 days after the event had taken place. In 1976 the first tries at instant polling received national attention as reactions to the presidential candidate debates were reported the same night as the debates! Quick implementation of telephone surveys has been demonstrated several times by users of the TDM. In one instance, when input to a tax policy issue was needed, a survey was completed, from drafting the questionnaire to reporting the final results, in only 2 weeks. Another survey of faculty members required only 35 hours to complete once the questionnaire was designed. These examples clearly demonstrate the potential for rapid surveying by telephone.

Mail surveys, on the other hand, are usually locked into a definite time schedule of printing, folding, stuffing, and mailing dates. Follow-ups are also rigidly scheduled. The TDM for mail surveys requires some 8 weeks to complete the implementation process. Only in the case of very large surveys is the mail technique competitive with telephone surveys. The limited facilities generally available for telephone surveys mean that only a certain number of interviews can be completed each day. To illustrate the break-even point, a recent survey may be used. In this study completed interviews averaged about 20 minutes each, with the result that each interviewer completed about five interviews during each night's 3-hour calling period. The use of 15 telephones resulted in the successful completion of 75 calls per night. Assuming that calls were made only 5 days a week, roughly 3000 interviews could (at least theoretically) be completed during the 8 weeks required to do a mail survey.

The time required for implementing face-to-face interview surveys varies greatly. The factors of sample size, geographic dispersion, and effort required to recruit and train interviewers suggest that the time required is generally far closer to that required for mail surveys than telephone surveys. In any case, the major factors in such a determination are the sample size and geographical dispersion.

Can the Cost Be Afforded?

Frequently cost is the only factor taken into consideration in deciding among methods. Only part of its nearly overwhelming importance stems from a simple and direct determination of costs per respondent associated with each technique. Cost is the major determinant of whether an evaluation of many of the other performance characteristics favors one method over another. For example, the face-to-face interview was judged least sensitive to substitution. However, the cost of not substituting in face-to-face interviews is often very high, whereas for the telephone it is minimal. The result is that the relevant issue changes from the sensitivity of the technique to substitution, as we consider it, to a consideration of whether one must do it. A very similar argument can be made with respect to the cost implications of efforts to locate respondents to achieve high response rates in face-to-face interviews. Budget considerations may mean that call-backs must be abandoned for face-to-face interviews, whereas that would not be necessary for telephone surveys. In short, although cost is handled separately in this chapter, it is difficult to weigh it in isolation from other factors considered here.

We cannot provide concrete cost estimates that can be recommended as a basis for others to use in determining their probable costs. There are several reasons for this. First, the costs per respondent associated with each method vary widely, depending on a number of factors, including the type of sample and the geographical dispersion of the sample. Second, as discussed later, the costs are affected quite differently by increases in sample size. Third, major costs associated with each type of survey are expended in different categories (e.g., interviewer salaries and travel expenses in face-to-face interviews versus printing and postage for mail studies), and these categories are affected differently by recent inflation. Finally, each researcher faces a somewhat different cost situation. Whereas one researcher may have free access to typewriters, printing equipment, and secretarial services, another may have to charge them to the study. For these reasons we concentrate on identifying the kinds of costs associated with TDM studies for which essential characteristics such as sample size for the study and cost-free services to the researcher will be identified.

The costs associated with statewide mail public surveys in four different states using the TDM are reported elsewhere.[28] Sample sizes for these 1970, 1971, and 1973 surveys ranged from 2250 to 8037, and completion time of the questionnaires averaged 30 minutes. The surveys were conducted at different universities by different investigators. Thus a range of cost situations is presented, that is, differences in printing costs, equipment that had to be rented, and so on. The costs for the mail surveys done when first class postage was 8 cents per ounce or less ranged from $1.60 to $2.84 per completed questionnaire. Cost calculations included processing onto computer tape, but did not take into account fixed departmental costs (e.g., telephone and typewriters) nor the principal investigator's time. The costs for these surveys could be expected to run somewhat higher if they were conducted today inasmuch as clerical personnel wages are now some 20–30 percent higher, postage has nearly doubled, and other costs have also increased. Further analysis showed that the relative costs for the major expenditure categories varied considerably across studies. Without exception, however, the cost of labor (most of which was of a clerical nature) exceeded that for any other single category of expenditure, and on the average was slightly more than all other expenditures combined. The two major components of these other expenditures were postage and printing.

If the surveys had been done by telephone using the TDM, the cost would have been about $7.00 per interview, well over half of which would have been for telephone toll charges. Another one-quarter of the estimated cost was for the interviewer's time, with the balance attributable to printing, drawing the sample, monthly charges for the telephones, and other miscellaneous expenditures. However, certain aspects of the investigator's situation could radically alter these costs. For example, leased lines such as those available to some agencies and academic institutions might make it possible to reduce toll charges substantially, in some cases by half. The location of the survey operation near the center of a state or in the midst of the most densely settled area would also substantially reduce the toll charges.

Changes in the nature of the survey itself might substantially affect the relative costs of each type of survey. For example, reducing the length of the questionnaire by half would not be likely to decrease postage or processing costs and would have a very minor effect on printing costs. Only coding costs would be substantially reduced. The important cost implication, and one that we tend to follow in practice, is that the telephone is better for shorter surveys than long ones. Another situation that dramatically affects costs occurs when the geographical area surveyed has no toll charges associated with it, removing altogether the usual major cost for doing telephone surveys. In contrast, costs for implementing TDM surveys by mail are not much greater for state or national surveys than for those in single communities.

Still another factor that affects relative costs is sample size. For very small sample sizes, for example, less than 150, the printing costs may make mail surveys exceedingly expensive, because the TDM depends for its effectiveness on certain printing methods (discussed in Chapter 4) that are costly in small quantities. The telephone method has no special requirements other than readability for the interviewer, and the printing method we use is usually the cheapest one available. The costs of doing mail surveys become smaller as size increases. The reasons are lower printing costs for producing questionnaires and correspondence in large quantities and the efficiency that can be achieved when processing large quantities of questionnaires for mailing. In contrast, the costs per interview for doing telephone surveys decrease only slightly for large samples, inasmuch as the major costs per interview--toll charges and interview time—are not subject to economies of scale.

Although there are situations in which telephone interviews cost less (e.g., small sample size and no long distance calls), they are not common. Thus mail surveys are usually cheaper than those done by telephone, with the advantage growing larger as the sample size and geographical dispersion increase. The economies of scale possible in mail surveys present a decided advantage for that technique.

It is decidedly more expensive to conduct face-to-face interview surveys than either of the others. However, because of normal study design differences, direct cost comparisons are extremely difficult to make. We are reminded here of a remark by the director of a national survey organization: "You can no more talk about the price of *a* survey than the price of *a* car. It all depends on the model you want."[29] Costs vary enormously depending on such important design considerations as how many call-backs are to be made for not-at-homes and whether one member of a household can be substituted for another.

Another methodological difference that confounds cost comparisons is the use of the area probability sampling methods for face-to-face interviews. This means that subgeographical units are sampled first, and households are sampled within each subunit. This is done to decrease the two major costs for face-to-face interviews—interviewer wages and travel expenses. Although it is a virtual necessity for keeping costs to an acceptable level, it also decreases the efficiency of the sampling design (the confidence that can be placed in estimates based on a given sample size).

Even when area probability samples are used and sampling costs are at a minimum, the costs of doing face-to-face interviews are not competitive with other methods. Neither the mail nor telephone techniques entails travel costs—mileage, meals, and lodging—all of which have been increasing rapidly in recent years. In addition, doing face-to-face interviews requires greater training and skill than telephone interviews or the processing of mail questionnaires. Thus the hourly wages are likely to be considerably more; in our experience they are twice as great.

The costs of doing face-to-face interview surveys compare most favorably with the other methods when there is minimal geographical dispersion. The sensitivity of face-to-face interviewing costs to geographical dispersion can hardly be overemphasized. The contrast to mail surveys is especially great. The postage rate and most other costs associated with mail surveys are virtually the same regardless of whether the survey sample is one community or scattered across the entire nation. The telephone is intermediate, with the cost increase reflected only in toll charges, which increase with distance from the calling location.

The extremes of cost differences are suggested by the recent experience of a colleague. To conduct interviews for a national area probability sample of households, with each interview lasting approximately 45 minutes, the cost estimate provided by a reputable national survey organization was nearly $100 per case. The cost for the alternatives of using directories as a sample source (and thus sacrificing the area probability sample design) was estimated at about $20 per case for telephone interviews, most of which was taken up by toll charges, and $6 per case for mail questionnaires. For some samples, those for which only one or two respondents are located in a given community (e.g., mayors, agency directors, alumni of a university), the cost per respondent for a national face-to-face interview survey would be even greater.

At the other extreme, the cost of a local community face-to-face interview survey, which would have minimal mileage costs and few interview expenses, might compare very favorably with those for the other two methods. In this regard it is relevant to note costs for a one-county survey reported by Hochstim in which each of the three methods were used for part of the sample. He reported, for two surveys done in 1961 and 1962, that face-to-face interviews cost $9.04 and $10.35, telephone interviews $4.49 and $6.84, and mail questionnaires $4.05 and $6.01.[30]

Our discussion of costs assumes that the researcher plans to conduct his or her own study from beginning to end. Another possibility for some researchers who want to do face-to-face interviews is to contract with an existing survey organization to collect data as part of a study planned for their purposes. The piggy-backing of questions onto a survey that contains the questions of one or perhaps several other researchers places a quite different perspective on the cost of face-to-face interviews. Most (if not all) survey organizations that regularly conduct national surveys of the general public sell space in surveys on the basis of interview minutes. The advantage to the researcher who has only a few questions to ask are obvious. As long as the survey population is a common one, this procedure may occasionally make face-to-face interviews very competitive with mail and telephone methods, allowing one to avoid the multitude of problems of creating his or her own survey organization for a one-shot effort.

Similar possibilities may become increasingly available for telephone and mail surveys. However, the notion of piggy-backing questions onto surveys already planned is not as likely to be the crucial element to reducing costs as in the face-to-face interview. Firms that routinely conduct telephone surveys are likely to use WATS lines, which permit unlimited long distance calls after payment of a minimum charge. The more surveys that are conducted the cheaper the toll charges attributable to each. Coupled with the availability of sample frames and trained interviewers, this may make the cost of having someone conduct a survey compare favorably with mounting a local effort.

Although the costs for doing each type of survey vary greatly and comparisons are difficult to make, it is clear that in most cases face-to-face interviews are the most expensive and mail questionnaires the least. In spite of the fact that the differences are occasionally small, there is little doubt that costs represent the greatest, and sometimes most insurmountable, barrier to the utilization of face-to-face interviews.

CONCLUSION

After discussing 24 factors that seem important in evaluating the merits of each method, we now return to the elusive question of which method is best. Table 2.2 summarizes the discussion. Each performance characteristic is reported, and a "rating," based on the previous discussion, is provided for each method on each characteristic. Although it seems a useful way of bringing together the many and wide-ranging considerations to which this chapter is devoted, it is done with full recognition of the subjective elements that any rating system of this sort entails.

Table 2.2 shows each method to have "high" capabilities in some areas and "low" capabilities in others. With respect to the four general areas of concern about which this chapter is organized it is apparent that the face-to-face interview ranks highest in two of them—obtaining a representative sample and questionnaire construction and design. In contrast, the mail question-naire appears to perform most adequately with respect to obtaining accurate answers and the administrative factors we identified.

Table 2.3 provides another way of looking at the ratings. It presents the number of dimensions on which we judge each technique to be better than another technique. (Ties are ignored.) When all 24 of the dimensions for which ratings were made are considered, we find that the face-to-face and telephone interview techniques both rank above the mail technique about twice as often as the reverse is true (13 to 6 dimensions and 11 to 5 dimen-sions, respectively). However, the comparison shows that face-to-face inter-views rank above the telephone interview (7 dimensions) in about the same number of cases as it ranks below it (8 dimensions). These data suggest that the mail technique has more specific weaknesses than either of the other two, which themselves are about on a par with one another.

Although this is instructive, we would be among the first to argue that these numerical comparisons should not be used to arrive at the conclusion that face-to-face and telephone surveys are in fact about "equal" for any or all studies, nor that they are always superior to the mail survey. The strongest conclusion we allow ourselves to reach is that each method has merits as well as shortcomings. Furthermore, some items on the list are undoubtedly more important than others, and our ranking omits any consideration of relative weightings. Decisions as to which method is best, or at least adequate, cannot be made in the abstract; they must always be based on the needs of the specific survey.

There are few surveys in which every dimension covered in this chapter is relevant, and even fewer (if there are any at all) in which they can be weighed equally. In some cases the decision to use a particular method may rest with a single dimension from Table 2.2. For example, the inability to accept a sam-ple less adequate than that obtainable by area probability sampling methods may dictate the need for face-to-face interviews. On the other hand, the cost limitations may mean that only the mail method is acceptable. In still other cases speed may be the dominant consideration. Neither the mail nor face-to-face techniques can come close to matching the speed with which tele-phone surveys can be executed.

In summary, it is likely that the selection of the most appropriate method for a study will involve considerations of many or perhaps most of the per-formance characteristics discussed here. For example, a decision may involve evaluating questions to decide whether it is possible to ask them by mail or telephone and whether they are of the type in which the social desirability of response is a likely problem. The advantages of area probability sampling may have to be weighed against the necessity to accept a lower sample size

Table 2.2   Rating of Face-to-Face Interviews, Telephone Interviews, and Mail Questionnaires for Selected Performance Characteristics

METHOD

Performance Characteristics	Face-to-Face Interviews	Mail Questionnaires	Telephone Interviews
I. Obtaining a Representative Sample			
A. Known opportunity for all members of population to be included in the sample.			
1. Completely listed populations.	High	High	High
2. Populations which are not completely listed (e.g., household occupants).	High	Medium	Medium
B. Control over selection of respondents within sampling units.	High	Medium	High
C. Likelihood that selected respondents will be located.	Medium	High	High
D. Insensitivity to substitution of respondents and households.	Medium	Low	Low
E. Response rates.			
1. Hetrogeneous samples (e.g., general public).	High	Medium	High
2. Homogeneous, specialized samples (e.g., agency directors, ministers, students).	High	High	High
F. Likelihood that unknown bias from refusals will be avoided.	High	Low	High
II. Questionnaire Construction and Question Design			
A. Allowable length of questionnaire.	High	Medium	Medium
B. Type of question.			
1. Allowable complexity.	High	Medium	Low
2. Success with open-ended questions.	High	Low	High
3. Success with screen questions.	High	Medium	High

Table 2.2 Continued

Performance Characteristics	Face-to-Face	Mail	Telephone
4. Success with controlling sequence.	High	Low	High
5. Success with tedious or boring questions.	High	Low	Medium
C. Success in avoiding item non-response.	High	Medium	High
D. Insensitivity to questionnaire construction procedures.	High	Low	Medium
III. Obtaining Accurate Answers			
A. Likelihood that social desirability bias can be avoided.	Low	High	Medium
B. Likelihood that interviewer distortion and subversion can be avoided.	Low	High	Medium
C. Likelihood that contamination by others can be avoided.	Medium	Medium	High
D. Likelihood that consultation will be obtained when needed.	Medium	Medium	Low
IV. Administrative Requirements			
A. Likelihood that personnel requirements can be met.	Low	High	High
B. Potential speed of implementation.	Low	Low	High
C. Keeping costs low.			
1. Overall potential for low per interview costs.	Low	High	Medium
2. Insensitivity of costs to increasing geographical dispersion.	Low	High	Medium

Table 2.3   Number of Performance Characteristics for which Each Method Rates Higher Than Other Methods [a]

Comparative Rank	Face-to-Face Interviews	Telephone Interviews	Mail Questionnaires
1. Number of dimensions Face-to-Face ranked higher than others.	--	7	13
2. Number of dimensions Telephone ranked higher than others.	8	--	11
3. Number of dimensions Mail ranked higher than others.	6	5	--

[a]Based on information reported in Table 2.1.

(with its limits on generalizing results for sugroups) and fewer call-backs (with lower response rate).

The unavoidable fact is that the final decision requires the subjective weighing of one consideration against another. However, it is our hope that the material presented in this chapter will enable researchers to go about making that decision in a systematic way, and further that they will be prevented from picking a method that cannot possibly produce the desired results. Most of all, we wish to prevent survey researchers from deciding to use either the mail or telephone TDM, and then, with a report outline and stacks of computer printouts in front of them, discover an unforeseen inadequacy that leads to the lament, "if only I had known . . ."

NOTES

1. Many textbooks on social research include descriptions of area probability sampling. For example, see Charles H. Backstrom and Gerald D. Hursh, *Survey Research* (Evanston, Ill.: Northwestern University Press, 1963), Chapter 2; and Leslie Kish, *Survey Sampling* (New York: John Wiley, 1965). A less theoretical treatment than that of Kish, and one extremely useful for the practitioner, is Seymour Sudman, *Applied Sampling* (New York: Academic Press, 1976).
2. U.S. Bureau of the Census, *Statistical Abstract of the United States: 1975,* 96th ed. (Washington, D.C.: U.S. Government Printing Office, 1975). p. 516. The percentage of households with telephone service may be a slight overstatement, as evidenced by the following highs: Connecticut—101 percent, New Hampshire—103 percent, New Jersey—100 percent, and Vermont—102 percent.

3. U.S. Bureau of the Census of Housing: 1970, *Housing Characteristics for States, Cities, and Counties,* Vol. 1 (Washington, D.C.: U.S. Government Printing Office, 1972).

4. James A. Zrunner and G. Allen Brunner, "Are Voluntary Unlisted Telephone Subscribers Really Different?" *Journal of Marketing Research, 8,* 1971, pp. 121–124.

5. Sanford L. Cooper, "Random Sampling by Telephone—An Improved Method," *Journal of Marketing Research, 1,* 1964, pp. 45–48.

6. U.S. Bureau of the Census, *General Demographic Trends for Metropolitan Areas, 1960 to 1970, Final Report,* PHC (2) (Washington, D.C.: U.S. Government Printing Office, 1971).

7. Cooper, *op. cit.*

8. These trends were noted by a recent report of the American Statistical Association entitled, "Report on the ASA Conference on Surveys of Human Populations," *The American Statistician,* 28, February 1974, pp. 30–34.

9. Leslie Kish, "A Procedure for Objective Respondent Selection Within the Household," *Journal of the American Statistical Association, 44,* 1944, pp. 380–381; Verling C. Trodahl and Roy E. Carter, Jr., "Random Selection of Respondents Within Households in Phone Surveys," *Journal of Marketing, 1,* 1964, pp. 71–76.

10. W. Edward Deming, "On a Probability Mechanism to Attain an Economic Balance Between the Resultant Error of Response and the Bias of Nonresponse," *Journal of the American Statistical Association, 18,* 1953, pp. 743–744.

11. Kish, 1965, *op. cit.*

12. Alfred St. Louis, *The Texas Crime Trend Survey,* Statistical Analysis Center, Texas Department of Public Safety, August 1976, p. 4.

13. Don A. Dillman, Jean Gorton Gallegos, and James H. Frey, "Reducing Refusal Rates for Telephone Interviews," *Public Opinion Quarterly, 40,* 1976, pp. 66–78.

14. Don A Dillman, James A. Christenson, Edwin H. Carpenter, and Ralph M. Brooks, "Increasing Mail Questionnaire Response: A Four-State Comparison," *American Sociological Review, 39,* 1974, pp. 744–756.

15. Willis J. Goudy, "Interim Nonresponse to a Mail Questionnaire: Impacts on Variable Relationships," Journal Paper No. J-8456, Iowa Agriculture and Home Economics Experiment Station, Ames, Iowa, 1976.

16. This is a common criticism found in major textbooks on social research. See, for example, Fred N. Kerlinger, *Foundations of Behavioral Research* (New York: Holt, Rinehart, and Winston, 1965); Mildred Parten, *Surveys, Polls, and Samples* (New York: Harper and Row, 1950); and Claire Sellitz, M. Jahoda, M. Deutsch, and S. Cook, *Research Methods in Social Relations* (Chicago: Holt, Rinehart and Winston, 1959).

17. Charles Glock and Rodney Stark, *Christian Beliefs and Anti-Semitism* (New York: Harper & Row, 1966).

18. Paul Erdos, "How to Get Higher Returns From Your Mail Surveys," *Printers Ink, 12,* February 22, 1957, pp. 30–31.

19. John Colombotos, "Personal Versus Telephone Interviews: Effect on Responses," *Public Health Reports, 84,* 1969, pp. 773–782.

20. Donald R. Field, "The Telephone Interview in Leisure Research," *Journal of Leisure Research, 5, 1973, pp. 51–59.*

21. Rex Warland, Personal Communication, 1973.

22. Dillman, Gallegos, and Frey, *op. cit.*

23. Dillman, Christenson, Carpenter, and Brooks, *op. cit.,* p. 750.

24. Herbert H. Hyman, *Survey Design and Analysis* (Glencoe: The Free Press, 1955), p. 138. For a more complete discussion of this problem, see Derek C. Phillips and Kevin J. Clancy, "Some Effects of Social Desirability in Survey Studies," *American Journal of Sociology, 77,* 1972, pp. 921–940.

25. Joseph R. Hochstim, "A Critical Comparison of Three Strategies of Collecting Data From Households," *Journal of the American Statistical Association, 62,* 1967, pp. 976–989.

26. Colombotos, *op. cit.*

27. Frederick Wiseman, "Methodological Bias in Public Opinion Surveys," *Public Opinion Quarterly, 36,* 1972, pp. 105–108.

28. Dillman, Christenson, Carpenter, and Brooks, p. 754. This average includes only out-of-pocket costs and not salaries of the investigators.

29. James A. Davis, "Are Surveys Any Good, And If So, For What?" in H. Wallace Sinaiko and Laurie A. Broedling (Eds.), *Perspectives on Attitude Assessment: Surveys and Their Alternatives* (Champaign, Illinois: Pendilon Publications, 1976). p. 34.

30. Hochstim, *op. cit.,* p. 981.

Chapter Three

WRITING QUESTIONS:
....
Some General Principles

Subsequent chapters present the step-by-step details of the TDM for mail and telephone surveys. However, implementing these detailed procedures is *not* the most difficult problem faced by many users of the TDM. Their predicament is that some of the questions they propose to ask cannot possibly produce the kind of information they need. Without good questions, the details of the TDM become nothing more than the pursuit of one useless step after another.

A fortunate few know exactly what questions must be asked, perhaps because they are replicating a previous study. However, for every such person, there are many others who come to the survey situation with questions that are only tentatively formulated. Still others, we have discovered, are far less prepared, having little more than a study topic and a vague idea of what they want to ask. Although a discussion of the formulation of questions can hardly substitute for knowing what is needed from respondents to meet one's survey objectives, it can provide a basis for clarifying the types of data obtained from surveys and the subsequent examination of proposed questions.

The writing of questions can be conveniently divided into three parts, each of which requires separate decisions. They are (1) the kind of information sought, (2) the question structure, and (3) the actual choice of words. Failure to consider any one of the three can prevent users of the TDM from obtaining the information necessary for achieving their study objectives. For example, we have frequently observed people struggling to find just the right wording for their question when, regardless of the words chosen, the question could not fill their needs. The problem was that one kind of information (e.g., attitudes) was being requested when another (e.g., behavior) was called for by the study objectives. Similarly, we have seen the objectives of research thwarted by relying on one question structure (e.g., open-ended) when another (e.g., close-ended with ordered categories) was essential.

The purpose of this chapter is to help the user of the TDM identify the nature of problems frequently encountered in writing questions and to provide guidelines for overcoming them. However, our objectives are admittedly modest. There is no generally agreed on set of principles for writing questions. Indeed, the question that serves one study best may be totally inappropriate for another. Every survey represents a combination of study topic, population, and objectives that make it unique. Consequently, space limitations prohibit adequate treatment of the many specific concerns researchers are likely to encounter. Thus we focus on the concerns faced most frequently by previous users of the TDM.

Unlike the chapters that follow, the subject matter of this chapter applies to both mail and telephone questionnaires. Specific adaptations required for the two methods are discussed in Chapter 4 (for the mail questionnaire) and Chapter 6 (for the telephone questionnaire).

THE KIND OF INFORMATION BEING SOUGHT

The first step in writing a question is to identify exactly what kind of information is desired from survey respondents. Questions can usually be classified as requesting one or more of these types of information:

1 What people say they want: their *attitudes*
2 What people think is true: their *beliefs*
3. What people do: their *behavior*
4. What people are: their *attributes*

It is important to understand the differences among these types of information. Otherwise, efforts to write questions may inadvertently result in obtaining a different type of information from that which the researcher needs for a particular study.

Attitudes

Attitudes describe how people feel about something. They are evaluative in nature and reflect respondents' views about the desirability of something. Attitude questions require respondents to show whether they have positive or negative feelings about the "attitude object." Words typically used in attitude questions to indicate the direction of one's feelings include favor versus oppose, prefer versus not prefer, should versus should not, good versus bad, right versus wrong, and desirable versus undesirable. Attitude questions can be asked in a variety of ways, as shown in Example 3.1 for a study concerning abortion. Clearly, each question in this example asks respondents to register their views on the desirability of a particular course of action. As shown here, that desirability can be reflected in either the wording of the question (Examples 3.1A and 3.1C) or in the answer categories (Example 3.1B).

Beliefs

Beliefs are assessments of what a person thinks is true or false. There is no implied goodness or badness in beliefs, but only an assessment of what one thinks exists or does not exist.[1] Choices that are typically implied by belief questions include correct versus incorrect, accurate versus inaccurate, and what happened versus what did not happen. Belief questions can also be expressed in a variety of ways, as shown in Example 3.2. In some cases belief questions are designed to test people's knowledge of specific facts (Example 3.2A and 3.2B). In other cases they deal with issues for which no one knows the "correct" answer (Example 3.2C). In all cases belief questions are designed to elicit people's perceptions of past, present, or future reality.

It is not always easy to distinguish between questions that are designed to

Example 3.1 Questions that Elicit Attitudes

```
A.   Should all abortions be outlawed?

     1 NO
     2 YES

B.   In general, how do you feel about nationwide legal-
     ization of abortion in the United States?

     1 STRONGLY OPPOSE
     2 MILDLY OPPOSE
     3 NEITHER OPPOSE NOR FAVOR
     4 MILDLY FAVOR
     5 STRONGLY FAVOR

C.   Do you tend to agree or disagree with this statement?
     "Anyone who wants an abortion should be able to get it."

     1 AGREE
     2 DISAGREE
```

Example 3.2   Questions that Elicit Beliefs

A. Is this statement true or false? "Last year the number
    of abortions obtained in our county hospital was greater
    than the number of babies delivered there."

        1 TRUE
        2 FALSE

B. In your opinion does getting an abortion usually prevent
    someone from having another child?

        1 ALWAYS YES
        2 USUALLY YES
        3 SOMETIMES
        4 SELDOM
        5 ALMOST NEVER
        6 NEVER

C. Do you think that making abortions legal everywhere in
    the United States will lead to an actual decrease in
    our country's population?

        1 NO
        2 YES

---

elicit beliefs from those designed to tap attitudes. For example, consider the
questions, "Why did you decide not to get an abortion?" Strictly speaking,
respondents are being asked to register a belief about why they chose a
particular course of action. It can be expected that some respondents would
answer with a belief, for example, "I was unable to afford it." However,
another respondent might just as reasonably respond with an attitude, for
example, "I felt that obtaining an abortion is immoral, and no one should be
allowed to get one."

Questions are sometimes stated in a way that elicits responses constituting
a combination of beliefs and attitudes, as in this example:

To what extent is the obtaining of illegal abortions a problem in this community?

    1 NOT A PROBLEM AT ALL
    2 A SLIGHT PROBLEM
    3 A MODERATE PROBLEM
    4 A SERIOUS PROBLEM

Some people might respond "a serious problem" because of their beliefs that
many abortions are obtained, and these produce many medical problems.

Others might possess no knowledge about the extent to which illegal abortions occur, but respond with "a serious problem" because they feel it is wrong for anyone to obtain an abortion. It seems most likely, however, that responses will reflect both an assessment of the prevalence of abortions and feelings about whether they should be allowed to occur.

Questions that elicit both beliefs and attitudes may lead one to wonder whether it is useful to distinguish between attitude and belief questions in the first place. In our view, the gray area in which they become intertwined does not justify ignoring the fairly clear conceptual distinction that can be made between them.[2] Further, it is a distinction that many survey researchers have found helpful in writing their questions. However, because there is a point at which the distinction begins to fade, an awareness of it may help to alleviate undue consternation at finding the appropriate categorization for every single question that one might wish to ask in a survey.

Behavior

The third kind of information commonly obtained in surveys consists of reports about respondents' behavior. Strictly speaking, these questions elicit people's "beliefs" about their behavior. On this basis it might be argued that behavior should not be considered a distinct type of information. However, in our opinion there is a substantial difference between asking people to describe their own behavior and asking for their view about something they have experienced only in a cognitive (as opposed to a physical) sense. Thus the identification as a separate kind of information seems warranted (Example 3.3). Behavioral questions may concern what people have done in the past (Example 3.3A), what they are currently doing (Example 3.3B), or what they plan to do in the future (Example 3.3C).

Attributes

The fourth type of information that surveys seek to gather concerns attributes, which are often referred to as personal or demographic characteristics. People tend to think of attributes as something they possess, rather than something they do. Virtually all surveys ask for a number of them. Among the most frequently requested attributes are age, education, occupation, income, sex, marital status, family composition, home ownership, race, politics, and religion. The usual purpose for collecting this information is to explore how the other kinds of information (i.e., beliefs, attitudes, and behavior) differ for people with various attributes. The questions shown in Example 3.4 are ones that might reasonably be asked in a survey about abortion.

Example 3.3   Questions that Elicit Behavior

A. Have you ever had an abortion?

    1 NO
    2 YES

B. Are you currently taking birth control pills?

    1 NO
    2 YES

C. Do you think you will try to become pregnant again
    at some time in the future?

    1 NO
    2 PROBABLY NO
    3 PROBABLY YES
    4 YES

Example 3.4   Questions that Elicit Information on Attributes

A. Are you currently married?

    1 NO
    2 YES

B. What is your present age?

    _____YEARS

C. How many children have you had?

    _____NUMBER

The Importance of Distinguishing Among Types of Information

Why is it important to distinguish among the four types of information? Our experience with many people preparing to conduct surveys suggests that what appears on the surface to be a desire to obtain one kind of information frequently turns out to be desire for another. The objective, "to find out people's opinions on abortion," may in fact reflect a desire to describe people's beliefs, attitudes, or actual behavior. In such cases the clarification of one's objectives is a necessary first step that must be satisfactorily accomplished before one can proceed to write specific questions. Otherwise, attempts to reword questions may unwittingly lead not only to a change in wording, but perhaps to a complete change in the kind of information that will be elicited. We can recall, for example, the startled look of disbelief on the face of an agency director when he discovered that a study aimed at exploring people's actual behavior resulted in a questionnaire in which nearly three-quarters of the questions concerned beliefs and attitudes. Another reason for distinguishing among the types of information is that questions of each type tend to pose different writing problems. In general, attitude questions are far more sensitive to wording variations than other types of questions. For example, Schuman and Duncan report these answers obtained from two attitude questions asked in 1969.[3]

President Nixon has ordered the withdrawal of 25,000 troops from Vietnam in the next three months. How do you feel about this—do you think troops should be withdrawn at a faster rate or slower rate?

42% faster
20% same as now (not mentioned as an alternative, but accepted if offered)
16% slower
13% no opinion

In general do you feel the pace at which the president is withdrawing troops is too fast, too slow, or about right?

28% too slow
49% about right
6% too fast
18% no opinion

Clearly, whether one concluded that people supported the President depended on which question was used.

We should not be too surprised when attitude questions with slightly different wordings elicit somewhat different responses. People's attitudes on a specific subject are often complex and intertwined with other attitudes and beliefs they hold. Further, attitudes are held in varying degrees and are subject to considerable fluctuation. Thus when people are asked to express their attitudes on a given subject, they are likely to engage in considerable contemplation that involves carefully considering how well the particular wording of the question reflects the degree to which they hold the attitude under investigation.

In contrast, questions about behavior and attributes are usually much less sensitive (although not immune) to wording variations. People can usually state quite unequivocally whether they have, for example, visited a family planning clinic in the last 6 months or whether they are married. As one would logically expect, belief questions are intermediate between attitude and behavior questions in terms of their sensitivity to wording variations.

The variations in sensitivity to wording hold a major implication for how one goes about ascertaining information. When a question seems likely to be sensitive to wording variations, it is advisable to ask another or perhaps several questions. Thus people interested in attitudes, and to a certain extent beliefs, often ask a number of similar questions from which they try to construct attitude scales by combining the responses in certain ways. At the other extreme, it is seldom necessary to ask for information on attributes in more than one way. For example, one would not ask respondents to indicate their age in years and then ask them to indicate the year of their birth.

Efforts to get survey sponsors to recognize the differences among the kinds of information sought sometimes result in a conscious effort to include all four types of questions in a questionnaire. Obtaining all four types of information does not make a survey either good or bad. It depends on the type of information that is called for by the study objectives, something that researchers must decide for themselves. Until one specifies what kind of information is needed, efforts to write specific questions are destined to be futile.

DECIDING QUESTION STRUCTURE

The second major decision in writing questions is to determine question structure. Our basis for distinguishing among question structures is the nature of response behavior asked of the respondent. Using this as our criterion, four basic types of question structures can be identified.

1. *Open-ended*

    These questions have no answer choices from which respondents select their response. Instead, the respondents must "create" their own answers and state them in their own words.

2. *Close-ended with ordered choices*

    For these questions answer choices are provided; each is a gradation of a single dimension of some thought or behavior. The respondent's task is to find the most appropriate place on an implied continuum for his or her response.

3. *Close-ended with unordered response choices*

    Here answer choices are provided, but no single dimension underlines them. Respondents must choose from among discrete, unordered categories by independently evaluating each choice and selecting the one that best reflects his or her situation.

4. Partially close-ended

Such questions provide a compromise. Although answer choices are provided, respondents have the option of creating their own responses. The choices provided are almost always unordered choices, although we occasionally see ordered choices with this structure.

Virtually all questions that might be asked in a survey fit into one of these categories. Further, each type of information described in the preceding paragraphs (i.e., attitudes, beliefs, behavior, and attributes) can be requested using each structure, as we illustrate later (Examples 3.5–3.8). However, as we also show, some structures tend to be more suitable for obtaining certain types of information than others. Each question structure requires respondents to engage in a different kind of response behavior and has certain advantages and disadvantages.

Open-Ended Questions

Open-ended questions are likely to be used in two distinctly different situations. One is a situation in which respondents can express themselves freely (Examples 3.5A and 3.5B). The other common use is to elicit a precise piece of information that respondents can recall without difficulty when there are a very large number of possible answers and listing all of them would increase the difficulty of answering (Examples 3.5C and 3.5D).

Open-ended questions of the first type are most often employed when the researcher cannot anticipate the various ways in which people are likely to respond to a question. They are used to stimulate free thought, solicit suggestions, probe people's memories, and clarify positions. Further, they give respondents a chance to vent frustrations and state strong opinions. They are indispensible for exploratory studies in which the researcher's main purpose is to find the most salient aspects of a topic, perhaps in preparation for developing close-ended questions for a later survey. However, open-ended questions of this type also exhibit some problems.

Example 3.5   Open-Ended Questions

A. What should be done in order to improve this community?
    (Attitude)

B. In your opinion what is the biggest barrier to getting
    young people to help improve this community? (Belief)

C. What community organizations have you joined since
    moving to this town? (Behavior)

D. In what county is your residence located? (Attribute)

Perhaps the biggest disadvantage is that these kinds of questions can be very demanding. People are asked to recall past experiences, reorganize them, and find the terms with which to express them. The task of creating and articulating answers is difficult for most respondents, especially those with low educational attainment or who lack experience in communicating ideas to other people. Such people may well become embarrassed and thus incur considerable social cost when required to respond. Therefore, the successful use of open-ended questions of this type usually requires persistent probing by a sympathetic interviewer. Otherwise, answers may be incomplete, uninterpretable, or irrelevant. For these reasons they are generally unsuited for mail questionnaires.

Another frequent disadvantage of open-ended questions that encourage free expression is the difficulty of constructing meaningful variables for statistical analysis (regardless of whether collected by mail or telephone). Unfortunately, open-ended questions usually produce relatively few mentions of any one topic; thus efforts to test hypotheses usually end up by comparing a few people whose views on a topic are known against the vast majority whose views are not known. Suppose, for example, that 15 percent of the respondents who answered Example 3.5A suggested that a swimming pool was needed to improve their community, and the researcher desired to determine whether "support" for this idea is greater among respondents with school-age children. Although an appropriate comparison could be made, it would provide a very weak test of the hypothesis. It cannot be assumed that those who failed to "volunteer" swimming pool as an answer are opposed to the idea. The most that can be assumed is that these people did not happen to think of it when asked about possible community improvements. Included among the group of respondents who did not mention this idea could be a greater number who favor the idea than oppose it. A more adequate test of support would be provided by a specific question that asked every person how they felt about that topic, clearly dividing opponents and proponents into separate categories.

However, questions that encourage free expression do not always inhibit the construction of variables for meaningful statistical analysis. For example, suppose that respondents in a survey are asked, "What leisure time activity do you most enjoy doing?" The researcher may be less interested in the specific activity than its general nature. It may be possible to classify most respondents according to whether the activity they mention is "passive" or "active," producing a useful dichotomous variable that can be subjected to statistical analysis.

The second type of open-ended question is not designed to encourage free expression. It seeks a specific fact, usually (but not always) a behavior or attribute that is known to the respondent. The only barrier to providing answer categories, and thus turning it into a close-ended question, is that it would be unnecessarily time consuming for the respondent and, in the case of mail questionnaires, would require a great deal of precious space. Most people, for example, can name the kind of car they drive and the county in which they live, making it unnecessary to read through a list of perhaps 50–100 names to find the answer that fits. Also, responses to open-ended questions of this type do not usually provide any problems for statistical analysis.

However, even these questions are not without their problems. Sometimes people cannot recall all the possible answers (e.g., the voluntary community organizations to which they belong), and underenumeration becomes a problem. Second, people do not always read or hear questions correctly. In such cases the double exposure to content provided by close-ended questions prevents mistakes. In a mail survey of the general public, we were surprised to discover that several people listed "United States" in response to the question, "In what county do you live?" This apparently happened because they misread the word "county" as "country." Finally, illegible handwriting poses problems for the user of this type of open-ended question, underscoring the difficulties created by the use of open-ended questions in mail surveys. On the other hand, good interviewing can usually overcome these disadvantages of underenumeration and misunderstanding.

Close-Ended Questions with Ordered Answer Choices

The feature that distinguishes close-ended questions with ordered answer choices from all other forms of questions is that each choice offered for a particular question represents a gradation of a single dimension of some concept. This question structure is ideally suited for determining such things as intensity of feeling, degree of involvement, and frequency of participation (Example 3.6).

Questions with ordered choices tend to be quite specific, restricting respondents to thinking about a very limited aspect of life in a very limited way. They are often as narrow as open-ended questions are broad. To answer these questions, respondents must identify the response dimension that underlies the answer choices and place themselves at the most appropriate point on a scale that is implied by the answer choices. Questions of this nature are only appropriate when a researcher has a well-defined issue and knows precisely what dimension of thought he or she wants the respondent to use in providing an answer.

This type of question uses the information supplied by respondents to determine the extent to which each respondent differs from every other one. Thus responses to such questions are well suited for many forms of sophisticated analyses (e.g., regression analysis). Researchers also find this question

Example 3.6 Close-Ended Questions with Ordered Answer Choices

---

A. How do you feel about this statement? "I wish this community had more tennis courts." (Attitude)

   1 STRONGLY DISAGREE
   2 MILDLY DISAGREE
   3 NEITHER AGREE NOR DISAGREE
   4 MILDLY AGREE
   5 STRONGLY AGREE

B. In general, how well do you get along with your next door neighbors? (Belief)

   1 NOT AT ALL WELL
   2 NOT TOO WELL
   3 ABOUT AVERAGE
   4 FAIRLY WELL
   5 VERY WELL

C. How often do you attend church services? (Behavior)

   1 ONCE A WEEK OR MORE
   2 TWO OR THREE TIMES A MONTH
   3 ABOUT ONCE A MONTH
   4 LESS THAN ONCE A MONTH

D. What is your present age? (Attribute)

   1 UNDER 25 YEARS
   2 26-35 YEARS
   3 36-45 YEARS
   4 46-55 YEARS
   5 56-65 YEARS
   6 OVER 65 YEARS

---

structure particularly attractive for asking series of attitude and belief questions when their goal is to combine answers to form a multiple-item scale. Thus the questions in a single questionnaire often use the same type of answer choices (e.g., strongly agree to strongly disagree) for many items. Another attractive feature of questions with ordered response choices is that they are usually less demanding than questions of any other type, a result of the precisely prescribed response expectations.

Close-Ended Questions with Unordered Answer Choices

The essential difference between close-ended questions with ordered answer choices and those without is that the latter do not limit respondents to choosing among gradations of a single concept. Each choice is an independent alternative representing a different concept. To answer questions with unordered answer choices it is necessary to evaluate individually each alternative in relation to every other one. Questions of this type are often used to establish priorities among issues and decide among alternative policies. As shown in Example 3.7, they too can be used to collect all four kinds of information. These questions are generally more difficult to answer than those containing ordered answer choices, inasmuch as respondents must often balance several ideas in their minds at the same time. Sometimes the mental demands of these questions are enormous, as when respondents are asked to rank 10−20 items, or when each set of response choices differs only slightly from the others.

The shortcomings of these questions are quite similar to those of questions

---

Example 3.7   Close-Ended Questions with Unordered Response Choices

A. Who should be most, second, and third influential in deciding whether this community obtains a downtown shopping mall? (Attitude)

(Put appropriate number in each box)

```
┌───┐  MOST
└───┘  INFLUENTIAL              1 THE MAYOR
                                2 THE CITY MANAGER
┌───┐  SECOND MOST              3 THE CITY COUNCIL
└───┘  INFLUENTIAL              4 THE CHAMBER OF COMMERCE
                                5 THE DOWNTOWN MERCHANT'S
┌───┐  THIRD MOST                 ASSOCIATION
└───┘  INFLUENTIAL              6 THE GENERAL PUBLIC
```

B. Which one of the following do you think is most responsible for inflation? (Belief)

1 UNION DEMANDS FOR HIGHER WAGES
2 BUSINESS DEMANDS FOR HIGHER PROFITS
3 THE PUBLIC'S DEMANDS FOR MORE GOVERNMENTAL SERVICES
4 FOREIGN COUNTRY DEMANDS FOR HIGHER PRICES FOR OIL, MINERALS, AND OTHER PRODUCTS THEY EXPORT

C. On which of the following have you spent the most time during the past week? (Behavior)

1 DOING COMMUNITY SERVICE ACTIVITIES
2 WATCHING TELEVISION
3 WORKING AROUND HOUSE AND YARD
4 VISITING WITH FRIENDS AND NEIGHBORS

D. Which best describes the kind of house in which you live? (Attribute)

1 SINGLE FAMILY DWELLING
2 DUPLEX OR TRIPLEX
3 APARTMENT
4 MOBILE HOME

with ordered answer choices. Unless the researcher's knowledge of the subject allows meaningful answer choices to be stated, useful results cannot be obtained. Perhaps the most frequent criticism is that the preferred options of all respondents are not stated, as shown in Example 3.7B. For example, the respondent might feel that the biggest cause of inflation is poorer productivity among workers, which is not included in the list of options. However, this shortcoming can be overcome by the use of the question structure described next.

Partially Close-Ended Questions

The fear that certain options will be overlooked by researchers has led to the widespread use of the partially close-ended question. This attempt to attain the best of the open and closed formats is a natural compromise, allowing the building of variables and the testing of hypotheses, but not forcing people into boxes in which they clearly do not fit. This format is almost always limited to unordered, close-ended questions, as shown in Example 3.8. However, we have seen a few cases in which a researcher gave respondents the option of rejecting the predefined dimensions of ordered questions.

We should not expect too much with respect to the yield of the open-ended option for statistical analyses. Although we often use this format, we seldom obtain a sufficient number of additional responses to warrant their inclusion in the planned analyses. Usually the vast majority of respondents select one of the offered categories rather than create their own, especially if the researcher does a good job of identifying the most appropriate categories.

However, turning a close-ended question into one that is only partially closed may provide very useful information. If, for example, a number of respondents insist that none of the categories fit them, it can be assumed that there are numerous others who, although they did not choose the open-ended version, probably chose one of the close-ended versions reluctantly. In short, an unusually high number of volunteered responses to partially closed questions suggests that something is amiss and that an evaluation must be made before attempting to reach conclusions.

Choosing the Most Appropriate Structure

Any of the four structures may be the "best" one for a particular question. Consider, for example, the general question of who people want to be elected governor of their state. This question is posed in Example 3.9 using each alternative structure. Depending on the researcher's plans for using responses to the question, any structure might be the most desirable one.

The open-ended version would seem most appropriate prior to the begin-

Example 3.8   Partially Closed Questions

A. Which of the following areas of expenditures do you want
    to have the highest priority for improvement in this
    community? (Attitude)

    1 STREETS AND ROADS
    2 SEWAGE TREATMENT
    3 PARKS
    4 OTHER

    _____

B. For what reasons did you retire before age 65? (Belief)

    1 HEALTH REASONS
    2 DESIRE FOR MORE FREE TIME
    3 WAS ASSURED OF A MORE THAN ADEQUATE INCOME
    4 SPOUSE STRONGLY ENCOURAGED ME TO DO IT
    5 PLEASE LIST AS MANY OTHERS AS YOU CAN THINK OF

    _____

    _____

C. Which of these community recreational facilities do
    you most frequently use? (Behavior)

    1 PARKS
    2 TENNIS COURTS
    3 SWIMMING POOL
    4 OTHER (PLEASE SPECIFY)

    _____

D. What do you consider yourself to be? (Attribute)

    1 REPUBLICAN
    2 DEMOCRAT
    3 INDEPENDENT
    4 OTHER (PLEASE SPECIFY)

    _____

ning of a campaign, when the candidates are unknown. It probes people's memories to find out if any particular individual is making an impression on the citizenry and might be in an advantageous position for mounting a campaign. Questions of this nature are often used in seeking an answer to the question of who would be the strongest candidate, but it would not be very useful if the candidates have already been selected, and one wants to know for whom people plan to vote. Sometimes people cannot "volunteer" the name of their preference, but can easily select it from a list of candidates.

The close-ended version with ordered response categories is useful for quite a different purpose. People are asked to independently evaluate each

Example 3.9   A Question on One Topic Structured Four Different Ways

---

OPEN-ENDED

Who would you like to see elected Governor in this year's election?

CLOSE-ENDED WITH ORDERED RESPONSE CHOICES

How well do you think each of these candidates would perform if elected Governor?

1.	Karns------------Poor	Fair	Good	Excellent
2.	White------------Poor	Fair	Good	Excellent
3.	Caldwell---------Poor	Fair	Good	Excellent
4.	Sweeney----------Poor	Fair	Good	Excellent

CLOSE-ENDED WITH UNORDERED RESPONSE CHOICES

Which of these four candidates would you most like to see elected Governor?

(Circle Number of Your Answer)

1 KARNS

2 WHITE

3 CALDWELL

4 SWEENEY

PARTIALLY CLOSE-ENDED

Who would you like to see elected Governor?

(Circle Number of Your Answer)

1 KARNS

2 WHITE

3 CALDWELL

4 SWEENEY

5 OTHER (PLEASE SPECIFY)

---

possible candidate and provide a rating of how they expect the candidates to perform if elected. The responses to this question would allow the researcher to assess whether the differences between candidates are large or small, information that would be particularly helpful in deciding how to conduct a campaign. Large differences would suggest that changing voter opinions would require a substantial effort. Small differences would suggest that minor events might switch voter preferences.

The close-ended version with unordered response categories is the type that most closely resembles what people are asked to do at the polls, where the issue is who one prefers, not the extent to which one candidate is preferred over another (as implied by the close-ended version with ordered response categories). This structure is most likely to be used when the candidates are known and the researcher is attempting to predict the outcome of an election. The partially closed version would be appropriate if write-in candidates are likely to be a significant factor in the election.

Each question shown in Example 3.9 provides a different kind of information. We should not be surprised to find all four types asked in the same survey as the researcher tries to gain as much knowledge as possible about the probable outcome of an election. Yet question structure cannot be decided apart from what the researcher is attempting to find out in the survey. Selecting the wrong structure can result in a failure to meet one's research objectives just as easily as it can result from asking for the wrong kind of information (already discussed in this chapter) or using the wrong words, the topic to which we turn next.

COMMON WORDING PROBLEMS

The third decision researchers face in writing questions is how to word them. After a number of futile tries at wording a particularly difficult question, a colleague threw his pencil across the room and declared, "writing questions would be a lot easier if we did not have to use words!" Anyone who has conducted a survey can probably sympathize with his frustration. The wrong choice of words can create any number of problems—from excessive vagueness to too much precision, from being misunderstood to not being understood at all, from being too objectionable to being too uninteresting and irrelevant. No one would deny that it is important to find the right choice of words. However, the right choice in any given situation and how to know when you have achieved it are two things on which agreement is far less likely to occur.

Our confidence in being able to provide satisfactory guidelines for wording questions is not bolstered by the experience of Payne, discussed in his classic book, *The Art of Asking Questions.* In one chapter he presents 41 versions of a single question before finding one that he considers acceptable for a survey. Even this question is cautiously labeled "passable," and the reader is admonished that pretesting might shoot this 41st version "full of holes" (p. 227).[4] The concluding chapter of the book summarizes Payne's rules for wording questions, with the subtitle of the chapter providing a good description of the survey researcher's dilemma, "A *Concise* Check List of 100 Considerations" (my italics).

The rules, admonitions, and principles for how to word questions enumerated in various books and articles present a mind boggling array of generally good but often conflicting and confusing directions about how to do it. There is no shortage of simple admonitions on what to do and what not to do. For example,

Use simple words.
Do not be vague.
Keep it short.
Be specific.
Do not talk down to respondents.
Avoid bias.
Avoid objectionable questions.
Do not be too specific.
Avoid hypothetical questions.

The problem is that these "how to do it" rules often get in one another's way. "Use simple words," is usually good advice, but it frequently interferes with advice to "keep it short." It is interesting, for example, to note that Payne's 41st version of the question mentioned previously was expanded from only eight words to 28, as difficult words were changed to simple ones.[5] Using simple words also increases the risk of "talking down to the respondents." The well-founded advice not to be vague often produces questions that are too specific. The advice to keep questions from being too direct and therefore objectionable sometimes results in not heeding the advice to avoid hypothetical questions. In addition, although biased wording is certainly to be avoided, it is precisely those questions that may be required for building many kinds of attitude scales.

The reason that seemingly good advice, taken literally, may turn out to be bad advice is that questions are not written in the abstract. Writing questions for a particular questionnaire means doing them for (1) a particular population, (2) a particular purpose, and (3) for placement next to other questions in the questionnaire. Words that are too difficult for use with some populations may be perfectly acceptable for others. A question that is fairly vague may satisfy the exploratory objectives of one study, but not the analytic ones of another. A question that makes little sense by itself may be quite clear when asked after the ones which precede it in the questionnaire.

A list of admonitions, no matter how well intended, therefore cannot be considered as absolute principles that must be adhered to without exception. Thus our discussion of common wording problems is organized as a series of questions that can and should be asked about each item the researcher considers for inclusion in his or her study.

Will the Words Be Uniformly Understood?

To make a question mean the same thing to everyone—the goal in writing each survey question—it is usually important to keep the wording as simple as possible. Some words are needlessly complex, and substitutes can be found. For example, the words listed on the left can often be replaced by the simpler words to the right.

exhausted	tired
candid	honest
priority	most important
leisure	free time
employment	work
supervision	care
courageous	brave
assistance	help
preserve	protect
virtually	nearly
rectify	correct

When a word exceeds six or seven letters, chances are that a shorter and more easily understood word can be substituted, although we should not automatically assume that all shorter words are acceptable. For example, it would not be advisable to substitute "deter" for "discourage," or "yield" for "production." Further, many simple words have more than one meaning (e.g., fast, place, and note) and must be used with care, being certain that their use does not increase rather than decrease chances for misunderstanding.

Substituting simple for complex words often has the paradoxical effect of turning simple sentences into complex ones (Example 3.10). This trade-off cannot be overlooked in deciding how a particular question should be worded. Our effort to substitute simple words for "prescription drugs," and "percent," resulted in more than doubling the length of the question from 16 to 38 words. One barrier to using simple words is that the more complex ones have very precise meanings that make conversations more efficient by eliminating long, burdensome phrases. The more complex the subject matter of the survey, the more likely that we must wrestle with the trade-off between the complexity of words and the burden of length.

Sometimes it is unnecessary to find substitutes for what appear to be difficult words. Virtually all occupational groups share a particular vocabulary that is not understood by outsiders. The use of such a vocabulary facilitates efficient communication, and the use of simpler words would only confuse matters. In a survey of city planners it seems quite reasonable to talk about "annexation," instead of "an addition." Similarly, in surveying physicians it seems reasonable to talk about "pharmaceutical companies," instead of "companies that sell medicines." To do otherwise may even suggest a lack of knowledge and understanding of the topic of the survey. However, the fact remains that people who do surveys are far more likely to overestimate than underestimate the vocabularies of respondents. Thus when in doubt, it seems prudent to use the simpler of the available alternatives.

A thesaurus is an indespensible tool for finding synonyms that might be used. There is no substitute for asking someone with less education than most respondents are likely to have to go through a questionnaire and identify words that they find confusing. Pretesting with actual respondents (not the commonly used students or secretaries) is also very important, because it helps one find the commonly shared vocabulary of the study population.

Do the Questions Contain Abbreviations or Unconventional Phrases?

Few would argue for the use of abbreviations, foreign phrases, or slang in a questionnaire, and we certainly agree that they should be avoided. However,

Example 3.10   The Trade-off Between Difficult Words and Question Length

---

```
Problem:  Difficult words

      Should the state sales tax on prescription drugs be
      reduced from 5 percent to 1 percent?


Problem:  Excessive length

      Should the state sales tax on those medicines that can
      only be bought under a doctor's order be lowered so that
      people would pay 1 cent tax instead of 5 cents tax for
      every dollar spent on such medicine?
```

---

they are sometimes employed in surveys because they refer to something that can be communicated far more efficiently by the use of such terms. Although we usually avoid the use of any abbreviations or slang in questionnaires sent to the general public, we cautiously use them in other questionnaires. For example, we see nothing wrong with using "blitz" and "slant" in a survey of football coaches. Even though the "ABA" refers to both the American Bar Association and the now defunct American Basketball Association (plus a number of other organizations), we doubt that the use of this abbreviation would cause confusion in a survey of attorneys.

Sometimes the desire to use abbreviations derives from having to repeat a particular term many times throughout a questionnaire. We recall, for example, one mail survey of the general public in which the name "Washington State University" was repeated 50 times. In this case it seemed quite reasonable to use the abbreviation, being very careful to note the full name in conjunction with that abbreviation, "Washington State University (WSU)," once on every page.

Some terms are considered so common that they are not thought of as abbreviations or jargon. However, the meaning of two of the most common such terms, "etc." and "i.e.," are often confused and thus should be avoided. Needless to say, we feel the same about common expressions from foreign languages (e.g., *quid pro quo*) that frequently appear in journalistic and literary work.

Are the Questions Too Vague?

Vague questions invariably produce vague answers. The problem is that people interpret vague terminology in so many different ways that their responses are equally varied. Consider, for example, the questions in Example 3.11. The first of these three questions does not specify which level of government (federal, state, or local), what policies, or the age of the "older" people. The next one specifies federal government, programs, and retired people so that the question's meaning is clearer. The last question is even more specific, naming some specific programs and specifying retired people over 65 years of age as the target group. If the last alternative is still too vague, one might wish to abandon the open-ended format altogether. A series of close-ended questions could be posed about specific proposed changes, for example, "a 20 percent increase in the social security benefits for people over 65 years of age."

We cannot unequivocally say which revision is most desirable. If the researcher has some specific programs in mind, it seems suitable to switch to a close-ended format. If, on the other hand, the questionnaire is basically a "fishing expedition" to find out what is on people's minds, the first alternative may be the most appropriate. Vagueness is a matter of degree. Instead of eliminating it from a questionnaire, the issue is often deciding how much of it is useful.

Excessive vagueness is not a matter that applies only to open-ended questions. It is often apparent in the answer categories chosen for close-ended questions of the graded variety, as in the question on religious attendance (Example 3.12). Whereas some people may consider "regularly" to be weekly or even daily, others may consider it to be once a month. The fact that respondents answer from different frames of reference means that vague categories often result in different responses from people who want to report similar behavior.

When evaluating the vagueness of terms and the overall meaning of questions, it is very important that the questions not be isolated from others in the questionnaire. For example, taken by itself the term "state" is a vague term and could have different meanings. However, if a series of questions precedes it in which it is made abundantly clear that one is referring to, say, Alaska, "state" may be a very appropriate term.

Is the Question Too Precise?

The desire to avoid vagueness sometimes results in questions being so precise that people are unable to answer them. Consider, for example, the open-ended question about reading habits in Example 3.13. People's lives are usually not so well ordered that they can recall exactly how many times they performed a particular act, whether it was reading books, attending church, or going out to dinner. Thus the use of broad categories, as suggested in Exam-

Example 3.11   Vague Terms

Problem:

> What changes should the government make in its
> policies toward older people?

A Revision:

> What changes, if any, do you think the federal govern-
> ment should make in its programs for retired people?

Another Revision:

> What changes, if any, do you think the federal govern-
> ment should make in social security, medicare, and
> other programs for retired people over 65 years of
> age?

Example 3.12   Answer Categories that Are Too Vague

Problem:

How often did you attend religious services during the past year?

1 NEVER
2 RARELY
3 OCCASIONALLY
4 REGULARLY

A Revision:

How often did you attend religious services during the past year?

1 NOT AT ALL
2 A FEW TIMES
3 ABOUT ONCE A MONTH
4 ABOUT TWO TO THREE TIMES A MONTH
5 ABOUT ONCE A WEEK
6 MORE THAN ONCE A WEEK

Example 3.13   Too Much Precision

Problem:

How many books did you read last year?

_____NUMBER

A Revision:

How many books did you read last year?

1 NONE
2 1-10
3 11-25
4 26-50
5 MORE THAN 50

ple 3.13, represents an essential compromise between too much vagueness and too much specificity.

Is the Question Biased?

A biased question is one that influences people to respond in a manner that does not accurately reflect their position on the issue under investigation. Some people refuse to answer questions that appear to them to be slanted in a particular direction. Others may be negatively affected by the wording of a question so that they intentionally respond with an answer that does not reflect their actual opinion. Still others may be unaware that a question is biased and may be influenced to respond in the direction encouraged by the wording. Unfortunately, such biased questions cannot always be easily identified, primarily because there are a number of different ways in which a question can be biased. One type of biased question implies that the respondent should have engaged in a particular behavior and thereby gives the impression that "everyone is doing it" (Example 3.14). Respondents who are concerned about being different from other people may be influenced to say "yes" to the first question, even though they have never seen the movie.

Another way in which questions are biased is if unequal comparisons are requested, as in the first question in Example 3.15. It is much easier to blame a small group of privileged people than to blame a whole category of people. This particular question could have been loaded just as easily in another direction by listing the choice "big corporate farmers" or "union leaders."

Not only do some phrases create bias, but some specific words have such a strong emotional appeal that they tend to bias questions no matter how they are used. Some words with a strong positive appeal in our culture are "freedom," "equality," "private enterprise," "justice," and "honesty." Words with a strong negative appeal are "bureaucrat," "socialist," "boss," and "government planning." These words should be avoided if it is at all possible. It is especially difficult to balance the choices in close-ended questions when terms with such a strongly emotional flavor are incorporated into one of the answer categories.

Words can bias a question in more than one direction, leading some unwary respondents to answer in one direction, whereas others, who are

---

Example 3.14   Bias from Establishing a Behavioral Expectation

---

Problem:

More people have attended the movie, <u>Gone With The Wind</u>, than any other motion picture produced in this century. Have you seen this movie?

   1 YES
   2 NO

A Revision:

Have you ever seen the movie <u>Gone With The Wind</u>?

   1 YES
   2 NO

Example 3.15   Bias from Unequal Comparison

```
Problem:

    Who do you feel is most responsible for the high
    price of meat in our grocery stores?

        1 FARMERS
        2 LABORERS
        3 EXECUTIVES OF THE MEAT PROCESSING PLANTS

A Revision:

    Who do you feel is most responsible for the high
    price of meat in our grocery stores?

        1 FARMERS WHO PRODUCE IT
        2 LABORERS WHO PROCESS IT
        3 BUSINESS MEN WHO OPERATE THE MEAT PROCESSING PLANTS
```

equally unaware of the biased wording, are led to respond in another direction. Consider, for example, the political candidate question in Example 3.16. Identifying the candidates according to who is the incumbent and who is the challenger provides an additional basis for people to respond and may differentially influence respondents' choices. If respondents are not very familiar with either candidate, they may retreat to selection criteria that have little or nothing to do with the candidates. Whereas some respondents retreat to such criteria as "proven leadership" (opting for the incumbent), others resort to "desire for change" (choosing the challenger). Consequently, it may be best not to give the identifying information.

Unfortunately, the problem of whether to provide identifying information cannot always be resolved easily. If the candidates for governor were to be identified on an election ballot according to who was the incumbent, the original question in Example 3.16 would accurately reflect the stimulus to voters and would therefore be appropriate. For this reason it is often approp-

Example 3.16   Bias in More Than One Direction

```
Problem:

    If the election were being held today, who would you
    vote for:  John Jones, our present governor, or
    David Smith, the present challenger?

A Revision:

    If the election for governor were being held today,
    who would you vote for:  John Jones or David Smith?
```

riate to identify candidate choices in surveys according to political party affiliation.

Still another type of loading is a lack of balance among positive and negative categories from which respondents are asked to choose in close-ended questions with ordered categories (Example 3.17). The first version of this question would tend to encourage respondents to select a "decrease" option inasmuch as there are three degrees of that choice from which to choose, compared to only one "increase" option. Thus the middle position on the implied scale is one of the decrease options instead of a neutral "stay the same" category. A lack of balance among answer choices is more likely to produce a substantial bias when the issues addressed by the question are not salient to respondents.

Occasionally it is necessary to use unbalanced questions, because balancing them would create unrealistic answer choices. For example, "Should our company's management set as its objective to get worker productivity to (1) stay the same, (2) increase a little, or (3) increase a lot?" If we balance this question with some "decrease" categories, many people would judge the question to be inappropriate and even frivolous.

In handling question bias of any type, it is useful to remind ourselves that our task is less one of removing bias than it is to strive for balanced questions. It is simply not possible to strip all questions of affective terminology that might predispose respondents to answer in one way or another. Further, the concepts measured in social surveys do not usually have precise, ultimately

***

Example 3.17   Bias from Unbalanced Categories

Problem:

    Currently our country spends about 35 billion dollars
    a year on defense. Do you feel this amount should be:

       1 INCREASED
       2 STAY THE SAME
       3 DECREASED A LITTLE
       4 DECREASED SOMEWHAT
       5 DECREASED A GREAT DEAL

A Revision:

    Currently our country spends about 35 billion dollars
    a year on defense. Do you feel this amount should be:

       1 INCREASED GREATLY
       2 INCREASED SLIGHTLY
       3 STAY THE SAME
       4 DECREASED SLIGHTLY
       5 DECREASED GREATLY

correct definitions. Thus the total elimination of words that can bias responses is just not possible.

Is the Question Objectionable?

There are several reasons that respondents find questions objectionable. Perhaps the most frequent reason is that the information requested (e.g., how much money did you earn last year?) is considered quite personal, and no one has the right to that information. A second source of objections is that words and phrases convey implications about which the respondents have very negative feelings (e.g., are any of your friends homosexuals?). Still another source of objection is that answers to certain questions are considered incriminating (e.g., have you ever stolen anything?). It takes only one or two highly objectionable questions to produce a complete refusal to answer a questionnaire. Although it seems reasonable to suggest complete elimination of such objectionable questions, we doubt that many would find this suggestion very useful, because if such questions were not important, researchers would not propose to ask them. Thus we concern ourselves here with various ways one might make objectionable questions less of a problem.

One method is to ask people to respond to broad categories instead of writing down or verbalizing a precise piece of information they prefer not to divulge. This method is extremely helpful for income questions, as shown in Example 3.18. For many people there is a substantial difference between revealing their exact financial status and divulging what many people can probably guess just by knowing their occupation or by observation of the home in which they live. Our advice *not* to use open-ended questions on

Example 3.18   The Use of Broad Categories to Overcome Objections

---

Problem:

How much was your total family income in 1976?

_____DOLLARS

A Revision:

Which of the following categories best describes your total family income during 1976?

1 LESS THAN $5,000
2 $ 5,000 to $ 9,999
3 $10,000 to $14,999
4 $15,000 to $24,999
5 $25,000 OR MORE

---

income items has occasionally led researchers to use as many as 25 categories (each with $1,000 increments) for income questions. This tends to magnify the importance of the income question and does little to reduce its objectionable nature. In fact, some respondents may interpret it to be exactly what it often is, a thinly veiled attempt to get one's exact income. Therefore, they may find it even more objectionable than the open-ended procedure.

Another method of reducing objections to questions is to establish a context that softens their impact. For example, consider the question in Example 3.19 that contains an implication (the church is a parasite) to which some people might object. As first stated, the strongly negative view could be repulsive to some people, making them wonder what the researcher might be trying to prove with the study. They may conclude that the question reveals the researcher's opinions about the church and become very guarded in their responses. The lengthy introduction to the revised version prepares the respondent for strongly worded questions and suggests that the statements that follow do not necessarily reflect the researcher's view.

The most difficult questions for which to reduce objections are those requiring answers that could conceivably lead to the person being condemned by

---

Example 3.19   The Use of Contextual Material to Overcome Objections

---

Problem:

    "The church is a parasite on society." Do you agree
    or disagree with that statement?

      1 AGREE
      2 DISAGREE

A Revision:

    Next, I want to ask how you feel about the relationship
    between the church and society. Here are various opinions,
    both negative and positive that we have heard people give
    on the topic and we would like to know whether you agree
    or disagree with each.

    "The church teaches people to help one another."

      1 AGREE
      2 DISAGREE

    "The church is a parasite on society."

      1 AGREE
      2 DISAGREE

    "Etc."

---

others (e.g., knowledge of being a homosexual) or that reveal illegal behavior (e.g., smoking marijuana). If the research objectives do not permit switching from a behavioral question (have you done it?) to a less threatening one (how do you feel about people who do it?), the procedure in Example 3.20 might be considered.

Example 3.20 The Use of a Series of Questions to Overcome the Objectionable Nature of a Question

---

Problem:

Have you ever shoplifted anything?

    1 NO
    2 YES

A Revision:

As you may know, there is now a great deal of discussion about shoplifting in this community, and questions as to how it should be handled. Some people feel it is a serious problem about which something should be done, others feel it is not a serious problem. How about yourself? Do you consider shoplifting to be a serious, moderate, slight, or no problem at all in our community?

    1 SERIOUS
    2 MODERATE
    3 SLIGHT
    4 NOT AT ALL

During the past few years do you think the frequency of shoplifting has increased, stayed about the same, or decreased in this community?

    1 INCREASED
    2 STAYED ABOUT THE SAME
    3 DECREASED

Please try to recall the time when you were a teenager. Do you recall personally knowing anyone who took something from a store without paying for it?

    1 NO
    2 YES

How about yourself? Did you ever consider taking anything from a store without paying for it?

    1 NO
    2 YES
    (If yes)
    Did you actually take it?

    1 NO
    2 YES

Sometimes the researcher is caught in the dilemma of not being able to select any term without alienating some people. This problem is most clearly illustrated by the current difficulties of obtaining racial and ethnic identification (Example 3.21). Some people adamantly reject the terms describing their ethnic identity used in the first question (e.g., Negro). Others would just as adamantly reject (or not recognize) the alternatives. Therefore, the solution may have to be a compromise of listing both terms. Still another solution, not shown here, is to list each term in our revised alternative on a separate line so that, for example, a person could choose either the category "Black" or the category "Negro." However, the category "Native American" cannot be used by itself. Invariably many white people, as well as American Indians, consider this an appropriate category for themselves.

Is the Question Too Demanding?

Occasionally researchers propose to ask questions that demand so much that they would try the patience of even the most enthusiastic respondents. An

Example 3.21   Overcoming Objections to Terms for which There Are No Substitutes

```
Problem:

    Which of the following best describes your racial or
    ethnic identification?

        1 BLACK
        2 CHICANO
        3 NATIVE AMERICAN
        4 WHITE
        5 ORIENTAL
        6 OTHER--SPECIFY_____

(An alternative set of choices)

        1 NEGRO
        2 MEXICAN-AMERICAN
        3 AMERICAN INDIAN
        4 CAUCASIAN
        5 ORIENTAL
        6 OTHER--SPECIFY_____

A Revision:

    Which of the following best describes your racial
    or ethnic identification?

        1 BLACK (NEGRO)
        2 CHICANO (MEXICAN-AMERICAN)
        3 NATIVE AMERICAN (AMERICAN INDIAN)
        4 WHITE (CAUCASIAN)
        5 ORIENTAL
        6 OTHER--SPECIFY_____
```

example is a request to rank 25 government programs from first to 25th in terms of importance to society. Although we do not doubt the potential value of *accurate* answers to such a question, we seriously doubt whether most people are capable of providing them. Fortunately, few questions of this nature survive pretests, and researchers often solve the problem by switching to another format (e.g., making each item into a close-ended question with ordered response categories) or simply limiting the ranking to the top three choices.

Researchers can sometimes obtain the information they want in a far less demanding manner than first proposed, as in Example 3.22. Reporting the percentage of monthly income spent on rent would require most respondents to do the appropriate mathematical calculation, if an accurate answer is to be provided. The two alternative questions provide enough information so that an answer to the original question can be calculated by the researcher. Since it relies on specific facts, it is likely to be a more accurate answer than if the respondent had had to guess at the answer.

Is It a Double Question?

Separate questions are sometimes combined into one, and the respondent is asked to give a single answer. The result is an ambiguous question that inevitably produces an ambiguous answer. Consider, for example, the question about the legalization of marijuana in Example 3.23. People who favor home use but oppose public use could provide a clearly interpretable answer of "yes." Other people who felt any of these ways could not: (1) favor both home and public use, (2) oppose both uses, or (3) oppose home but favor public use. The question could be revised in either of the ways shown in Example 3.23.

Example 3.22 A Question that Is Unnecessarily Demanding

Problem:

What percent of your monthly income is spent on rent (or house payments)?

A Revision:

How much is your monthly rent (or house payment)?

_____DOLLARS

How much is your average monthly income?

_____DOLLARS

Example 3.23　　A Double Question

```
Problem:

    Do you favor legalization of marijuana for use
    in private homes but not in public places?

        1 NO
        2 YES

A Revision:

    Do you favor or oppose legalization of marijuana for
    use in private homes?

        1 FAVOR        ·
        2 OPPOSE

    Do you favor or oppose legalization of marijuana for
    use in public places?

        1 FAVOR
        2 OPPOSE

Another Revision:

    Which of the following best describes how you feel
    about the legalization of marijuana for use in
    private homes and public places?

        1 OPPOSE LEGALIZATION FOR BOTH HOME AND PUBLIC USE
        2 OPPOSE LEGALIZATION FOR HOME USE BUT FAVOR FOR
          PUBLIC USE
        3 FAVOR LEGALIZATION FOR HOME USE BUT OPPOSE PUBLIC USE
        4 FAVOR LEGALIZATION OF BOTH HOME AND PUBLIC USE
```

Our concern with double-barreled questions extends beyond interpretability of answers. Such questions tend to discredit the researcher's questionnaire in the eyes of respondents, and make the completion of it seem like a worthless activity, jeopardizing the completion of the remainder of the questionnaire. However, despite our objections, there are certain cases in which such questions might be appropriately used. Consider, for example,

Congress is considering whether to pass a law that would make the use of marijuana legal in the home but keep its use illegal in public places. Would you favor or oppose passage of this proposed law?

1 FAVOR
2 OPPOSE

In this case the research question has to do with attitude toward a particular policy and not with a complete description of all attitudes. Thus its use seems quite appropriate, and it is doubtful whether respondents would object. Questions about public policies are more likely than not to have contingencies. To break questions down into their component parts when the concern is with receptivity to the overall package is not very beneficial.

Does the Question Have a Double Negative?

In a conversation it is unnatural to say yes when the answer really means no. Yet respondents are sometimes asked to do exactly that, as in Example 3.24. Questions that imply a double negative are often asked because a change from the present is being considered. If we were simply to reverse the question (and ask if the city manager should be responsible to the mayor) some people might be puzzled because they recognize that the question implies no change. Thus our solution is to switch from an ordered to unordered response category. The result of this change is to clarify the question and improve its communicability by the elimination of the double negative.

Are the Answer Choices Mutually Exclusive?

Sometimes questions are worded in a way that requires respondents to give more than a single answer when only one is requested, for example, when a numerical category begins with the same number as the last number of the previous category (e.g., 18–35 years of age, 35–45 years, etc.). Although this kind of error affects relatively few people (at least when the categories are broad), it should be avoided. In some cases the lack of exclusiveness is more subtle and can cause serious problems, as in Example 3.25. The first question asks for two kinds of information—the place and the actual source. Some

---

Example 3.24   A Question with a Double Negative

```
Problem:

    Should the city manager not be directly responsible
    to the mayor?

    1 NO
    2 YES


A Revision:

    To whom should the city manager be directly responsible,
    the mayor or the city council?

    1 THE MAYOR
    2 THE CITY COUNCIL
```

Example 3.25   Answer Choices that Are Not Mutually Exclusive

```
Problem:

    How did you first hear about the proposed freeway?

        1 FROM A FRIEND OR RELATIVE
        2 AT A MEETING OF AN ORGANIZATION TO WHICH I BELONG
        3 AT WORK
        4 FROM MY SPOUSE
        5 OVER TELEVISION OR RADIO
        6 NEWSPAPER


A Revision:

    From whom (or what) did you first hear about the
    proposed freeway?

        1 FROM A FRIEND OR RELATIVE
        2 FROM MY SPOUSE
        3 OVER TELEVISION OR RADIO
        4 FROM THE NEWSPAPER

    Where were you when you first heard about it?

        1 AT A MEETING OF AN ORGANIZATION TO WHICH I BELONG
        2 AT HOME
        3 AT WORK
```

people could have heard about the freeway from a friend at work. Our solution is to break the question into two parts.

Have You Assumed Too Much Knowledge?

Typically, questions assume that a certain amount of knowledge is possessed by the respondent. Sometimes too much knowledge is assumed, as in Example 3.26. Respondents may become embarrassed at not knowing something that the researcher seems to feel he or she should know. Rather than admit that they have no idea of the governor's stand on gun control, they are likely to base their answer on whether they agree with the governor on most other issues or on whether they like the governor. One way of handling this problem is to break the question into two or more parts, as shown. In the revision the respondents are asked to articulate the governor's stand as they understand it before they are asked whether they agree with it.

The problem of assuming too much knowledge in surveys is quite prevalent. There are few issues on which at least a few respondents lack the knowledge assumed by the question. Some people cannot recall the make of car they drive or the last time they visited a doctor. Polls have shown that a few

Example 3.26   A Question that Assumes Too Much Knowledge

Problem:

    Do you tend to agree or disagree with the governor's
    stand on gun control?

      1 AGREE
      2 DISAGREE

A Revision:

    The governor has recently taken a stand on gun control.
    Were you aware that he had taken a stand on that issue?

      1 NO
      2 YES⟶
            (If yes) please describe in your own words
            what you consider his position to be.

    Do you tend to agree or disagree with his stand?

      1 AGREE
      2 DISAGREE

---

people cannot recall the name of the President of the United States, and many do not know their senators. Thus it is important to scrutinize each question to determine whether an "I don't know" response should be offered.

At the same time, we have often been surprised at how much knowledge most people in a study sometimes possess. A number of years ago, while we were conducting a survey of farmers, we were pleasantly surprised to find that they could tell us in minute detail how they had previously mixed chemicals to apply to their crops, even though they were interviewed many months after they had actually done it. The conclusion we reach is that only very thorough pretesting can provide an adequate basis for resolving the question of how much knowledge can safely be assumed.

Has Too Much Been Assumed About Respondent Behavior?

The problem of assuming too much is not limited to attitude, belief, or attribute questions; it occurs just as often in behavioral questions. The question in Example 3.27 has little meaning to people who can barely remember the last time they ate at a restaurant. The first revision simply precedes the preference question with a screen question that establishes the frequency of the behavior being investigated. This solution is probably the most common and is applic-

Example 3.27   A Question that Assumes a Particular Behavior

Problem:

> When you go out to restaurants, which kind of restaurants do you most often go to?
>
> 1 THOSE THAT SERVE FOREIGN STYLE FOODS
> 2 THOSE THAT SERVE AMERICAN STYLE FOODS

A Revision:

> How frequently have you eaten out in restaurants during the last year?
>
> 1 NONE
> 2 ONCE OR TWICE
> 3 SEVERAL TIMES BUT LESS THAN ONCE A MONTH
> 4 ONCE A MONTH OR MORE
>
> (If several times or more) Which kind of restaurants do you most often go to?
>
> 1 THOSE THAT SERVE FOREIGN STYLE FOODS
> 2 THOSE THAT SERVE AMERICAN STYLE FOODS

Another Revision:

> If you were planning to eat out in a restaurant soon, do you think you would most likely go to a restaurant that serves:
>
> 1 FOREIGN STYLE FOOD
> 2 AMERICAN STYLE FOOD

able to virtually all questions in which assumed behavior could conceivably be a problem. The second revision converts the question into a hypothetical format, switching it from a behavioral question to an attitudinal one. This is only acceptable if such a change in the kind of information being gathered is acceptable to the researcher. We are less enthusiastic about this revision than the preceding one, but we show it because of its frequent use.

Is the Question Technically Accurate?

Questions often provide information as well as ask for it. Thus it is important that this information be accurate, leaving no doubt that the researcher accurately comprehends the topic under investigation. The inaccurate information contained in Example 3.28 could be devastating to a study. Someone who is

Example 3.28   A Question That Contains Inaccurate Information

```
Problem:

    Another activity of the police department is the
    catching and fining of traffic violators.  Should
    this activity receive greater, about the same, or
    less emphasis than at present?

        1 GREATER
        2 SAME
        3 LESS


A Revision:

    Another activity of the police department is to
    catch traffic violators.  Should this activity receive
    greater, about the same, or less emphasis than at
    present?

        1 GREATER
        2 SAME
        3 LESS
```

knowledgable about police activities would be quick to point out that police only catch traffic violators, and it is the judge (or judicial system) that is responsible for fining them. Sometimes it takes only a slight error like this one to discredit an entire survey, endangering response and later uses that might be made of the survey results.

We cannot overemphasize the problem of inaccurate questions inasmuch as surveys often concern issues with which the surveyor has only a passing acquaintance. As we emphasize in later discussions of pretesting (Chapters 4 and 6), this represents one of the most important aspects of evaluating early drafts of a questionnaire.

Is an Appropriate Time Referent Provided?

Questions may include a time referent that introduces unwanted variation into answers. The question shown in Example 3.29 could be particularly troublesome for a survey conducted over a period of several weeks. If the first people reached in a survey are contacted in April and the last ones are surveyed in July, chances are great that the reported frequency will have increased steadily throughout the survey. The two suggested revisions differ substantially. One specifies a precise time period, whereas the other eliminates a time referent altogether and asks the respondent to do some mental

Example 3.29   A Question with an Inappropriate Time Referent

---

```
Problem:

    How many times have you played golf this year?


A Revision:

    How many times did you play golf during 1976?


Another Revision:

    On the average, how many times a year do you play
    golf?
```

---

averaging. As a general rule we prefer the specificity of the first revision, feeling that a given time referent is better than none. However, we would use the latter if for some reason we felt that people's participation varied greatly over years and we wanted to avoid the constraints of any particular one.

Can the Responses Be Compared with Existing Information?

Questions must sometimes be phrased in such a way that answers can be compared with existing information. For example, researchers frequently want to compare income levels (and other information) reported by respondents with the known characteristics (from U.S. Census data) of the general public as a check on the representativeness of those who responded to a survey. If a researcher intends to make such a comparison (and we strongly recommend it), it is imperative that the same response categories be used in the questionnaire as in the U.S. Census. In many cases personnel records, directory listings, or other records are available for comparison; thus the survey questions must be comparable. Comparability is also necessary when one wants to compare results with those of another survey. Some researchers are tempted to "improve" on the wording of questions used in other surveys, even though they would like to make comparisons. There is no middle ground on this issue. As one researcher noted, "In a serious replication one will repeat faithfully the 'errors' of the original study as well as adhere to its 'good ideas.' "[6] Thus the need to compare responses with existing information may sometimes (depending of course on the researcher's objective) override any other wording considerations noted in this chapter.

Are the Questions Too Cryptic?

During the process of editing a questionnaire, words are sometimes deleted in an effort to keep the questions simple. The result is that the questions can no longer stand alone, as in Example 3.30. The first question clearly requests the number of years lived in Idaho. The intent of the ones that follow is to obtain the names of the city and county in which people currently live. However, there was a carry-over effect from the first question, and nearly 20 percent of the respondents repeated the number of years they had lived in these places instead of their names. Care must be taken to avoid the possible carry-over from one question to another. The best way to do this is to avoid incomplete sentences.

CONCLUSION

In this chapter we have posed three questions that researchers must ask about every survey question, regardless of the method they have chosen for doing a particular survey. They are

---

Example 3.30   Questions that Are Too Cryptic

```
Problem:

    Q-30  Number of years lived in Idaho.

          _____YEARS

    Q-31  Your city or town.

          _____CITY OR TOWN

    Q-32  Your county.

          _____COUNTY

A Revision:

    Q-30  How many years have you lived in Idaho?

          _____YEARS

    Q-31  In what city or town do you live?

          _____CITY OR TOWN

    Q-32  In what county do you live?

          _____COUNTY
```

Will it obtain the desired *kind* of information?
Is the question *structured* in an appropriate way?
Is the precise *wording* satisfactory?

A negative answer to any of these questions suggests that the writing task is not complete. Unless all three are answered affirmatively, the question cannot produce the information the researcher wants.

Our treatment of these three issues could not, nor was it intended, to serve as a cookbook with specific directions on how to write questions. The differences in population to be surveyed, study objectives, and the questionnaire context in which each question is placed provide for too much variation on what is most desirable for one's survey. Further, there remains much that is not known about how questions affect respondents and what questions are most satisfactory for particular situations. Thus we have attempted to raise critical questions that will help identify flaws and to suggest some possible ways to overcome them.

In this chapter we make only incidental reference to the specific requirements of mail and telephone questionnaires. Thus an effort to write questions based on this chapter can only be considered tentative, pending later discussion of how to adapt them for the mail questionnaire (Chapter 4) and the telephone questionnaire (Chapter 6).

NOTES

1. Our distinction between beliefs and attitudes is based on that made by Martin Fishbein, "A Consideration of Beliefs, and Their Role in Attitude Measurement," in Martin Fishbein (ed.), *Readings in Attitude Theory and Measurement*, (New York: John Wiley and Sons, 1967), pp. 257–266.
2. *Ibid.*
3. Howard Schuman and Otis Dudley Duncan, "Questions About Attitude Survey Questions," in Herbert L. Costner (ed.), *Sociological Methodology*, 1973-1974, (San Francisco: Jossey-Bass, 1974), pp. 232–251.
4. Stanley Payne, *The Art of Asking Questions*, (Princeton, N.J.: Princeton University Press, 1951), p. 227.
5. *Ibid.*
6. Otis Dudley Duncan, *Toward Social Reporting: Next Steps* (New York: Russell Sage, 1969).

Chapter Four

CONSTRUCTING MAIL QUESTIONNAIRES

....

Too often the construction of mail questionnaires has been accorded only slightly more attention than one would give to the preparation of a shopping list. As long as the needed items were included, little else seemed to matter. General appearance, the order in which items appeared, and the type of paper used were unimportant. The attitude of some researchers about questionnaire design seems to have been that if the wording was scientifically sound and the recipient could understand the questions, the questionnaire was satisfactory—thus neglecting most of what the questionnaire construction process is about.

The mail questionnaire, more than any other type of questionnaire, requires careful construction, for it alone comes under the respondent's complete control. It must truly be its own advocate. The absence of the interviewer, the traditional crutch for poorly constructed questionnaires, means there is no way to gloss over construction deficiencies or to respond to typical respondent queries, such as

Is this a sales gimmick?
What does this have to do with me and my problems?
How long will it take?

Is this worthwhile?

Are the questions difficult?

Answers to these questions are provided (sometimes implicitly) by a multitude of questionnaire attributes. Size, shape, weight, color, paper quality, cover design, question order, and layout are among the numerous features, offering clues to the worth of the questionnaire. The total design method (TDM) principles of mail questionnaire construction discussed in this chapter are based on the identification of how each aspect of the questionnaire, from the most obvious to the least obvious, may affect the recipient's decision to respond.

Because we are concerned with the overall effect, and in particular the motivational appeal of the questionnaire, it seems appropriate to describe our purpose in terms outside the usual realm of scientific inquiry. The difference between a list of questions and a questionnaire is much like the difference between individual flowers and a floral arrangement. Not only is a poorly arranged display of flowers unattractive, but it detracts from the beauty of individual flowers contained within. The essence of an aesthetically pleasing arrangement of flowers is in the balance that exists among the flowers and the display materials that bring them together. The corresponding task in questionnaire construction is to find a balance among all the various elements that make up the questionnaire, of which the questions are only one. Leaving small, seemingly insignificant, yet visible attributes unattended will make the overall effect less appealing.

Our efforts to find a balance among the elements that comprise a questionnaire concentrate on both the cost and reward sides of the social exchange process discussed in Chapter 1, although primarily on the former. Efforts to decrease costs to respondents focus on reducing the time required for completing the questionnaire, the time the respondent *thinks* it will take, the mental effort needed for comprehension, and any hint of embarrassment from failure to understand directions for answering questions. The provision of rewards concentrates mostly on making the questionnaire appear interesting.

THE BASIC CONSTRAINTS: BOOKLET FORMAT AND PRINTING PROCEDURES

The respondent's first exposure to the look and feel of the questionnaire provides the first of several critical tests that the questionnaire must pass. This brief experience may answer a host of questions posed by its delivery to the respondent. To encourage further examination the questionnaire must be designed to provide immediate *and* positive answers to concerns over its importance, difficulty, and length. Our preeminent concern with this initial impact leads us to discuss first something that is ordinarily considered last —how the questionnaire is to be printed and the size and shape of paper to be used. These visually observable characteristics form the basic constraints within which all other TDM design considerations are couched.

1. *The questionnaire is printed as a booklet.* It consists of 8¼" × 12¼" sheets of paper folded in the middle and stapled (when more than one sheet is used) to form a booklet, the dimensions of which are 6⅛" × 8¼".
2. *No questions are permitted on the front or back pages (the "cover" pages).* These spaces, the ones most likely to be seen first by respondents, are reserved for material that has the specific purpose of stimulating interest in the questionnaire. The result is that the number of pages available for questions is always two less than the number of pages available for printing. For example, three sheets of paper folded to form a booklet provide twelve pages, ten of which (as we shall see) can be used for questions.
3. *The questionnaire pages are printed in a photographically reduced form.* Each page of the questionnaire is typed on a regular typewriter with a carbon ribbon, using 12-point (elite) type in a 7" × 9½" space on regular 8½" × 11" paper. To fit the booklet format, each page is photographically reduced to 79 percent of the original size.
4. *The questionnaire booklet is reproduced on white or off-white paper by a printing method that provides quality very close to the original typed copy.* White or off-white paper, which is somewhat lighter and more opaque than the widely used 20 pound mimeo paper, is preferred. We prefer 16 pound paper of a type normally used when printing on both sides is required. A wide variety of printing machines produce quality work and the preferred method depends on what is available to the researcher.

The exactness of our prescription is justified by diverse yet specific requirements that must be met by questionnaires. If a random sampling of people were asked to list the words they associate with "bad" questionnaires, their descriptions would likely include bulky, long, formidable, barely readable, messy, boring, disorganized, or confusing. The TDM construction process seeks to overcome these common objections by presenting an attractive, well-organized questionnaire that looks easy to complete. Printing questionnaires as booklets with photographically reduced pages requires less paper and makes them appear far shorter than they really are. Yet by reducing the size to just over three-quarters of the original typed pages, readability is retained for nearly everyone.

The professional appearance achieved by the booklet format, the carefully designed cover pages, and the quality printing job tells the respondent that a great deal of work went into the questionnaire. This enhances the importance of the survey in the respondent's eyes. Further, the gimmickry of garish colors and designs is avoided to keep anyone from associating the questionnaire with advertisements or other unsolicited mail.

Readers experienced with printing methods will find the recommended dimensions of the questionnaire unusual, requiring trimming of normally used printing stock. They might reasonably ask why the slightly larger and readily available 8½" × 14" legal-size paper is not folded to form booklets. The reason is that we have found the recommended dimensions to be the largest possible that can be used for the commonly employed twelve-page questionnaire and still allow it to be mailed along with cover letter and return envelope for the minimum (i.e., less than one ounce) first-class postage. Postage savings invariably exceed any additional cost for wasted paper or trimming. Further, the folded questionnaires also fit nicely into the monarch size (7½" × 3⅞") envelopes and slightly smaller (6½" × 3¾") business reply envelopes.

Let us pause a moment to fully consider the implications of our concern with precise questionnaire and stationery sizes. We do not wish to suggest that slight deviations on any one element will have a major effect on response. However, the TDM for mail questionnaires is a carefully integrated system. This means that each part is designed to fit with every other part. A change in one part may make it necessary to change other parts. The end result of this domino effect may be a substantial effect on both response rates and costs. For example, as already noted, our prescribed size dimensions are designed to get a questionnaire into the mail at the minimum postage rate. The consequences of using a questionnaire that has slightly larger dimensions is, at the current rate of 13¢ per ounce for first-class postage, about $400 for a sample of 1000 people by the time the TDM has been completely implemented. However, this is by no means the only likely implication.

The questionnaire is also designed to fit the recommended sizes for mailout and return envelopes. The use of a larger questionnaire will require larger envelopes, resulting in a mailout package that inevitably projects a more imposing image, increasing the perceived social costs of responding. Perhaps the ultimate in this regard is a switch from regular business stationery to manilla envelopes. Their bulky and impersonal appearance is inconsistent with the total image we try to project. Thus what the reader may at first see as an excessive preoccupation with details is, in our view, justified. Our task is not unlike that of the engineer who wants to design a more efficient engine. The chances of achieving that goal are greatly increased when each part is precisely engineered to fit with every other part. Taking the liberty of borrowing a part from another engine often means having to adjust numerous other parts to achieve an acceptable fit. Although a fraction of an inch more or less for our questionnaire dimensions may seem trivial, the implications may be anything but trivial.

Our printing constraints literally demand that the questions be made to fit the available pages. We would be among the last to carry this statement to the extreme of deciding that crucial questions had to be omitted, making it impossible to achieve study objectives. Rather, a predetermined process is followed, which begins with deciding approximately how many units of four pages (unfolded sheets of paper) are needed. When questions run a little bit over the allotted number of pages, we work to condense spacing and eliminate the least important questions to achieve a good fit. If the number of questions is such that no amount of juggling and condensing will make them fit the allotted number of pages, we move to the next higher unit of four, taking advantage of any excess space to distribute our questions in a more attractive manner.

ORDERING THE QUESTIONS

A recommendation often given for ordering the questions in a questionnaire is to begin with something "easy." Supporting this admonition is the belief that if respondents are able to answer early questions quickly, fears that the questionnaire contains difficult and time-consuming questions are overcome. This principle of building respondents' confidence with early questions has sometimes led to the practice of beginning questionnaires with such items as age, sex, marital status, and education. In our view, this is a very poor procedure.

Suppose, for example, that a survey is conducted on opinions about the establishment of a national health care program. A cover letter (the need for which is explained in Chapter 5) has been prepared that emphasizes how important it is for citizen opinions to be taken into account in designing such a national program. A sense of importance is further communicated by the cover of the questionnaire, which carries an interest-stimulating title, "Should the United States Have a Health Care Program? A Nationwide Study of Citizen Preferences." When respondents open the questionnaire to page 1 and discover no queries about their opinions, but rather that the researcher wants to know their age, sex, and so forth, any initial enthusiasm is likely to vanish.

There is no need for innocuous questions, personal or otherwise, to serve as icebreakers in the mail questionnaire. An interviewer is not present to generate nervousness or a fear of saying or doing the wrong thing. In fact, the interviewer's absence creates the need to determine question order on the basis of motivational considerations. There are several specific principles that are followed under the TDM.

First, questions are ordered along a descending gradient of social usefulness (or importance); those which the respondent is most likely to see as useful come first, and those least useful come last. For example, the question of whether the United States should pass legislation to establish a health care program supported entirely by taxes is likely to be seen as socially useful, inasmuch as respondents are likely to identify with the United States and be concerned about their health care. Although a question that asks a person to agree or disagree with the statement, "Private enterprise is basically good," may be very important to the study's purpose (perhaps as part of an attitude scale on the appropriateness of government to handle health care), it lacks obvious social utility. Every effort is made to place questions of this nature later in the questionnaire.

The second ordering principle is to group questions that are similar in content together, and within content areas, by type of question. This means that several questions concerning the financing of a government health care program would be placed together rather than intermingled with others. Further, within content areas, questions requiring an answer of "yes" or "no" would be placed together, as would items requiring respondents to indicate their extent of agreement or disagreement. Two purposes are served by this principle. The first is to ease the mental effort required for constantly switching from one kind of question to another. The second is to encourage well-thought-out answers, something that is more likely to occur if respondents are asked questions in an order that seems logical to them.

The third principle used in deciding the order of questions involves taking advantage of cognitive ties that respondents are likely to make among groups of questions. In this way we can build a sense of flow and continuity through-out the questionnaire. For example, questions about whether the United States should establish a health care program lead nicely into questions about how government should finance such a program, which in turn could lead into a series of seemingly unrelated questions about government responsibil-ity in various areas of life. The principle of building on cognitive ties is of special importance, because most questionnaires consist of a variety of ques-tions, many of which strike respondents as quite unrelated to the study topic as communicated to them by the cover letter and cover page of the question-naire.

Thus TDM questionnaires do not follow the commonly used procedure of making respondents randomly switch from one topic to another and back again, or change answer formats for the ostensible reason of keeping their answers to some questions from affecting answers to others. Presumably that procedure avoids the tendency for respondents to make their answers consis-tent with one another and to use certain response categories while avoiding others. In our view the evidence that less valid answers are obtained is not strong. Allowing people to dwell on any one topic for more than a few seconds at a time may in fact produce answers that are better thought out and hence more valid. We recognize that the objectives of some studies literally demand that certain topically related questions be separated, as in the extreme case in which the same question is repeated as a consistency check. However, in such cases even wide separation does not prevent respondents from looking back at their previous answers, as noted in Chapter 2.

The final TDM ordering principle is that the questions in any topic area that are most likely to be objectionable to respondents should be positioned after the less objectionable ones. This does not mean that all objectionable questions are relegated to the last page of the questionnaire. Rather, such ordering is done within the topical order and flow suggested by adherence to the first three principles. The application of these four principles is illustrated by Example 4.1 with the complete list of questions from a study about community size preferences. The rationale for question ordering is provided in the column beside each group of questions.

To apply all four ordering principles at the same time, certain compromises must be made. We doubt that there is a single *best* ordering for the questions shown in Example 4.1 or, for that matter, in most other studies. Rather, the best we can hope for is an ordering that strikes a balance among the concerns we have addressed and can later be embellished by appropriate transitions (discussed in the section of this chapter entitled Formulating the Pages). The final ordering of questions is often suggested by decisions concerning the cover letter and the statement it contains about the study topic and its social usefulness. At the same time, considerations concerning question order may also influence the content of the cover letter, that is, how to best explain the purpose of the study to the respondents.

One aspect of ordering that we have never found necessary to modify is the placement of demographic questions (i.e., questions that elicit personal information such as age, sex, income, etc.). These questions are always placed at the end of the questionnaire. Users of the TDM have sometimes been tempted to place these questions earlier in the questionnaire because of their crucial importance. It is often believed that moving these items forward results in fewer nonresponses to them. However, this assumption is not well founded. Nonresponse to these items on TDM questionnaires has been found to be as low, and sometimes lower, than for all items placed earlier in the questionnaire. For example, in five statewide TDM studies the item nonresponse for seven personal characteristics (income, occupation, age, sex, marital status, education, and home ownership) placed on the last pages of the questionnaire averaged 2.1 percent versus 3.7 percent for items related to the study topic in the first half of the questionnaire. Further, examination of a large number of questionnaires in which the TDM has been completely used reveals no tendency for the item nonresponse rate to be significantly higher for any particular pages in the questionnaire. Therefore, efforts to place ques-

Example 4.1 Order of Questions for Community Size Preference Study

Pages of Questionnaire	Questions on Each Set of Facing Pages	Reasons for Question Order
1-2	Where would respondent most and least like to live: Q-1 Region of country Q-2 Size of region Q-3 Size of community Q-4 Residential location in most preferred community	All questions on these pages have obvious relationship to purpose of study, as explained in cover letter: "Bills have been introduced in Congress and our State Legislature aimed at encouraging the population growth of rural and small town areas and slowing down that of large cities . . .,could greatly affect the quality of life . . . no one really knows in what kind of communities people like yourself want to live or what is thought about these proposed programs." As a result the questions appear socially useful.
3-4	Q-5, Q-6 How important is each of 10 attributes (e.g., being near relatives, quality of schools) in choosing a community in which to live. Q-7 What size of community is believed to offer best quality of life for each of 18 community characteristics (e.g., availability of good jobs and adequacy of police protection).	First questions clearly related to stated purpose of study and appear socially useful. Something of a subtle change in Q-7 from asking what respondent wants (stated purpose of study) to what he or she believes to be true (not a stated purpose). However, general topic of Q-7 is clearly related to the stated purpose of study.
5-6	Q-8, Q-9 Proposed population redistribution policy explained and respondents asked to register attitudes toward 7 programs for achieving redistribution goals. Q-10 Name of respondent's county Q-11 Name of respondent's community Q-12 Years lived in community Q-13 Where residence located Q-14 How satisfied respondent is with present community Q-15, Q-16 How respondent would feel about moving away from community	Both Q-8 and Q-9 have obvious relationship to study purpose. However, substantive content is somewhat removed from people's past experiences and therefore judged as being harder to answer. Also, Q-8 itself was long (wordy) due to the necessity of providing information to respondents. Q-10 is a crucial transition. Starting with this question the remainder of the questionnaire asks for personal characteristics. Those on this page were there because they were most closely related to the topic, and seem least objectionable. Many respondents may not be aware of this change to questions asking personal information.
7-8	Q-17 Names of voluntary associations belonged to, if any Q-18 Number of organizations in which an officer Q-19 Belief about whether have enough voice in community activities (list of 7) Q-20 Times per month involved in 6 different community activities Q-21 Number of years lived in various sized communities other than own	No obvious relationship to study objectives in these questions or any that follow. However, all of these pages concern community activities in some way, and therefore may appear to respondent to have some relevance. The community focus represents a continuation, rather than a break, from thought processes generated by previous pages.

Example 4.1   Continued

Pages of Questionnaire	Questions on Each Set of Facing Pages		Reasons for Question Order
9-10	Q-22	Sex	Strictly personal data with no apparent relationship to study topic. Ordered so the most objectionable questions are asked last. Such questions as religion and politics were asked because they affect where people may wish to live.
	Q-23	Marital status	
	Q-24	Childrens' ages	
	Q-25	Respondent's age	
	Q-26	Home ownership	
	Q-27	Years of service in armed forces	
	Q-28	Education	
	Q-29	Employment status	
	Q-30	Occupation	
	Q-31	Income	
	Q-32	Religious preference	
	Q-33	Religious attendance	
	Q-34	Political party	
	Q-35	Political stand	

tions on pages on which the lowest item nonresponse rate occurs are simply not warranted.

The reason for the low nonresponse to personal questions placed last may be that filling out the early pages of the questionnaire is viewed by respondents as an investment. Thus unless they answer the personal items, the investment may be lost, that is, the questionnaire might not be counted. In addition, they are faced with admitting that the time they spent filling out the earlier pages was wasted. A second possibility may be that people's resistance to providing information on their personal characteristics is not all that great *if* they are given a reasonable justification for such questions. It is one thing to ask people for their income when they do not know why it is wanted; it is quite another to ask them to give it for the implied reason of examining differences among people with high and low incomes on issues that the respondent finds interesting. Some respondents may even find themselves wondering about such differences and may be more than willing to provide the requested information.

CHOOSING THE FIRST QUESTION

No single question is more crucial than the first one. It is more likely than any other to determine whether a questionnaire is destined for the mailbox or the garbage. Thus it warrants special attention.

The ordering principles already discussed suggest that the first question be clearly related to the survey topic and have socially useful implications. However, several additional criteria are also applied in an effort to increase the likelihood that all who read the first question will answer it and continue answering the questions that follow.

The first criterion is that it be *easy*, so that virtually all respondents will need only a few seconds to comprehend it and another few seconds to answer it. Therefore, open-ended questions (Question A in Example 4.2) are never used. Long close-ended questions with lengthy answer choices are also avoided (Question B in Example 4.2).

Further, the opening question, more than any other question, must clearly convey a sense of neutrality. Any question that might suggest in the slightest way that the researcher leans toward a particular view is avoided. Therefore TDM questionnaires never begin with statements with which respondents are asked to express agreement or disagreement. The appearance of such an item may lead respondents to infer that the way the statement is worded reflects the researcher's position and they are being asked whether they agree with that position (Question C in Example 4.2). It is better to locate any such questions later in the questionnaire so that they will be viewed in the context of several other questions, rather than as the only indicator of the subject of the study.

The first question should also be clearly *applicable to everyone*. Any item that logically requires a "does-not-apply" category (for example, "What kind of car do you own?") should be avoided. The fact that the only question read by the respondent does not apply to him or her may lead to the conclusion that most of all the remaining questions do not apply, a convenient excuse for going no further (Question D in Example 4.2). This matter of applicability involves far more than the simple fact of whether it logically requires a "does-not-apply" category. A question may draw an "I don't know" response because it concerns something that the respondent has not thought about seriously. The respondent's belief that he or she knows very little about a subject (and thus is inclined to say "I don't know") or the belief that there are others far better qualified to answer the questions are major contributors to nonresponse.

In addition to applying to all respondents, the first question should be *interesting to everyone*. Finding such a question is especially difficult in surveys of heterogeneous populations like the general public, where there may seem to be nothing that can appeal so broadly. However, it is usually possible to construct a question that is clearly related to the stated purpose of the survey and is likely to arouse a fair amount of interest in most respondents.

Some of the difficulties of selecting a first question are illustrated by the selection process for the one used in a community size preference study, the question order for which is shown in Example 4.1. When decisions about the

Example 4.2 Development of the First Question for a Community Size Preference Study

NOT ACCEPTABLE: . . . . AND, THE REASONS WHY

A. Think for a minute about the kind of community in which you would most like to live. Then, very briefly describe it by listing a few of the characteristics it would have.

Open-ended; too demanding.

B. Here are some descriptions of different kinds of regions in which one might choose to live. Each choice contains a different size major city, different amounts of open-country, and some include suburbs or smaller towns. Suppose you could live in some part of any of these regions. In which one would you most like and least like to live.

Too demanding; question is complex and categories are too long.

(Circle Number of One Choice in Each Column)

Region most like	Region least like	
1	1	LARGE METROPOLITAN: CONTAINS CITY OF 500,000 OR MORE, MANY SUBURBS, VERY LITTLE OPEN-COUNTRY
2	2	MEDIUM METROPOLITAN: CONTAINS CITY OF 150,000 TO 499,999, SEVERAL SUBURBS, SOME OPEN-COUNTRY
3	3	SMALL METROPOLITAN: CONTAINS CITY OF 50,000 TO 149,999, FEW SUBURBS, CONSIDERABLE OPEN-COUNTRY
4	4	SEMI-URBAN: CITY OF 10,000 TO 49,999, FEW SMALLER TOWNS AND CONTAINS MUCH OPEN-COUNTRY
5	5	SEMI-RURAL: CONTAINS CITY OF 2,500 to 9,999, ONE OR TWO SMALLER TOWNS, MOSTLY OPEN-COUNTRY
6	6	RURAL. CONTAINS TOWN OF LESS THAN 2,500, SURROUNDED ENTIRELY BY OPEN-COUNTRY

C. Think for a minute about the kind of community in which you would most like to live. Then, indicate the extent to which you agree or disagree with the following question:

Respondent may view it as reflecting the researcher's point of view.

My ideal community would be completely free of industrial air pollution.

1 STRONGLY DISAGREE
2 SOMEWHAT DISAGREE
3 NEITHER AGREE OR DISAGREE
4 SOMEWHAT AGREE
5 STRONGLY AGREE

D. Thinking for a minute about the kind of community in which you would most like to live, which do you think the school system should emphasize the most: basic skills such as reading and writing, or the social and emotional development of children.

May be seen by some respondents as inapplicable to them (perhaps because of no children in schools).

1 EMPHASIZE BASIC SKILLS THE MOST
2 EQUAL EMPHASIS ON BOTH
3 EMPHASIZE SOCIAL AND EMOTIONAL DEVELOPMENT THE MOST

Continued

Example 4.2   Continued

ACCEPTABLE . . . . .AND, THE REASONS WHY

-1-

E.   Suppose you could live wherever you wanted in the United States.
     Please use the map below and indicate where you would <u>most like</u>
     and <u>least like</u> to live.

Neutral, applies to
everyone, fast, easy,
and interesting.

(Circle Number of One Choice
in each column)

Most like to live	Least like to live	
1	1	PACIFIC NORTHWEST
2	2	PACIFIC SOUTHWEST
3	3	ROCKY MOUNTAINS
4	4	SOUTHWEST
5	5	PLAINS
6	6	GREAT LAKES
7	7	SOUTH
8	8	FAR SOUTHEAST
9	9	MIDDLE ATLANTIC
10	10	NEW ENGLAND

general question order were made, it seemed most reasonable to start the
questionnaire with several items aimed at ascertaining the size of community
in which respondents would like to live. However, none of these questions
(one of which is Item B in Example 4.2) seemed appropriate as a first question, being too long and difficult. Further, these questions were statistical
(contained numbers) and looked boring. The question finally selected (Item E
in Example 4.2) was not among the list of questions originally prepared for
the study. It was specially prepared to stimulate interest and meet the other
requirements for being placed first in the questionnaire. Respondents to pretests found this question interesting, partly because of the map. In addition,

the question was easy to answer. Further, the generous spacing—a full page for one question—contributed to the entire questionnaire having a fast and easy look about it. In addition, it clearly applied to everyone, and despite its relative lack of importance to our objectives, respondents seemed likely to view it as integrally related to the purpose of the survey. Finally, and of great importance, the question provided a convenient means of introducing respondents to a procedure for registering both a "most" and "least" liked preference, a format used for the next several questions. Thus this "throwaway" question effectively bridged the gap between the cover letter and the front page of the questionnaire on the one hand and the main body of the questionnaire on the other. This more than justified its use of space.

Sometimes the special characteristics of a study require first questions that emphasize one dominant consideration. We encountered this in a study of the general public on the topic of the policy that should be followed by the State Land Grant University in a variety of areas, from priorities for athletics to rules for student behavior. Our primary concern was the fact that most state residents had no previous contact with the university and that they would see the entire questionnaire as inapplicable to them. The only connection they seemed to have with the university was the indirect one of paying taxes, the major source of university funding. We focused on that connection, explaining this fact in the cover letter and offering it as a reason for their being surveyed. The first question became one about how much influence respondents felt the general public currently had on university policies and activities. It was followed by a few others that continued the theme by asking whether there should be a change in the public's influence and how important it was for the university to consider the needs and desires of specific groups, for example, alumni, farmers, and other interest groups, in formulating policy. Thus to establish applicability to all potential respondents, the issue of finding a good first question was broadened to finding several good first questions.

A frequently encountered situation that calls for a special first question is one in which a questionnaire is sent to many people who are for some reason ineligible for a study. This may occur when, for example, a survey of registered voters is the study's goal but the sample is drawn from the telephone directories which of course contain many unregistered voters. In such cases we use the first question to determine eligibility, directing those to whom it applies to continue with the remaining questions.

Situations like this present multiple problems that do not have an entirely satisfactory solution. The possibility exists that, on seeing that some people do not have to fill out the questionnaire, respondents will be tempted to include themselves among that group and thus be excused from the study. There are others who, although ineligible, may find the questionnaire intriguing and want to complete it. They "make" themselves eligible to get their views included. A further problem is that those who are ineligible discard the questionnaire without letting the researcher know they are ineligible, making it difficult to calculate meaningful response rates.

This problem was faced in a study of sociologists employed outside a college or university setting. The sampling of names from professional directories made it likely that a fairly large number of academically employed persons would be included. In an attempt to encourage the response of everyone, making it possible to eliminate ineligible respondents and calculate the response rate, the first question was carefully worded to explain why the responses of some questionnaire recipients were not needed and at the same time requested a positive response (i.e., something other than just discarding the questionnaire) of everyone (Example 4.3).

Example 4.3   Development of First Question for Survey Sent to Sample, Including Many People to Whom It Did Not Apply

NOT ACCEPTABLE:

Q-1 Are you employed as a teacher, researcher, or administrator
      (e.g., chairman or dean) in a college or university?
      (Circle one)

               1 NO

               2 YES

               (If yes) This study only applies to persons
               employed outside the usual academic positions.
               Therefore you do not need to answer this
               questionnaire.

ACCEPTABLE:

Q-1 Are you employed as a teacher, researcher or administrator (e.g.,
      chairman or dean) in a college or university? (Circle one)

               1 NO

               2 YES

               (If yes) Inasmuch as our purpose is to learn
               more about the work of sociologists outside the
               usual kinds of academic positions, we do not
               need your answers to the remainder of the
               questions. However, we would appreciate any
               comments you might like to make that would help
               us learn how graduate training programs should,
               if at all, be adjusted in order to prepare
               sociologists adequately to assume nontraditional
               roles. Above all, please return the questionnaire
               to us so we know you are employed in the usual
               kind of academic position.

Finally, we must note that question order and the selection of the very first question are decisions that can only be made tentatively. Final decisions must wait until efforts to formulate individual pages of the questionnaire have been made. That is the task to which we now turn.

FORMULATING THE PAGES

Arranging the questions on each page of the questionnaire is inevitably a slow process and must be done with painstaking care. The problem is that several goals must be met satisfactorily and simultaneously. First, the end result must be aesthetically pleasing and look easy to do to motivate respondents to complete it. At the same time, the structure of precisely worded questions must be preserved. Third, the pages must be constructed in a way that keeps respondents from skipping individual items or whole sections. To accomplish all three goals, we adhere strictly to a number of principles of page construction. Underscoring all of them is consistency and attention to even minute details that might affect respondent behavior.

The usefulness of following these principles can be seen by comparing pages from questionnaires in which they have been used with those in which they have not. Example 4.4 shows a page of commonly asked personal characteristics placed in a format quite similar to that used in numerous questionnaires. Besides being crowded and uninteresting, there is a considerable risk that wrong answers will be checked and some items missed altogether. The defects in this page and the revisions aimed at overcoming them are elaborated below in relation to the principles of construction used to remedy them.

Use Lower Case Letters for Questions, Upper Case for Answers

All questions are distinguished from answer categories by the use of lower or upper case letters. This psychological guide for responding aids the respondent, yet it is sufficiently subtle that most respondents are probably not consciously aware of the difference. Lower case letters are always reserved for questions, which are usually longer than answers, because of their somewhat greater readability. Although the use of upper case letters makes answer categories (especially the longer ones) somewhat more difficult to read, it seems a small cost compared to the value of having this convenient guide to help respondents through the questionnaire.

Identify Answer Categories on Left, with Numbers

Although answer categories can be identified in several ways, the consistent use of numbers is preferred over the commonly used blanks or boxes. One

Example 4.4   Page Formulation Principles Applied to Commonly Asked Survey Questions

UNACCEPTABLE

Q-22   Your Sex: __Male __Female

Q-23   Your present marital status: __Never Married __Married __Divorced
__Separated __Widowed

Q-24   Number of children you have in each age group: ___Under five years
___5-13 ___14-18 ___19-25 and over

Q-25   Your present age: _____

Q-26   Do you own (or are you buying) your own home? __No __Yes

Q-27   Did you serve in the armed forces? __No __Yes (year entered_____,
Year discharged_____)

Q-28   Are you presently: __Employed __Unemployed __Retired __Full-time
homemaker

Q-29   Please describe the usual occupation of the principle wage earner in
your household, including title, kind of work, and kind of company or
business. (If retired, describe the usual occupation before retirement.)

Q-30   What was your approximate net family income, from all sources, before
taxes, in 1970?

Less than $3,000 __   10,000 to 12,999 __   20,000 to 24,999 __
3,000 to 4,999 __   13,000 to 15,999 __   25,000 to 29,999 __
5,000 to 6,999 __   16,000 to 19,999 __   Over $30,000 __
7,000 to 9,999 __

Q-31   What is the highest level of education that you have completed?

No formal education   __   __ Some college
Some grade school   __   __ Completed college. . .major_____
Completed grade school   __   __ Some graduate work
Some high school   __   __ A graduate degree. . .degree and
Completed high school   __   major_____

Q-32   What is your religious preference? __Protestant denomination __Jewish
__Catholic __Other _____Specify __None

Q-33   How frequently did you attend religious services in a place of worship
during the past year: __Regularly __Occasionally __Only on special days
__Not at all

Q-34   Which do you consider yourself to be? __Republican __Democrat __Independent
__Other __Specify

Q-35   Which of these best describes your usual stand on political issues?
__Conservative __Liberal __Middle-of-the road __Radical

ACCEPTABLE:

Q-22   Your sex. (Circle number of your answer)

1 MALE
2 FEMALE

Q-23   Your present marital status. (Circle number)

1 NEVER MARRIED
2 MARRIED
3 DIVORCED
4 SEPARATED
5 WIDOWED

134

Example 4.4   Continued

Q-24 Number of children you have in each age group. (If none, write "0")

Number of children

_____ UNDER 5 YEARS OF AGE

_____ 5 TO 13

_____ 14 TO 18

_____ 19 TO 24

_____ 25 AND OVER

Q-25 Your present age: _____ YEARS

Q-26 Do you own (or are you buying) your own home? (Circle number)

1 NO
2 YES

Q-27 Did you serve in the armed services? (Circle number)

1 NO
2 YES. . . Year entered _____

Year discharged _____

Q-28 Are you presently: (Circle number)

1 EMPLOYED
2 UNEMPLOYED
3 RETIRED
4 FULL-TIME HOMEMAKER

Q-29 Please describe the usual occupation of the principal wage earner in your household. (If retired, describe the usual occupation before retirement.)

TITLE: _____

KIND OF WORK YOU DO: _____

KIND OF COMPANY OR BUSINESS: _____

Q-30 What was your approximate net family income from all sources, before taxes, in 1970? (Circle number)

1 LESS THAN $3,000
2 3,000 TO 4,999
3 5,000 TO 6,999
4 7,000 TO 9,999
5 10,000 TO 12,999
6 13,000 TO 15,999
7 16,000 TO 19,999
8 20,000 TO 24,999
9 25,000 TO 29,999
10 OVER $30,000

Q-31 Which is the highest level of education that you have completed? (Circle number)

1 NO FORMAL EDUCATION
2 SOME GRADE SCHOOL
3 COMPLETED GRADE SCHOOL
4 SOME HIGH SCHOOL
5 COMPLETED HIGH SCHOOL
6 SOME COLLEGE
7 COMPLETED COLLEGE. (specify major) _____
8 SOME GRADUATE WORK
9 A GRADUATE DEGREE
(specify degree and major) _____

Continued

Example 4.4   Continued

Q-32 What is your religious preference? (Circle number)

    1 PROTESTANT (specify denomination)_____
    2 JEWISH
    3 CATHOLIC
    4 OTHER. . . (specify)_____
    5 NONE

Q-33 How frequently did you attend religious services in a place of worship during
      the past year? (Circle number)

    1 REGULARLY (once a week or more)
    2 OCCASIONALLY
    3 ONLY ON SPECIAL DAYS (Christmas, etc.)
    4 NOT AT ALL

Q-34 Which do you consider yourself to be? (Circle number)

    1 REPUBLICAN
    2 DEMOCRAT
    3 INDEPENDENT
    4 OTHER. . .(specify) _____

Q-35 Which of these best describes your usual stand on political issues (Circle number)

    1 CONSERVATIVE
    2 MIDDLE-OF-THE-ROAD
    3 LIBERAL

reason for this preference is that the assignment of a number for each answer
category provides a convenient form of precoding (that is, assignment of a
number that represents the response in the computer analyses). This is one of
our few concessions to the researcher's data processing needs. It compen-
sates partly for the elimination of all other precoding information from the
questionnaire to eliminate potentially confusing information extraneous to the
respondent's needs. The second reason for choosing numbers is that they can
be produced by all typewriters, whereas boxes require special equipment.

The identifying numbers are always placed to the left of the answer
categories for two reasons. First, some answer categories are longer than
others and placing the numbers to the right would result in their being located
some distance away from the answer, increasing the chance for error. Placement only one space to the left of the first word of the answers helps ensure
that respondents will circle the answer they in fact want to indicate. Second,
respondents who pick certain answers are sometimes asked to give additional
specification or explanation (e.g., denomination for those who indicate "Pro-
testant," as in Example 4.4). It is convenient to ask for specification to the
right of the answer without having to extend answer numbers even further
away to provide the needed writing space. Although for some questions
(those with "yes/no" answers) it makes little or no difference on which side
the answer numbers are placed, the importance of consistency and the likelihood that the questionnaire will contain many different types of response
categories make this a rule that should be followed without exception.

Specific rules are also followed in deciding which numbers to assign to the various answer categories. First, we always try to use the same number for the same answer. For example, in "yes/no" questions a "1" is assigned to "no" and "2" to "yes." In "agree/disagree" questions, "1" is assigned to "strongly disagree" and "5" to "strongly agree." It makes no difference whether the lower numbers are on the negative or the positive side. The important point is that the same number be retained throughout the study for a given answer category. This procedure further eases the respondent's task in completing the questionnaire and prevents errors. For example, it prevents the respondent who has associated "1" with "no" early in the questionnaire from making an inadvertent error when it is switched to indicate "yes."

The use of numbers to represent all categories and the consistent assignment of numbers to particular categories throughout the questionnaire run counter to the practice of some researchers. Their supporting argument is that numbers infer an order of desirability and might lead some respondents to simply choose certain numbers (presumably lower ones) despite the categories they represent. We have not seen convincing results to confirm this effect on self-administered questionnaires. Further, we believe that being required to use numbers throughout the questionnaire to represent various kinds of categories tends to reduce any propensity to pick certain numbers over others. In addition, the risk of confusion from switching assignments of numbers appears to outweigh the risk of bias toward picking numbers regardless of the words associated with them.

Establish a Vertical Flow

Response categories and the numbers that represent them are arranged so that answers are registered in a vertical line on each page. Only rarely does the structure of certain questions (such as the occupation question in Example 4.4) not allow it. The purpose of vertical flow (besides nice appearance) is to prevent inadvertent omission, something that occurs often when respondents are required to move back and forth across the page with their answers, as in the poorly constructed version of Example 4.4. The revision makes it more difficult to skip a question without being aware of doing so. Support for this notion comes from the finding that a page of questions (quite similar to this one) has consistently produced an item nonresponse rate of well under 2 percent in our surveys of the general public.

Such a vertical flow also prevents the common error of checking the space on the wrong side of the answers when answer categories are placed beside one another rather than underneath. Still another reason for adopting a vertical flow pattern is that it appears to have the positive psychological effect of enhancing the respondent's feeling of accomplishment—each question means moving further down the page so that a sense of making progress comes with each answer. Finally, vertical flow usually results in considerable white space remaining on each page. This is desirable, giving the questionnaire the image of being easy to complete.

Provide Directions for How to Answer

The need for clear directions on how to provide answers is often easy to overlook. On the surface, it seems unlikely that respondents would provide unclear answers to numbered categories, making the addition of the phrase, "Circle number of your answer," unnecessary. However, without such directions, respondents sometimes revert to "Xs," checks, or simply lines to indicate which number they are choosing. The encirclement process results in fewer ambiguous markings and should thus be encouraged.

It is important that the same marking procedure be used throughout the questionnaire. Although it hardly seems necessary to repeat directions for every question, we prefer to repeat them too many times rather than too few. It is especially important that the directions be repeated for most questions if respondents are sometimes asked to circle more than one answer and in other cases to circle only one.

The importance of complete directions was made abundantly clear to us in a study that asked the number of children in each of five age groups (Question 24 in Example 4.4). In that study, the direction "If none, write 0" was omitted, with the result that nonresponse to this item was 9.7 percent, higher than for any other item in the questionnaire. The addition of the instruction "If none, write 0" in a later survey resulted in the item nonresponse for an identical population falling to less than 2 percent. As a result of this experience, we examine each question individually to see whether specific directions are needed to ensure that every respondent will answer the question in an appropriate way.

Finally, directions for answering are always distinguished from the questions by putting them in parentheses. Lower case letters are preferred because of their greater readability and to avoid confusion with answer categories.

Special Procedures for Items in a Series

A frequently used questioning procedure is referred to as the items-in-a-series format, that is, a number of individual questions for which responses are to be made by choosing among identical response categories. For example, respondents may be asked to read a series of 20 statements and for each one choose among such categories as "strongly agree," "somewhat agree," "undecided," "somewhat disagree," and "strongly disagree." Close adherence to the vertical flow principle means that much space is required for the repetition of the answer categories after each item. Thus a special procedure has been developed for questions of this nature that retains an easy-to-do look, but greatly condenses the space needed.

Example 4.5 shows an undesirable format for items-in-a-series questions that we have frequently seen used. Not only does it make the questions unnecessarily difficult to complete, but the chances of error (e.g., marking an "X" in the wrong row or column) are considerable. This example exhibits the further difficulty of asking respondents to do two separate tasks for the same question, which results in directions that are unduly complicated and confusing. It requires the respondent to refer back to the question, an action that

Example 4.5   More Page Formulation Principles, Primarily for Items-in-a-Series Questions

NOT ACCEPTABLE: 245

Q-7   Much has been said about the quality of life offered by various sizes of cities. We would like to know how you feel. First, please show which city size is best for each of the characteristics by putting an "X" in the appropriate column by each item. Second, please look back over the list and show which three of these characteristics would be most important to you if you were selecting a new community in which to live by ranking them from 1 (most important) to 3 (third most important).

	city below 10,000 people	city of 10,000 to 49,999 people	city of 50,000 to 149,999 people	city over 150,000 people	Rank Three Most Important Here
Equality of opportunities for all residents, regardless of race					
Place in which to raise children					
Community spirit and pride					
General mental health of residents					
Adequacy of medical care					
Protection of individual freedom and privacy					
Adequacy of public education					
Friendliness of people to each other					
Adequacy of police protection					
General satisfaction of residents					
Respect for law and order					
Lowest costs for public services (like water, sewer, and police)					
Recreational and entertainment opportunities					

Example 4.5   Continued

ACCEPTABLE:

Q-7   Much has been said about the quality of life offered by various sizes of cities. Which of the following do you think is best for each of the characteristics listed below?

SMALL <u>means</u> below 10,000 people is best
MEDIUM <u>means</u> 10,000 to 49,999 people is best
LARGE <u>means</u> 50,000 to 149,999 people is best
VERY LARGE <u>means</u> 150,000 or more people is best

		Size of city which is <u>best</u> (Circle your answer)			
1	Adequacy of medical care . . . . .SMALL	MEDIUM	LARGE	VERY LARGE
2	Adequacy of public education . . . . . .SMALL	MEDIUM	LARGE	VERY LARGE
3	Adequacy of police protection. . . . . .SMALL	MEDIUM	LARGE	VERY LARGE
4	Place in which to raise children . . . .SMALL	MEDIUM	LARGE	VERY LARGE
5	Protection of individual freedom and privacy. . . . . .SMALL	MEDIUM	LARGE	VERY LARGE
6	<u>Lowest</u> costs for public services (like water, sewer, and police). . . . .SMALL	MEDIUM	LARGE	VERY LARGE
7	Friendliness of people to each other . .SMALL	MEDIUM	LARGE	VERY LARGE
8	Community spirit and pride . . . . . . .SMALL	MEDIUM	LARGE	VERY LARGE
9	Equality of opportunities for all residents, regardless of race. . . . . .SMALL	MEDIUM	LARGE	VERY LARGE
10	General mental health of residents . . .SMALL	MEDIUM	LARGE	VERY LARGE
11	Recreational and entertainment opportunities. . . . . .SMALL	MEDIUM	LARGE	VERY LARGE
12	General satisfaction of residents. . . .SMALL	MEDIUM	LARGE	VERY LARGE
13	Respect for law and order. . . . . . . .SMALL	MEDIUM	LARGE	VERY LARGE

Q-8   Which of the above community characteristics would be most important to you if you were selecting a new community in which to live? (Put number of item in appropriate box)

☐ MOST
    IMPORTANT

☐ SECOND
    MOST
    IMPORTANT

☐ THIRD
    MOST
    IMPORTANT

runs contrary to the previously discussed principle of vertical flow. Admittedly, it is tempting to place two questions using the same items side by side because much space is saved. However, the result is a question structure that is among the most frustrating to respondents that we know of, leading to a higher item nonresponse. To overcome these problems, several principles of page formulation are applied.

Ask One Question at a Time.   The respondent should only be asked to do one thing at a time. The problem of asking two questions is that each request interferes with the other. Some respondents may even try to answer both questions at the same time, which at worst they will find impossible and at best very demanding, with frustration the inevitable result. Breaking the question into its two logical parts does more to ease the respondent's task than any other possible revision. It makes giving directions simpler for both the researcher and the respondent. Also, being asked to go through a question more than once tends to diminish the respondent's sense of progress and induces discouragement with the overall task.

Dividing such a question into two parts requires either that the items in the series be stated twice or that a cross-reference be made. The latter option is followed in Example 4.5 because only three items are to be ranked. If a response were required for each item in the list, it would likely be more efficient to restate the items in the next question. The referral to items in the preceding question imposes certain requirements of its own. One is that the questions either be listed on the same page or, if the questions are too long for that, on facing pages. A few tries at flipping pages back and forth to answer a ranking question like that in Example 4.5 should make it abundantly clear to the reader that this too can be quite a nuisance and one that respondents should not be expected to tolerate. A second important requirement for questions that require referring back to an earlier question is that respondents be given an easy procedure for marking choices. For this reason, items are always numbered and directions provided for respondents to indicate choices by means of these numbers.

Use Words for Answer Choices.   Matching rows with columns to place an "X" in an appropriate space is a needlessly difficult and tiring task, with a high risk of error. The common problem of limited questionnaire space means that in this example (the unacceptable format of Example 4.5) the answer choices provided in column headings had to be turned sideways to fit, further increasing the difficulty of the respondent's task. In contrast, the acceptable version uses only a word or two to represent each category and places them horizontally beside each item in the series. The choices are left unnumbered to conserve space and avoid the possible confusion of which number goes with which of these horizontally listed categories. Further, and consistent with other answer choices, they are typed in upper case letters. When the complete category descriptions are too long to be placed in the allocated space, as in this question, a "key" must be provided. Placed at the top of the question, it can easily be referred to if needed.

A method we have often seen used to overcome spatial limitations for placing answer categories to the side of the items is to substitute numbers or abbreviations (e.g., SA for strongly agree) for the words, relegating the words to a position at the head of each column. We avoid this procedure for all questionnaires directed to the general public and as far as possible for all others, because the use of numbers or letters imposes a difficulty on some respondents and increases the likelihood of error. Remembering what each number or letter represents may be quite easy for persons with above average intellectual capabilities, but not for others. Also, persons in a hurry sometimes forget what a "1" or a "5" means, especially if it meant something else in a previous question.

Identify Answer Categories with a "Hat".   At first glance even the revision of the question in Example 4.5 may strike respondents as a little confusing. The format is decidedly different from that used for most other questions. Respondents are asked to answer to the right of the items rather than to the left. Further, they are asked to choose among horizontally placed categories that run contrary to the principle of vertical flow. Therefore, the way to mark answers may not be sufficiently clear to respondents. The "hat" technique has been found to be an effective device for guiding respondents into this different way of answering questions.

As shown in Example 4.5, the "hat" is placed over the answer column that contains a concise restatement of the question, carefully done so as to closely represent the original question and also include the direction to circle answers. Besides informing respondents how to answer, the "hat" tends to break up the type on the page, improving its overall appearance.

Show the Connection Between Items and Answers.   Several specific actions can be taken to clearly show the linkage of each item in a series to its appropriate answer category and to improve the appearance of the page. Each is seemingly minor, yet together their impact is quite significant. First, items are numbered to show how many are in a series and to help provide a sense of organization. The items in the series are usually of varying lengths and some may require more than one line, as in Example 4.5. When the first and all subsequent lines of each item are started at the same left-hand margin (as in the unacceptable version of Example 4.5), temporary confusion may arise in ascertaining where each item begins and ends. Further, there is the danger that respondents will circle answers after reading only the first line of the item, not realizing there is more. To prevent this, three procedures are followed. First, the second and all subsequent lines for a given item are indented two spaces from the margin used for the first line. Second, the response categories are printed on the same typed line as the last line of each item, enabling the respondent to move easily from the last line of the item to the answer choices. Finally, as still another guide, a dotted line extends from the last word of each item to the appropriate answer categories.

As shown in the example, the vertical space between each item is adjusted to make equal vertical distances between successive sets of answer categories. Varying the vertical space between items has very little consequence because of the other guides written into the questions. However, varying the distance between answer categories tends to interfere with the consistent method of circling answers and gives the page a less aesthetic look.

Use the Multiple Column Technique to Conserve Space

This page formulation technique is normally used only when it is imperative that a questionnaire be shortened and when two or more questions can be written as one using identical answer categories. Example 4.6 illustrates this format for finding the education of a respondent's parents. It involves using the previously discussed "hat" technique to indicate where each answer is placed. It is important that this technique be carefully distinguished from our method of handling items in a series. This one is used only when the respondent is to choose items in one column irrespective of items in other columns. Thus it involves choices among vertically arranged answer categories in contrast to the item-in-a-series technique which requires choosing among horizontally arranged answer categories.

When both the multiple column technique and the items-in-a-series technique are used, respondents may become confused about whether they are to choose among horizontally arranged categories or vertically arranged categories. To help prevent confusion, the multiple column technique always uses numbers (rather than words) that are placed to the left of the answer category. Thus it represents a logical extension of the normal answering procedure whereby people circle numbers to the left of vertically aligned response categories.

Example 4.6   Another Page Formulation Principle: The Double-Column Technique

Q-1   What is the highest level of education that your parents have completed?

(Circle Number of One Choice in Each Column)

FATHER	MOTHER	
1	1	NO FORMAL EDUCATION
2	2	SOME GRADE SCHOOL
3	3	COMPLETED GRADE SCHOOL
4	4	SOME HIGH SCHOOL
5	5	COMPLETED HIGH SCHOOL
6	6	SOME COLLEGE
7	7	COMPLETED COLLEGE
8	8	SOME GRADUATE WORK
9	9	A GRADUATE DEGREE

Show How to Skip Screen Questions

Screen questions, those which direct some but not all respondents to skip one or more questions, depending on the answer they provide, present a special construction problem. Specifically, the problem is how to make clear who is to answer the question that follows and what should be done by those who are not supposed to answer it. Special instructions are always required for such questions. This problem is made especially difficult when there are many such questions, and respondents must be directed to skip several sections of the questionnaire.

An unacceptable method of giving directions for screen questions is illustrated in Example 4.7. It depends on describing in words what the respondent should do. The main drawback is that the necessarily complex instructions are easily misunderstood. The TDM procedure for handling them involves three elements: the use of arrows to direct respondents from the screen question to the next question that applies to them, the indentation of all questions that may be screened from respondents as a kind of psychological guide, and finally the use of boxes to direct respondents past the question or series of questions they should not answer. All three elements are shown in Example 4.7. Not shown, but of equal importance, is that a similar box is placed by the question at which individuals who are instructed to skip certain questions should begin again. Similar boxes are also used at the top of each page that applies only to some respondents indicating to whom it applies. Besides serving as a convenient signpost in the process of filling out a questionnaire, the attention-drawing character of these boxes helps communicate quickly to respondents who have not yet started the questionnaire that it may be shorter than it first looks.

In cases in which respondents are asked about the same number of questions no matter which of two ways they are directed, an alternative method is used. The questionnaire page is divided in half, as shown in Revision 2 of Example 4.7, and respondents are directed by arrows to the appropriate column of the question. This approach is very desirable inasmuch as no skipping of sections is required of any respondent. However, its use is considerably more limited than the approach just discussed, for seldom do screens result in all respondents being asked the same number of follow-up questions.

Make Questions Fit Each Page

Turning pages in the middle of a question creates confusion and invites errors. It also makes the questionnaire less attractive to respondents, especially when (as may often happen) respondents scan the questionnaire before sitting down to fill it out and find it necessary to read several lines down some

Example 4.7   Page Formulation Principles: Screen Questions

NOT ACCEPTABLE:

Q-5 Do you own or rent the home in which you now live?

        1   OWN HOME
        2   RENT HOME

Q-6 (If you rent it, answer these questions. If you own it, skip
     straight to Question Q-14 on Page 4.)

     How much is your monthly rent?

        1   LESS THAN $100
        2   $100 TO $199
        3   $200 TO $299
        4   $300 OR MORE

ACCEPTBLE: Version 1

Q-5 Do you own or rent the home in which you now live?

        1   OWN HOME ──────→   IF YOU OWN YOUR HOME,
        2   RENT HOME   SKIP FROM HERE TO Q-14
                           ON THE NEXT PAGE

    (If you rent)
Q-6 How much is your monthly rent?

        1   LESS THAN $100
        2   $100 TO $199
        3   $200 TO $299
        4   $300 OR MORE

ACCEPTABLE: Version 2

Q-5 Do you own or rent the home in which you now live? (Circle number of
     your answer)

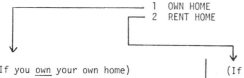

        1   OWN HOME
        2   RENT HOME

(If you <u>own</u> your own home)	(If you <u>rent</u> your home)
Q-6a How much is your monthly house payment (without property taxes)?	Q-6b How much is your monthly rent?

1   LESS THAN $100
  2   $100 TO $199
  3   $200 TO $299
  4   $300 OR MORE
	1 LESS THAN $100
	  2 $100 TO $199
	  3 $200 TO $299
	  4 $300 OR MORE

Q-7a How much per month do you pay for electricity, garbage collection, heat, and water?	Q-7b Which, if any, of these are included in your monthly rent? (Circle <u>all</u> that are included)

1   LESS THAN $25
  2   $25 TO $74
  3   $75 TO $124
  4   $125 OR MORE
	1 ELECTRICITY
	  2 GARBAGE
	  3 HEAT
	  4 WATER
	  5 NONE OF THE ABOVE

145

pages before they can make sense of the questions. Thus we consider it very important to have questions fit the pages of the questionnaire, allowing overlap only after all acceptable alternatives are exhausted.

Usually, it is easy to prevent a question from continuing onto the next page. One approach to the problem is to rearrange the question order slightly. This must be done cautiously so as not to break continuity, but it can usually be done without violating the ordering principles already discussed. A second technique, which applies when the lack of fit is not great, is to manipulate spacing. The distance left between preceding questions, or even the lines within a question, can sometimes be contracted (or expanded). Switching from double space type to single space, or even to half space is common. If the questions still do not fit, the page margins may be narrowed slightly.

Sometimes question rearrangements and space adjustments leave portions of pages blank. This is undesirable because of the unprofessional look and the resultant connotation of poor planning. In such cases, the spaces between lines can be expanded, or, if minor adjustments are not sufficient, the space may be labeled with an invitation for the respondent to elaborate on the previous answer. In some cases the extra space may be used for a more general, open-ended question about the survey topic.

However, it is not always possible to prevent questions from continuing onto a second page, especially for questions of the items-in-a-series variety. When it is necessary to make a page continuation, every effort should be made to place the entire question on facing pages. Not only does this placement help the respondent, but it saves space by eliminating the need to restate the question and answer choices, as would be necessary for back-to-back pages.

Use Transitions for Continuity

The final task of page formulation is to write transitions, the connective material that provides a sense of flow and continuity to the questionnaire. Well-written transitions add a conversational tone, serving much the same purpose for the mail questionnaire that impromptu interviewer comments do for telephone and face-to-face interviews. They guide respondents from one part of the questionnaire to another, giving warning that a change is imminent.

If everyone who picked up a questionnaire were unalterably committed to filling it out, there would be little need for good transitions. However, since that is not the case, the judicious use of transitions is essential. Transitions represent one of the few opportunities the researcher has for building motivational qualities into the questionnaire.

Transition statements are used in three situations. One is when a new line of inquiry starts. Here they serve as a signaling device, warning that some change in thought patterns is required. Sometimes they are added for individual questions, but usually each transition introduces several items, for example, "Next we would like to ask several questions about the community in which you live." When used to introduce new kinds of questions, transitions help overcome the negative effects of surprise, notably the tendency to skip entire sections or to quit altogether.

The second situation calling for transitions is the start of new pages, particularly the first of two facing pages. Their purpose here is quite different from introducing a new line of inquiry. They are aimed at the preliminary page-flippers, the people who want to see what the entire questionnaire is about before committing themselves to the task of answering. When scanning a questionnaire, the respondent is likely to focus first on the tops of the pages, particularly the one on the left, which is the natural starting place. Well-written transitions located at the top of this page help convince the respondent that the questionnaire is well thought out, reasonable, and that each question has a purpose—beliefs that contribute greatly to motivating respondents.

The third use of transitions is to break up the monotony of a long series of questions on a single topic. They are added to give a conversational tone to what otherwise might sound like an inventory list of questionnaire items, beginning with such standard and demanding phrases as: "How much," "How often," "Which of the following," "Describe," and so on. These are not the kinds of words that motivate respondents to go from one question to the next, then to the next, and so forth to the end of the questionnaire.

However, a questionnaire with too many transitions can be just as annoying as one without them. Thus it is useful to have a single transition serve more than one purpose. In practice this means that when beginning a series of questions on the same topic we strive to place them at the beginning of a page, especially the left of two facing pages. Trying to get new lines of inquiry to coincide with the start of two facing pages is another matter. At this point, the researcher, having already spent considerable time in ordering questions according to the previously discussed principles, may experience some frustration. Although a serious effort to get new topics to coincide with new pages should be made, scrapping the principles of ordering or leaving partial pages blank is not warranted. This brings us to an important point that we can now emphasize—writing transitions, deciding question order, and formulating pages, the major substance of this chapter, are not tasks that routinely follow one another in a definite order. One of the main challenges of questionnaire construction is to achieve a reasonable balance among these objectives, the effect of which is to maximize response. This can only be done by working them out together.

The words used in transitions are just as important as whether transitions are included in the questionnaire. The wrong words can produce biased answers or even refusals, the very opposite of their intended effect. In general, major transitions attempt to convey in a simple way the notion that the ensuing questions are very important to the study's purpose. This has sometimes been construed to mean that respondents are given a precise analytic reason, telling them, for example, that their answers to the questions that follow affect certain behaviors asked about in other questions (Example 4.8A). This is not a good practice. Such statements may very well induce consistency-conscious respondents to develop congruence between these and previous answers rather than providing their true opinions. Excessively long transitions should also be avoided (Example 4.8B). Although a lengthy transition is appropriate when it seems essential to convey explanatory information about the study, there is a risk that respondents will find them burdensome to read and will only skim them. Still other kinds of transitions that may do more harm than good are ones that sound inappropriately demanding or that establish a false sense of importance (Examples 4.8C and 4.8D).

Transitions must also fit the situation. It is useful to distinguish between major and minor transitions. When introducing a very minor change of topic, a single question on a topic, or providing a break in a long series of questions on a single topic, a short phrase at the beginning of the question will usually suffice (Examples 4.8E–4.8H). The simple word "next" is especially helpful at the beginning of two facing pages. It suggests to the preliminary page scanner that this question is preceded by others, and implicitly, that if he or she does not understand the question or reason for it, turning to earlier pages (where the most interesting and socially useful questions are located) might alleviate their concern. The simplicity of such transitions should not lead one to conclude that they are unimportant.

When a major change of topic occurs, it is important to note that change in a way that justifies the new questions. The ways in which this may be accomplished include relating the ensuing section to the one that preceded it (Example 4.8I) or inserting a social utility statement (Example 4.8J). When the change is such that the respondent is not likely to sense a major shift, one can simply state that the question fills another important purpose of the study (Example 4.8K).

Into the latter part of the questionnaire, particularly the section on personal characteristics, the need for full transitions is less important. By that time respondents have committed themselves to finishing the questionnaire, and social utility arguments are not needed. Thus the personal information questions always located at the end of the questionnaire are introduced by nothing more than one sentence that asserts that this information will help understand and interpret the study results (Example 4.8L and 4.8M). Statements that this information is an important part of the study should be avoided. Rather, these

Example 4.8   Examples of Transitional Statements

NOT ACCEPTABLE: . . . . .AND, THE REASONS WHY

A. People's leisure time activities affect how they feel about the kind of community in which they would like to live. So, next we want to ask how you spend your free time.

May bias answers.

B. People are different with respect to their leisure time activities. Some have a lot of leisure time. Others have very little. Some are involved mostly in outdoor activities, whereas others spend most of their time indoors. Regardless of your own situation and preferences we would like to learn more about them. So, next we want to ask several questions about how you spend your free time.

Unnecessarily long; risk that only part will be read, and produce bias. Makes questionnaire more rather than less difficult.

C. Now we want you to answer some questions about your leisure time activities.

Has demanding tone that may alienate respondent.

D. It is essential for this study that we learn about people's leisure time activities.

Establishes sense of importance that respondent may feel is unwarranted.

ACCEPTABLE: Minor transitions, for introducing specific questions or breaking routine of a long series on the same topic.

E. Next, we would like to ask about your visits to parks and playgrounds.

Lends conversational tone to questionnaire, and a sense of informality.

F. Our next concern is outdoor activities.

G. Now, would you please indicate how many times you visited a state park last year.

H. Could you please tell us how you feel about the number of city parks in your town.

ACCEPTABLE: Major transitions, for topic change.

I. Another important part of understanding the kinds of communities in which people live has to do with their leisure time. So, next we would like to ask some questions about how you spend your leisure time activities.

Relates next question to ones that preceded it.

ACCEPTABLE: Major transitions, for topic change.

J. Another important purpose of this study is to learn more about how people spend their leisure time.

Simple appeal to study purpose; best when change of topic is not great.

K. Policy makers concerned with designing communities in which people want to live need to better understand how people spend their leisure time. Therefore, we would like to ask several questions about your leisure activities.

Defends usefulness of study in terms of social utility.

ACCEPTABLE: For prefacing personal questions on last pages.

L. Finally, we would like to ask a few questions about yourself for statistical purposes.

Short and to the point. The end is in sight!

M. Finally, we would like to ask some questions about yourself to help interpret the results.

149

questions are portrayed as being of secondary interest. This helps to mitigate their inherently threatening nature.

DESIGNING THE FRONT COVER

The questionnaire covers, especially the front cover, are likely to be examined before any other part of the questionnaire. Therefore, each is carefully designed to create a positive first impression. The front cover receives the greatest attention and contains (1) a study title, (2) a graphic illustration, (3) any needed directions, and (4) the name and address of the study sponsor.

The title is designed to convey, in a few words, the topic of the study and to make it sound interesting. A project title as submitted to a funding agency, for example, "A Multivariate Analysis of the Determinants of . . ." would *not* make a good title for a questionnaire. Likewise, something eye catching such as "This is your last chance to influence government," is threatening and suggestive of deceptive advertising. Titles that imply some form of bias, such as anti-urbanism implied in the title, "Do our cities have to keep on growing?" should also be avoided. Thus the title of the study of community size preferences referred to throughout this chapter became, "Developing communities in which people want to live." Whatever the chosen title, it must convey an accurate impression of the content, make the questionnaire sound interesting, and do it in a neutral manner.

Subtitles are often useful. Their specific purpose is to convey the research nature of the project, for example, "A 1975 study of the opinions of Washington residents." The subtitle is placed separately from the main title, because it is usually difficult to make this phrase sound appropriate as part of the main title.

A graphic illustration is a very crucial aspect of the questionnaire cover. Its purpose is to add interest. Its mere presence tends to set TDM questionnaires apart from others the respondent may have seen before, thereby stimulating interest. The design may be quite simple (Example 4.9A) or more complex (Example 4.9B). The detail is far less important than its presence. Most important, the illustration must convey a sense of neutrality. A view of a pristine wilderness area on a questionnaire cover would be highly inappropriate for a study seeking to determine the relative priorities for economic growth versus environmental preservation. At the very least a balance should be struck. However, one difficulty of achieving neutrality by striking a balance is that people read their own interpretations into an illustration, sometimes focusing on only a portion of it. For this reason we favor the more abstract and simpler kinds of illustrations shown in the examples. Sometimes we try to find a symbol that appeals to a specific population, and one that has relatively little to do with the study topic itself. Outline maps of the state in which a study is being done is one example. A study of university alumni used a drawing of a campus tower known to virtually everyone who had ever been on the campus for even a short time.

The inclusion of the return address of the study sponsor is important for practical reasons. Sometimes questionnaires are separated from the cover letters and return envelopes; in such cases respondents would not be able to return the completed questionnaire even if they so desired. The importance

Example 4.9   Front Covers of TDM Questionnaires: A Simple Design and a More Detailed One for Studies on Public Issues

THE NEXT 5 YEARS: A STATEWIDE SURVEY OF WASHINGTON CITIZENS ABOUT

CRITICAL ISSUES FACING OUR STATE AND NATION

This survey is one of several we have done to better understand how Washington residents feel about a wide variety of important issues now confronting us. Please answer all of the questions. If you wish to comment on any questions or qualify your answers, please feel free to use the space in the margins. Your comments will be read and taken into account.

Thank you for your help.

Department of Rural Sociology
Washington State University
Pullman, Washington 99163   *Continued*

Example 4.9   Continued

Deciding Washington's Future:

Which Direction Do **You** Prefer?

A 1974 statewide effort to determine what citizens want for the future of Washington. What should be our goals for: job opportunities? industrial growth? population growth? use of natural resources? health? education? transportation? government? other concerns?

Please answer all of the questions. If you wish to comment on any questions or qualify your answers, please use the margins or a separate sheet of paper.

"Alternatives for Washington," of which this research is a part, is sponsored by the State of Washington, Office of Program Planning and Fiscal Management.

Return this questionnaire to:
Department of Rural Sociology
Washington State University
Pullman, Washington 99163

of this return address was emphasized in some isolated instances when our business reply envelopes were used to return questionnaires that were for some other study, which we could not forward to the study sponsor because of the lack of identification.

The return address does *not* include the name of the researcher. Including it on the questionnaire would be inconsistent with the way in which the researcher is portrayed to the respondent in the cover letter (see Chapter 5). Our goal is to have the respondent view the researcher as an intermediary between the respondent and the accomplishment of a socially useful activity. We seek to broaden the exchange relationship to include the researcher's sponsoring agency (or institution); its legitimacy contributes to the creation of trust. The respondent seems more likely to trust that promises will be kept if such promises are "backed" by a known organization than if reliance must be placed on an unknown person.

DESIGNING THE BACK COVER

The back cover of TDM questionnaires is deceptively simple (Example 4.10). It consists of an invitation to make additional comments, a thank you, and plenty of white space. If copies of the results are to be sent to respondents, a statement to that effect is also included. However, despite the simplicity, the considerations that go into deciding how this page is used and the exact wording are as important as those which go into the front cover.

Our first concern is that this page not compete for attention with the front cover or detract from it in any way. We would much prefer that a respondent look first at the front cover and then go immediately to page one of the questionnaire. A design that extends from the front to the back cover increases the likelihood that the respondent will examine both covers before starting the questionnaire, and as a result may do so by flipping open the questionnaire near the back so that the first questions he or she sees are those on personal characteristics.

Questions are *never* included on the back page. If our ordering principles are strictly adhered to, the questions that would appear there—income, education, religion, or politics—are those which respondents are most likely to find objectionable. Not only would their placement on the back cover increase the chance of nonresponse, but experience has shown that the item nonresponse for those who do respond increases as well.

Of course, one solution to the potential problem of drawing attention to the back cover is to leave it blank. However, we believe that this page should be used in more positive ways. The request for any additional comments on the topic of the study seeks to overcome one of respondents' most frequent objections to questionnaires—questions written in ways that do not allow a complete answer. The wording of the initial part of the request, "Is there anything else?" clearly implies that this question should be completed last, and thereby refers people to the front of the questionnaire. The solicitation of comments that might help in future efforts is based on an exchange principle, that is, many people are rewarded by being asked for their advice in a consulting manner. The expression of appreciation and the promise of a summary of results also represent attempts to reward the respondent for completing the questionnaire.

Example 4.10   Back Cover of a TDM Questionnaire

     Is there anything else you would like to tell us about the kinds of communities in which you would like most to live? If so, please use this space for that purpose.

     Also, any comments you wish to make that you think may help us in future efforts to understand what Washington residents want from their communities will be appreciated, either here or in a separate letter.

Your contribution to this effort is very greatly appreciated. If you would like a summary of results, please print your name and address on the back of the return envelope (NOT on this questionnaire). We will see that you get it.

It should be noted that the back cover is more than simply another inducement to fill out the questionnaire. It can help overcome one of the serious weaknesses of the mail questionnaire, the lack of interviewer impressions and unsolicited comments that provide insights into the questionnaire itself. For example, comments provided here have helped us identify inadequate questions, and they have also provided interpretations and insights useful in writing study reports.

Also, the possible value of the back page to respondents should not be overlooked. This space (and additional sheets of paper they attach) have often been used by respondents to air their views on topics that are only tangentially related to the questionnaire and perhaps serves a therapeutic value to them. Others have used it to ask questions about the university (or a problem they think someone in the university could help them with). On several occasions we found ourselves in the role of seeking answers for them from other units of the university.

In summary, the unique location of the questionnaire covers place them in an often underestimated position of giving both the first and last impression of a study's worth. A questionnaire that must stand alone should not be without them.

PRETESTING

Pretesting to identify construction defects is a highly touted part of questionnaire design. However, in practice it is often done haphazardly, if at all. Some researchers even view it as a ritual, something to be delegated to their research assistants with directions to, "See if the respondents have any problems with this questionnaire." There are no generally agreed on requirements for pretesting. Instead, each researcher seems to have his or her own. Yet pretesting is especially important for mail questionnaires, because there are no interviewers to report defects and inadequacies to the researcher conducting the study.

Unfortunately, the nature of mail surveys makes pretesting an activity that is likely to be done poorly, if at all. This is especially true in light of the prevailing climate that allows the vague statement, "I pretested this with some respondents," suffice as a defense that adequate pretesting was done. The pretest dilemma is this. It is costly and time consuming to print a few questionnaires and run through the several carefully timed mailings such as are called for by the TDM. Even if this is done, the results are destined to be of very limited value because the researcher does not observe the respondents while they are answering the questionnaire. In addition, the researcher achieves no insight into respondents' difficulties that may have led some of them not to respond at all. Finding that all questions on a questionnaire have been answered and that the return rate is satisfactory often gives a misleading sense of security, leading the researcher to the erroneous conclusion that all questions are understood and are successfully measuring what they are intended to assess.

Our dissatisfaction with the reliance on pretest surveys and concerns with both the time and money costs of conducting them led to the development of a specific set of TDM pretest procedures. These greatly improved questionnaire quality. The methods are based on recognition that any pretest of a mail survey must answer several questions, only some of which concern the adequacy of individual questions:

Is each of the questions measuring what it is intended to measure?

Are all the words understood?

Are questions interpreted similarly by all respondents?

Does each close-ended question have an answer that applies to each respondent?

Does the questionnaire create a positive impression, one that motivates people to answer it?

Are questions answered correctly? (Are some missed, and do some elicit uninterpretable answers?)

Does any aspect of the questionnaire suggest bias on the part of the researcher?

Although this list does not exhaust the concerns a thorough pretest is designed to evaluate, it should suffice to say that a pretest is designed to "test" the questionnaire as well as the questions. General impressions of the questionnaire are just as important, if not more so, as the precise wording of questions in stimulating the return of mail questionnaires.

Prior to the pretest every effort is made to produce a questionnaire that looks final, that is, the questions are ordered according to the principles already discussed, cover pages are in "final" form, and individual pages are constructed in accordance with the TDM procedures. However, in lieu of actually printing the questionnaire, a mock-up is prepared. This can be done at very little cost by taping the questions on regular-sized paper, reproducing them on a copy machine, and taping the pages back-to-back to form booklets. The questionnaire is then submitted to the scrutiny of three types of people.

The first of these groups may be described as colleagues, that is, other similarly trained professionals who understand the study's purpose, including the hypotheses to be tested. The role of this group is to evaluate the questionnaire in terms of whether it will accomplish the study objectives. In our experience, colleagues invariably provide feedback not available from any other group. In one case a colleague pointed out that some of our answer categories did not coincide with those used by the U.S. Census Bureau (which had been recently changed), which meant that our plan to compare respondent characteristics to those of the general public (which we had described to the colleague) would have been difficult. Surprisingly, in another instance a colleague quite familiar with the topic of another survey suggested that we not use census categories for our answers to certain questions, notably age. Inasmuch as that study was concerned with entry into the labor force and retirement, to which the age at which each of these occurred was important, he advised switching to an open-ended question in response to which people would write down their exact age. This would allow us to make finer distinctions among types of people than the broad census categories would allow.

These nearly opposite recommendations illustrate one of the most essential aspects of pretesting by colleagues. They must understand the nature of the study. A question format that seems most suitable in one study may not be at all satisfactory in another. Also, a simple request to "take a look at my questionnaire," will probably result in a superficial examination that focuses on clerical problems and directions to respondents. The lack of in-depth criticism may lull one into complacency concerning whether the questionnaire will achieve the objectives of the study. Most, and probably all, veterans of numerous surveys can cite examples of questions that, if they had been more thorough in their pretesting, they would have asked differently. No amount of pretesting is likely to eliminate all problems, but thorough examination of questionnaires by colleagues represents one of the best ways of minimizing them.

The second pretest group consists of potential "users" of the data. This may include politicians, policy makers, agency administrators, or professionals in other fields. Our primary interest is to find people with substantive knowledge of the survey topic. Feedback from this type of person often differs substantially from that provided by those having similar training and employment as the researcher. In a survey about tax policies we conducted, this meant having the questionnaire examined by people responsible for collecting and analyzing tax revenue for the state. This examination prevented the inclusion of some questions that might have revealed the obvious ignorance of the investigator concerning a subtlety of tax laws and thus discredited the entire survey among knowledgeable respondents and potential users of the results.

The third group from which pretest information is sought are those people drawn from the population to be surveyed, the group that pretests have traditionally focused on to the exclusion of the other two groups. People selected for this pretest are chosen to represent a cross section of potential respondents. They are told in general terms that a survey is to be done and they are being asked to help pretest it. They are then given a questionnaire accompanied by a cover letter and asked to fill it out in the presence of the researcher. This pretest has two crucial aspects. One is the verbal feedback, "I don't know what you want here," "None of these answer categories seem to fit me," "The cover letter sounds awfully demanding," and so on. The second aspect is the observations made while the respondent fills out the questionaire. Nonverbal feedback, that is, hesitating before answering, erasures, and a skipped question that is returned to later give direct evidence of problems that might be solvable. Often it is this help, which many pretest respondents do not even realize they provide, that proves most valuable. Our major expectations from this pretest is *not* for respondents to specifically tell us how to improve the questionnaire (although many do that). Rather, it is to let us know in any way they can, consciously or unconsciously, what is wrong with the questionnaire. This information provides the starting point for revision and subsequent pretesting.

A variation of the pretest with prospective respondents is to bring them together in small groups and, after having them fill out the questionnaire under the watchful eye of the researchers, to go through an extensive "debriefing" in which group discussion is generated for the purpose of stimulating the respondents to identify problems that might otherwise be overlooked. This has been particularly helpful in identifying questions that are interpretable in more than one way.

Perhaps the most crucial aspect of pretesting with the actual survey population is that its diversity be represented. This means searching for people who represent each major segment of the population, for example, high and low income, rural and urban, Republican and Democrat, and so on. It is especially important that variations in people's reading and writing abilities, for which achieved levels of education is one of the few available indicators, be represented.

It is desirable to complete the pretesting process with a small scale survey, in which *all* the procedures to be followed in the actual survey are used. However, the cost and time constraints referred to earlier often preclude this. If the other pretests have been done adequately, a pretest survey probably provides very little additional insight into questionnaire defects. However, it can be extremely useful in helping to estimate probable response rates and to pretest the ability of the organization to handle the survey, both of which may be extremely beneficial for planning a study.

CONCLUSION

A good questionnaire is seldom drafted in one sitting, or even two or three. We often went through 8, 10, or even 12 revisions before sending the questionnaire to the printer.

When a questionnaire nears its final form, it is useful to sit back and reflect on the original study objectives to be certain that, in one's zealousness to have a questionnaire look good and be interesting to the respondent, content has not been sacrificed. At this point, it is important to remind yourself that a questionnaire is a means to a particular end, not the end itself. This chapter deals with how to construct a questionnaire to which people will want to respond, with only an occasional reference to whether substance is being sacrificed. However, this was done to elevate what has often been viewed as an afterthought to the status of a carefully planned effort, which, if well done, should increase the usefulness of the mail questionnaire for most researchers. Yet whether mail questionnaires are viewed as an acceptable survey method hinges on whether valid responses to questions important to a study can be obtained. Turning boring but important questions into interesting but meaningless trivia is not useful to anyone. No aspect of constructing a questionnaire can be considered more important than guarding against such a possibility.

Chapter Five

IMPLEMENTING MAIL SURVEYS

No matter how good a questionnaire is made to look, feel, and read, this will not in itself ensure the success of a mail survey. Poor response often occurs for reasons that have nothing to do with the questionnaire's appearance or content. The problems that prevent the retrieval of completed questionnaires sometimes occur long before the potential respondent is contacted, sometimes not until the questionnaire is completed. The causes of nonresponse include

The questionnaire never reached its destination, because a wrong address and a postage rate did not provide for its return to the sender.

The questionnaire arrived at the prospective respondent's address, but was discarded without being opened because it resembled "junk" mail.

The envelope was opened, but, because there were no instructions about which member of the household should respond, the questionnaire was never filled out.

It was clear who should complete the questionnaire, but another person opened the letter and failed to bring it to the right person's attention.

The desired person received the questionnaire, but because he or she found no convincing explanation about why it should be completed, it was thrown away.

The prospective respondent decided to fill out the questionnaire, but temporarily laid it aside and just never got back to it.

The questionnaire was filled out, thoughtfully and completely, but the return address was misplaced, and the prospective respondent did not know to whom it should be returned.

Some problems, such as failing to indicate which member of a household should complete the questionnaire, seem almost too trivial to mention. Others, such as developing a cover letter explanation of the survey that will be most convincing, are perplexing and sometimes difficult to solve. However, nonresponse is a serious problem under any circumstances. Thus each element that might help to prevent it—no matter how trivial—is worthy of design considerations. The realization that virtually any step in the process of sending and retrieving questionnaires may produce a refusal constitutes the frame of reference from which the procedures for implementing the Total Design Method (TDM) mail surveys—reported in step-by-step detail in this chapter—were developed.

The major difficulty in the development of the implementation process was less one of finding *individual* techniques to solve problems (e.g., how to encourage people to open the envelope) than how to build a *set* of complementary techniques that together would produce a high quantity and quality of response. For example, a shocking pink envelope embellished with a humorous cartoon may serve quite nicely to get the envelope opened. It could even get some people to pause, probably in surprise at finding a mail questionnaire inside, and eventually decide that such originality should be rewarded with a response. However, the initial curiosity of some who were first attracted by the envelope's external appearance may switch to bewilderment or rejection when they find a request for help on a serious topic from a respected organization. Or, even worse, they may provide answers that are as frivolous as the envelope that originally attracted their attention. Thus our efforts to develop implementation procedures for the mail TDM focused on designing an implementation *system* that is consistent with the usual aims of social research, and not on producing a collage of gimmicks.

OVERVIEW OF THE IMPLEMENTATION PROCESS: THE BASIC APPEAL

Consistency among the individual elements of an implementation system cannot be achieved in the abstract. Rather, consistency must be developed in accordance with a theme, which determines the costs and rewards associated with each individually applied technique. Various themes might provide the foundation of the appeal through which potential respondents are approached.

An implementation theme followed by some researchers with reasonable success is a personal appeal to people's altruistic inclinations. It depends on asking potential respondents, "Would you do me a favor?" This appeal is based on the fact that it is not out of the ordinary in our society to ask a favor of complete strangers. Provided that the request is not very demanding, people often comply with it. The users of this approach usually send a brief and easy to read letter that emphasizes the writer's personal appreciation of their help, but mentions in only the briefest and most general way, if at all, why the favor is asked. Typically, the questionnaire is quite short, and no obligations are incurred by the respondent, as would be implied by a lack of anonymity (e.g., identifying questionnaires with a numbering system) and being asked to divulge highly personal items of information (e.g., religious and political participation). A small token of appreciation (e.g., a quarter) might also be enclosed to further convey the impression that the researcher appreciates the respondent's effort to respond. No doubt this is a useful approach in some survey situations, and the method consists of much more than an arbitrary juxtapositioning of implementation techniques.

However, this altruistic appeal also has certain insurmountable weaknesses for the kind of study usually of interest to social scientists. First, the power of the appeal to "do me a favor," is strong only as long as the person being asked does not have to go out of his or her way to comply. The questionnaires typically needed for social research studies are ones which require a great deal of effort on the part of the respondent. Many of the questions they contain are boring, and people are asked to divulge considerable amounts of personal information. Further, appealing to altruism tends to make difficult the use of follow-ups—perhaps the most powerful individual stimulator of response—because persistently repeating a request for a favor tends to turn into a demand that the respondent feels the researcher has no right to make. Thus we have developed a quite different appeal to use with the TDM.

The appeal of the TDM is based on convincing people first that a problem exists that is of importance to a group with which they identify, and second, that their help is needed to find a solution. The researcher is portrayed as a reasonable person who, in light of the complexity of the problem, is making a reasonable request for help, and, if forthcoming, such help will contribute to the solution of that problem. The exchange relationship the researcher seeks to establish is broader than that between him or herself and the questionnaire recipient, that is, if you do something for me, I'll do something for you. Rather, the researcher is identified as an intermediary between the person asked to contribute to the solution of an important problem and certain steps that might help to solve it. Thus the reward to the respondents derives from the feeling that they have done something important to help solve a problem faced by them, their friends, or members of a group including community, state, or nation, whose activities are important to them.

Many specifics flow from this basic appeal and intertwine to comprise the TDM implementation procedures. First, a cover letter is prepared that communicates the appeal. It emphasizes a reasonable explanation of the subject of the study, its benefit to a group with which the recipient identifies, and the individual importance of the respondent to the study's success. Length is only a secondary consideration in preparing the cover letter, although one full page is considered a maximum. The letter is reproduced on appropriate letterhead stationery, *and* the recipient's name and address is added. It is completed by adding, in normal business letter fashion, the exact date the letter is mailed and the researcher's individually applied signature. An identification number, an explanation of which is included in the letter, is stamped on the cover of the questionnaire, where it is visible to the respondent. Then the cover letter and a business reply envelope are carefully folded in a predetermined fashion and placed for mailing into a regular business stationery envelope on which the respondent's name and address are individually typed. First-class postage is affixed (either by stamp or meter) to the envelope, and the mailing is dispatched.

Exactly 1 week later a postcard follow-up is sent to all recipients of the first mailing. Preprinted, but with an individually typed name and address on one side and an individually applied signature on the other, the note on this postcard is written as a thank you for those who have already returned their questionnaires, and a reminder to those who have not. A second follow-up is mailed to nonrespondents exactly 3 weeks after the original mailout. It consists of a cover letter that basically informs them that their questionnaire has not yet been received and includes a restatement of the basic appeals from the original cover letter, a replacement questionnaire, and another return envelope. The third and final follow-up is mailed 7 weeks after the original mailing. It consists of a cover letter and still another questionnaire and return envelope, and it is sent by certified mail to the remaining nonrespondents.

The additional detail necessary for the implementation of the TDM oail survey comprises the remainder of this chapter. However, before proceeding with the ensuing step-by-step discussion, we must explain a fundamental principle that gives form to the method and makes the emphasis on consistency among elements a meaningful concern, and not simply a platitude with a hollow ring.

The TDM for mail surveys relies heavily on personalization throughout the implementation process. It is the major vehicle for conveying to the respondent the critical messages that the study is important and that the respondent's participation is important to its success. Personalization involves much more than putting a respondent's name and a real signature on the cover letter, the simplistic way in which it is often viewed. The test of whether personalization is achieved rests not with individual techniques, but with the overall effect that is produced, that is, whether respondents feel that they are accorded individual attention. Any impression of individual interest in respondents created by techniques such as typing their names on the cover letter, providing the researcher's signature, and so on, may be neutralized in a number of ways. One of them is a date on the letter that precedes (or for that matter follows) the date of arrival by a week or two. Another is a mimeographed address label on the envelope. Likewise, the use of the "bulk" mailing rate privilege automatically signifies a mass mailing. In fact, it is not legal to use this postage rate for personal correspondence, something known by many people, thus making it an unfailing indicator that, regardless of appearances to the contrary, the letter is not actually a personal appeal.

One of the strongest elements of personalization available to the researcher is to explicitly inform the respondent in follow-ups that "as of today we have not yet received your questionnaire." This message acts as a kind of feedback that indicates in an urgent way that the researcher views the respondent's completed questionnaire as quite important. Every effort is made to personalize the letter to the fullest extent by using all available techniques, taking great care not to overlook even the smallest detail that could possibly detract from the effect we wish to create.

Personalization must be viewed as relative. Whether a specific technique gives the impression of individual attention depends greatly on current methods for producing mass mailed materials. Computer technology makes it possible to mass produce letters that not only include name, address, and salutation, but the computer writes, "Dear Mr. Roberts," repeats his name as many times as desired in the body (possibly with the variation of the "Roberts family"), refers to his home on Maple Street, and informs him that he is one of very few families in Wallace, Washington asked to participate in the survey. The letter can be produced automatically, in seconds, by a very high speed printer. This extreme personalization is increasingly common in advertising efforts and may soon become equally impersonal as once was the faintly dittoed, "Dear citizen." Indeed, people are likely to judge such efforts at mechanical sincerity as quite insincere, and even cynical.

The standard toward which we strive is to make our appeals comparable in appearance and content to what one business person would send to another whom he or she knows only slightly, or not at all, to ask for help on an important project. The letter is honest, straightforward, and offers a reason for the appeal in terms of the hoped for outcome of the project. It is processed as any business letter would be. In this situation a letter that repeats the individual's name several times would sound artificial. Likewise, a business person would not write a letter by hand, for to do so would seem inefficient and unwarranted, because there was no preexisting personal relationship.

WRITING THE COVER LETTER

Ideally, the cover letter is the first part of the mailout package to be examined by the respondent. It serves to introduce the survey and hopefully motivates the respondent to immediately pick up the questionnaire, fill it out, and, just as expeditiously, return it. However, in practice the cover letter must do much more. Some people scrutinize and reread it several times, using it as the sole basis for deciding what to do with the questionnaire. At the other extreme, some ignore it, at least until they have a question (e.g., "these questions are pretty personal, do I really want to answer them?"); then it will be used as a reference document.

The cover letter is virtually the only opportunity the researcher has for anticipating and countering respondent questions. Composing the cover letter is made even more difficult by the realization that excessive length will, regardless of anything else, cause the cover letter to be skimmed with little or no comprehension of its content, or even ignored altogether. Thus the researcher is caught in the dilemma of whether to prepare a short "snappy" letter that is high on motivation or an informational letter that is long and, as a result, low on appeal. Our solution is to strike a balance and make *every* paragraph, indeed *every* sentence, serve a distinct purpose. We never set a word limit on our TDM letters except that we keep them to a length that fits attractively onto a single page.

This Is a Useful Study

The first paragraph of the letter is designed to do two things—(1) explain what the study is about and (2) convince the respondent that the study is useful. The latter is the primary focus, but it cannot be accomplished without first providing adequate information about the study's purpose.

To establish in the respondent's mind that the study is important, it is described as useful to some group with which the respondent identifies. Fundamentally, the letter rests on the assumption that doing something useful is rewarding to the respondent. Thus in surveys of the general public, reference is usually made to meeting the "needs of citizens throughout the state," or perhaps "residents of your county." In studies involving people with a common organizational membership, reference would likely be made to "helping your organization better serve the needs of its members." It is imperative not to build an appeal for usefulness around a group that is rejected by some of those surveyed. The end result of such an appeal might well be selective nonresponse. Suggesting that a survey is being done to help the Democratic (or Republican) Party better serve the needs of all Americans is not very helpful in getting those who identify with the other party to respond, especially since the last thing each party's members probably want is for the opposing party to grow and prosper at the inevitable expense of their own. The resultant respondent selectivity could be quite detrimental to the survey's success. Thus careful consideration is given to using the benefit to specific organizations or segments of the population as the basis for an appeal. When such a reference is made, we focus on the benefit to members (of which the respondent is one) or people served by the organization, rather than to the organization itself.

There are many ways in which the social usefulness argument can be stated. Our procedure for developing such an argument starts with considerable reflection on what a study is about and how it might serve the needs of people. That is often easy, inasmuch as many studies are conceived and financed because of the belief that they will serve the needs of certain people. Sometimes, however, the human implications of the research are forgotten in the rigor of daily efforts to build theoretical models of human behavior. Thus there may be no substitute for extensive contemplation about ways to explain the importance of a study to nonsocial scientists. When developing social utility arguments, we have found it particularly useful to read newspapers and magazines, searching for current issues around which the social utility theme might be developed.

Social utility arguments can readily be formulated for most topics, even the very theoretical. Some of those which have been developed by researchers for studies on widely differing topics are shown in Example 5.1. In each TDM survey the researcher tied the concern of the research to the concerns of the people surveyed. Once, when planning a study on community size preferences, bills to accomplish population distribution had been introduced in the Washington Legislature as well as in the U.S. Congress (Example 5.2). These events provided us with an excellent means of introducing our study to the public (not to mention the increased importance the results would have to policy makers themselves). Thus the first paragraph is usually formulated at the same time the first questions for the questionnaire are selected. Our goal is to make the questions appear very natural in light of the study purposes described in the cover letter. Preparing them together provides maximum flexibility for building this critical tie.

Certain features that commonly appear in the lead paragraph of cover letters are intentionally avoided. Stock phrases such as these, which sometimes get used in the first line of a cover letter are avoided:

Enclosed is a questionnaire	A guaranteed turn-off. Besides "questionnaire" being a word to avoid, the respondent can see what is enclosed.
This is a survey	"Survey" is another word to avoid.
I am a research sociologist.	Who the researcher is does not have as much importance as what he or she wants. Besides, this can probably be noted as a title under the signature.
The Citizen's Committee for a New Tax Policy is a group of local people banded together for the purpose of	May be important, but if so, later would be better.
Your help is needed	Important, but wait until a good reason has been given. Besides, they probably surmise such a request is coming; other- wise, why the letter?
To complete the Ph.D. degree at my university I am required to write a dissertation. The topic is	Some people may be sympa- thetic, but most will not, and the general image of dissertations is that they are more often eso- teric than useful.

Finally, it is essential that any hint of bias be avoided. Conducting a study to find out "how the citizens of this state feel about our organization's stand on this issue" is quite different from saying, "we don't know how citizens feel on this issue, and believe it important that their voices be heard." The former tends to suggest the possibility that results will be shaped to fit the researcher's political needs rather than letting the data speak for themselves. As a result, respondents who are suspicious of the researcher's motives may try to out-guess him or her, and therefore do not respond in line with their true feelings.

Example 5.1   Selected Social Utility Arguments Included in Cover Letters Developed by Users of the Total Design Method

Crime victimization survey of general public[a]	Nearly everyone in America is alarmed about crime. Unfortunately, we have only a sketchy idea of what crimes are being committed, how frequently, and what kinds of persons are victims of various kinds of crimes. Without such information, and without a clear understanding of what citizens want their government to do about crime, sensible and effective crime prevention programs are difficult to formulate
Evaluation of educational program by former students[b]	As a former student, your school is interested in how well the vocational and non-vocational programs met your needs to make a living. The only way we know to find out is to ask you. The information you provide will be used to help improve programs for your fellow students.
Family roles study of general public[c]	Never before has there been so much discussion about the American family and what's happening to it. No doubt it is changing, but it is not clear how fast and in what direction. Furthermore, many are wondering whether these changes are desirable. For example, should husbands and wives both work outside the home? Should household duties be shared? Should more of the family functions be done outside the home by other agencies?
	Knowing what residents of Washington think about the responsibilities of husbands and wives and what the family of the future might be like is important to all of us. But it is especially relevant to counselors, teachers, and legislators since it may help them make decisions about day care centers, divorce laws, and other legislation affecting family life.
Views on University activities: general public[d]	In the past few years there has been a lot of discussion about what the policies and activities of our state's colleges and universities should be. Some of the questions being asked here at Washington State University (WSU) include these: is WSU meeting the needs and desires of the state's residents; should more attention be given to teaching and less to research; should men and women be allowed to live in the same dormitories; and who should decide these questions. We are conducting this study because we feel that the residents of Washington, all of whom support WSU through the taxes they pay, should have their opinions heard on these important matters.

[a] Stuart Gould, personal communication, 1973

[b] Roy Lyn Schmidt, "The Development and Validation of Follow-Up Instruments for Secondary Schools and Vocational-Technical Institutes in the State of Washington," unpublished Ph.D. dissertation, Washington State University, 1974.

[c] F. Ivan Nye and Viktor Gecas, personal communication, 1973.

[d] Linda Kay Smith, "Attitudes Held by Students, Their Parents, and the General Public on the In Loco Parentis Position of the University," unpublished M.A. thesis, Washington State University, 1973.

You Are Important to the Success of This Study

The second paragraph of the cover letter seeks to convince the respondent that his or her response (or that of someone else in the household) is important and that no one else's can be substituted (Example 5.2). This paragraph is designed to counter one of the most frequent respondent objections given in all kinds of surveys, "my opinions on this subject aren't very important,"

Example 5.2 Example of Cover Letter for Household Survey

Official letterhead	**WASHINGTON STATE UNIVERSITY** PULLMAN, WASHINGTON 99163

DEPARTMENT OF RURAL SOCIOLOGY
Room 23, Wilson Hall

Date mailed   April 19, 1971

Inside address in   Oliver Jones
matching type   2190 Fontana Road
                           Spokane, Washington 99467

What study is about;   Bills have been introduced in Congress and our State Legislature
its social usefulness   to encourage the growth of rural and small town areas and slow
                           down that of large cities. These bills could greatly affect the
                           quality of life provided in both rural and urban places. However,
                           no one really knows in what kinds of communities people like your-
                           self want to live or what is thought about these proposed programs.

Why recipient   Your household is one of a small number in which people are being
is important   asked to give their opinion on these matters. It was drawn in a
(and, if needed,   random sample of the entire state. In order that the results will
who should complete   truly represent the thinking of the people of Washington, it is
the questionnaire)   important that each questionnaire be completed and returned. It
                           is also important that we have about the same number of men and
                           women participating in this study. Thus, we would like the ques-
                           tionnaire for your household to be completed by an <u>adult female</u>.
                           If none is present, then it should be completed by an <u>adult male</u>.

Promise of   You may be assured of complete confidentiality. The questionnaire has
confidentiality;   an identification number for mailing purposes only. This is so
explanation of   that we may check your name off of the mailing list when your ques-
identification   tionnaire is returned. Your name will never be placed on the ques-
number   tionnaire.

Usefulness of study   The results of this research will be made available to officials and
                           representatives in our state's government, members of Congress, and
"Token" reward   all interested citizens. You may receive a summary of results by
for participation   writing "copy of results requested" on the back of the return en-
                           velope, and printing your name and address below it. Please <u>do not</u>
                           put this information on the questionnaire itself.

What to do if   I would be most happy to answer any questions you might have. Please
questions arise   write or call. The telephone number is (509) 335-8623.

Appreciation   Thank you for your assistance.

                                                           Sincerely,

Pressed blue ball
point signature

                                                           Don A. Dillman
Title   Project Director

or, "I don't know much about this so why don't you get someone else who does." Our argument of individual importance states that representativeness is essential, a theme that we believe is better understood by the general public as each year goes by. The most immediate objective of this paragraph is to prevent the questionnaire from being passed to someone else. A more forceful presentation of why it is important for that particular person to respond, rather than ignore it, can be saved for follow-up mailings.

Household surveys of the general public sometimes present special problems for developing the argument about individual importance. Usually the composition of the household is not known in advance, for example, when the sample is drawn from telephone listings; thus the person the researcher wants to complete the questionnaire may not be the one to whom the letter is addressed. To handle this situation, the individual importance of the household is stressed, and then it is stated who from that household should respond, as in Example 5.2. This example asks for an adult female, but provides for the possibility of none being at this address by indicating an adult male would in that case be acceptable. When selection procedures of this nature are used, different cover letters must be prepared and randomly assigned to households in the survey.

The random selection of respondents from households is a problem for which completely satisfactory methods have yet to be worked out.[1] The method of alternating between adult males and females is not as adequate as the methods normally used in face-to-face interview surveys or the procedures described in Chapter 7 for telephone surveys. The difficulty stems from the complexity of the respondent selection procedure and how to provide those directions to respondents. The development of such procedures and evaluating whether respondents follow them correctly represents a high priority concern for the further development of the TDM.

Your Questionnaire Will Be Treated Confidentially

The third paragraph promises confidentiality, a concern for increasing numbers of respondents (Example 5.2). Part of the fear held by many respondents is generated by the concern that their answers will be used for purposes other than research and will have later repercussions for them. Some researchers have fanned the flames of this fear by using invisible ink, although their motive for doing so was probably to cut the cost of follow-ups and to avoid sending a questionnaire to someone who had already responded. Indeed, one representative of the market survey industry has described the use of invisible ink as a standard practice.[2] The fear that comes with the disclosure that respondent information has been misused in only one out of literally thousands of surveys is probably enough to keep respondents wary. This makes it difficult for researchers, whose interest in specific respondents stops the moment the questionnaire is returned, to convince respondents that their promise of confidentiality will be honored.

There is, of course, no reason to be concerned about the issue of confidentiality unless questionnaires are identified by respondent. The TDM uses an identification system that is discussed later in this chapter. The presence of an identifying number on the questionnaire is explained to respondents in a straightforward, honest manner (Example 5.2). The sole reason for employing such an identification system is to facilitate the sending of follow-ups, a practice that is essential for producing a high response rate. In addition to cutting costs, the identification system prevents earlier respondents from being bothered by follow-ups and avoids the possibility that they will complete a second or even a third questionnaire—a problem that is sometimes (although infrequently) encountered. It also avoids the possibility of the questionnaire being passed to another family member or friend, who completes and returns it. We have found no reason to vary this paragraph on confidentiality from one study to another.

Other Important Messages

The fourth paragraph of our cover letter reemphasizes the basic justification for the study—its social usefulness. A somewhat different approach is taken here, however, in that the intent of the researcher to carry through on any promises that are made, often the weakest link in making study results useful, is emphasized. In Example 5.2 the promise (later carried out) was made to provide results to government officials, consistent with the lead paragraph, which included a reference to bills being considered in the State Legislature and Congress. Our basic concern here is to make the promise of action consistent with the original social utility appeal. In surveys of particular communities, a promise is often made to provide results to the local media and city officials.

The respondents are also promised a copy of the results (if at all possible) for several reasons. One reason is an explicit attempt to reward respondents in a manner consistent with something they found interesting to do. We are under no illusion that such an offer will have reward value for every respondent. However, the fact that requests are generally made by from one-half to two-thirds of the respondents suggests that many respondents value the opportunity to see the survey results. Additional evidence of the importance of results to some respondents stems from the fact that in surveys we have conducted without offering copies of the results, many respondents have asked for them.

Respondents who want results are instructed to put their name and address on the back of the return envelope, rather than on the questionnaire itself. This does two things. First, it simplifies clerical procedures by having all requests for results written in one place. Second, it is a convenient way of reinforcing the promise of confidentiality made in the preceding paragraph. It might be reasoned that the respondent's task could be simplified even further by a box that could be checked as a means of requesting results. Our reasons for not doing this are practical ones. Addresses frequently change, and by asking respondents to supply their addresses, we are assured of having the most current ones.

When a business person makes a request of someone, it is appropriate to indicate a willingness to answer any questions that arise. We believe that it is important to include this perfunctory message. When potential respondents do ask questions, it provides one more opportunity to convince some people to respond. However, the number of situations in which we were able to do this is small. Relatively few letters and telephone calls are ever received, usually well under 1 percent of the sample. In fact, a letter very similar to the one in Example 5.2 elicited only one telephone call and perhaps 20 letters from a sample of 4500. Even when people are told they may call collect, the number remains relatively small. The main value of the message is that it adds credibility to the study. Although few make the effort to call or write, merely knowing that the possibility exists suggests that the study is legitimate and that respondents are important to it. Finally, we found one other reason for always including this message. One of the major shortcomings of surveys by mail is the near total lack of communication with respondents. The few inquiries we received, as well as notes on the questionnaire given as comments rather than questions, sometimes pointed out ambiguities we missed in the pretest.

The letter is completed with a simple statement of thanks, a closing, the sender's name, and the sender's title (Example 5.2). These are added just as they would be for a normal business letter.

In summary, the cover letter is not something to be written at the last minute, as if it were an afterthought. There is precious little space to get across so many messages—study topic, social utility, individual importance of respondent, explanation of identification, promise of anonymity, promise of results, willingness to answer questions, appreciation, and sponsorship. Most users of the mail TDM find themselves going through several drafts of the cover letter before producing one that is acceptable. However, its crucial role in serving as the main, and perhaps the only, communication link between researcher and respondent makes such time well spent.

PREPARING THE COVER LETTER FOR TRANSMITTAL

When preparing cover letters for transmittal to respondents, it is important that four conditions be realized. The first is to add the date the letter is to be mailed (Example 5.2). This is a simple and quite natural thing to do. Yet the number of letters we have seen that either list a date far different from the actual date of mailing, list only the month, or omit the date altogether, suggests that this simple procedure is often overlooked. To do so is inconsistent with, and detracts from, the various other efforts to make the letter appear important.

Second, the name, address, and salutation (if one is used) must be individually typed onto the letter (Example 5.2) in normal business letter position. There are several situations in which the salutation is not used. One is in the case of household surveys in which the name of the person listed at the top may not be the person in the household who will be asked to respond. Another consists of situations when it is not known whether a person's name is that of a male or female, for example, when initials only are available or when the listed first name is "Pat." Still another problem is deciding whether to address a female as Miss, Mrs., or Ms. Whenever uncertainty exists about the appropriate salutation, the typed inside address appears exactly as it occurs on the sample list, but two lines closer to the body of the letter; thus the absence of the salutation will be less noticable.

The third condition to be achieved when reproducing cover letters is to use the sponsoring organization's normal business stationery or a very close fac- simile that is of monarch size, 7¼ × 10½ (Example 5.2). It would be nice if every organization had a crisp bond stationery with a colored insignia by its name. The high quality of such stationery would immediately distinguish it from any mass mailing. However, stationery of this nature is now a vanishing species, especially in large organizations such as universities for whom the cost savings from black ink on lighter weight paper are substantial. The let- terhead used by many organizations is now so simple that a facsimile, virtually undetectable from actual stationery, can be produced at the same time as the body of the cover letter, by multilith or other inexpensive printing methods. In any event, every effort is made to produce a cover letter that is, if not the same, virtually identical to the stationery used by the researcher for all regular business correspondence.

The final touch is to add a real signature to each respondent's letter, using what is descriptively called the "pressed blue ball point pen" method (Exam- ple 5.2). It is simple, although somewhat time consuming. Each letter is signed on a soft surface with sufficient pressure applied to the ballpoint pen that indentations in the paper are made. Rubbing one's finger over the back of the page provides unmistakable evidence that the signature is real, and has neither been preprinted or applied by means of a signature machine. Of the many aspects of personalization used in processing cover letters, this remains one of the most important, because it is the most difficult to imitate by mass production methods.

PRINTING THE COVER LETTER

We have used four different types of printing methods to reproduce cover letters, and this by no means exhausts all possibilities. The best method depends primarily on the facilities one has available and the cost. One method is to type each letter separately. The individuality of these letters, corrected errors and all, can hardly be questioned. However, this method is prohibitively costly, except for the smallest of samples. Further, the recent availability of memory typewriters has hastened the obsolescence of this time-consuming practice.

When memory typewriters, of which there are many varieties on the market, are used, the letter is entered into the typewriter and at the punch of a button, individual letters are automatically typed. The operator adds names, addresses, and salutations individually for each respondent. On some machines, this information can be stored in a separate memory bank and recalled when needed; thus the entire letter is produced automatically.

Another method we have used is to type one master copy of the letter and then reproduce the desired number of copies by a multilithing technique. Names, addresses, and salutations are then added by a typist using the same type as the original letter. This is the least expensive method of any that we have used. Success in making the letters appear highly personalized depends on control of the ink flow during the multilithing process, so that letters are neither darker nor lighter than natural type, and whether typists are adept at aligning inside addresses with the margin of the letter. Most of our studies used this method, and good results were obtained. It is particularly cost effective because the letterhead of our university is black and can be printed at the same time as the letter, alleviating the need for the separate purchase of stationery.

Still another method for printing cover letters is to store the text of the letter and respondent addresses in a computer, and print both through a high-speed printer connected to a computer terminal. Both stationery and envelopes can be printed in continuous perforated rolls to achieve maximum speed. Letters equal in quality to those produced by the memory typewriters can be expected. Finally, we should note that it is possible to use a combination of machines, storing all the necessary information in the computer, but linking a memory typewriter to the computer for the purpose of typing the letters.

The most important point to make about reproducing cover letters is that the situation facing one researcher may differ markedly from that of another. We know of some who would consider no alternative except the computer, and others who zealously avoid it because of cost and the lack of control over gaining access at the precise times it is needed. Others avoid memory typewriters for similar reasons. There is no substitute for assessing one's own situation with respect to the availability and cost of all methods before choosing the most appropriate one.

PREPARING THE ENVELOPE

If one's goal were to give people an early warning signal that something pretty unimportant was being sent to them, there are several ways to do it. One would be to choose an envelope that is unusual in size, shape, or color, perhaps embellished with other hallmarks of advertising, for example, "dated materials enclosed," or "immediate reply requested." Another way is to attach a mimeographed (or carbon copy) address label, with the last name first, so that the unmistakable source of the mailing address appears to be an alphabetized list. Still another warning of unimportance is a bulk rate insignia or a stamp with a denomination below the current first class rate.

The role of the envelope in the TDM is to attract only enough attention to guarantee that it will be opened and to convey an impression consistent with the message contained inside. It should look about the same as an envelope containing an individually written business letter from one person to another.

Business envelopes that match the cover letter stationery are always used. The dimensions of the questionnaire (8¼" × 6⅛") are such that when folded into thirds it will fit nicely into a monarch sized envelope (3⅞" × 7½"), the smallest we have found practical to use. Our preference for this size is dictated by purely practical efforts to bring the weight of the mailout package within the bounds of the minimum first-class rate. The smallness of the package and minimum postage are important indicators that normal business mail is being sent. Further, the envelope gives the impression that the questionnaire it contains should not take very much time to complete. Although manilla envelopes just slightly larger than the folded questionnaire are available and would eliminate the need for folding, they are zealously avoided because extra postage is likely to be needed and they project the undesirable image of "bulk."

Names and addresses are individually typed onto the envelope itself with the surname placed last as is the standard correspondence practice. At this point in the process, the advantages of a memory typewriter or computerized printer become apparent, inasmuch as this will be the second of perhaps seven times that the full name and address of each potential respondent is to be typed before the survey is completed.

ADDING POSTAGE

First-class mail is always used. The reasons for using it extend well beyond the image of importance it creates. Next to special delivery, it has the highest handling priority by the U.S. Postal Service. If the recipient has moved, it will be forwarded automatically for 1 year after the change of address. If it cannot be delivered for any reason, the letter will be returned to the sender, often with notations that may be helpful in tracing respondents or calculating return rates. Such notations are "no such address," "left no forwarding address," "refused," "deceased," and so on.

Bulk rate, besides symbolizing a lack of importance, receives a very low handling priority. According to Postal Service regulations, it may be held up to 24 hours at each handling point through which it passes. As a result, the delivery of questionnaires may easily take a week or longer. Because of great variations in the speed by which bulk mail is moved, we have not found it unusual for a follow-up mailing to reach respondents about the same time as the original questionnaire, thus amplifying even further the study's lack of importance. Another problem is that bulk rate mail cannot be forwarded or returned unless postage is guaranteed by the sender.

In light of the reported success of more expensive postage rates—certified and special delivery—it seems natural that their use be considered.[3] Their effect on initial mailings using the TDM is, to our knowledge, untested. We do not use certified or special delivery for two reasons. One is the current cost of certified and special delivery, which varies from 60¢ to $1.25 plus regular first-class postage. The other is the seeming inconsistency with the contents of this initial mailing—a polite request for help. It is not our purpose at this time to convey a sense of urgency. As discussed later in the description of follow-ups, the appeal is intentionally conveyed at a low key; the intensity of the appeals can be increased at a later time, when the certified mailing is used.

As a matter of convenience the envelope is metered instead of stamped. At first it was thought the meter might serve as one more symbol of a deper-sonalized society and thereby adversely affect response. However, experimental data showed no differences in the effects of the meter versus multicolored stamps.[4] We cautiously suggest that the meter is now routinely used for business correspondence, and sometimes for personal mail; thus the image is not as negative as it once was.

Another decision to make about postal procedures is whether to request "address corrections" from the U.S. Postal Service. If requested by stamping envelopes with the phrase "address correction requested," the Postal Service will return a form to the sender with a respondent's new address at the same time that it forwards the letter on to that address. The current cost of this service is 25¢ for each new address provided. Requests for address corrections do not increase the chances that a respondent will be contacted, inasmuch as this service is provided only for the 1-year period during which first class mail is automatically forwarded. However, the resultant updating of the address list helps ensure that the follow-up mailings reach respondents as rapidly as possible, bypassing the inevitable delay created by the need to readdress and reroute the mailings. The use of the address correction request sometimes helps to eliminate ineligible respondents from later mailings, for example, those who are shown by the new address to have moved away from the geographic area being surveyed. In our view, the address correction service is helpful, but it is unnecessary unless a substantial number of address changes are expected.

IDENTIFYING THE QUESTIONNAIRE

Normally, TDM questionnaires are stamped with individual identification numbers so that follow-up mailings need be sent only to those not responding to earlier mailings. This lowers costs considerably and ensures that only one questionnaire is returned by each respondent. Our procedure is to stamp an identification number onto the front of the questionnaire. The number corresponds to one similarly stamped next to the recipient's name on the mailing list. The number is placed in the upper right hand corner of the cover page, a position in which it is easily visible.

Positioning the identification number on an inside page, or perhaps the bottom of the back cover page, could create the impression that the researcher is attempting to hide it. Its prominent display, on the other hand, is consistent with the straightforward manner in which its use is discussed in the cover letter. Also, should a respondent wish to remove the identification number, this placement allows it to be clipped off without the loss of any of the answers on the back of the page. The printing of identification numbers on questionnaires can be done by hand, but is greatly facilitated by the use of an inexpensive mechanical hand-held numbering machine. Models are available that automatically change from one number to the next each time an impression is stamped on the page.

The case for the use of this identification system is strengthened by the lack of objections we have received in conjunction with the high response rates. Although respondents sometimes remove the identification numbers, this does not present a formidable problem, since it occurs in less than one-half of 1 percent of the cases. Interestingly enough, some of those who removed the identification numbers wrote in response to later follow-ups to indicate that their questionnaires were returned earlier after the identifying number was removed.

We cannot overemphasize the importance of being very careful with any identification process. Many researchers we know can relate stories of frustration about how a number was used twice (or not at all), and they found it necessary to open stacks of sealed envelopes to correct the error. In one case it was not discovered at all until a number of complaints came from persons who had already sent in their completed questionnaires but were still receiving follow-up mailings. To help prevent problems of this nature, the numbering of questionnaires is usually the last step in preparing the mailout and is carefully done in conjunction with the envelope stuffing process.

Some researchers are exceptionally reluctant to use any type of identification system at all, either as a matter of principle or because they feel that their topic is an extremely sensitive one. An alternative approach has been developed for that purpose. Instead of identifying the questionnaires in any way, a separate return postcard is included in the mailout package. The cover letter is modified to ask respondents to return the postcard separately when their questionnaire is returned (Example 5.3). The postcard contains only the respondent's pretyped name (or an identification number) matched with the name of the mailing list and a statement about the postcard's purpose (Example 5.3). The frequent illegibility of signatures prevents their use as the sole means of identification.

Our reluctance to make greater use of this method as a standard means of separating respondents from nonrespondents stems from several concerns. One is the additional cost for printing, processing, mailing (the weight of the return postcard is often enough to push the cost of the mailout above the minimum rate for first-class postage), and the return postage. Another is the concern that some respondents will return the postcard without returning the questionnaire. Although several studies have shown that the number of returned postcards about equals the number of returned questionnaires, it seems quite possible that a certain number of people who return their postcards do not bother to return their questionnaires, and that number is offset by others who do the opposite.

PREPARING RETURN ENVELOPES

The final element of the mailout package is the preaddressed, postage-paid return envelope. Without it response rates would suffer significantly. Business reply envelopes (6½" × 3½") preprinted with the researcher's return address are used. This eliminates the time-consuming activity of procuring, safely storing, and applying stamps to the envelopes. Further, the cost of unused stamps from each mailing (one-half to three-fourths of the total) is avoided inasmuch as no postage costs are incurred when a business reply envelope is discarded. There are also some disadvantages to the use of business reply envelopes that should be recognized as well. A permit must be purchased, although this is no problem for many researchers, because their employers already have them. A second important factor is that return postages are higher (either 16.5¢ or 25¢ per ounce depending on the type of permit) than the current 13¢ first-class postage rate.

Example 5.3   Separate Return Postcard Used to Make Questionnaire Anonymous, and Explanatory Paragraph to be Substituted in Cover Letter (see Example 5.2)

Identification number	1428
Purpose	I have returned my questionnaire separately.
Name	
	your name (please print)
Appreciation	Thanks again for your help with this important study.

Paragraph substituted in cover letter

You may be assured of complete anonymity. There is no way we can identify from whom the questionnaires are returned. Instead, we ask that you print your name on the enclosed postcard and mail it back separately so that we may remove your name from our mailing list. Only the questionnaire should be returned in the postage free envelope.

An experiment was recently conducted in which all aspects of the TDM were used, except that half the respondents were sent self-addressed stamped reply envelopes instead of business reply envelopes. The group receiving the stamped envelopes showed a slightly higher return rate than the group receiving business replies (76 versus 72 percent).[5] The results were from a community problems survey in a single county and were used in a survey utilizing a franking privilege mailout. We consider the results suggestive but in need of replication on other populations under regular mailout conditions before they can be considered conclusive.

ASSEMBLING THE MAILOUT PACKAGE

Insisting, which we do, that there is a "best" way to fold the cover letter, questionnaire, and business reply envelope together and stuff them into an envelope may strike some as rather fastidious. Nonetheless, we believe it is important and worthy of mention. The contents are folded together rather than inserted separately (another sure-fire indicator of a mass mailing); thus when the envelope is opened all contents are removed together, and the recipient's attention comes first to the cover letter (Example 5.4). This is accomplished by first folding the questionnaire into thirds so that the top portion, containing the study title and respondent identification number, is visible. The bottom part of the folded questionnaire is tucked under the flap of the business reply envelope, which has been laid on the table with the address side down. Then both the questionnaire and business reply envelope are placed on the middle third of the cover letter. To complete the folding, the bottom third of the cover letter is folded over the questionnaire first and the top third last. The completed packet is then inserted into the mailout envelope with the questionnaire resting right-side up.

SELECTING THE MAILOUT DATE

A mailing date early in the week is recommended. We prefer to have the respondent receive the questionnaire as soon after the mailout date as possible. Putting questionnaires into the mail on Monday or Tuesday makes it possible for even those questionnaires that must be forwarded to a new address to arrive the same week they are mailed. However, Monday mailout also presents some problems. Because of the weekend buildup, mail is heavier that day than any other day of the week. We prefer not to add to that burden and the increased likelihood of clerical errors it entails. Also, we prefer that all mailings (follow-ups) go out on the same day of the week, and a Tuesday mailing is most helpful when sending questionnaires only to nonrespondents (as desired in later mailings). This allows for convenient handling of the weekend mail and the removal of a substantial number of additional names from the follow-up mailouts.

Finally, we avoid mailing close to holidays and during the entire month of December. Any holiday means a temporary back-up of mail and an increased likelihood that people are temporarily away from home. During the month of December people write and receive more letters than at any other time of the year, thus increasing the chances that a questionnaire will lie unanswered. This is *not* a good time to do a survey by the mail or any other method.

FOLLOW-UP MAILINGS

Without follow-up mailings, response rates would be less than half those normally attained by the TDM, regardless of how interesting the questionnaire or impressive the mailout package. This finding, based on numerous

Example 5.4   How to Fold the Mailout Package

Step 1:   Fold the questionnaire
          into three parts.

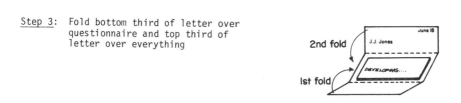

← upper right
  hand corner

Step 2:   Insert flap of business reply
          envelope over bottom of
          front page.

Step 3:   Fold bottom third of letter over
          questionnaire and top third of
          letter over everything

2nd fold

1st fold

Step 4:   Place in mailout envelope.

surveys, makes a carefully designed follow-up sequence imperative. A well-planned follow-up is more than a reminder service. Each mailing provides a fresh opportunity for the researcher to appeal for the return of a questionnaire, using a slightly new approach. The TDM follow-up procedures include three carefully timed mailings, each of which differs substantially from the others.

The follow-up procedures in the TDM are based in part on a consideration of how successful face-to-face interviewers go about persuading prospective respondents to be interviewed. Ordinarily an interviewer introduces him or herself, briefly describes the reason for being there, and politely asks for permission to begin the interview, all of which may take as little as a minute or two. If the respondent agrees, the interviewer's attempts to persuade cease, and most of the arguments that could have been employed will go unused. Giving the entire sales pitch to someone who is unlocking his or her screen door is not only unnecessary, but can make an otherwise receptive person become quite hostile. If, on the other hand, the prospect hesitates or says no, the interviewer will likely give more information about the study, offer more reasons why it is important, and emphasize why that particular respondent is essential to the study's success. When difficulties are encountered, most interviewers attempt to react to the concerns they detect in the respondent's behavior. Various arguments are used until they find one that works. In the decisive moments that determine whether the result will be reluctant acquiescence or total refusal, the interchange may become emotionally charged. Finally, in a last ditch effort to turn a near certain refusal into a completed interview, the interviewer may broach the limits of allowable behavior, perhaps disassociating him or herself somewhat from the sponsors of the study and asking for a personal favor that will "help me get paid." In short, the interviewer's attempts at persuasion are sometimes minimal and sometimes great, often building to a crucial and decisive conclusion.

The design of our follow-ups seeks to emulate certain (but not all) aspects of the successful interviewer's behavior. Specifically, each follow-up mailing differs somewhat from the one that preceded it, as attempts are made to invoke new and more persuasive appeals. Further, the appeals are designed to crescendo, with later follow-ups being stronger attempts at persuasion than preceding ones. The obvious difficulty that distinguishes the situation of the face-to-face interviewer from that of the mail researcher is that the latter has little or no feedback from respondents. This lack of feedback, other than the knowledge that a previous message did not get the desired response, makes it impossible to vary the appeal to hit the major concerns of each respondent. At best, the researcher can only guess at the predominant reasons for nonresponse and incorporate appeals to overcome them into all follow-up correspondence.

The realization that every respondent must be appealed to in the same way leads to our use of a relatively "reserved" approach throughout. Although emotionally intense arguments may sometimes produce results, we believe they would appear reckless and offensive when handled over a period of weeks, rather than in a few short and easily forgotten moments on someone's doorstep. Therefore, we avoid them, attempting instead to increase the intensity of the appeals only to a level that is not threatening and that stays within the bounds of normal business practice when a voluntary, yet important matter of business is pursued.

The three mailings that comprise the complete follow-up sequence are given here, identified by the number of weeks that elapsed after the original mailout.

One Week: *A postcard reminder sent to everyone. It serves as both a thank you for those who have responded and as a friendly and courteous reminder for those who have not.*

Three Weeks: *A letter and replacement questionnaire sent only to nonrespondents. Nearly the same in appearance as the original mailout, it has a shorter cover letter that informs nonrespondents that their questionnaire has not been received, and appeals for its return.*

Seven Weeks: *This final mailing is similar to the one that preceded it except that it is sent by certified mail to emphasize its importance. Another replacement questionnaire is enclosed.*

The First Follow-Up

Most people who answer questionnaires do so almost immediately after they receive them. A questionnaire that lies unanswered for a week or more is not very likely to be returned. In repeated studies we observed that half the return envelopes are postmarked within two or three days after being received by respondents. After that time, the number of postmarked returns declines, sharply at first and then gradually, but nonetheless persistently.

The inevitably high nonresponse to any given mailing is probably due less to conscious refusals than either unrealized good intentions or the lack of any reaction at all. Questionnaires that are well constructed and accompanied by a carefully composed cover letter are often laid aside with firm plans to look at them later. As each day passes without the questionnaire being looked at, it becomes a lower priority, until it is completely forgotten, lost, or unknowingly thrown away.

Thus the postcard follow-up is not written to overcome resistance, but rather to jog memories and rearrange priorities. It is timed to arrive just after the original mailing has produced its major effect, but before each person's questionnaire has had time to be buried under more recent mail. One week is an appropriate interval of time for making an appeal that, if carefully worded, conveys a sense of importance. At the same time it does not sound impatient or unreasonable.

The precise wording of the card reflects still another concern. The first lines simply state that a questionnaire was sent to the respondent the previous week, and why (Example 5.5). This may appear to be a waste of precious space. However, for some respondents (the number of which surprised us at first) this is the first time they learn that a questionnaire was sent to them. The reasons for the original questionnaire not reaching them extend well beyond loss in the mail. The previous mailout is sometimes addressed incorrectly or is not forwarded (whereas for some unexplained reason the postcard is). In still other cases, another member of the family opens the envelope containing the questionnaire and fails to give it to the desired respondent, or it may have been skipped over and not opened at all. Whatever the reasons, we have often received letters in which we were advised that the sender would be delighted, or at least willing, to fill out a questionnaire—if only we would be kind enough to send them one.

Undoubtedly, most people who do not recall receiving a questionnaire will not bother to write for one. However, the knowledge that one was sent may stimulate them to query other members of their family (or organization), leading to its discovery. For others, the card may increase receptivity when a questionnaire finally does arrive in the mail, as a result of having been delayed for some unknown reason or as a matter of routine in the next follow-up. For those respondents who are fully aware of having received the questionnaire and still have it in their possession, the lead paragraph serves to remind them of it by coming quickly to the point.

The second paragraph of the card contains the crucial message the postcard is designed to convey. People who have already returned their questionnaires are thanked and those who have not are asked to do so "today," a time reference consistent with importance. This is followed by a sentence that

Example 5.5   Postcard Follow-up Sent 1 Week After Original Mailing

Date mailed	April 26, 1971
Tie to previous letter	Last week a questionnaire seeking your opinion about community growth problems now facing our country was mailed to you. Your name was drawn in a random sample of households in Washington.
Thanks to early responders	If you have already completed and returned it to us please accept our sincere thanks. If not, please do so today. Because
Why recipient is important	it has been sent to only a small, but representative, sample of Washington residents it is extremely important that yours also be included in the study if the results are to accurately represent the opinions of Washington residents.
Invitation to get replacement questionnaire	If by some chance you did not receive the questionnaire, or it got misplaced, please call me right now, collect (509-335-8623) and I will get another one in the mail to you today.
	Sincerely,
Pressed blue ball point signature	*Don A. Dillman*
Title	Don A. Dillman Project Director

amplifies the message of how important each recipient is to the success of the study, originally contained in the initial cover letter.

The third and final paragraph is an invitation to call for a replacement questionnaire if one is needed. It is aimed at both those who did not receive the original questionnaire and those who discarded it. The postcard is completed by the routine statement of appreciation and the researcher's name, title, and the pressed blue ball point pen signature.

The main reason for choosing a postcard over a letter for the first follow-up is convenience to both the researcher and the respondent. Also, it introduces variety by contrasting with the envelopes that contain the mailings that precede and follow it. The postcard is printed, usually by a multilith process, with slightly reduced type, a necessity for getting the message to fit. Actual postcards (rather than a postcard stock that would have to be stamped or metered) are normally used, but this is also a matter of convenience.

The respondent's name and address are individually typed on the reverse side, exactly as was done for the envelope of the initial mailout. The name is not repeated on the message side because this would require a further reduction of the print used for the message and, if typed on with a regular typewriter, would exhibit an awkward contrast.

The decision to send this postcard to all questionnaire recipients, whether they have responded or not, is simply a practical one. One week after the initial mailing is when the maximum number of returns usually arrive. It is simply too confusing to attempt to sort returns to save the minor postage costs of the cards. Even in small surveys with a sample of, say, a few hundred, there is usually no time to wait until a significant number of returns are in before addressing the postcard follow-up and still get it out on schedule. Another significant advantage of the blanket mailing is that the postcards can be (and should be) printed and addressed even before the first mailout and stored so that this work does not interfere in any way with the often confusing task of processing early returns.

The users of the TDM often ask what percentage of returns they should achieve by the end of the first and second mailings to know whether they are "on schedule" with what the method usually produces. The question is difficult to answer. To begin, we should note that the short span of time between the initial mailing and postcard follow-up makes it difficult to separate the response-inducing effects of the first two mailings. Typically, however, the reminder postcard is followed by a response burst that almost equals and occasionally surpasses that achieved by the first mailing. However, it must be recognized that some questionnaires whose return is triggered by the postcard would ultimately have been returned anyway. In five surveys of the general public conducted in four states, from 19 to 27 percent of questionnaires were mailed back prior to receipt of postcards.[6] After the postcard, but prior to the next follow-up, the percentage increment of responses ranged from 15 to 25 percent. It is significant that the range was so great, especially in light of the fact that the final response after the two remaining follow-ups was within a five point range from 70 to 75 percent. As we would expect, returns from the first two mailings tend to be greater in studies of specialized populations for whom final response rates are usually higher.

The Second Follow-Up

There is a marked difference between the content of the second follow-up and the mailings that precede it (Example 5.6). This letter has a tone of insistence that the previous contacts lack. Its strongest aspect is the first paragraph, in which recipients are told that their completed questionnaire has not yet been received. This message is one of the strongest forms of personalization, communicating to the respondent in an unequivocal way that he or she is indeed receiving individual attention. This strongly reinforces messages contained in previous letters that the respondent is important to the success of the survey.

However, most of this letter is devoted to a restatement of each respondent's importance to the study in terms quite different from those used in previous mailings. The social utility of the study is also emphasized once again, implying that the usefulness of the study is dependent on the return of the questionnaire. The recipient is also reminded which member of the household is to complete the questionnaire. The letter is completed by mention of the enclosed replacement questionnaire, the usual note of appreciation, and the now familiar pressed blue ball point pen signature. It is sent in the same type of envelope used for the initial mailing by first-class mail.

In developing the obviously stronger "sales pitch" of this letter, it is equally important not to over- or undersell. It is important that it show a greater intensity than preceding letters, but not be so strong that potential respondents become disgruntled. We believe the letter appears sterner and more demanding when considered in isolation than when read by the respondent in the context of having already been asked to make an important contribution to an important study. If the study lacked social importance or had a frivolous quality about it, the letter would probably seem quite inappropriate to the respondent and would produce a negative reaction.

Ordinarily this letter is not reproduced until questionnaires are returned from previous mailings in considerable quantity. This provides an excellent opportunity to gather feedback on problems encountered by respondents. For every respondent who writes to ask a question, it is likely that many more have a similar question but do not take time to write. Thus a postscript to the follow-up letter is sometimes added in hopes of answering questions that may

Example 5.6   Second Follow-up Letter

WASHINGTON STATE UNIVERSITY

PULLMAN, WASHINGTON 99163

DEPARTMENT OF RURAL SOCIOLOGY
Room 23, Wilson Hall

Date mailed

May 11, 1971

Oliver Jones
2190 Fontana Road
Spokane, Washington 99467

Tie to previous
communication

Recognize importance
of recipient

Usefulness of study

Why recipient is
important

Who should
complete it

Appreciation

Pressed blue ball
point signature

Title

Feedback based on
questions asked by
respondents

About three weeks ago I wrote to you seeking your opinion on the
kinds of communities in which you would like and not like to live.
As of today we have not yet received your completed questionnaire.

Our research unit has undertaken this study because of the belief
that citizen opinions should be taken into account in the formation
of public policies for the planning and development of communities
in which people will live in the future.

I am writing to you again because of the significance each questionnaire has to the usefulness of this study. Your name was drawn
through a scientific sampling process in which every household in
Washington had an equal chance of being selected. This means that
only about one out of every 375 people in Washington households
are being asked to complete this questionnaire. In order for the
results of this study to be truly representative of the opinions of
all Washington residents it is essential that each person in the
sample return their questionnaire. As mentioned in our last letter,
the questionnaire from <u>your household</u> should be completed by an
<u>adult female</u>. If there is no adult female present, then it should
be completed by an adult male.

In the event that your questionnaire has been misplaced, a replacement is enclosed.

Your cooperation is greatly appreciated.

Cordially,

Don A. Dillman
Project Director

P.S. A number of people have written to ask when results will be
available. We hope to have them out sometime next month.

have been suggested to the researcher by such feedback. The postscript also
suggests that the study is important inasmuch as the researcher is examining
early returns and trying to deal with respondent concerns.

It is essential to send a replacement questionnaire with the follow-up letter.
The 3 weeks that have elapsed since the first mailing make it probable that the
original questionnaire, if it has not been lost or thrown away, will at least be
difficult to find. In one of our early studies we made the mistake of not
enclosing a replacement questionnaire. Not only did we get a considerable
quantity of cards and letters requesting a copy of the questionnaire to which it
was necessary to respond, but even after this effort the total response was
only half that usually obtained for the second follow-up.

Unfortunately, a replacement questionnaire can create problems. It is possible that someone may fill out two questionnaires instead of only the one intended, or perhaps they will give it to a spouse or friend to complete. Although this occasionally happens (as evidenced by returns with duplicate identification numbers) the frequency is so low as to be of little concern. Perhaps the greatest difficulty rests with those respondents who *did* fill out and return the earlier questionnaire only to be informed that the researcher did not receive it. This underscores the great importance of an accurate identification system and the need to hold the follow-up mailing to the last minute so that respondents whose questionnaires have just been received can be deleted. Scheduling this follow-up a full 2 weeks after the postcard reminder allows responses to dwindle to a small trickle, considerably lowering the chance that someone who has sent in a questionnaire will receive another one. Further, the additional time and subsequently smaller number of required follow-ups reduces postage and clerical costs considerably.

The Third Follow-Up

This request, the final effort to elicit a response, exhibits a greater overall intensity than any of those which precede it (Example 5.7). However, this is not because of the wording of the cover letter, which in fact is somewhat softer than that of the preceding one. Rather, its insistent nature stems from the simple fact that it is a fourth request, *and* it is being sent by certified mail—a postage rate that requires the recipient to acknowledge delivery with his or her signature. Because these factors raise the intensity to a high level, the relaxed wording of the cover letter emphasizes explanations of why this additional follow-up is sent and why certified mail is used. The now familiar social utility argument and the message of individual importance are repeated once more, in words different from any used previously.

The use of certified mail entails several implications. The cost is considerable—60¢ plus regular first-class postage. This charge allows for delivery to the specified address and the securing of the signature of whoever happens to be there and is willing to accept delivery by signing for it. This is the minimal service, and the one we use. However, for an additional 45¢, a receipt acknowledging delivery can be requested, and for still an additional fee of 60¢ it is possible to specify that the addressee be the one to sign for the letter. If no one is available to sign for it, the delivery person leaves a "notice of attempt to deliver certified mail," and the recipient must go to the post office to get it. The letter is held for 10 days before being returned to the sender as "unclaimed."

The effectiveness of the certified mailout is substantial. Its use in five statewide surveys of the general public was responsible for raising response

Example 5.7   Third Follow-up Letter

WASHINGTON STATE UNIVERSITY

PULLMAN, WASHINGTON 99163

DEPARTMENT OF RURAL SOCIOLOGY
Room 23, Wilson Hall

Date mailed

June 7, 1971

Oliver Jones
2190 Fontana Road
Spokane, Washington 99467

Tie to previous
communications

I am writing to you about our study of citizen preferences for community living. We have not yet received your completed questionnaire.

Recognize importance
of recipient

The large number of questionnaires returned is very encouraging. But, whether we will be able to describe accurately how Washingtonians feel on these important issues depends upon you and the others who have not yet responded. This is because our past experiences suggest that those of you who have not yet sent in your questionnaire may hold quite different preferences for community living than those who have.

Why recipient
is important

Usefulness of
the study

This is the first statewide study of this type that has ever been done. Therefore, the results are of particular importance to the many citizens, community planners, and lawmakers now considering what kinds of community growth should be encouraged (and for that matter discouraged) so as to best meet the needs of persons like yourself. The usefulness of our results depends on how accurately we are able to describe what the people of Washington want.

Importance of recipient
to study's usefulness

Why sent by certified
mail

It is for these reasons that I am sending this by certified mail to insure delivery. In case our other correspondence did not reach the person in your household whose response is needed (adult female, unless there is none in which case an adult male should respond), a replacement questionnaire is enclosed. May I urge you to complete and return it as quickly as possible.

Reminder

I'll be happy to send you a copy of the results if you want one. Simply put your name, address, and "copy of results requested" on the back of the return envelope. We expect to have them ready to send early next Fall.

Appreciation

Your contribution to the success of this study will be appreciated greatly.

Most sincerely,

Pressed blue ball
point signature

Don A. Dillman
Project Director

Title

rates from an average of 59.0 percent to 72.4 percent, an increase of more than 13 percentage points.[7] On the average, then, the certified mailing elicited about one-third of the remaining unanswered questionnaires. The certified mailing produced a greater *relative* return, that is, the percentage of those dispatched in each mailing, than any mailing that preceded it. Its relative return was 33 percent, compared to a range of 24 to 29 percent of the number mailed for the earlier mailings. These results are even more impressive when we realize that those who responded to it had ignored three previous mailings and therefore might be classified as "hard core holdouts."

The benefits of the certified mailout extend beyond simply improving response rates. It tends to pick up greater portions of older, less-educated, and lower-income people, those most often missed by mail questionnaires. Thus our confidence in the representativeness of returns is improved. Another benefit of the certified letter is that it has proved very effective in eliciting explanatory notes from people who for some reason were ineligible for a study but had not previously considered it important enough to let the researcher know this. As a result, we are able to calculate response rates with greater accuracy.

It is to be expected that when an attempt is made to deliver certified letters, some respondents will not be at home, making a trip to the post office necessary. Although few are likely to be as inconvenienced or disgruntled as the cattle rancher who noted in rather colorful language on his completed questionnaire that he had to drive 40 miles to get it, some will likely be displeased.[8] Nonetheless, it is also true that the users of the certified letter follow-up have received relatively few complaints. We can only speculate about the reasons for its effectiveness and the general lack of negative response. However, we surmise that the use of certified mail probably does not seem unreasonable to respondents if they are convinced that the study is important, as intended by the wording of the earlier communications.

The possibility of inconvenience to some respondents has led some researchers to omit the certified mailout from their procedures and to use regular first-class mail for this final follow-up. Although less effective, such a follow-up invariably elicits some additional responses, perhaps half as many as the certified letter.[9] Another alternative that might be considered, although we know of no one who has used it in conjunction with the TDM, is the use of special delivery mail for the third follow-up. At a cost of $1.25 plus regular first-class postage, the U.S. Postal Service will make one attempt to contact the recipient. Unlike delivery of the certified letter, this attempt is not a part of regular delivery activities, except in certain rural areas. Instead, it is made individually just after the letter arrives in the local post office. If no one is at home to receive the letter, for which no signature is necessary, a note is left on the door, and the letter is placed in the mail box. The obvious drawback to the use of special delivery is its high cost, more than double that for certified mail. However, the aura of importance created by special delivery seems likely to enhance response, perhaps as much or more than the certified technique.

Still More Follow-Ups?

Three follow-ups is the maximum we have used. However, we know of two TDM studies in which additional follow-ups were made. Goudy, in conducting some small community studies in Iowa, followed the third mailing with attempts to conduct face-to-face interviews.[10] In his survey of the general public he was successful in raising the obtained response rate from 78.2 percent (following the certified mail follow-up) to 96.0 percent. Thus he was successful in completing interviews with three out of every four of those who had failed to respond to the mail questionnaire. The obvious problem with this technique is cost, which in many instances is the reason face-to-face interviews were not used in the first place.

The effectiveness of a telephone call as an additional follow-up has also been demonstrated. In a crime trend survey in Texas conducted by St. Louis, who for the most part followed the procedures of the mail TDM, those who had not responded after the certified mail follow-ups were contacted by telephone. Of the 50 people contacted, 31 interviews were completed over the telephone, and several additional mail returns were obtained.[11]

These two studies suggest that it is possible to increase the response rate more than we have by our regular follow-up procedures. Nevertheless, the additional benefits of a higher response rate must be weighed against the cost and the value of the additional follow-ups to the analyses to be conducted. These are questions that only the researcher can satisfactorily answer.

DYNAMICS OF THE IMPLEMENTATION PROCESS

There is more to implementing a mail survey than the ordered series of events described in this chapter. Once the first mailing is dispatched, feedback from respondents and other events, only some of which can be anticipated, require considerable attention from the researcher. Sometimes on-the-spot modifications of the implementation process are necessary. Such concerns extend through all four mailings.

Handling Undelivered Questionnaires

Usually one of the first problems to present itself is the return of undelivered questionnaires. Immediate attention often makes remailing possible and prevents wasting scheduled follow-ups. As shown in Example 5.8, the reasons provided by the U.S. Postal Service for nondelivery generally fit into four categories. The first relates to a change of residence by respondents. Occasionally people move without leaving a forwarding address. Most movers leave a forwarding address, but U.S. Postal Service regulations keep it on record for only 1 year. If the move was within the same city or county, it is sometimes possible to locate the person by consulting the local telephone or city directories. The latter sometimes contains employment information that allows tracing the person to a new address through his or her employer.

Example 5.8   Reasons Given by U.S. Postal Service for Undelivered Letters and Some Possible Actions for Handling Them

Problem	Some Possible Actions
Moved	
Moved, left no address	Place call to respondent
Moved, not forwardable	
Forwarding address expired	Check city directory and try listed place of employment for new address
Possible Errors	
Not known at address	
Not deliverable as addressed	
Addressee unknown.	Check for clerical errors
Insufficient address	Try calling respondent's household
No such street	
No such number	
No such office in the state.	Check with Postal Service
Refusal	
Refused.	Usually none
Unclaimed.	Remail at a later date
Deceased.	Drop from sample

Through these various efforts it is often possible to remail a sizable portion of the questionnaires that were not forwarded.

The second general reason for undelivered questionnaires is categorized here as "possible errors." This categorization seems appropriate because the main causes for "addressee unknown," "no such street," and so on, are clerical errors. When a questionnaire is returned for any of these reasons, we first check our processing procedures and sample sources to see if an incorrect address was used. If this procedure does not identify the problem, an attempt is made to locate the respondent's telephone number and to call the household, thus reverting to the procedures used for those known to have moved. Some problems are unique to certain surveys. In one of our statewide surveys nearly all the letters for one rural community were returned. The reason for this problem was that the addresses reported in the sample list (telephone directory) were different from those used by the U.S. Postal Service. In one state it was found that nearly 10 percent of the addresses taken from telephone directories were inadequate for mailing purposes.[12] A consultation with the local post office was required to solve that problem. In another case the sample list for a metropolitan county reported an unincorporated community that had no post office. This too required consultation with the post office and ultimately telephone calls to the respondents to get the questionnaire correctly mailed.

A third category of problems reported in the notation system used by the U.S. Postal Service are letters that are refused or unclaimed. Generally, refusals are not a problem until later mailings, part cularly the one that is certified, when respondents recognize the envelope and presumably choose not to accept delivery. In these cases follow-up attempts are usually not made. The questionnaires that are unclaimed from earlier mailings may have simply lain in the mailbox for a period of time without being picked up. This suggests that the person may be temporarily gone, and remailing at a later time is often effective. However, some are clearly refusals, or the respondent chooses to leave the envelope in the mailbox, or, as in the case of the certified mailing, in the post office. Finally, the U.S. Postal Service marks letters of persons who are deceased with that notation and returns them to the sender unless other arrangements for handling the deceased person's mail have been made.

The success of our tracing procedures varies a great deal. As one would expect, they work best when sample lists are current and the number of undelivered letters is low. The remailing of questionnaires requires establishing new mailout dates for follow-up correspondence, creating additional work for the implementation of the study. However, the end result can be a significant increase of several percentage points in the final response rate.

Answering Respondent Questions

Another activity for which the researcher must be prepared is answering respondent inquiries and comments. Each mailing is likely to bring reactions other than a completed questionnaire from a few recipients. Among the more frequent are

The person you want is out of town for three weeks and cannot do it until he returns.

I would do the questionnaire except for the identification number on it.

I would do it except for the personal questions in it, which I don't think are any of your business.

I have only lived here for a few months, so I don't know enough about this community to answer your questionnaire.

I'm too old, but my son-in-law says he will fill it out if you really need it.

I filled out a questionnaire like this one 6 months ago and don't want to do it again.

Tell me how you got my name, and I'll do your questionnaire.

These comments are acknowledged, and our response to these various inquiries is determined both by philosophical concerns and response considerations. We feel that respondent questions, even "strange" ones, deserve a response, just as our request to complete a questionnaire deserves to be honored. Thus we make a point of answering them. In general, we respond as a well-trained interviewer would—attempting to convince people of their importance to the study. We explain why an identification number is used, why it is important to have old people as well as young people in the study, why the son-in-law would not be an acceptable substitute, and how we got their names. We feel the most appropriate approach is to be straightforward and honest and to thank them for writing to us.

Responding to Other Inquiries

Letters are also written to us by second parties on behalf of the questionnaire recipients. The most common of these indicate that the desired respondent is physically incapable of completing it, usually because of infirmities of old age. Another fairly typical one comes from the spouse of the requested respondents, who reports that the person is temporarily out of town. We respond to these letters in much the same way we answer respondent inquiries. Acknowledgement letters and "thank yous" go to the second parties who inform us that the desired respondent cannot complete the questionnaire. The aim of these letters is to thank them and also to assure them that the person's name is being removed from the sample list if that action is appropriate.

Still another kind of letter we have grown accustomed to receiving is from someone who has simply heard about the study, perhaps because a friend showed him or her a questionnaire. These sometimes come from media people or from those who would find the results useful in their work. These inquiries are handled in as helpful a way as possible, consistent with the study objectives. We found it particularly important to be prepared in large-scale surveys with a policy for handling requests for interviews or news stories. Our approach is to respond to such requests in much the same way we would answer respondents' questions, emphasizing the social utility of the study, the importance of every individual responding, and so on.

Scrutinizing Early Returns

When returns begin to come in, one of the first priorities is to open the business reply envelopes and scrutinize the questionnaires. Besides providing for the quick location of questions to which responses must be given in follow-up letters, certain problems can be identified. For example, in one study our questionnaires were trimmed in a way that produced a tendency for pages to stick together. This meant the return of several questionnaires for which sets of facing pages had been skipped. The immediate identification of this problem led us to institute a procedure whereby the missing two pages were photocopied, marked with the appropriate identification number, and returned to the respondent with a note stating, "In our routine check for completeness we noticed two pages were missed. It appears they may have stuck together and thereby been inadvertently missed . . ." Nearly two-thirds of those contacted returned the missing pages, significantly improving the quality of data. Usually, problems of this nature are not anticipated, making the close monitoring of early returns essential.

A second reason for checking early returns is that some problems may be identified that can be corrected by a follow-up letter. In one large survey of the "heads of households" conducted during the Vietnam War, in Washington (a state with numerous military bases), the first mailing elicited several responses indicating that the "head of the household" was out of the country. The realization that for each person writing to tell us of her situation there were probably a considerable number of others led us to include a postscript in our second follow-up. It began by noting, "A number of people have written to tell us . . ." *and* suggested that another member of the household complete the questionnaire.

Our discussion covers some, but by no means all, of the situations calling for special attention once the survey is underway. Each survey is different, with the survey topic, population, and sampling procedures all contributing to the existence of a unique set of circumstances. The important conclusion is that implementation activities do not simply take care of themselves once the survey questionnaires are in the mail. Much remains to be done.

THE IMPORTANCE OF PLANNING AHEAD

Observation of the attempts of others to utilize the mail TDM provides a seemingly constant reminder that the biggest problems do not stem from a lack of knowledge about what is to be done. Rather, the headaches come from the problems of getting everything to happen, and on time. The TDM is a carefully articulated set of procedures; the success of each is dependent on the success of others. The sources of the implementor's frustrations are many. For example, consider the following:

One researcher successfully obtained the monarch size stationery, ordered his letters printed, and only then discovered that no envelopes were available. They would have to be ordered and "might" be delivered in six weeks. Another underestimated the number of questionnaires and ran out when the certified mailout was being prepared. A reorder would have taken two weeks, putting her well behind schedule.

Still another underestimated his costs and had to completely forego the last follow-up.

In another instance the questionnaire was in a very rough draft stage when mailing dates were set and letters printed. In order to meet the mailout deadline, the questionnaire had to be sent to the printers with a number of glaring deficiencies.

The processing of return questionnaires was ignored in one study, until too close to the second follow-up, with the result that a considerable number of people who had already returned their questionnaires in ample time to be processed were informed that "As of today we have not received your questionnaire."

When working with users of the TDM, our optimism about the probable success of their proposed study increases greatly when the line of questioning begins to switch from "what to do" to how they should plan to "get it done." Many questions of this nature concern the staff required for the study and when each event should be accomplished. A frequent dilemma for those doing fairly large surveys, say samples of a thousand or more, is whether to depend on a regular secretarial staff or to hire temporary personnel. Sometimes dependence on a regular secretarial staff that handles work for a number of people creates the hazard that just when their time is most needed, for example, a few days prior to the second follow-up when letters to nonrespondents must be processed, the staff is preempted for other work. Hiring completely different people also creates difficulties, however. Besides the usual problems associated with working with new people, the work flow for the TDM is inherently uneven, going from periods of crisis just before each mailing, to periods of little to do after each has been dispatched.

People have worked successfully with both situations. The fear of having a regular secretarial staff preempted just when they were most needed led one researcher to have all four mailouts to all respondents typed prior to the beginning of the survey. Although this prevented the possibility of modifying a later letter, that risk was deemed worth it, as was the extra cost for questionnaires, letters, and envelopes. All deadlines were met without a hitch. Another researcher in a very similar situation hired a separate staff, but planned the workload so that the same people typed, processed returns, and coded questionnaires, thus maintaining an even work flow throughout the implementation process.

No matter whether researchers use an existing secretarial staff, hire their own, or do most of the work themselves, the time spent estimating how long it takes to address and sign each letter, stuff each envelope, code each questionnaire, and so forth, is time well spent. It may prevent having to make a decision to switch to a "Dear Citizen" type of letter, or make other deviations from the TDM that affect response rates. At the very least it should provide for a smoother flow of work and help avoid crises.

CONCLUSION

Recently, near the end of a long and somewhat tedious training session, a would-be user of the TDM leaned back in her chair and wearily observed, "It used to be that a mail questionnaire was a technique that would give a little something for almost nothing. What you have spent this afternoon telling us is that we can get a lot more, but to get it means we have to give a lot more." Her comment summed up rather concisely the reactions of many other users. Doing repeated drafts of questionnaires and cover letters, making conscious decisions about several dozen details of the implementation process, and managing a precisely timed series of events requires time and mental effort not usually associated with mail questionnaires. Yet, to maximize response, we doubt there is a simple alternative.

The reader may be tempted to search through this chapter for the half dozen "easy to apply" techniques that assure response. Indeed, some who have used the mail TDM have been very forthright in declaring their skepticism about the importance of a few seemingly minor omissions, for example, substituting address labels for individually typed addresses or a stamped signature for the recommended pressed ball point pen signature.

Our response to these queries is equally forthright—in many cases we simply do not know what the effect might be. It must be recognized that the mail TDM is based on a theory of response that must be evaluated empirically. Although we have found it successful on an overall basis, for the most part the effects of its constitutent parts have not been tested. Examining the relative effects of the several dozen elements involved in the TDM requires expensive experimentation that can only be done over a considerable period of time. This is because tests for the effects of specific elements in the TDM, none of which can be expected to be very large by itself, require large sample sizes. In addition, the possible interactions among techniques as well as the possible differing effects on various populations and study topics must be taken into account. Complicating these matters even further is the realization that effects on response quality are as important as effects on response quantity. Finally, cost effectiveness must also be considered.

It seems a high priority that carefully designed experiments be conducted to determine whether response rates and response quality are affected by

Substitution of computer-printed address labels, which can be printed quite cheaply, for individually typed names on envelopes.

Elimination of personalization procedures such as individual names on letters and the pressed ball point pen signature from *some* of the mailings.

Shortening the interval between follow-ups, thereby decreasing the possibility of contamination from events intervening between early and late returns.

Substitution of stamped return for business reply envelopes.

Monetary incentives.

Substitution of telephone calls for one or more of the follow-ups.

Use of colored ink and occasional illustrations in the questionnaire.

It takes little imagination to think of many more worthwhile experiments that might result in the improvement of the mail TDM.

Our concern with improvements for a method we refer to as "total" may strike some readers as somewhat contradictory. However, as noted in Chapter 1, we use the term "total" to emphasize our assumption that the best quality and quantity of response can be achieved when all aspects of the questionnaire construction and survey implementation processes are subject to design considerations. Thus "total" refers to our concern with the total survey process. The question of the maximum response mail questionnaires are capable of producing remains open and is expected to remain so for some time. To date we can only say that the response rates are much higher than those which gave the mail survey the reputation of being one of the step children of survey research, a view we now believe to be safely behind us.

NOTES

1. Such procedures were pioneered in a "Life Satisfaction" study conducted by Duane Alwin, John Finney, and Luther Otto at Washington State University, but evaluation of the effort is not yet available.

2. "Those Confidential Reader Surveys," *Los Angeles Times,* November 3, 1975

3. William M. Kephart and Marvin Bressler, "Increasing the Response to Mail Questionnaires: A Research Study," *Public Opinion Quarterly, 22,* 1958, pp. 123–132; W. L. Slocum, L. T. Empey, and H. S. Swanson, "Increasing Response to Questionnaires and Structured Interviews," *American Sociological Review, 21,* 1956, pp. 221–225.

4. Don A. Dillman, "Increasing Mail Questionnaire Response in Large Samples of the General Public," *Public Opinion Quarterly, 36,* 1972, pp. 254–257.

5. Deanna Rankos, personal communication, 1975.

6. Don A. Dillman, James A. Christenson, Edwin H. Carpenter, and Ralph M. Brooks, "Increasing Mail Questionnaire Response: A Four-State Comparison," *American Sociological Review, 39,* 1974, pp. 744–756.

7. *Ibid.*

8. Slocum, Empey, and Swanson, *op. cit.*

9. James S. House, Wayne Gerber, and Anthony J. McMichael, "Increasing Mail Questionnaire Response: A Controlled Replication and Extension," *Public Opinion Quarterly, 41,* 1977, pp. 95–99.

10. Willis J. Goudy, "Interim Nonresponse to a Mail Questionnaire: Impacts on Variable Relationships," Iowa Agriculture and Home Economics Experiment Station, Journal Paper No. J–8456, Iowa State University, 1976.

11. Alfred St. Louis, "The Texas Crime Trend Survey," Statistical Analysis Center, Texas Department of Public Safety, 1976.

12. James A. Christenson, personal communication, 1975.

Chapter Six

CONSTRUCTING TELEPHONE QUESTIONNAIRES

On the surface, conducting a telephone interview may appear simple—as easy as reproducing a mail questionnaire (or one used for face-to-face interviews), adding a few words of verbal introduction, drawing names from a telephone directory, dialing the telephone, and asking the questions. However, this is not a very realistic view of what is actually involved in telephone surveys.

For one thing, excellent mail questionnaires do not make very good telephone questionnaires. There are several reasons. First, telephone interviews depend entirely on verbal instead of visual communication. Thus concern with how a questionnaire looks gives way to a concern of how it sounds. Second, an interviewer who is heard, but never seen, becomes an intermediary between the questionnaire and the respondent. This means, on one hand, that some questionnaire construction requirements can be relaxed, including the requirement that the content be sufficiently enticing to serve effectively as the questionnaire's own advocate. On the other hand, it means there is a possibility that interviewers will read questions incorrectly and make other errors. A third difference is that the telephone is often chosen because the researcher has a very short time in which to complete a study. This means that ways to facilitate rapid completion of the survey and processing of results must be given careful attention. Fourth, special requirements are imposed by the use of random digit dialing, a sampling method that frequently leads to choosing the telephone method over mail methods for household surveys. These basic differences between mail and telephone surveys mean that the various aspects of conducting mail and telephone surveys are inherently different and must be treated as such.

Not only do telephone surveys differ from mail surveys, but, just as important, they differ a great deal from face-to-face interview surveys. Whereas the face-to-face interviewer can use visual aids to help explain questions and can observe the respondent's facial expressions for hints that something is misunderstood, the telephone interviewer can do neither. When interviewing by telephone, one is totally dependent on what can be verbally communicated, one word at a time. Thus questionnaires that are quite adequate for face-to-face interviews may be totally inadequate for telephone interviews.

Although the specific principles of questionnaire construction and implementation discussed here for the telephone are quite different from those discussed in Chapters 4 and 5 for the mail questionnaire, the principles of the Total Design Method (TDM) hold. Thus exchange theory provides the theoretical basis for shaping each aspect of the TDM telephone survey to create the most favorable impression of the study and its sponsors. The concern with planning and administration is even greater than for the mail TDM, because it is necessary to bring all aspects of the telephone process together at one time when the actual interviews are to be done. This chapter and the next one describe the telephone TDM for conducting surveys. This chapter concentrates solely on the process of constructing the telephone questionnaire. All aspects of the implementation process are discussed in Chapter 7.

SERVING THREE AUDIENCES

The design of the telephone questionnaire is shaped by the needs of three audiences: respondents, interviewers, and coders. Each audience has distinct needs that usually cannot be dismissed in favor of the questionnaire construction requirements imposed by the others. Therefore the construction process necessitates an understanding of the problems faced by each audience, where their needs conflict, and where necessary compromises must be made. This situation contrasts sharply with that for the mail questionnaire, in which the needs of the respondent are always deemed paramount.

Needs of the Respondent

The task of responding to a telephone interview is difficult. Often respondents are called to the telephone unexpectedly and are asked to do something that they do not yet fully understand. Their immediate feelings may be reluctance, anxiety, or even excitement. In addition, people may be caught in the midst of activities they seek to continue even while on the phone, for example, preparing dinner, opening mail, or watching television. As a result, the respondent's attention may be focused only partially on the interview. We are reminded here of one survey in which veterinarians were interviewed. A respondent was reached over his speaker telephone system while in the midst of surgery. Although he indicated his willingness to answer questions while continuing the operation, the surprised interviewer was relieved when her suggestion that she call back later was accepted. Although cases of divided attention are rarely so dramatic, the consequences of impaired respondent concentration for understanding questions and providing valid answers may be severe.

Being interviewed by telephone requires a skill that is not well developed in many people. Respondents must rely solely on what is heard to formulate a response. A mispronounced word or the failure of respondents to understand a word for reasons beyond the control of both interviewers and respondents (e.g., line static) may mean that a question becomes entirely incomprehensible. Whereas respondents to a mail questionnaire may visually scan it at their own pace, reread certain parts if needed, and hesitate on single words, this is obviously not possible in the telephone interview. Since the pace of the telephone interview tends to be set by the interviewer, the respondent is put under some pressure to reply sooner and in a less relaxed manner than is required under face-to-face interviews. Another occasional problem for telephone respondents is that anxiety, coupled with the need for intense concentration, causes them to tire quickly. Concentration may be impaired further by the location of the telephone in or near centers of activity that are relatively inconvenient for interviews. These include the kitchen where someone else is preparing a meal, the family room where children are watching television, or a hallway where, in addition to traffic, there may be no place to sit.

These considerations entail several implications. Subtle ways must be found to discourage respondents from beginning or continuing with other activities that may distract their attention from the interview. For example, some formats provide the opportunity for respondents to answer without really hearing the questions, for example, a long series of similar attitudinal items requiring a simple yes/no answer, a problem that can be corrected by insertion of open-ended questions that require respondents to formulate their own response. Our point here is not that the former types of questions should be avoided, but only that great care should be taken in deciding question order and format. In lengthy telephone interviews, questions that generate respondent interest should be included even though they may not be critically important to the study objectives. Whereas in the mail TDM interest getting questions are used to motivate respondents to begin the questionnaire, they are employed periodically in the telephone TDM to first obtain and then maintain the respondent's undivided attention. Our experience with telephone interviews suggests that the issue is not whether committed respondents will complete the interview (once they start, few respondents terminate in the midst of the interview), but whether they will lose their concentration and thus their ability to answer questions fully and accurately.

Great care must also be taken in wording questions to determine that they not only read well, but also sound well. Further, abruptly switching from one topic to another may momentarily confuse respondents. To avoid this, appropriate transitional statements may need to be added. Even redundancy that is out of place on a mail questionnaire or face-to-face interview may be necessary in a telephone interview. In summary, the complete dependence on oral communication requires that careful attention be paid to the communicability of questions and the overall questionnaire format to ensure respondent concentration.

Needs of the Interviewer

Worthless or inaccurate information can result just as easily from the incorrect reading of questions or erroneous recording of answers by interviewers as from respondents' misinterpretations. Thus the interviewer's task in seeing that good interviews are completed is at least as important as the respondent's task of maintaining concentration.

Consider what interviewers may be faced with when interviewing someone in a sample of the general public. Once they have read the introduction to whomever answers the telephone, they must determine who in that household is eligible to respond and get them to the phone. The initial few seconds of a call are very decisive in determining whether a successful interview will take place. It may be essential for the interviewer to respond quickly yet concisely to such respondent reactions as, "How do I know this is authentic?" "I don't know anything about what you want, so call someone else," or simply "I have something on the range and it is burning." Although some respondents eagerly run up the researcher's telephone bill, many others are likely to be nervous and proceed only with the utmost encouragement and coaxing.

As the interview proceeds it is necessary to simultaneously keep the conversation moving, write answers while mentally preparing to read the next question, avoid long blank spots created by the need to write lengthy verbatim answers, listen intently for indications of changing mood, record unsolicited comments that may be useful for purposes of the interpretation, hold the telephone receiver, and turn the pages of the questionnaire. Interviewers do not have access to nonverbal cues like a shrug of the shoulders or changes in facial expressions. In general, interviewers are unaware of interruptions to a respondent's concentration unless they are verbally communicated to them or can be heard in the background. At the same time, unless the interviewer provides the appropriate feedback, the respondent cannot tell how long it is taking the interviewer to write down answers and thus when to provide the next bit of information.

Under these conditions it should come as no surprise that conducting one interview after another and going repeatedly over the same questions can be quite exhausting. The result is that interviewer mistakes are not only possible, but highly probable. A questionnaire that (1) includes word combinations that are hard to read, (2) requires memorizations of which questions to skip if certain answers are given, (3) necessitates frequent turning of pages, and (4) has irregular placement of questions on pages, invites interviewer mistakes. Taking into account the interviewer's comfort and convenience is not a matter of luxury, but an essential part of telephone survey design.

The fact that respondents never see the questionnaire means that it is possible to design its physical appearance almost exclusively with the interviewer in mind. In practice, this means adopting practices consciously avoided in mail questionnaires, for example, full-size rather than photographically reduced page format, occasional use of partially filled pages to separate sections, and color coding of various sections of the questionnaire. The construction practices outlined in this chapter place a high priority on meeting the needs of the interviewer.

Needs of the Coder

Since the telephone survey is often chosen over the mail or face-to-face survey because of its speed of implementation, methods of facilitating rapid data compilation are important. Precoding, that is, identifying the computer card columns and punches for each response category on the questionnaire, is highly desirable. Although this practice is avoided in our mail questionnaire procedure because we wish to eliminate all information not relevant to the respondent, the fact that respondents never see the telephone questionnaire makes this practice acceptable. Although the coder's needs are of lower priority than those of the interviewer, precoding marks and additional instructions for coders usually do not interfere with the requirements of the interviewer.

WORDING THE QUESTIONS:
THE SPECIAL PROBLEMS OF TELEPHONE QUESTIONNAIRES

The fact that one can ask certain kinds of questions over the telephone that cannot be handled very well by mail questionnaires often leads to the telephone survey being chosen over the mail survey. A major example of such advantages is the likelihood of getting far better responses to open-ended questions in telephone interviews. With skillful probing by interviewers high-quality responses to such questions are probable, overcoming one of the most nagging limitations of mail questionnaires. Another advantage is the ability to exercise complete control over the order in which questions are asked. This prevents respondents from scanning the entire questionnaire before settling down to complete it and thereby being predispositioned to answer certain questions in ways they otherwise would not. An additional advantage concerns the interviewer's ability to obtain answers to "objection-able" questions. A good telephone interviewer can often overcome a respondent's reluctance to answer particular questions. The interviewer's presence also helps to prevent difficult questions from being skipped and others from being inadvertently missed. Still another advantage of telephone interviews is the ease with which large numbers of screened questions, that is, questions that apply to some respondents but not others, may be handled. The complicated directions required for skipping sections of mail question-naires and the intimidating bulky appearance often necessitated by such sections are features of which the telephone respondent need not be aware.

Unfortunately, these advantages are often overshadowed by several problems of telephone interviews, a common denominator of which is complexity. The total reliance on the respondents' retention of what they hear, at a pace set by someone else, places very clear limits on what and how much can be asked to obtain adequate answers. In some cases, questions can be restructured to decrease and perhaps circumvent these difficulties. In the paragraphs that follow we identify common problems of complexity and suggest ways they have been overcome in telephone TDM surveys. Further, we concern ourselves with construction problems that result from the presence of an interviewer between the questionnaire and the respondent. Consistent with our theory of respondent behavior, our goal is to reduce the social costs associated with responding, including mental effort, embarrassment, and the belief that one's answers to unclear questions are worthless.

Questions That Are Too Long

The most common form of complexity is length. Long questions containing several ideas are highly prone to being misunderstood, with the possible result that the respondent arbitrarily chooses one of the offered response categories to prevent a lengthy repeat. Strict dependence on oral communication means that many questions that work in mail questionnaires simply cannot be asked in the same form on the telephone.

A seemingly easy solution to excessively long questions is found in the advice to "keep them short and simple." In general, we would endorse this prescription, but it is frequently impossible to follow without adversely affecting the research objectives. A survey on citizen reactions to a proposed change in state tax laws is a case in point.[1] Since data were to be collected for use by the state legislature, it was deemed essential that none of the key elements of the proposed tax package be omitted. After a number of attempts, the question was placed in a mail questionnaire format that was acceptable from the technical viewpoint of the tax analysts and at the same time understandable to respondents. Efforts to incorporate the same question in a companion telephone survey proved quite frustrating to respondents and interviewers alike. A second reading was usually necessary before respondents could answer.

The solution to this problem seemed paradoxical. It involved building in redundancy by summarizing the questions so respondents heard the essential parts more than once (Example 6.1). We call this a "key word summary." The obvious result was an even longer question, but the added length, combined with slight changes to put it in a more conversational form, helped the respondents mentally organize the entire question before attempting to answer. The key word summary has wide applicability, making it possible to utilize questions that might otherwise have to be simplified beyond recognition or omitted altogether.

Interviewers report another desirable effect of this key word summary. It concerns the fact that some respondents think they understand the question, but actually do not. Hearing a summary that they recognize as inconsistent with their understanding of the question results in a request for clarification. This gives interviewers an opportunity to repeat the question, with a good chance that they will have a respondent's undivided attention.

Too Many Response Categories

The problem of excessive length is not limited to the question itself. Researchers often want to identify many gradations of response to obtain a wider distribution of responses. This involves the use of several response categories (see Example 6.2). There are two fundamental problems with the use of many categories to record the responses of telephone interviewees. Remembering the categories is one, but this can usually be overcome through repetition. The other problem is potentially more serious. The listed order of the response categories often implies an order of feeling from extremely negative

Example 6.1   Reducing Complexity through Reorganization and Addition of a Key Word Summary

Recently a proposal to change the kinds of taxes we pay was made in our state legislature. Here is what it would do:

1. Eliminate all special property tax levies for the maintenance and operation of schools.

2. Eliminate the sales tax on groceries and prescription drugs.

3. Replace the revenue money lost with a new state graduated income tax. This would leave the total amount of taxes the same.

4. Fix the maximum rates of the graduated income tax and the present sales tax in the State Constitution so neither can be increased except by voter approval.

How do you feel about this proposal?
    (Circle number of answer that best describes your opinion)

        1 STRONGLY OPPOSED
        2 SOMEWHAT OPPOSED
        3 UNCERTAIN
        4 SOMEWHAT FAVORABLE
        5 STRONGLY FAVORABLE

Recently a proposal to change the kinds of taxes we pay was made in our state legislature. I would like to tell you about this proposal and find out how you feel about it. Here is what it would do.

First, two taxes would be eliminated, these include all special property tax levies for the operation of schools and all sales tax on groceries and prescription drugs.

The money lost would be replaced by a new state graduated income tax, which would leave the total amount of taxes collected the same.

Finally, the maximum rate for both the new income tax and the sales tax would be fixed in the State Constitution so neither could be increased except by voter approval.

So, what has been proposed is to eliminate all special property tax levies for schools and the sales tax on groceries and prescription drugs, and replace them with a state income tax and a sales tax rate fixed in the State Constitution.

How do you feel about the proposal? Are you strongly opposed, somewhat opposed, uncertain, somewhat favorable or strongly favorable?

        STRONGLY OPPOSED....1
        SOMEWHAT OPPOSED....2
        UNCERTAIN...........3
        SOMEWHAT FAVORABLE..4
        STRONGLY FAVORABLE..5

to extremely positive. Because the respondent can see the choices on a mail questionnaire or can read them from a list during a face-to-face interview, the implied order can easily be seen. It is unlikely that respondents could err by choosing an intermittent category, for example, "quite" as stronger than "very" in the mail questionnaire version of the community satisfaction question (which we have seen used in several surveys), shown in Example 6.2. However, it is not surprising for a telephone respondent to become confused over the categories. Although reducing the number of categories, as shown in Example 6.2, results in a loss of information, it may be advisable.

The difficulty of finding words to connote intensity of feelings frequently leads researchers to use hypothetical scales. For example:

Please indicate on a scale of zero to ten the extent to which you agree or disagree with each of the following statements. Ten means completely agree, zero means completely disagree. Five means you are "neutral" or "undecided." Use the other numbers to indicate degrees of feeling.

Our experience with this is mixed. Although some people are quick to grasp the technique, interviewers often have great difficulty explaining it to others. To date, we have not found it acceptable for obtaining considerable gradations in response categories, particularly on surveys of the general public.

Another method sometimes used in TDM telephone questionnaires to simplify a question with too many response categories is to break the question into two parts, first asking respondents for the direction of their feelings and then asking them the degree (or intensity) of their feelings. Breaking the question into two parts results in a reduction in memory requirements and thus the potential for respondent confusion.

This type of format adjustment is not limited to attitudinal statements. In one TDM telephone survey, we were faced with a question taken from a previous mail questionnaire for which each of the six answer categories were of considerable length, making the question nearly incomprehensible over the telephone (Example 6.3). Because of certain policy objectives of the survey, each answer category had to contain three pieces of essential information—the size of the largest city, the nature of surrounding suburbs or towns, and the amount of open country. Breaking the question into the two-step sequence greatly decreased the memory requirements, and respondents were able to handle it easily.

In theory, the two-step method has very wide applicability, because many questions can be so divided. However, this technique should not be used if there is a chance that answers to the first part would be affected by knowledge of the options offered in the second part. A question on population growth taken from recent mail and telephone surveys illustrates this problem. In the

Example 6.2   Reducing Complexity by Providing Fewer Response Categories

MAIL FORM:

How satisfied are you with your community?

```
1  VERY SATISFIED
2  QUITE SATISFIED
3  SOMEWHAT SATISFIED
4  SLIGHTLY SATISFIED
5  NEITHER SATISFIED NOR DISSATISFIED
6  SLIGHTLY DISSATISFIED
7  SOMEWHAT DISSATISFIED
8  QUITE DISSATISFIED
9  VERY DISSATISFIED
```

REVISED FOR TELEPHONE:

How satisfied are you with your community? Would you say you are very satisfied, somewhat satisfied, neither satisfied nor dissatisfied, somewhat dissatisfied, or very dissatisfied?

```
VERY SATISFIED . . . . . . 1
SOMEWHAT SATISFIED . . . . 2
NEITHER SATISFIED NOR
   DISSATISFIED . . . . . . 3
SOMEWHAT DISSATISFIED  . . 4
VERY DISSATISFIED. . . . . 5
```

mail version, respondents were asked whether they would like the population to

```
1  INCREASE AT A FASTER rate than the population of the United States
2  INCREASE AT THE SAME rate as the population of the United States
3  INCREASE AT A SLOWER rate than the population of the United States
4  STAY THE SAME as it is now
5  DECREASE
6  I DON'T KNOW
```

In the telephone version, respondents were first asked whether they wanted the population to increase, stay the same, or decrease. The second step of the sequence was to ask those who selected an "increase" response category to choose from among the three rates of increase options stated above. As revealed in Table 6.1, the results were dramatically different for the two surveys.

In the telephone questionnaire, over twice as many respondents chose "stay the same" than in the mail version. The proportion choosing "decrease" was about the same in both surveys. Thus the effect on other categories was for the most part limited to reducing the number who had chosen some rate of increase in the mail version. A plausible explanation for this difference is that, when asked to choose in a telephone interview among the three general categories of "increase," "stay the same," and "decrease," the lack of definition for *how much* increase discouraged responses in that

Example 6.3   Reducing Complexity by Dividing One Question into Two Steps

| MAIL FORM: | Here are some descriptions of different kinds of counties in which you might like to live. Each choice contains a different sized major city, different amounts of open-country, and some include suburbs or smaller towns. Suppose you would live in some part of any of these counties, in which one would you <u>most</u> like to live? (Circle number of choice) |

    1 <u>LARGE METROPOLITAN</u>: LARGEST CITY OF 500,000 OR
           MORE, MANY SUBURBS, VERY LITTLE OPEN-COUNTRY
    2 <u>MEDIUM METROPOLITAN</u>: LARGEST CITY OF 150,000
           TO 499,999, SEVERAL SUBURBS, SOME OPEN-COUNTRY
    3 <u>SMALL METROPOLITAN</u>: LARGEST CITY OF 50,000 TO
           149,999, FEW SUBURBS, CONSIDERABLE OPEN-COUNTRY
    4 <u>SEMI-URBAN</u>: LARGEST CITY OF 10,000 to 49,999,
           FEW SMALLER TOWNS, AND CONTAINS MUCH OPEN-COUNTRY
    5 <u>SEMI-RURAL</u>: LARGEST CITY OF 2,500 to 9,999, ONE OR
           TWO SMALLER TOWNS, MOSTLY OPEN-COUNTRY
    6 <u>RURAL</u>: LARGEST TOWN OF LESS THAN 2,500, SURROUNDED
           ENTIRELY BY OPEN-COUNTRY

| REVISED FOR TELEPHONE: | Next I want to ask about the kind of county in which you might like to live. Would you prefer a <u>metropolitan county</u>, i.e., one with a largest city of 50,000 or more people, plus suburbs and some open-country, or a <u>non-metropolitan county</u>, one with a largest city of less than 50,000 people, plus smaller towns and much open-country? |

                                   NON-METROPOLITAN....1
                                   METROPOLITAN........2

Which of these three sizes of metropolitan counties would you most prefer?

        a) one which has a largest city of 500,000 or more
            people, many suburbs, and very little open-country,
        b) one which has a largest city of 150,000 to 499,999
            people, several suburbs, and some open-country, or
        c) one which has a largest city of 50,000 to 149,999
            people, few suburbs, and considerable open-country.

                                500,000 plus........1
                                150,000 to 499,999..2
                                50,000 to 149,999...3

Which of these three sizes of non-metropolitan counties would you most prefer?

        a) one which has a largest city of 10,000 to 49,999
            people, few smaller towns, and contains much open-
            country,
        b) one which has a largest city of 2,500 to 9,999 people,
            one or two smaller towns, and is mostly open-country,
            or
        c) one which has a largest town of less than 2,500
            people surrounded by open-country

                                10,000 to 49,999....1
                                2,500 to 9,999......2
                                less than 2,500.....3

category. The respondents who were willing to accept some increase, for example, natural growth, but who do not want much of it, may have thought that "the same" was closer to their true feelings than some undefined increase. Thus they quite appropriately avoided any of the increase categories. This interpretation is supported by the observation that of the three increase

Table 6.1 **Comparison of Responses to Mail Questionnaire and Two-Step Revision for Telephone Surveys**

Response Categories	Mail Version	Telephone Two-Step Version
1 INCREASE AT A FASTER rate than the population of the United States	1.7	2.1
2 INCREASE AT THE SAME rate as the population of the United States	23.4	13.3
3 INCREASE AT A SLOWER rate than the population of the United States	30.9	7.3
4 STAY THE SAME as it is now	29.2	66.3
5 DECREASE	10.8	9.2
6 I DON'T KNOW	4.1	1.7

categories the choice closest to the "stay the same" category shows the greatest difference—nearly 24 percentage points—between the mail and telephone formats.[2]

Our conclusion is that breaking a question into two parts, with the first part consisting of three categories, thereby leaving the respondent to define the general boundaries among them, should be avoided. It seems best to limit the two-step method to questions in which an unmistakable dichotomy is declared in the first step, for example, increase-decrease, agree-disagree, or satisfied-unsatisfied. However, in reference to the larger problem of complexity, the two-step solution is generally more desirable than reducing the number of categories. The latter results in a loss of information and precision.

Problems in Ranking Categories

It is one thing to hand a list of, say, six or seven items to respondents and ask that they rank them from top to bottom, and quite another to read the same list over the telephone and ask for a similar ranking. Not only must telephone respondents remember all the items, but they must also perform the decidedly more difficult task of remembering the order in which they assign a rank to each item until the task is finished. Relatively few people have the memory capabilities to complete the task. The longer the list and the less familiar the items, the harder it is to rank them. Fortunately, there are several means of simplifying the task.

One mechanical solution to this problem is to ask the respondents to get a pencil and paper and write down the list when it is read over the phone. This has the advantage of retaining the precise question structure, but imposes an additional burden on respondents that they may not be willing to accept. In some households, paper and pencil are always kept by the telephone. In others, as noted by a friend who has young children with a penchant for drawing, the only way a sharpened pencil and pad of paper can be kept available is to have them under lock and key! Although perhaps a bit over-stated, we believe it unwise to operate under the assumption that paper and pencil will always be handy to the respondent.

Some researchers have suggested to us that response categories or even a copy of the questionnaire could be sent to respondents ahead of time to be used for reference when they are called. We have not seen the results of such trials and do not know how workable this approach might be. Although it would require considerable cooperation on the part of respondents, it seems to be a promising possibility and deserves consideration. Still another possibil-ity, and one we have found quite workable, is to change the format to a two-step sequence (Example 6.4). First, a new question is formulated in which the respondent is asked to evaluate each item, for example, in terms of whether they are favorable or unfavorable. This question is followed by a request to rank them. The first question is aimed at fixing each item in the respondent's mind, along with his or her general evaluation of it, making the ranking task that follows easier. This format also produces additional informa-tion that may be useful. It not only allows establishing an overall ranking, but it measures intensity of feeling in a way that shows the psychological distance between rankings.

Further modifications can be made, as shown in Example 6.4. After achiev-ing a rating for each item in terms of four categories, interviewers can ask respondents to rank only those groups to which they answered "much." Then they could be asked to do the same for those rated "some," and so on, until all seven groups are ranked. The example shown is a version prepared for the mail questionnaire. However, the general concept embodied in this revision, that is, asking for intensity of response and then for a ranking, is one we prefer for mail questionnaires as well, particularly where there is a large number of items. It helps prevent superficial scanning and assigning of rank without careful thought. Further, mail respondents can refer back to those items to which they reacted most favorably and then choose the ones to rank the highest. The reason we place greater emphasis on the format in this chapter is that the reasons for adopting it are somewhat more compelling for the telephone interview than the mail questionnaire. The greatest drawback to the use of this format involves the time required to administer it. However, we know of no better way to fix each item firmly in the respondent's mind before asking for the ranking.

Items in a Series

Writing questions that can be asked via the telephone also requires adapta-tions not strictly related to the reduction of complexity, such as how to ask the

Example 6.4   Reducing Complexity for Rank Order Questions by Changing to an Extended Format

| MAIL FORM: | Listed below are seven groups which currently influence our state university's athletic program. Please indicate which group you believe should have the most influence, second most influence, and third most influence by putting numbers in the appropriate boxes. |

	SHOULD HAVE MOST INFLUENCE	1. State Legislature 2. Board of Regents 3. University Administration
	SHOULD HAVE SECOND MOST INFLUENCE	4. University Faculty 5. Students 6. Parents of Students
	SHOULD HAVE THIRD MOST INFLUENCE	7. Alumni of the University

| REVISED FOR TELEPHONE: | I am going to read to you seven groups which currently influence our state university's athletic program. For each please indicate whether you think this group should have much influence, some influence, very little influence, or no influence on the athletic program. |

	NO	LITTLE	SOME	MUCH
1. First, do you think the legislature should have much, some, very little or no influence on the athletic program? 1		2	3	4
2. Should the Board of Regents have much, some, very little or no influence? 1		2	3	4
3. The next group is the University Administration 1		2	3	4
4. What about the University Faculty? . . 1		2	3	4
5. Students? 1		2	3	4
6. Parents of Students? 1		2	3	4
7. Alumni of the University? 1		2	3	4

Now, of these groups we have just discussed which one do you think should have the most influence? If you like, I would be happy to read the names of the groups to you once more

| | MOST INFLUENCE |

Which should have the second most influence?

| | SECOND MOST INFLUENCE |

Which should have the third most influence?

| | THIRD MOST INFLUENCE |

same question for each of several items in a series. In mail questionnaires the listing of items in one column and answer choices at the side are sufficient to show the respondent what is to be done. However, all this information must be communicated orally in the telephone questionnaire. The interviewer faces the problem of being certain that response categories are understood, yet avoiding needless repetition, which may irritate some respondents. A possible solution, shown in Example 6.4, is to present the first item (Legislature) as a full question, the next one (Board of Regents) in an abbreviated form, but with a complete list of response categories, and from that point on leave it to the interviewer's discretion. The fact that full question formats are provided for the first items tends to encourage the interviewer to ask the rest of the list of the items in a consistent manner.

Maps, Diagrams, and Pictures

It is often assumed that questions that incorporate visual aids cannot be asked by telephone. However, in some cases the information conveyed by maps, diagrams, and even pictures can be translated into words without a loss of meaning. For example, in a mail questionnaire study on recreational use of a reservoir area, a map was included for people to mark the route they drove through during their visit to the area. The purpose of this question was to determine whether certain points of interest were seen and which combination of entrances and exits were used. The map provided a convenient and interesting (for the respondent) means of obtaining this information. This question was easily adapted to the telephone questionnaire by explicitly asking people their points of entrance and exit and whether each of several points of interest was visited along the way (Example 6.5). Similarly, in Chapter 4, a question was shown that consisted of a map of the United States divided into 10 regions. Respondents were asked to indicate in which regions they would most like to live. One means of adapting this question to the telephone is to ask in which state people would most and least like to live.

Whenever the form of a question is modified, there is a chance that responses will not be equivalent. For example, delineation of the United States map into regions, which encourages people to think at that level of abstraction, may result in some choosing a region other than the one containing the particular state they would otherwise choose. Needless to say, such modifications should be carefully done and tested for equivalency. However, we believe that many visual questions can be successfully adapted to telephone interviews, thereby removing one objection to telephone surveys.

Incorporation of Response Categories Into the Wording of the Question

Each of the preceding examples (6.1–6.5) includes a simple, but nonetheless essential, aspect of question adaptation not yet mentioned. The response categories are incorporated into the question stems, as well as being listed separately. This allows the researcher to maintain better control over how the interviewer reads the response alternatives to the respondent. A simple listing of categories, such as that used in the TDM mail questionnaires, is somewhat unnatural to read. The result is that interviewers frequently and inconsistently add their own introductory remarks such as, "The choices are" or "There are

Example 6.5   Changing from a Map to Words

MAIL FORM:

Below is a map of Lilac Park. We would like to know the route you followed while visiting the park. Please do the following:

1) Put an "X" by the spot you entered the park, and an "O" by the one where you left (regardless of whether it was the same).
2) Starting from the "X," use arrows to show the path you followed in driving through the park. If you went over the same route more than once, show that by putting more arrows beside the previous ones.
3) Write "stop" beside the places you stopped and got out of the car, if any.

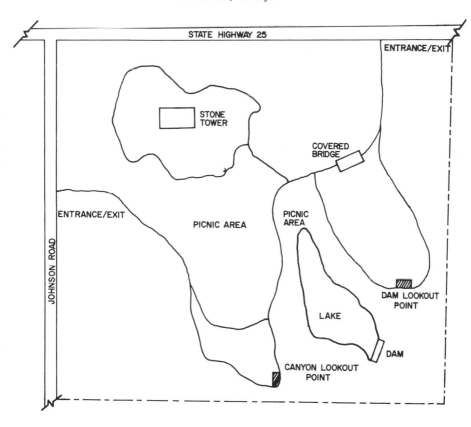

four possible answers for this question." Thus they may unwittingly alter the meaning of a question. The incorporation of response categories into the question itself promotes consistency in voice inflection as well as wording and, if well done, helps maintain a smooth natural flow in the manner in which questions are asked.

Example 6.5   *Continued*

REVISED FOR
TELEPHONE

Next I want to ask some questions about your visit to Lilac Park?

1. Did you enter the park from the state highway which is paved, or Johnson Road which is graveled?

    STATE HIGHWAY 1

    JOHNSON ROAD 2

2. When you left the park did you leave from the same gate that you entered, or the other one?

    SAME 1

    OTHER 2

I am going to read to you some points of interest that people frequently visit at the park. For each, I would like to know whether or not you visited it.

3. First, did you drive by the Lookout Point from' which you can see the dam of the lake?

    NO 1

    DOESN'T REMEMBER 2

    YES 3

    3a. When you got to this Lookout Point, did you get out of the car to look around?

    YES 1

    NO 2

4. Did you drive over the covered bridge?

    NO 1

    DOESN'T REMEMBER 2

    YES 3

    4a. When you were near the covered bridge, did you get out of the car to look around?

    NO 1

    YES 2

Rotation of Answer Choices

The last adaptation to telephone questionnaires we discuss represents an occasional problem. It occurs when there is concern that the order in which answers are read to the respondent will influence the response. Perhaps the most common situation in which this is a concern is election surveys, in which there is a series of candidates. If the order is deemed important by the researcher, the names of the candidates may be presented on a rotated basis, as shown in Example 6.6. If the sample is small, it may be most efficient to simply underline the first name by hand, as suggested by the example. If it involves a very large sample or if several questions are rotated, a more efficient means may be to randomly assign pages on which answer choices appear in different orders.

ORDERING THE QUESTIONS

The order in which questions are asked is considered very important in TDM telephone interviews. For example, a researcher may want to establish the respondent's perceptions about the most pressing problem facing the nation in a survey that is devoted mostly to questions about the state of the economy. If respondents become aware of pages of detailed economic questions before answering the most pressing problem questions, as is likely for a mail questionnaire, their response to the latter might be affected. A second situation in which question sequence is important develops when large numbers of screen questions must be placed prior to those questions which apply only to certain respondents.

Example 6.6 Answer Category Rotation

| Mail Form |

If the primary election were held today which of the following candidates for Governor would you vote for? (Circle number of your answer)

1 MARTIN KENNITS
2 HAROLD LACEY
3 ELEANOR LINDEN
4 DAVID ROY
5 J.S. TIMMONS

| Revised for Telephone |

If the primary election were held today, which of the following candidates for Governor would you vote for?

(INTERVIEWER: START WITH NAME THAT IS UNDERLINED IN RED AND END WITH NAME JUST ABOVE IT IF ANY. INSERT "or" BEFORE LAST NAME IS READ)

Martin Kennits	KENNITS 1
Harold Lacey	LACEY 2
Eleanor Linden	LINDEN 3
David Roy	ROY 4
J.S. Timmons	TIMMONS 5

Beyond these rather obvious needs to order questions in a certain way, the importance of question order in telephone interviews is frequently dismissed. The source of this tendency is the belief that the interviewer can be depended on to cajole respondents into completing difficult series of questions. Admittedly, question order (except perhaps for the crucial first questions) has less importance for telephone interviews than mail surveys. The fact that once an interview is underway relatively few respondents terminate before completion diminishes (but does not eliminate) the need to analyze the motivational qualities of each page of the questionnaire. However, concern with question order is justified by the likelihood that data quality, that is, the accuracy and completeness of answers, can be increased by following the principles of ordering, outlined below, which correspond closely to those used for mail questionnaires (see Chapter 4).

General Principles of Question Order

The major contributions that question order can make to data quality are to ease the task of the respondents and to reduce any resistance to participation. We have noted repeatedly how difficult it can be to comprehend questions over the telephone. Not understanding a key word at the beginning of a question may make the rest of it completely unintelligible. Respondents who feel some embarrassment at having to ask that a lengthy question be repeated or who lack the patience for such a repeat, may simply "guess" at one of the suggested answer categories. Frequent and haphazard changes of topics, for example, starting from "Which candidate do you prefer?" and going to "How satisfied are you with your present job?" and then to "Do you favor the Equal Rights Amendment?" demand more of respondents than does covering all the questions on a single topic before continuing to the next one. Similarly, question-by-question changes in response category formats, for example, from "agree/disagree" in one question to rank order in the next, to a cafeteria selection from among several categories in the next, increase the respondent burden and thus the chance of error. Logically, the greatest respondent difficulty can be expected when each question in a sequence entails both topic changes and response format changes from the preceding one. Thus we recommend that within the sequence requirements set by the study objectives, questions be grouped by topic and within topic by consistent formats, just as for the mail questionnaire (Chapter 4).

The researcher can do a great deal with question order to reduce respondent resistance. Few would tell a respondent that an important study was being conducted about major societal problems, and then start with items about income and religion, two frequently asked questions that many respondents find objectionable. However, our concern here extends well beyond the placement of specifically objectionable items. Questions can be ordered in a manner whereby one set of questions seems to lead logically into the next and conveys to the respondent early in the interview a sense of doing something worthwhile. The objectionable qualities of a question often stem as much from the context in which it is asked as from its specific substance.

The ordering principles followed include beginning the questionnaire with items central to the topic, about which the respondent is informed in the introduction to the interview, and which appear interesting and socially important. A gradient of descending importance relevant to the topic (as likely viewed by the respondent) is established. All topical questions are asked before the beginning of the questions related to personal characteristics. Any topic-related questions likely to be substantively objectionable are placed just prior to the personal characteristic items. The personal characteristics positioned last are, of course, ordered with the ones least likely to be objectionable coming first.

The First Few Questions

No aspect of the question writing and ordering process is given more attention than the phrasing and content of the first few questions. There are several reasons for this. First, if a response can be obtained to these questions the likelihood of a subsequent termination of the interview is greatly decreased. Second, interviewers are frequently able to use the first question or two to overcome respondent objections to the interview since, if properly related to the topic, they draw the respondent's attention away from other concerns. The third reason for the importance of these questions is that the way they are asked and answered tends to set the pace and tone of the interview.

Experience has led us to a "first question" format that involves a series of two or three questions rather than only one. The first question is close-ended, with no more than two or three answer categories. Further, it meets the criteria of being relevant, interesting, easy to answer, and applicable to everyone in the study, just as required for TDM mail questionnaires.

A simple first question helps get the interview started. Frequently respondents will state their unwillingness to be interviewed, but rather than immediately hanging up remain on the line and respond to the interviewer's attempts to overcome their objections. A common objection, especially in studies of the general public, is that "I don't know anything about the topic so I won't be able to answer the questions." Some will even ask to hear the first question, perhaps in an effort to confirm that point. In other cases, an interviewer can bolster the argument that the respondent's opinion is really important and the respondent will be able to answer the questions by reading the first one. A good first question can convince the respondents that they know enough to state their opinions. This is definitely not the place for a long question, a complicated two-step question, or one in which items are ranked.

The first question is generally followed by an open-ended one in which respondents are required to formulate a response and express it in their own words. Some respondents approach an interview in a very relaxed manner and may answer every close-ended question in great detail, as if it were open-ended. For them, the inclusion of an open-ended question at this point is not really essential. Others, however, quickly state their willingness to be interviewed but are apprehensive and a little bit nervous. This often leads them to answer each question quickly, as if they felt impelled to punctuate every question the interviewer asks. This sets a very fast pace for the interview, which leads in turn to the respondent not providing carefully reasoned answers. The early inclusion of this open-ended question helps nervous respondents find their telephone voice and helps establish a pace for the interview. In addition, this type of question encourages respondents to express themselves fully throughout the remainder of the interview and provides the interviewer with a feel for the respondent that can be used in establishing better rapport.

An example of an initial question sequence that meets these criteria is taken from a study of reactions to a proposal for a new taxing structure in the state of Washington (Example 6.7). These questions were added simply to elicit interest. It may be noted in this example that a screen question is involved, making the open-ended question inapplicable to some respondents. An additional open-ended question was added to make sure that every respondent would have the opportunity to start talking "in his or her own words" very early in the interview.

CONSTRUCTING THE PAGE

A well-constructed telephone questionnaire leaves as little as possible to chance and is designed to maximize the probability that interviewers will administer it in exactly the same fashion to each respondent. This means doing everything possible to decrease the likelihood that interviewers will be uncertain about question order or the exact words to use in asking questions. Efforts are also made to minimize instances in which interviewers must make on-the-spot improvisations. It should come as no surprise that the TDM telephone questionnaire looks quite different from one done for a TDM mail study, since visual attractiveness is irrelevant for telephone questionnaires. On the other hand, detailed guides to interviewers are absolutely essential. Indeed, instructions to the interviewers often take up as much space as the questions. The rules followed in questionnaire construction for TDM telephone surveys are outlined in the following paragraphs.

Example 6.7   First Question Sequence

1. First I would like to ask you how you feel about the amount of state and local taxes you now pay. Do you feel the amount you pay is too much, about right, or not enough?

    NOT ENOUGH 1

    ABOUT RIGHT 2

    TOO MUCH 3

2. Of the taxes which you now pay is there any one tax you particularly object to paying?

    NO 1

    ———————— YES 2

    2a) Which tax is that?

    _____

    2b) Why do you particularly object to paying it?

    _____

    _____

    _____

3. Discussion is now going on about whether the kinds and amounts of taxes paid by Washington residents should be changed. In general, what kinds of changes, if any, do you think should be made in the kinds and amounts of taxes paid by Washington residents?

    _____

    _____

    _____

    _____

Use Lower Case Letters for Questions; Upper Case for Answers

All words and phrases to be read to respondents are typed in lower case letters. Those which are only read occasionally, such as probes to open-ended questions, are similarly typed, but set off by parentheses. All words that are *never* read to respondents, such as interviewer instructions and coding information, are typed in upper case letters (Example 6.7).

Distinguishing between what is to be read and what is not to be read is essential to gain consistent administration of the questionnaires by interviewers. It is far easier to train interviewers to observe a rule without exception, for example, only read the words in small letters, than to teach them the structure of each question so that they will know which parts to read and which to not read. It also avoids some of the strain involved in thinking far enough ahead to maintain fluency. Simply put, this procedure routinizes the reading of the telephone questionnaire, allowing interviewers to concentrate on other aspects of the interviewing process.

List Answer Categories Not Provided to Respondent

Answer categories the researcher does not want to bring to the attention of respondents are listed with an identifying number below each question (Question 1 of the telephone version in Example 6.8). This is done to be sure there is an appropriate category for interviewers to mark no matter how respondents answer.

The kinds of additional categories that are used depends on the question and the researcher's needs. We normally find it useful to distinguish between the "don't knows" (those who indicate they either cannot decide or simply have no opinion) and the "refusals" (those who indicate they do not want to answer the question). Although it is sometimes difficult for interviewers to distinguish between these categories, and the number of responses to each category is exceedingly small, usually less than 5 percent, we have found the information useful for evaluating the objectionable quality of items for use in future surveys.[3] The "don't know" category also serves as a rough index of whether a question makes sense to respondents. A "does not apply" category is added for questions that are not asked of certain people, because it is screened out as a result of an answer they provided to a preceding question.

Precoding the Answer Categories

Each response category is assigned an identifying number that is used to represent it on a computer punch card. Such precoding is always used on telephone questionnaires; this is another way that TDM telephone and mail questionnaires differ.

There are perhaps as many ways of assigning numbers to answer categories as there are researchers doing telephone surveys. Besides being partly a matter of preference, certain coding schemes work better with some computer systems and computer programs than with others. Thus we strongly suggest that the person who plans to use a computer but lacks familiarity with it obtain local help in establishing his or her precoding scheme. Bearing this "caveat" in mind, the precoding procedures used in Example 6.8 are discussed to illustrate how certain problems encountered in precoding might be handled.

One precoding procedure shown in Example 6.8 is the consistent use of certain numbers for specified purposes throughout the questionnaire. In the system we have established for our own research, 7 is always reserved for

Example 6.8   Comparisons of Mail and Telephone Techniques for Page Construction

```
MAIL VERSION:
```

Q-1 We would like to begin by asking how you feel about Washington as a state in which to live? Do you consider it: (Circle number of your choice)

      1 VERY DESIRABLE
      2 SOMEWHAT DESIRABLE
      3 SOMEWHAT UNDESIRABLE
      4 VERY UNDESIRABLE

Q-2 Over the past five years would you say that, as a state in which to live, Washington has become? (Circle number of your choice)

      1 MORE DESIRABLE
      2 STAYED ABOUT THE SAME
      3 LESS DESIRABLE
      4 I DON'T KNOW

(If you circled either _more_ or _less_ desirable) What do you think is the main reason for this change?

Q-3 The purpose of Alternatives for Washington is to find out what goals citizens want for the future of our state. A few possibilities are listed below. Do you feel each one should _NOT_ be a goal, or should be a _HIGH_ priority, _MEDIUM_ priority, or _LOW_ priority goal for Washington?

GOAL NUMBER	POSSIBLE GOALS FOR WASHINGTON	How much priority, if any, should these goals have? (Circle your answer)			
1	Increase the variety of job opportunities by promoting the growth of business and industry	NOT	HIGH	MEDIUM	LOW
2	Protect the natural environment, such as rivers, shorelines, wilderness, and scenic areas from economic activities that might damage it	NOT	HIGH	MEDIUM	LOW
3	Increase family incomes so people may purchase more of the consumer goods and services they want	NOT	HIGH	MEDIUM	LOW
4	Keep population growth of the state small by discouraging people from moving to Washington from other states	NOT	HIGH	MEDIUM	LOW
5	Decrease the total amount of energy used by industry and individual consumers	NOT	HIGH	MEDIUM	LOW
6	Increase the amount of services government provides to people of the state	NOT	HIGH	MEDIUM	LOW
7	Decrease the amount of unemployment below the present level, and keep it there	NOT	HIGH	MEDIUM	LOW
8	Conserve natural resources, such as minerals, land and timber, so that future supplies are insured	NOT	HIGH	MEDIUM	LOW

Q-4 Of the possible goals listed above, which three do you feel are most important for Washington? (Put _number_ in the appropriate box)

[ ] MOST IMPORTANT   [ ] SECOND MOST IMPORTANT   [ ] THIRD MOST IMPORTANT

"does not apply," 8 for "I don't know," and 9 for "refusal." Zero is used for the occasional slip-up when no information is recorded by the interviewer. This leaves six punches for the coding of answers. When the number of possible answers exceeds six, a two-column rather than one-column field is employed, and double digits are used to represent the special codes, that is,

Example 6.8   Continued

REVISED FOR
TELEPHONE:

		Computer Code
1.	We would like to begin by asking how you feel about Washington as a state in which to live? Do you consider it to be very desirable, somewhat desirable, somewhat undesirable, or very undesirable?	Deck:Column

```
                    VERY UNDESIRABLE . . . . . . . . 1
                    SOMEWHAT UNDESIRABLE . . . . . . 2
                    SOMEWHAT DESIRABLE . . . . . . . 4
                    VERY DESIRABLE . . . . . . . . . 5
                    (Don't Know) . . . . . . . . . . 8
                    (Refusal) . . . . . . . . . . . 9        1:11
```

2. Over the past five years would you say that as a state in which to live Washington has become <u>MORE</u> desirable, <u>LESS</u> desirable or stayed about the same?

```
                    LESS DESIRABLE . . . . . . . . 1
                    STAYED ABOUT THE SAME . . . . . 2
                        (Go to Q-5, top of the page)
                    MORE DESIRABLE . . . . . . . . 3
                    (Don't Know) . . . . . . . . . 8
                        (Go to Q-5, top of the page)
                    (Refusal) . . . . . . . . . . 9        1:12
```

2a. What do you think is the main reason Washington has become more desirable as a place to live? [PROBE IF NECESSARY, E.G., "Can you think of any reason at all?"]   [IF MORE THAN ONE REASON GIVEN, ASK FOR RESPONDENT TO IDENTIFY MOST IMPORTANT ONE, E.G., "Which of those reasons you mentioned do you consider the main reason for Washington becoming more desirable as a place to live? CIRCLE IT]

```
_____
                                                      1:13-14
_____

_____
```

2b. What do you think is the main reason Washington has become less desirable as a place to live? [PROBE IF NECESSARY, E.G., "Can you think of any reason at all?]   [IF MORE THAN ONE REASON GIVEN, ASK FOR RESPONDENT TO IDENTIFY MOST IMPORTANT ONE, E.G., "Which of those reasons you mentioned do you consider the main reason for Washington becoming less desirable as a place to live? CIRCLE IT]

```
                                                      1:15-16
_____

_____
```

77 for "does not apply," and so on. The consistent use of these numbers reduces the possibility of coding error.

Another procedure we use is to assign lower numbers to the negative responses and higher numbers to the positive responses. Thus 1 is always assigned to "no" and 2 to "yes," 1 to "disagree" and 2 to "agree," 1 to

Example 6.8　Continued

| REVISED FOR |
| TELEPHONE: |

3. Before asking the next question, I want to explain a little more about the purpose of this study. Last spring and summer more than 1500 state residents from all walks of life met in state and area conferences where they discussed what they wanted for Washington to be like in the future. A wide variety of possible goals for the future were stated. Tonight we want to ask your opinion on some of the goals more frequently discussed, to find out what you think is most important for the future of the state.

I will begin by reading to you eight of the possible goals for the state. For each one I read, would you indicate whether you think it should NOT be a goal for Washington, or if it should, whether you would like it to be a LOW priority, MEDIUM priority, or HIGH priority goal for our state.

	NOT (1)	LOW (2)	MEDIUM (3)	HIGH (4)	(Don't Know) (8)	(Refusal) (9)	Computer Code Deck:Column
The first of these possible goals is to increase the variety of job opportunities by promoting the growth of business and industry. Should it NOT be a goal, or be a LOW, MEDIUM, or HIGH priority goal for the state?	.1.	. 2	. . 3	. . .4.	. . 8	. . . 9	1:17
The next one is: Protect the natural environment, such as rivers, shorelines, wilderness and scenic areas from economic activities that might damage it. Should it NOT be a goal, or should it be a LOW, MEDIUM, or HIGH priority goal?	.1.	. 2	. . 3	. . .4.	. . 8	. . . 9	1:18
[INTERVIEWER: FROM THIS POINT ON, REPEAT CATEGORIES AS YOU DEEM NECESSARY]							
The next goal is: Increase family incomes so people may purchase more of the consumer goods and services they want	.1.	. 2	. . 3	. . .4.	. . 8	. . . 9	1:19
The next one is: Keep population growth of the state small by discouraging people from moving to Washington from other states	.1.	. 2	. . 3	. . .4.	. . 8	. . . 9	1:20
Decrease the total amount of energy used by industry and and individual customers	.1.	. 2	. . 3	. . .4.	. . 8	. . . 9	1:21
Increase the amount of services government provides to people of the state	.1.	. 2	. . 3	. . .4.	. . 8	. . . 9	1:22
Decrease the amount of unemployment below the present level and keep it there	.1.	. 2	. . 3	. . .4.	. . 8	. . . 9	1:23
Conserve natural resources, such as minerals, land and timber, so that future supplies are insured	. . .1.	. 2	. . 3	. . .4.	. . 8	. . . 9	1:24

"unfavorable" and 2 to "favorable," and so on. When gradations of response are represented, the numbering sequence starts with the most intensely negative category assigned 1 and the highest number, except for the special categories mentioned above, assigned to the most intensely positive category. The use of this system helps when attempting to interpret the computer output. Reference to codes identifying the number represented by each response is needed far less frequently.

Precoding is completed by the assignment of card and column numbers for each computer punch. In most computer systems, each card has 80 columns within which punches can be made. The number of the card (if more than one card is required) and the columns to be used are listed beside each question. In Example 6.8, two columns are reserved for each open-ended question because the number of punches needed is not known until after the survey is completed.

The result of the precoding effort is the ability to go quickly from the questionnaire to computer cards for analysis. We have conducted numerous surveys in which the key punchers who transferred data from questionnaire to cards kept pace with interviewers; the data were submitted for computer analysis each evening, minutes after the last interview was completed.

Place Precoding Information to the Right of the Answer Categories

A seemingly small but important distinguishing feature of the TDM telephone questionnaire is the placement of the "precoded" response category numbers. Response categories, that is, punch numbers, are always placed to the right of the answer category rather than the left as in the TDM mail questionnaire. Several considerations dictate this change. First, interviewers are less likely than respondents to circle the wrong category when the number is further removed from the beginning of the item. Second, it is easier, since placement on the right requires less back and forth movement of the hand and keeps the hand from covering the next question on the page. Finally, this method allows the punch number to be located in the most convenient location for the data analysts, that is, immediately next to the card and column number.

Use Special Format for Screen Questions

All questions that apply to every respondent are typed beginning at a standard left-hand margin of the page (Question 2, Example 6.8). Questions that apply only to those respondents who answer a screen question in a certain way are indented 10 spaces from the margin used for the preceding question. As a further and very explicit guide to the interviewer, an arrow is used to connect the selected response category in the screen question to the appropriate subsequent question. The absence of any direction beside a response category automatically means that the next question to be asked is the first succeeding one printed at the standard left-hand margin of the page. It is an understood rule that *all* questions printed here are to be asked of everyone, with one exception. If a turn of pages is required, and it may not be obvious that that question is printed at the normal left-hand margin, a written instruction (e.g., go to Q−5, top of next page) is provided under the relevant answer categories, as shown in Example 6.8, Question 2. The use of pictorial directives, arrows, and margins means that there are fewer things for interviewers to remember and therefore less chance that mistakes will be made or that the fluency of the interviewer will be broken.

Put Interviewer and Coder Instructions Onto Questionnaire

Placing interview instructions onto the questionnaire means that they can be located where they are most apt to be needed, rather than on a separate sheet of paper where they must be searched out each time. These instructions may range from an explanation of how to pronounce a word (e.g., an election candidate's name) to detailed directions on when a probe should be used (as shown in Question 2a of Example 6.8). Consistent with an earlier procedure, all such instructions are printed in upper case letters, clearly distinguishing them from all material that is read to the respondent. (Although we see no need to overload questionnaires with detail, particularly with material repeated in numerous places throughout the questionnaire, this is the handiest location to place information specific to a particular question.)

Use Transitions and Explanatory Material Freely

During the page construction process, questions are frequently modified and material added to improve the flow of the interview and, ultimately, the quality of the results. This includes simple lead-in statements and occasional lengthier transitions. Again, running counter to the frequent admonition to "keep it brief," we have been influenced by Laurent.[4] His experiments showed that doubling the length of questions by introducing the subjects of the inquiry and adding redundant remarks prior to the actual question did not increase the length of response duration, but responses contained more valid information. For example, increasing recall time by placing a filler between an introductory statement and the question was accomplished thus:

> Our next question asks those things people do to protect their health. This is an additional subject we are gathering a few data on. What are the things you do to protect your health?

This item produced significantly more items than a simple reading of the last statement of the question. In seeking to explain his findings, Laurent notes:

... a longer question may inform the respondent that the interviewer is not in a
hurry, thus releasing perception of time constraints which might be detrimental
to adequate search activity. . . . Finally, the responding behavior may also gain
ineffectiveness because some of the initial ruminating-type activity has already
taken place during the time the question was being asked. The respondent is
given more time for rehearsal activity and response polishing.[5]

Although Laurent's results were obtained from face-to-face interviews, we
believe that the respondents' need for time to organize their thoughts is even
greater for the telephone interview. The unexpected occurrence of the telephone interview, the respondent's desire to get it over with so that interrupted
activities can be continued, and the lack of the interviewer's presence to aid in
building rapport, leads us to use restatement and warning of what is to come
extensively.

Thus questions are often introduced with phrases such as, "Next we would
like to ask you a question about," and "Now let's turn to . . ." Whenever a
major change in question topic or response format is about to occur and
whenever else deemed necessary, even lengthier statements of transition are
employed, such as that which precedes Question 3 of Example 6.8. In this
example, which comes shortly after the beginning of the interview, a little
more information is provided about the purpose of the study in an effort to
build respondent interest. Also, it precedes a question that contains several
items; thus it is also used to set the stage for it. Telling how many items are in
the next question gives the respondent a clear expectation of what is about to
occur. The use of transitions whenever a major change of topic takes place
prevents a carry over of thoughts from preceding questions that could interfere with the respondent's understanding of what is about to occur.

Break Pages Where Convenient for the Interviewer

The rule on turning from one page to another is simple—make turns where
they will interfere least with the interviewing process. If possible, they are
never made in the midst of a question where an interviewer would be required to continue reading as a page is turned. Also, turning pages in the
midst of a series of screen questions should be avoided. This reduces the
possibility that the interviewer will become confused. Thus it is not unusual to
have pages with only one or two questions on them. Partially blank pages
have no effect on data quality, as in TDM mail questionnaires, and entail
nothing more than a small paper and duplication cost. Allowing for such
pages further eases the task of conveniently making page breaks. The rear-
rangement of questions or the elimination of certain items, as is occasionally
deemed necessary for TDM mail questionnaires, is not a problem in tele-

phone interviews. One can even shift to legal paper size (8½″ × 14″) if necessary to get the questions to "fit."

PRETESTING

The philosophy applied to the pretesting of TDM mail questionnaires, discussed in Chapter 4, is rigorously adhered to for telephone studies. This means that a systematic pretest design is followed, using professional researchers, policy makers, and people with sample characteristics. Pretests are made under a variety of conditions, sometimes with respondents advised that they are pretest subjects, and other times without that knowledge.

It is easier to pretest a questionnaire for a telephone survey than for mail or face-to-face interview surveys. A random (or systematic) sample of the actual survey population can be contacted as easily and efficiently as special pretest groups drawn from the locality in which the research operation is based. For this reason we routinely overdraw our survey sample so that a portion of it may be used for pretesting purposes. Further, pretesting need not be the one-shot effort it often becomes for mail or face-to-face interview surveys. The feedback from an hour or two of pretest calls can be used to make immediate revisions. More pretest calls using the revised format can then be made the same day.

It is absolutely essential that telephone questionnaires be tested over the telephone. Having respondents fill it out themselves or reading it to them in a face-to-face situation, *does not* provide an adequate pretest. In fact, it may do more harm than good. The face-to-face situation results in both the interviewer and respondent relying on visual cues; the questionnaire deficiencies may be missed. Asking someone to self-administer a telephone questionnaire often results in suggestions (e.g., more parsimony and layout changes) that make a questionnaire more, rather than less, difficult to comprehend over the telephone. Testing over the telephone means that such things as normal line noise and the respondent's ability to concentrate while completley dependent on a verbal oral message are components of the test situation, as should be the case.

PRINTING

The method of reproducing telephone questionnaires is relatively unimportant, the main consideration is that they be quite legible. The conditions under which telephone interviewing is frequently done, that is, severe resource constraints and the desire for quick results, suggests that poorer quality duplication facilities widely available to individual agencies and college departments are used more than print shops, but this should present no problem.

The color coding of the questionnaires through the use of different colors of paper is highly desirable. In studies that involved the skipping of entire sections for some respondents, we found that it helps interviewers if such sections are color coded. Occasionally color has been used to distinguish questionnaires from one another, for example, surveys to be completed with agency directors versus those to be administered to the general public as part of the same study. The rule has been "if it helps, use it." Finally, to ease eye strain, brightly colored papers are avoided in favor of the widely available pastels.

CONCLUSION

The TDM telephone questionnaire contrasts sharply with the TDM mail questionnaire. It is "heard" but never "seen" by the respondent. Thus it does not need the visual attractiveness and self-sustaining detail that are essential to the TDM mail questionnaire. However, neither can it be formulated recklessly. If anything, the construction requirements are more rigorous. Words must be found to compensate for what is usually done by visual display in mail questionnaires and, for that matter, face-to-face interviews. The interviewer, who necessarily becomes an intermediary between researcher and respondent, is the major audience for the printed questionnaire.

The complete dependence on verbal communication between the telephone interviewer and respondent requires that each word be delivered and comprehended one at a time. This places substantial constraints on how questions are written for telephone surveys. Thus our major focus in this chapter is making the telephone questionnaire suitable for the requirements imposed by sole reliance on this one mode of communication. Reducing question complexity, rotating response categories, and incorporating response categories into stems are three such adjustments that must usually be made.

Once the essential difference in the mode of communication between mail and telephone questionnaires is recognized, a number of similarities become evident. For example, the principles of ordering questions and pretesting, discussed only briefly in this chapter, are very similar for both types of surveys. Further, the concern over not leaving anything to chance in the mail questionnaire applies equally to the telephone questionnaire. We also try to take advantage of every opportunity to make the questionnaire interesting and to reduce "costs" to respondents, such as embarrassment over personal questions, a sense of worthlessness resulting from not being able to answer some questions, and feelings of frustration from not being able to understand what the interviewer is trying to say. The principles of social exchange are used to the fullest extent. Thus, despite the contrast exhibited by printed mail and telephone questionnaires, their underlying principles are the same.

NOTES

1: Don A. Dillman, W. Williams, and D. Stadelman, Preliminary Report of WSU/UW Tax Surveys, Social Research Center, Washington State Univeristy, 1972.

2. The structure of this particular question suggests another, in our view less plausible, explanation for the response distributions. The study was designed to find out from citizens what goals they would like for the future of Washington State and included questions for a wide number of policy areas. The policy alternatives, as defined by program participants, were how fast the state would increase in relation to the rest of the United States or whether it would increase at all. Graduations of decrease were neither an issue they explored nor one that could be expressed in terms comparable to the increase gradations. The result was an unbalanced question, that is, more options on one side (increase) than the other (decrease) of the neutral point. As a general rule, it is recommended that unbalanced questions be avoided because of the possibility that people will be encouraged by the mere presence of more categories on one side to shift in that direction. If the unbalanced structure was the major factor in the response distributions we obtained, we would expect that the percentage in the decrease categories in the telephone version be greater than for the mail version. As can be seen in Table 6.1, that is not the case. Thus we believe the explanation offered in the text is more tenable.

3. Item nonresponse rates for telephone studies conducted by the Public Opinion Laboratory at Washington State University have shown that refusals to answer rarely occur. "I don't knows" are also reduced because of the presence of interviewers and their probing ability.

4. Andre Laurent, "Effects of Question Length on Reporting Behavior in the Survey Interview," *Journal of the American Statistical Association,* 67, 1972, pp. 298–305.

5. *Ibid.*, p. 305.

Chapter Seven

IMPLEMENTING TELEPHONE SURVEYS

A few years ago I was surprised by a request to conduct a statewide survey of the general public on a tax policy issue. There was nothing unusual about being asked to do such a survey, and the officials who made it had the quite reasonable objective of reporting public reaction to a proposal for changing the state's tax structure to a legislative committee. However, the surprise came when I was informed that the results would have to be available in only 15 days, an extremely short time to prepare a questionnaire, implement a survey, and report the results.

However, the task was accomplished. The entire first week was spent drafting, redrafting, and pretesting the questionnaire. Simultaneously, a statewide sample of households was drawn, interviewers hired, and interviewing sessions scheduled. The eighth day was spent finalizing the questionnaire, training interviewers and setting up computer programs to analyze the results. Interviews commenced the next evening, as did subsequent coding and data processing.

Because we desired the earliest possible results, the 750 households in the sample were divided, and a random sample of the total sample was called the first evening. The results of the first night's interviewing were fed into the computer less than a half hour after the last interview was completed, and a complete printout of frequency distributions and cross-tabulations was obtained within the hour. These partial results from some 150 interviews were phoned to the sponsors of the survey the same evening, less than 10 full days after their request.

The remainder of the survey was completed and reported over the course of the next four days, and complete printouts were delivered on the fifth day. The randomization procedure followed for selecting each night's calls meant that the final results showed remarkably little variation from the results obtained from the first evening's calls (less than 10 percentage points on any item).[1]

It is not our purpose to recommend that telephone surveys be conducted under time constraints as stringent as these or to suggest that this is the normal use for telephone surveys. Such haste compounds the possibility of error and unless one has considerable experience (or is willing to accept results of questionable quality), this situation should be avoided. However, the speed with which the surveys *can* be executed remains one of its primary virtues and cannot be ignored in developing an implementation method that is applicable to the needs of most researchers. The purpose of this chapter is to outline a method that can successfully pass a severe test like the one just described.

We must note a basic difference between the Total Design Method (TDM) mail implementation process described in Chapter 5 and the telephone process we are about to describe. The former is far more sensitive to modifications likely to be made because of the researcher's lack of resources. For example, cost saving efforts such as elimination of personalization, switching from first-class postage to another class of postage, or using a printing method less costly than the photoreduction booklet format seem likely to have negative effects on response. Thus the TDM mail method is a method without many options.

In contrast, implementation of TDM telephone surveys allows a number of options that may have little effect on the quality or quantity of response. For example, we know of some very sophisticated and fairly costly telephone survey operations in which questionnaires are computerized and appear on the screen of a cathode ray tube before the interviewer. The interviewer keypunches each answer into a terminal. Afterwards, the next question—which in the case of screen questions depends on the previous answer—automatically appears on the screen. Other researchers may literally operate on a shoe-string budget, doing everything themselves, from drawing the sample to conducting each of the interviews from their home telephone. The results obtained by such diverse procedures may not differ appreciably.

This chapter is written with full awareness of these diverse cirumstances. The method we describe is one that makes full use of the resources likely to be available to a researcher in a college, university, or agency at a reasonable cost and is one that can be implemented under a tight time schedule. Thus certain sections, for example, recruitment and training of interviewers, are important to some researchers and not others. Although the methods are for the most part adaptable to sophisticated operations not yet available in most universities, it is our purpose to describe a method that is not dependent on their use.

DECIDING HOW THE SAMPLE IS TO BE DRAWN

The specifics of the TDM implementation process are largely determined by the procedure used for selecting respondents. Thus a discussion of the basic sampling alternatives and the advantages of each is our point of departure.[2]

For some populations, a complete listing is available, and sampling becomes a simple process of randomly or systematically selecting a sample of the desired size from the total population. Examples include lists of ministers, dentists, voluntary association members, parents of children at a particular school, directors of counseling agencies, and university professors. For populations whose members are not listed, the sample selection is more difficult, requiring a two-step procedure that first identifies sample units and then selects respondents within each unit. Surveys for which a representative sample of the general public is desired represent the most common and problematic case. Two methods for selecting sampling units are commonly used: (1) sampling of published directories and (2) calling lists of randomly generated telephone numbers. Each has advantages as well as disadvantages.

Sampling Telephone Directories

One procedure for drawing a sample from telephone directories is to select each name randomly, perhaps through a two-step sequence of employing random numbers to generate a directory page number and then a name on that page. Another acceptable method is to systematically sample the directories, that is, starting near the beginning of each directory and taking every nth name from throughout the directory. Systematic samples are acceptable provided that there is no "periodic" repetition of people with certain characteristics in the listings that coincides with the sample interval,[2] an assumption we believe quite tenable for alphabetical listings. Systematic samples can be drawn in several ways, one of which is outlined below. This is a method that strives for convenience while protecting the systematic nature of the selection procedure.

1. *Acquire all relevant telephone directories.* When doing a survey of one community, this may be as simple as walking into the nearest telephone company office and picking up the needed directory. When an entire state or region of the country is involved, it may be necessary to order directories from the many telephone companies—a procedure that often requires several weeks.
2. *Determine the number of names needed from each directory.* When only one telephone directory covers the entire sample area, this task is quite simple. The number of names is the same as the sample size. However, when two or more directories are involved, it is a much more complicated task to accomplish.

   Perhaps the most common procedure is to estimate the number of residential listings contained in each directory and draw the same proportion of names from all of them. This of course requires one to estimate the number of residential listings in each directory. To make this estimate the residential listings on several pages are counted (3–4 for directories containing less than 15 pages, and as many as 20 for directories of very large cities). The average number of listings per page is then multiplied by the number of pages of residential listings contained in the directory. Any large blocks of governmental and commercial listings are duly marked (for future reference) and deleted from this page count. The results from each directory are totaled to determine the total number of residential listings for the entire sample area. The proportion of each directory's listings to be drawn for the sample is determined by simply dividing the desired sample size by the total number of residential listings in the sample area.

   The chief drawback to the procedure just outlined is that the number of listings contained in each directory may not be in close correspondence to the number of households (or the number of adults) known to live in that area. This sometimes happens because of variations in the percentage of households with telephone service, unlisted telephones, listings in more than one directory, or number of adults per household. The researcher may wish to determine the geographic coverage of each directory to estimate the population covered by it, and base the number of respondents to be drawn from each directory on that estimate. Although desirable for the pursuit of certain research objectives, this procedure is not as easy as it might sound, because the boundaries of telephone systems often do not correspond very well to the political boundaries on which population counts are based. The variation among states and even regions within states is enormous.

3. *Determine the sample interval.* The sample interval is the number of listings to be skipped between each listing selected. First calculate the number of column inches of listings contained in each directory, omitting from this count any blocks of governmental or other listings identified in step 2.[3] The sample interval is then determined by dividing the total column inches of listings in each directory by the number of names we wish to sample from it (which was also determined in step 2).

4. *Select the first listing.* The first interval within which a listing will be selected is measured off in the directory. For example, if division of total column inches in a directory by the number of names needed resulted in a sampling interval of 67 inches, that number of inches is measured off, starting with the first listing under "A." The actual number of listings in that 67-inch interval is determined. Let us assume that the number is 645. Then a table of random numbers is consulted, and a three-digit number within the interval 001–645 is randomly picked. Selection of 146, for example, means the 146th listing will be the first listing to be included in the sample.

5. *Select subsequent listings.* Starting at the exact point of the 146th name, 67 inches are measured off and at that point the next listing is selected. This procedure is repeated for sampling of all subsequent listings. In measuring intervals throughout the directory, any large blocks of listings deleted in step 2 are skipped.

6. *When to substitute.* There are two situations in which substitutions are needed. The first is when the interval falls on an obviously nonresidential listing. In this case, the person drawing the sample systematically alternates between selecting a residential listing one inch above the nonresidential listing and the same distance below it. The second situation concerns all listings that require two or more lines. This usually happens with professional people, such as doctors, who maintain an office number, a residential listing, and perhaps an emergency number. It frequently occurs because of long names. To avoid the possible bias of overrepresenting such households, they are selected only if the interval falls precisely on a predetermined position, such as the line that has the residence telephone. Should the interval fall on any other line, the substitution procedure for nonresidential listings is followed. The next interval following a substitution is started from the point the previous interval ended rather than the point of the substituted listing.

Modifications in the above procedure may have to be made because of the lack of correspondence between the manner in which directories are published and the researcher's needs. Directories sometimes integrate the listings for several communities, some of which are not to be covered by the survey, making it necessary to delete some listings. Sometimes this task is expedited by the use of different central exchanges (i.e., three-digit prefix numbers). Also, some directories indicate the community name (usually in abbreviated form) as part of the individual listings. Failing that, other address information may be helpful.

To some readers the procedure outlined for drawing a systematic sample from telephone directories is likely to seem excessively detailed. The reaction may be to wonder why a "close your eyes, turn the page, and point a finger" method of identifying households would not do just as well. If most humans were capable of the conscious exercise of random behavior on lengthy and uninteresting tasks, perhaps the finger method would be acceptable. However, we believe that people's normal behavioral tendencies may produce a biased sample without their realizing it. For example, left to their own devices, people drawing samples may unconsciously tend to pick from the center of the directory (and bias against certain ethnic names), avoid long names (and bias against other ethnic groups), consciously avoid listings that require two or more lines (and bias against professionals), or tend to pick streets with numbers for names (and in some cities bias against new subdivisions usually of higher socioeconomic status). Thus we see a need for detailed structure in the sampling methods.

Despite its simplicity, there are several shortcomings in relying on telephone directories for sampling. The first is the omission of those who have acquired a telephone or moved since the directory was published. In one study of a large city, Cooper estimated that the proportion of households with telephone service were listed in the directory declined from 90−94 percent (due to deliberately unlisted telephones) at the beginning of the directory year to 82 percent at the end of that year.[4] Our experience suggests that his estimate of those missed may be lower than for some areas of the country. Statewide surveys in Washington for which some directories are always nearly new and others nearly a year old (due to the rotation of publishing dates) have consistently resulted in 9−14 percent of the sampled numbers being disconnected. This fact, coupled with problems caused by new listings not yet in the directory, suggests that a very substantial portion of households may be missed through directory sampling.

The problems associated with missed numbers are of particular concern because those who move tend to differ from the general population. Census data reveal that movers tend to be younger and have more education than nonmovers. Likewise, those without school-age children are more likely to move than those with them.[5] Further, separation and divorce are becoming increasingly important as factors precipitating moves and thus a source of bias in sampling from directories.

Intentionally unlisted numbers is a second problem associated with directory sampling. The problem tends to vary by community; it is especially severe in large metropolitan areas and virtually nonexistent in many rural areas. Brunner and Brunner reported that, contrary to popular belief, those most likely to have unlisted numbers are less educated, more likely to be employed in blue collar jobs, younger, more likely to be divorced, and less frequent joiners of voluntary associations.[6] Contact with telephone company personnel in the study area usually provides a means of obtaining rough estimates of the proportions of subscribers with unlisted numbers. If such efforts are not successful, a method suggested by Sudman for using census data to calculate the extent of unlisteds might be considered.[7]

A third problem is multiple listings. Cooper reported that 3 percent of all private telephone subscribers had listings in more than one directory.[8] This problem is most likely to exist in metropolitan areas and may provide reason for concern inasmuch as those who are listed in more than one directory tend to be professional or business people, introducing a potential bias. With considerable effort, this problem can sometimes be mitigated by examining the central exchanges (three-digit prefix) for each number drawn in a sample and eliminating those known to be exchanges not used in the geographic area covered by the study. Usually this information can be secured from the local telephone company.

Random Digit Dialing

The existence of the problems just mentioned has stimulated many researchers to utilize the technique of random digit dialing. This technique was developed for the explicit purpose of accessing *all* working telephones regardless of whether their numbers are published in directories. Several ways of implementing this approach to sampling have been developed, and these methods are described elsewhere in considerable detail.[9] The interested reader would do well to read them before deciding whether to use a random digit approach and how to implement it. The treatment here is somewhat brief because of the accessability of most of these references.

In simplified form, random digit dialing is implemented thus:

1. All working telephone exchanges, that is, the three-digit prefixes immediately preceding the last four numbers, are identified for the geographical area of concern through an examination of telephone directories and/or contact with the relevant telephone company(ies).
2. Tables of random numbers or a computerized version of the same are used to generate a list of four-digit numbers for each exchange. In studies that incorporate large numbers of exchanges, a sample of exchanges can be drawn by random methods and then a sample of four-digit numbers for

each sampled exchange can be drawn, resulting in a type of cluster sample.

3. Interviewers call each of the resultant seven-digit numbers, discarding those which are not working numbers.

Perhaps the single biggest drawback to this approach is the wasted effort for checking out unused and nonresidential phones. A national study found only one-fifth of the dialings connected with residential telephones.[10] The problem stems from the fact that entire blocks of numbers within exchanges frequently are unused. For example, in a particular exchange, the numbers from the first two blocks (i.e., 0000–1999) might be the only ones in use. Thus four-fifths of the 10 blocks in the exchange consist of nonworking numbers. In theory, it would be possible to determine unused blocks, but researchers have seldom reported success in gaining that information from telephone companies, and our experience has been no different.

Another problem encountered, mostly in large metropolitan areas, is that new exchanges are sometimes added after the directory is printed. Unless the researcher can secure such information, one of the reasons for using random digit dialing, that is, getting unpublished listings, is compromised.

Sudman has suggested a technique for greatly improving the efficiency of random digit dialing through the use of telephone directories.[11] The current directory is systematically sampled for residential telephone numbers. The last three digits of each number are ignored, and the resultant partial numbers (the three-number exchange plus the first of the last four numbers) are treated as banks. Random numbers are then used to generate complete telephone numbers from the 1000 possible numbers (e.g., 2000–2999) within each bank. A sample drawn in this way is self-weighting in the sense that a bank with all 1000 numbers in use is 10 times as likely to be included in the sample as one for which only 100 numbers are in use. The likelihood of this happening can be increased by drawing a larger number of listings from the directory, thus reducing the number of random digit calls made for each bank. A bank drawn eight times would be assigned that many more numbers than one sampled only once. By not selecting numbers for commercial listings from the directories, banks that consist mostly of commercial listings have less chance of being included.

The Sudman method markedly improves efficiency and successfully reaches unlisted numbers and most new listings. However, it still does not overcome the problem of newly added central exchanges. In addition, newly added banks within existing exchanges, a far more frequent occurrence than the adding of new exchanges, becomes a problem that is not present in the basic technique previously described. Nonetheless, we believe the method offers much promise and will be used increasingly in future research.

The users of random digit methods must be aware of other nagging, but not serious, problems to which attention may have to be given. Two such problems have been identified by Glasser and Metzger.[12] First, it may be difficult to determine the status of unanswered calls, making the calculation of response rates and decisions on follow-ups more difficult. Calls to nonworking numbers may produce a series of unanswered rings, no connection (silence or buzzer), or a recall signal (rapid busy signal). Determining what each means and thus how to categorize the results (not at home, malfunction, circuit overload, or disconnected) is sometimes difficult, especially when one study encompasses many telephone companies, each of which may handle disconnected phones with different signals. The second problem is that some households have two or more numbers, thus increasing their chance of being called. Although the number of such households is small (Glasser and Metzger report less than 3 percent),[13] they are likely to have atypical characteristics, that is, are more likely to have teenagers and be located in Eastern urban areas.

Choosing Between Directory Sampling and Random Digit Dialing: Which is Best?

We believe it unwise to decide between random digit and directory methods of sampling without consideration of the characteristics of the population surveyed, the constraints set by survey objectives, and a full consideration of the researcher's situation. In many regions of the country, notably rural areas, population turnover is slight and unlisted numbers infrequent. The bias introduced by sampling directories is likely to be so little as to make the added cost of random digit dialing unwarranted. For example, Sudman has noted that the fraction of unlisted telephones outside standard metropolitan statistical areas in Illinois is well under 5 percent.[14] He concludes that in these areas sampling of directories is preferable to random digit dialing.

Where population turnover is of particular concern and the area to be surveyed is covered by only one directory, it may be possible to time a study to occur very shortly after the directory is released. In other cases, although we expect them to be exceptions, telephone companies may be willing to provide an operator's directory that is completely up to date. In either case the argument favoring directory sampling is strengthened.

Although we do not doubt the ability of random digit dialing to pick up most listed numbers, the question of whether random digit dialing effectively elicits interviews from those who deliberately keep their numbers from being listed in published directories is still not answered. The reasons for requesting unlisted numbers undoubtedly vary but among this segment of the population are those who wish to avoid unsolicited telephone calls. Therefore we believe it is likely that this group will exhibit higher refusal rates than other groups. This raises the unanswered question of how effective random digit dialing is in gaining access to one of the major categories of households used to justify its use. This information is essential to making judgments about the proportion of unlisted numbers that warrants switching from directory listings to random digit dialing.

The survey objectives may also have some bearing on this decision. Bias against the young, the divorced, and new residents of a community, which one would expect as a result of sampling from directories, is less serious for some surveys than others. For example, a survey of people likely to vote in an upcoming local election may be little affected by missing those not in the telephone directory, inasmuch as these people are less likely to be registered voters. On the other hand, a survey of renters' views on barriers to buying homes may be greatly affected because of the considerable mobility of such people. The amount of bias that can be tolerated varies greatly by survey and in the end must be referred to the researcher's judgment.

A final consideration is response rate and data quality. We conducted two experiments in which statewide samples drawn from directories were randomly divided, and half were called under random digit conditions (knowledge of respondent's name was not revealed in any way) and half were called by a method in which knowledge of the respondent's identity was established before conducting the interview (i.e., the interviewer asked the person answering the telephone if this was the residence of the person whose name appeared in the directory).[15] Response rates and response quality for these two groups were virtually identical, suggesting that neither factor should be considered in selection of method. However, a third experiment was conducted in which half the names drawn from a directory sample were sent letters informing them that they would soon be called for a telephone interview, whereas the other half were called without prior warning. The refusal rate was cut from nearly 15 percent in the sample called without warning, to only 8 percent for those who recieved a letter notifying them of the subsequent call. Further, perhaps because the advance letter made them less nervous, respondents receiving letters provided somewhat more complete answers and cooperated more fully with the interviewer.[16] Since such prior letters can only be used when the household address is known, this procedure can only be used with a sample drawn from directory listings. Given the already high response rate without the prior notification and the lack of any differences in response quality, we suggest that, in general, the ability to use a prior letter is not a sufficient reason to reject random digit dialing in favor of directory sampling techniques. Rather, it should be one of several considerations.

The circumstances under which directory listings work best are the *same ones* under which random digit dialing can best be implemented and vice versa. In rural areas in which directories are usually adequate, random digit dialing also encounters few problems. In large metropolitan areas in which published directories are the least adequate, exchanges and blocks of numbers are most likely to be added, thus making random digit efforts subject to greater limitations or at least higher costs.

WRITING THE INTRODUCTION

Once the decision on sampling method has been made, the interviewer's introduction can be written to suit whichever sampling method has been selected. It seems difficult to overestimate the importance of what the prospective respondent hears in the introduction when he or she answers the telephone. A few appropriately chosen phrases must accomplish for the telephone interview what the packaging and cover letter do for the mail questionnaire. In a nutshell, the introduction must contain a statement of who is calling, what is requested, and why it is worth the time of the interviewee to respond.

Special significance is attached to the introduction of the telephone interview because it is at this point that most refusals occur. Once the actual interview begins, very few respondents terminate before the last question is asked.[17] Results from the TDM telephone surveys we have conducted show that most people who refuse will listen to the entire introduction before attempting to terminate. Consequently, the introduction provides an important opportunity to persuade the person on the other end of the line that the survey is worth his time. Thus it has come as a surprise to us that our efforts (via experimentation) to vary the wording of introductions produced negligible effects on response rates.[18] The lack of difference under conditions mentioning or not mentioning the respondent's name has already been noted. In some experiments we offered a copy of the results in the introduction because we thought this action would be interpretedd as a reward to at least some respondents and would promote an attitude of trust and willingness to cooperate. Again, there was no discernible effect on response rate.[19] In another experimental introduction, it was argued that the study was socially useful, an argument frequently found successful in mail questionnaire studies. Again there was no noticeable effect.[20]

However, before concluding that just any introduction will do, we should add that in each case we were attempting to write the best introduction possible within the constraints of the variables we were testing. Thus even the control introductions were written in an effort to convince the respondent to be interviewed. In all introductions, interviewers gave their names, the name of the institution and city from which they were calling, how we obtained the respondent's number, and a conservative estimate of how many minutes the interview would take.

Each of these elements may be quite important in convincing respondents to stay on the line. Often the association with a university tends to legitimate a study, leading the respondent to think, "The university would not be sponsoring this study if it were not important." Knowing the call is long distance also tends to increase its importance, inasmuch as the respondent knows each minute costs money. The statement of how his or her name was selected, although brief and somewhat innocuous, anticipates and perhaps satisfactorily answers one of the frequent questions asked by respondents, "Why me?" Finally, the estimate of time the interview will take answers the preeminent concern of some respondents. A knowledge of the time involved provides some notion of the size of the task before them, a fact that may encourage them to consent to the interview and, hopefully, not to terminate the call prematurely. Giving a conservative, but reasonable, estimate helps reduce the perceived costs of being interviewed.

The introductions we use in TDM telephone surveys incorporate all the basic elements just mentioned (see Example 7.1). In addition, the success of several (nonexperimental) efforts has led us to include a statement encouraging the potential respondent to ask questions at the outset. The goal of the introduction is to provide all the information most respondents would like to have before they agree to be interviewed and at the same time begin the process of establishing rapport. The final "ok?" included at the end of the introduction (Example 7.1) is a way of asking respondent permission to start the interview. Interviewers find this a natural way to end an introduction, and our explicit intent at this point is to avoid giving the respondent a feeling of being rushed into the interview, thus getting the questions started on a more relaxed note.

Depending on the survey design, the introductions may require modification. If an advance letter has been sent (the topic of the next section), respondents are asked whether it was received. If a respondent selection procedure is used to select respondents within the households (the topic of the section following the one on advance letters), it is inserted into the middle of the interview, as indicated in Example 7.1.

THE ADVANCE LETTER

Surprised by an unexpected telephone call and a request to be interviewed, respondents often react with suspicion. Some forthrightly state their belief that the call is some kind of joke. Others ask questions to satisfy their skepticism.

Example 7.1 Introductions Used Under Conditions of Random Digit Dialing and Directory Methods of Sampling

Introduction Used with Random Digit Dialing:

Hello. Is this _____? (IF NO, TERMINATE INTERVIEW WITH, E.G.: I
            (number)   am sorry I have the wrong number.)

Is this a residential telephone? (IF NO, TERMINATE WITH, E.G.: I
                                    am sorry I have the wrong place.)

This is _____ at Washington State University.
       (interviewer's name)
I am calling from our Public Opinion Laboratory in Pullman. We are
doing a state-wide research study in order to find out how people
feel about the communities in which they live and what can be done
to improve them. Your telephone number was drawn in a random sample
of the entire state.

INSERT SELECTION PROCEDURE IF USED[a]

The questions I need to ask should take about 15 minutes. I want
to add that I would be happy to answer any questions you might have
about the study, either now or later. Okay?

Introduction Used with Directory Sampling:

Hello. Is this the _____ residence?
             (last name)

(IF NO. The number I was calling is _____ and it was for
_____ residence.)
(first and last name)

(IF WRONG NUMBER, TERMINATE WITH, E.G.: I am sorry to have bothered
you.)

This is _____ at Washington State University. I am
       (interviewer's name)
calling from our Public Opinion Laboratory in Pullman. We are doing
a state-wide research study in order to find out how people feel
about the communities in which they live and what can be done to
improve them. Your telephone number was drawn in a random sample
of the entire state.

INSERT COMMENT ON PRIOR LETTER IF APPLICABLE[b]

INSERT SELECTION PROCEDURE IF USED[a]

[a]Selection procedure presented in Example 7.4.

[b]If prior letter sent this statement is inserted:
      Last week a letter was sent to you explaining a little about the study.
      Did you receive it?

      (IF NO. I'm sorry yours didn't reach you. It was a brief letter we
      sent so people would know that we would be calling them.)

Still others, and probably the majority, do not verbalize their concern, but reflect it by initially being extremely guarded in their responses. These reactions interfere with the respondent's ability to concentrate on questions and other information provided by the interviewer. It is reasonable to think that this element of surprise and uncertainty contributes both to refusals and the lowering of response quality. Sending an advance letter to notify potential respondents of the impending telephone call is a reasonable way to counter possible difficulties. It not only eliminates the element of surprise, but it also provides tangible evidence that the interviewer is legitimate and that the telephone call is neither a sales gimmick nor a practical joke. As previously noted, experimental evidence shows that advance letters positively affect response rates for samples of the general public.[21] The use of advance letters in later surveys has consistently produced response rates of over 90 percent for general public surveys. However, a prior letter does not seem to have much effect for some populations. In an experiment conducted by Tollefson, prior letters were randomly sent to half a sample of veterinarians being surveyed on clothing preferences.[22] The results showed no difference in response, with a rate for both groups of nearly 100 percent. Surveys of many specialized populations, such as students, ministers, and agency personnel, normally produce such high response rates that a prior letter cannot be expected to influence them.

It appears that a prior letter influences the quality of data obtained in household surveys. Several measures of data quality in the previously mentioned general public experiment showed a consistent trend to better results when the prior letter was used. For example, those who received the letter had a lower item nonresponse rate (1.11 versus 1.27 percent), were more likely to answer every question (59 versus 55 percent), were more likely to report voluntary association membership (41 versus 32 percent), and mentioned a higher average number of voluntary association memberships in response to an open-ended question (1.56 versus 1.26 percent).[23]

The letter also appeared to affect respondent cooperation as perceived by the interviewer. Respondents who received the letter were seen as more helpful and more interested in the interview. Another indication of interest was that respondents who received the prior letter were more likely to ask for copies of results. Further, it was found that interviewers reported more difficulty in beginning the interviews with respondents who did not have advance warning.

These results lead us to conclude that a prior letter informing sample members of the impending survey should be sent to samples of the general public whenever possible. Several guidelines can be offered for preparation of the letter. First, it need not be lengthy. In the aforementioned experiments three lengths of letters were used—83, 268, and 538 words, respectively.[24]

The longer letters involved more detailed descriptions of the study and in-cluded efforts to increase social rewards (emphasis on social utility, promise of copy of results, and the taking of a more consultative approach) and decrease social costs (stressing that the interview is short and easy, promising anonym-ity). The differences in response rates among the letters were small, leading the author to conclude that the important consideration is the fact that the letter was sent and not the amount of content.

These results influence the design of the typical advance letter used in TDM telephone surveys (see Example 7.2). The aim of the letter is to strike a balance between being complete enough to relieve potential anxiety as-sociated with the surprise of learning of one's inclusion in a survey, yet general enough to leave some questions unanswered and thus create a de-gree of curiosity. Several points are emphasized in the letter. The first mes-sage is that the household will be called very soon. The second message is that the person to be interviewed may not be the person to whom the advance letter was mailed, that is, the name appearing in the telephone directory. We believe it is very important to include this when the respondent selection procedure is used, to prevent some recipients from looking forward with anticipation to the interview, only to be disappointed when the call is made and the person is informed that his or her opinion is not the one being solicited.

The third message is a concise description of the study topic. It is important that the description be couched in general terms likely to be consistent with the value systems of most respondents, rather than specific terms that would appeal to a more limited group. Otherwise the letter could result in many respondents deciding before they are called that they know nothing about the topic and/or that it is of no interest to them personally. Thus, as shown in Example 7.2, respondents are told that the study concerns how they feel about their community and what can be done to improve it, rather than, for example, a study of satisfaction with present community and potential for moving to another community. Similarly, a survey that focuses heavily on the importance of athletics to universities might be described better in terms of a study about tax-supported universities and how they can best serve the peo-ple of the state, because many will have no interest in or knowledge of athletics. Whatever the description, it is important that it not create a false impression, which could result in subsequent apprehension and suspicion when the call is made and the topic seems different from that described in the letter.

The fourth message in the letter sets the time expectation and advises the respondent to have the interviewer call back if the interviewer's call comes at an inconvenient time. We consider this particularly important because bad timing is a major cause of refusals. Thus we attempt to prevent inconvenience from being used as an excuse to refuse to be interviewed.

Example 7.2   Example of Advance Letter to Respondents

WASHINGTON STATE UNIVERSITY
PULLMAN, WASHINGTON 99163

DEPARTMENT OF RURAL SOCIOLOGY
Room 23, Wilson Hall

April 1, 1973

Mr. J. F. Stevenson
718 North 48th Street
Yakima, WA 99222

Dear Mr. Carlson:

Within a week or so, we will be calling you from Pullman as part of a research study. This is a state-wide survey in which we are seeking to understand how Washington residents feel about the communities in which they live and what should be done to improve them.

We are writing in advance of our telephone call because we have found that many people appreciate being advised that a research study is in process, and they will be called.

When our interviewer calls, she (or he) will ask to interview an adult member of your family. In order that our results represent all of the people in Washington, we ask to interview a female in some households and a male in others.

Altogether the interview should only take about fifteen minutes. If by chance we should happen to call at an inconvenient time, please tell the interviewer and they will be happy to call back later.

Your help and that of the others being asked to participate in this effort to find out what people want from their communities is essential to the study's success. We greatly appreciate it.

If you have any questions, please don't hesitate to ask our interviewer. Or, you may contact me by phone at (509) 335-8623 or by mail.

Cordially,

Don A. Dillman

Don A. Dillman
Project Director

DAD:cjd

Finally, the letter attempts to build rapport by expressing appreciation to the respondents and opening the possibility to them of contacting the director of the survey. The letters are produced in a manner intended to convey to respondents that they are an important part of the study. A personalized appearance is achieved by processing the letter in the same manner as the cover letter of TDM questionnaires (see Chapter 5). It is printed on letterhead stationery, typed on an automatic typewriter or reproduced by a multilith process, and has names and addresses actually typed at the top and signatures individually applied using the pressed blue ball point method. Further, names and addresses are individually typed on the outside of the envelope in normal business letter fashion. Address labels are not used.

SELECTING RESPONDENTS WITHIN THE HOUSEHOLD

Many, if not most, surveys of the general public require that the interviewer go through a systematic process for selecting the member of the household to be interviewed. Research objectives often require that results be generalizable to the entire population of adults and not just households. Interviewing whoever happens to answer thwarts the achievement of this objective. For example, the results of many surveys we have conducted show that females answer the telephone about two-thirds of the time, even in the evening hours when the chance is greatest for all adults in a household to be at home. Further, it is possible that married males who answer the telephone tend to differ from those in households where the female tends to answer. For example, the chances of males answering the telephone seem likely to increase if they normally receive business calls at home during the evening, as is often the case with professionals and business men.

A variety of selection procedures may be used to avoid bias resulting from interviewing whomever answers the telephone. One way of systematically selecting respondents has been developed by Troldahl and Carter.[25] This procedure requires that four selection tables be prepared and randomly assigned to the numbers to be called (Example 7.3). To use these tables only two items of information need be obtained from those who answer the telephone—the number of persons 18 years or older living in the households and the number who are men. The interviewer uses this information to determine which respondent to interview by finding the intersection point of the row showing the number of men in the household and the column reporting the total number of adults.

The Troldahl and Carter procedure achieves simplicity, although it precludes the possibility of surveying persons in households with three or more adults (of the same sex) who happen to be neither the youngest nor oldest household member of their sex. Since very few households have three or more adult members of the same sex and there is a great deal of heterogeneity in the characteristics of those neglected, the bias is not usually serious.[26] A second minor bias exists for three-person households regardless of sex composition because of the use of only four selection tables. We do not believe that either source of bias is great enough to warrant more complex

Example 7.3   Four Versions of Selection Table Used in Trodahl and Carter Procedure [a]

Total number of men in household	Total Number of Adults in Household			
	1	2	3	4 or more
Version I				
0	Woman	Oldest woman	Youngest woman	Youngest woman
1	Man	Man	Man	Oldest woman
2		Oldest man	Youngest man	Youngest man
3			Youngest man	Oldest man
4+				Oldest man
Version II				
0	Woman	Youngest woman	Youngest woman	Oldest woman
1	Man	Man	Oldest woman	Man
2		Oldest man	Woman	Oldest woman
3			Youngest man	Woman or oldest woman
4+				Oldest man
Version III				
0	Woman	Youngest woman	Oldest woman	Oldest woman
1	Man	Woman	Man	Youngest woman
2		Youngest man	Oldest man	Oldest man
3			Oldest man	Youngest man
4+				Youngest man
Version IV				
0	Woman	Oldest woman	Oldest woman	Youngest woman
1	Man	Woman	Youngest woman	Man
2		Youngest man	Woman	Youngest woman
3			Oldest man	Woman or youngest woman
4+				Youngest man

[a]Reproduced by permission from: Troldahl, Verling C. and Roy E. Carter, Jr., "Random Selection of Respondents Within Households in Phone Surveys," Journal of Marketing Research, Vol. 1, May 1964, p. 72.

selection methods that would increase the burden for both the interviewer and potential respondent.

Equal numbers of each of the four versions are assigned randomly to the study households. Each version is incorporated into questionnaires, as shown in Example 7.4. The procedures of the preceding chapter apply to constructing this page. For example, arrows are used to direct the interviewer, and lowercase letters are used to identify what should be read to the respondent.

Example 7.4 Example of Respondent Selection Procedure

It is important that we interview a man in some households and a woman in others so that the results will truly represent all the people of your state. To find out who I need to talk to in your household, I need to ask two short questions.

Q-1 The first one is, how many people 18 years and older live in this household including yourself?————————————→ CIRCLE ANSWER IN THIS ROW

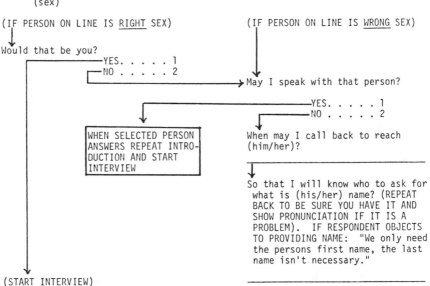

Q-2 How many of them are men?

CIRCLE ANSWER IN THIS COLUMN

		1	2	3	4+
0	WOMAN	OLDEST WOMAN	YOUNGEST WOMAN	YOUNGEST WOMAN
1	MAN	MAN	MAN	OLDEST WOMAN
2			OLDEST MAN	YOUNGEST MAN	YOUNGEST MAN
3				YOUNGEST MAN	OLDEST MAN
4+					OLDEST MAN

(INTERVIEWER: CIRCLE CATEGORY AT INTERSECTION AND USE IN THIS SENTENCE)

Okay, according to the method used by our university I need to interview the
_____ in your household.
        (sex)

(IF PERSON ON LINE IS <u>RIGHT</u> SEX)   (IF PERSON ON LINE IS <u>WRONG</u> SEX)

Would that be you?
            YES. 1
            NO 2   May I speak with that person?

                                                        YES. 1
                                                        NO 2

WHEN SELECTED PERSON ANSWERS REPEAT INTRODUCTION AND START INTERVIEW

When may I call back to reach (him/her)?
_____

So that I will know who to ask for what is (his/her) name? (REPEAT BACK TO BE SURE YOU HAVE IT AND SHOW PRONUNCIATION IF IT IS A PROBLEM). IF RESPONDENT OBJECTS TO PROVIDING NAME: "We only need the persons first name, the last name isn't necessary."

(START INTERVIEW)

The questions I need to ask should take about fifteen minutes. But before starting them I want to mention that I would by happy to answer any questions you might have about the study either now or later. Okay?

Putting in the selection table in the form shown in Example 7.4 reduces interviewer decisionmaking to a prescribed mechanical operation of following arrows and determining an intersection point. However, this portion of the interview remains one of the most difficult to administer. The interviewer must be very careful and prepared for any number of contingencies. Respondents are more likely to ask questions here than at any other place in the interview. If the person will not answer either of the key selection questions, the interviewer is faced with a serious dilemma. It is not possible simply to skip over these "troublesome" questions to others, as might be done later in a difficult interview.

THE NEED FOR CENTRALIZED INTERVIEWING FACILITIES

The concern that prompts us to discuss in some detail the issue of whether telephone interviews should be conducted from a central or dispersed facility (such as individual home telephones) has been aptly summarized by Eastlack and Assael:

> It is at the point of "human-to-human" contact that the bulk of survey research fails. The weakest link in the chain of decision-directed information gathering which we call survey research is after the well drawn sampling plan is put into action, the pretested and re-tested questionnaire is used, and the precise interviewing instructions are administered: *It is when the interviewer takes over.*[27]

A centralized interviewing facility in which all calls are made from the same room or adjacent rooms under the watchful eye of supervisors cannot prevent interviewer-related problems, but it offers the potential for greatly reducing them. Although this facility is obviously not essential to conducting interviews, its contribution to data quality leads us to view it as one of the most important components of the telephone TDM. Further, the costs of establishing such a facility are often surprisingly low. Sometimes it is even possible to develop one on a temporary basis without cost.

The close supervision makes it possible to quickly catch interviewer errors and take corrective measures. In addition, interviewer questions can be answered immediately. Further, by having the interviewers turn in each interview schedule as it is completed, it can be scanned for completeness, legibility in recording answers to open-ended questions, and so on. If there is an omission, an inconsistency, or an ambiguous response, it can be brought to the interviewer's attention while that particular interview is still fresh in the interviewer's mind. The chance of an interviewer being able to correct such problems is much greater in this situation than if he or she is asked about it after completing several more interviews or after several days have elapsed. Similarly, if clarification requires calling the respondent a second time, that contact can be made within a short time after the original interview, while it is still fresh in the respondent's mind.

An additional advantage of centralized interviewing facilities is apparent when respondents question the authenticity of the interview, ask questions the interviewer simply cannot answer, or even demand to speak to whomever is directing the survey. A centralized facility makes it possible for the supervisor to take over immediately in such situations and often obtain a completed interview.

Centralized interviewing also makes it more difficult for interviewers to falsify interviews or conduct them in any way other than that which is prescribed by the researcher. At the same time, constant supervision provides many opportunities for the supervisor to give positive reinforcement to the interviewers. In short, the centralized facility provides for both control and support of the interviewing staff.

A key advantage of centralized facilities is that it is possible to employ interviewers who have little or no previous experience. They can be quickly trained to a level adequate for conducting interviews in a supervised situation. The centralized laboratory makes interviewing by people with little experience possible in two ways. First, interviewers do not have to be trained to meet all possible situations and circumstances with only their own good judgment as a back-up. The interviewers can turn directly to the supervisor for help with, for example, special problems of eligibility, how to record an answer not enumerated in the coding scheme, or a respondent's esoteric question. Any tendency on the part of beginning interviewers to read questions in a biased manner or to misread them altogether are matters that can be quickly identified so corrective action can be taken.

The second way in which a centralized laboratory may be a substitute for elaborate training is that, instead of learning only the norms of the interviewing process in pretest training situations, interviewers are trianed "on the job." The actual interviewing activities serve as a training process, with continual feedback to interviewers from the supervisor and fellow interviewers (as well as from respondents) as the source of learning.

Centralized interviewing is also quite efficient, a feature of particularly great importance if the survey is conducted under severe time pressure. Although questionnaires may be parceled out equally to interviewers when interviewing begins, some will finish their share sooner than others, because of variation in the lengths of interviews and the number of not-at-homes, busy signals, and refusals. The supervisor of a centralized facility can easily reallocate uncompleted questionnaires to interviewers who finish ahead of schedule. Also, the special problems of continuous busy signals and wrong numbers may be directed to a person especially trained to handle them. Tentative refusals (someone who said "no" but did so in a way that suggests they might be convinced to continue) or other problematic call-backs can be reassigned to more experienced interviewers. In addition, unanticipated problems, such as a frequently asked question that interviewers are unprepared to answer, can be readily identified and instructions for handling them quickly disseminated.

The advantages of centralized interviewing are sufficiently great that it behooves every telephone researcher to consider developing such a facility. This is the case even where a small number of highly trained and trusted interviewers are to be used, because even they cannot handle all contingencies, nor are they immune from mistakes.

An example of an inexpensive centralized facility is the Washington State University Public Opinion Laboratory (Example 7.5). It is a converted seminar room of relatively small dimensions (24 by 17 feet), yet it is large enough for 14 interviewers to work comfortably and efficiently. The room was converted by building desks that extend outward only two feet along two of the walls. Acoustical dividers were placed every three feet along the benches to separate interviewing stations. To control sound, carpeting was added to the work desks. This supplemented the acoustical soundboard used on the dividers and wall above each desk. The conversion was completed by the installation of 14 telephone lines. The arrangement, despite being relatively open, makes it possible for each of the 14 interviewers to conduct interviews in such a way as not to disturb his or her neighbor. The compactness also makes it possible for the supervisor(s) to be no more than a few feet away from any interviewer.

The costs of this conversion included only the carpentry work required to build the wall desks and the standard charge of the telephone company for installing each telephone line. In this case, the telephones are attached to plug-ins so they can be removed for storage, and the room can be used for its original purpose when it is not needed for a survey.

A semicentralized facility can often be developed on a makeshift basis by arranging for the use of telephones in employee offices of a college or agency. If the offices are close to one another, the supervisor can always be nearby. Night interviewing, usually needed for household surveys, does not ordinarily interfere with the working hours of these offices.

We stress the simplicity of the arrangement because we believe sophistication in physical surroundings is not a necessary condition for quality interviews. However, there are ways in which the elements of a very basic laboratory can be improved. Monitoring equipment can be installed so that a supervisor can listen to both sides of an interview or even take part in a three-way conversation if required. Headphones can be substituted for receivers to allow interviewers to work with both hands. Speaker telephones

Example 7.5   Diagram of Telephone Laboratory Used by the Author

Blackboard for special Instructions

Coatrack

Work Table for Sorting Questionnaires

Carrels are separated by acoustically treated 1" thick panels. These panels measure 18¾" (width) X 19½" (height), and rest on individually collapsible desks which have been carpeted. Each carrel is equipped with two cabinets for equipment storage, black dial type phone w/shoulder rest, and phone jack on wall under desk.

24"

Room is 23'-10" x 17'-2¼

Windows

can be installed, enabling everyone in the room to listen to both sides of interviews used for training purposes. Recording equipment (complete with the necessary "beeper") can also be installed for purposes of preserving a record of interviews for further analysis, if appropriate. There are doubtless other improvements that can be worked out when cost is not a barrier, including computer terminals with cathode ray tubes on which the questionnaire is displayed.

RECRUITING THE INTERVIEWERS

At first, the task of recruiting and training interviewers may seem an extraordinarily difficult problem. Unless the researcher is located in an area in which telephone interviews are routinely conducted by others, it is doubtful that a supply of trained interviewers is readily available. Thus one is likely to be faced with the task of locating people without experience and training them to an adequate level of competence.

The problem is often exacerbated by the desire to complete a study as quickly as possible. This can best be done by hiring more interviewers and having each of them work a shorter period of time. Further, the nature of the telephone interviewing task tends to create a need of its own for more interviewers. Telephone interviewing is an exceedingly demanding activity, both physically and cognitively. Conducting one interview after another, interrupted only by the postinterview editing, causes interviewers to tire quickly. We have found that although many interviewers find the task quite enjoyable and can be called on for survey after survey, relatively few want to work seven to ten consecutive evenings, the time that may be required to complete a study. The result is that the number of interviewers needed for a survey may exceed by half or more the number of interviewer stations the researcher wants to have in operation at any one time.

However, the need to find a considerable number of potential interviewers is not as much of a problem as it first appears. For one thing, as noted earlier, the skill requirement is not as great as that for face-to-face interviewing. Face-to-face interviewers must learn how to conduct the interview itself, locate and sample households, handle travel expense reports, plan their own day, and to know when, for what reasons, and how to make contact with supervisory personnel. Also, they must learn to be their own decision makers in efficiently planning their call-backs. When they knock on the door of a household, they are essentially on their own; help from a supervisor is a few hours or even days away. Finally, a review of the interviewer's completed questionnaires and a chance to correct errors may not be possible until a good share of the interviews are completed. The researcher is in a position of getting very little direct feedback on the interviewer's performance other than the completed form itself. For all these reasons, the researcher must be very confident in the abilities of interviewers to handle all the problems they face; perhaps most important he must be able to trust that they will conscientiously conduct the interviews, before placing them in the field. In contrast, telephone interviewing from centralized telephone facilities allows one to recruit interviewers with little or no previous experience and provide them with the necessary skills in a few brief training sessions.

Finding an adequate number of applicants from which to recruit may not be at all difficult. It is most desirable to conduct household surveys in the early evening hours, about 6:00 to 9:00 p.m. This increases the efficiency of the task inasmuch as all members of the household are most likely to be at home. Because of the unusual work hours for interviewers and the temporary nature of the work, labor pools may be tapped that are not normally available for full-time work during the day. In particular, this includes home-makers with young children. During the day child care is more of a problem, whereas at night a spouse or school-age sitter may be called on. A certain number of already employed workers interested in "moonlighting" are also likely to apply. Finally, in college communities students provide an excellent source of help. In general this group is particularly desirable because of their generally high intellectual capacities, the flexibility of their schedules (day as well as night interviewing), and the likelihood that some have been exposed to social research methods in their course work.

Just as the telephone interviewing task differs markedly from face-to-face interviewing, the selection criteria for the two types of interviews are also different. Personal appearance and ability to organize a work day are not major concerns in selecting telephone interviewers. The skills that contribute to satisfactory telephone interviewing appear to be fewer than those needed for face-to-face interviewing. The basic requirements for telephone interviewing center around a person's voice, for example, clarity, and other communication abilities. However, even with a smaller number of requirements it is difficult to offer advice on hiring good telephone interviewers. We have yet to see experimental evidence that unequivocally shows that interviewers with certain characteristics produce better results than others. Thus our selection procedures are based in part on subjective judgments.

Our screening of prospective interviewers focuses on four criteria. The first is an ability to read questions fluently. Some people have considerable difficulty with this task. Even after several practice sessions they continue to read questions in a halting manner. The problem is sometimes reflected in a tendency to read questions in a word-by-word manner and is often compounded by the necessity for longer than usual pauses between questions to determine which question should be read next. Asking potential interviewers to carefully study a page from a questionnaire and then have them interview someone with it aids in identifying such difficulties.

The second criterion is the sound of the interviewer's voice over the telephone. Some voices are difficult to understand, and this is of special concern when long distance calls are made, because connections are often poor. Occasionally voices are quite understandable, but have a harshness or otherwise irritating quality that makes them difficult to listen to for a long period of time. The only real test of the degree to which a voice can be understood is to listen to it over the telephone. When possible, the voice is evaluated by someone who has not personally met the prospective interviewer. Thus they are in the position of judging the interviewer's voice on the same bases a respondent might. This task can be done simultaneously with an evaluation of the prospective interviewer's ability to read questions fluently.

The third criterion on which a prospective interviewer is evaluated is the extent to which his or her voice interferes with those of other interviewers. In a centralized facility an overly loud or harsh voice may make it difficult for other interviewers to conduct their own interviews. It becomes a serious problem when two interviewers are only a few sentences apart in their respective interviews, and the interfering voice causes the other interviewer to stumble or unconsciously skip a few sentences. Another problem is that such a voice may cause "evasive actions" in other interviewers (such as covering the ear not held to the receiver or talking louder), putting additional strain on an already difficult task.

The final criterion on which prospective interviewers are evaluated is quite distinct from the three preceding ones. It is the interviewer's ability to respond to questions from the respondent. Some prospective interviewers find it difficult to "ad lib" a necessary response and communicate it in a manner consistent in quality and tone with the remainder of the interview. Thus, as part of the evaluation of prospective interviewers, they are asked questions to which they must spontaneously formulate acceptable answers. For example, prospective interviewers might be asked as part of a test interview "How did you get my name?" or "How long will this take?"

It was originally supposed that females would get fewer refusals than males; we reasoned that the female voice would be considerably less threatening than the male's, especially when the phone call was unanticipated. In several statewide surveys we found no differences in response rates of male and female interviewers,[28] nor any interactional effect between the sex of respondent and that of the interviewer.[29] In particular, female respondents are no more likely to refuse when called by a male than by another female.

Although we have seen no experimental evidence to suggest limiting interviewers to females, we conclude that it is a good idea to avoid employing males for more than half the interviewing positions in a centralized laboratory. The lower pitch of their voices often results in a "masking effect" that leads them to talk more loudly. The result is more voice interference among interviewers.

TRAINING THE INTERVIEWERS

The comfort of having close supervision in a centralized laboratory should not lead one to conclude that interviewer training is an optional matter, or that the best way for interviewers to learn is to immediately start calling respondents. If the interview recruits lack experience and there is a fairly large number to train, it is essential that the training methods are worked out carefully, well in advance of the actual training. Our approach to training is based on an assessment of the skills an interviewer must have before dialing the first respondent.

Operating the Telephone

Operating a telephone is an essential part of interviewer training, and it is more complex than it appears on the surface. One aspect of this is simply the problem of dialing the respondents. If long distance calls are involved, interviewers must be instructed how to make them. If leased wires are being used, for example, the WATTS system, a special procedure may be required for using those lines. If calling from an agency or university with its own switchboard, a procedure not known to interviewers might also be required. In addition, interviewers must also be told how to recognize various wire signals. For example, in some telephone systems a "one beep per second" signal indicates the line is busy, and a two beep per second signal is known as a "reorder" and indicates that, for some reason, possibly mechanical, the call did not go through. Successive reorder signals suggest getting help from the operator, whereas a busy signal only suggests setting the questionnaire aside for a short while.

Finally, interviewers must be instructed on how to get information on new or changed numbers when necessary, if, for example, a recording informs them that a number has been changed. A few moments of instruction and a sheet on how to dial various types of calls has been found to increase interviewer efficiency markedly—especially in the early stages of a survey.

Answering Respondent Questions

Respondents are frequently interested in learning more about a study than interviewers would routinely tell them in the introductory remarks. Most often it is a matter of general curiosity. At other times, whether they agree to be interviewed depends on the answers they receive. Thus from the standpoint of public relations as well as successful interviewing, the interviewers must know much more about the survey than what questions are in the questionnaire and how to ask them. As part of their training, then, interviewers are given considerable background on the survey objectives and other likely concerns of respondents. This orientation frequently includes a description of the steps in the survey process that occur before the interviewing and what happens after, including a tour of the computer facilities.

A summary sheet of anticipated questions is also prepared. It is posted near each interviewer for easy reference. The first section of this summary sheet includes the questions that tend to occur in most surveys. As shown in Example 7.6, most concern the survey and the respondent's role in it. Questions about the specific survey likely to be raised at any point in the interview are included on the sheet in the second section, entitled, "This Survey in Particular." Answers needed for specific questions on the questionnaire are included on the questionnaire itself rather than on the sheet. An example might be the meaning of a word, for example, "metropolitan area," as used in the questionnaire. An inventory of frequently offered reasons for refusals and ways to counteract them makes up the final section. Interviewers, particularly new ones, find this section quite useful.

Interviewers are carefully trained to use this sheet by means of practice interviews in which the person being interviewed (usually the supervisor or project director) asks some questions that can be answered only by reference to the summary sheet. Emphasis is placed on getting a natural sound into the interviewer's voice when responding to one of the questions. To achieve this, they are encouraged to paraphrase rather than read the answer verbatim. This practice, rather than simply reading a programmed response, is essential, because the respondent's questions are seldom asked exactly as worded on the sheet.

The results from use of this back-up sheet are exceedingly positive. Many interviewers do not have to use it after the first night or two but find security in its presence. The researcher can also take some degree of comfort in knowing that the respondent's simplest questions will not be met with a nervous apology of the type "I don't know sir; I am just an interviewer and no one has told me that," making both the interviewer and research project look bad to the respondent.

Completing The Call Record

Most interviews are not completed on the first attempt. Many require three, six, or even more call-backs. Some calls may result in conversations with one or more members of the household. A "call record," which interviewers are trained to complete with great care, can prevent a number of embarrassing moments, such as recalling a husband who explains to an interviewer for the second time that evening that his wife—the selected respondent—is out of town for three days.

Each TDM telephone questionnaire contains a call record that takes up the major portion of the cover page (see Example 7.7). It is placed on that page regardless of how much of the introductory material must be relegated to other pages. This is because the call-back information is used by the interview supervisor and others to sort questionnaires into appropriate categories, such as disconnected phones, refusals, completed interviews, call back later tonight, call back tomorrow morning, and so on. Efficiency requires having that information on the front page of the questionnaire. It is important that interviewers be trained to report each requested piece of information in complete detail. A specification of the date and time each call is made helps in planning when to schedule call-backs. For example, a series of no answers every night for a full week between 6:00 and 9:00 p.m. would suggest that a household

Example 7.6   Example of "What the Respondent Might Like to Know" Sheet Provided to All Interviewers

Washington State University
Public Opinion Laboratory
Community Preference Study
April, 1973

WHAT THE RESPONDENT MIGHT LIKE TO KNOW
About This Study

ABOUT THE SURVEY

WHAT IS THE PUBLIC OPINION LABORATORY?

It is a division of the Social Research Center, which was established to do research that concerns state and local problems. The Laboratory is used for surveys like this one in which we are attempting to find out how people feel about various problems faced in our State.

WHO IS SPONSORING (PAYING FOR) THE SURVEY?

It is sponsored by the Department of Rural Sociology. And, is being paid for jointly by state and federal research funds allocated to it.

WHAT IS THE PURPOSE OF THIS SURVEY?

There is a lot that isn't known about what makes people satisfied with their communities. Studies such as this one are done to find out what it is that people especially like and don't like about the communities in which they live. We hope the results will be helpful in improving them. This survey is one of four being done throughout the United States right now.

WHO IS THE PERSON RESPONSIBLE FOR THE SURVEY? MAY I TALK TO HIM/HER?

The person is Dr. Don Dillman, a researcher for the Department of Rural Sociology. I am sure he would be happy to talk with you. I can have him call you, or if you like you can call him collect. His telephone number is 509-335-8623.

ABOUT THE RESPONDENTS ROLE IN THE SURVEY

HOW DID YOU GET MY NAME (TELEPHONE NUMBER)?

Everyone's number was drawn from the current telephone directories in use throughout the state. The method we use means that every telephone number has an equal chance of being drawn, and it is strictly by chance that your's is one of them.

HOW CAN I BE SURE THIS IS AUTHENTIC?

I would be glad to give you my telephone number here in Pullman and you may call me back collect.

(If that isn't acceptable) I can give you my supervisor's number and you can call him/her collect. That number is 509-335-4749.

Example 7.6   Continued

WHY DO YOU NEED TO KNOW HOW MANY PEOPLE LIVE HERE?

> Different households have different numbers of people living in them.
> And if our suvey is to be truly representative of all the people in
> the state then in some households I need to talk to a man and in others
> a woman. When more than two adults live in a household I need to talk
> to the oldest one in some and the youngest in others. So to find out
> who I need to talk to I first have to know how many adults live in
> your household and how many of them are men.

WHY DON'T YOU INTERVIEW MY (HUSBAND/WIFE/SON/DAUGHTER, ETC.)?

> We can't do that because it's one of the things that keeps our
> surveys from being representative of the entire state. If we didn't
> follow this selection procedure all of the time we would probably end
> up with too many men, or on the other hand too many women, of certain
> ages.

IS THIS CONFIDENTIAL?

> Yes, most definitely! After the interview is completed the answers
> are put onto computer cards without names. Then the questionnaires
> are thrown away. All information we release is in the form of a
> certain percent "yes" and a certain percent said "no." In this form
> no individual response can ever be identified.

> Also, the matter of confidentiality is terribly important to the
> success of our Laboratory, because we do a lot of surveys. Thus,
> we are very careful to protect people's anonymity.

CAN I GET A COPY OF RESULTS?

> Yes, we would be glad to send it to you, if you will give me your
> current address. We hope to have the results ready in about three
> months.

THIS SURVEY IN PARTICULAR

DOES THIS SURVEY HAVE ANYTHING TO DO WITH THE LAND USE PLANNING DEBATE
IN THE LEGISLATURE?

> No, there is no connection at all.

be called during the day, because members of that household might work at night.

Requiring the interviewer's name to be on the sheet lets the supervisor know who to talk to if a question arises about an earlier call or even a completed interview. The recall code shown in Example 7.7 reduces the uncertainty of how to start a conversation when one or more persons of a household have been spoken with previously. Without the code and further detail provided in the result column, the early moments of the recalls may be awkward, as the interviewer tries to determine how much or how little has previously been explained to the respondent. Thus interviewing personnel are instructed on the use of the code column and the result column of this call

Example 7.6   Continued

POSSIBLE ANSWERS TO REASONS FOR REFUSALS

REASONS FOR REFUSING	. . . AND POSSIBLE RESPONSES
TOO BUSY	This should only take a few minutes. Sorry to have caught you at a bad time, I would be happy to call back. When would be a good time for me to call in the next day or two?
BAD HEALTH	I'm sorry to hear that. Have you been sick long? I would be happy to call back in a day or two. Would that be okay?

(IF LENGTHY OR SERIOUS ILLNESS, substitute another member of household. IF THAT ISN'T POSSIBLE, excuse yourself and indicate they will not be called again.) |
TOO OLD	Older people's opinions are just as important in this particular survey as anyone else's. In order for the results to be representative for all residents of the state, we have to be sure that older people have as much chance to give their opinion as anyone else does. We really do want your opinion.
FEEL INADEQUATE: DON'T KNOW ENOUGH TO ANSWER	The questions are not at all difficult. They mostly concern how you feel about your community rather than how much you know about certain things. Some of the people we have already interviewed had the same concern you have, but once we got started they didn't have any difficulty answering the questions. Maybe I could read just a few questions to you and you can see what they are like.
NOT INTERESTED	Its awfully important that we get the opinions of everyone in the sample other-wise the results won't be very useful. So, I'd really like to talk with you.
NO ONE ELSE'S BUSINESS WHAT I THINK	I can certainly understand, that's why all of our interviews are confidential. Protecting people's privacy is one of our major concerns and to do it people's names are separated from the answers just as soon as the interview is over. And, all the results are released in a way that no single individual can ever be identified.
OBJECTS TO SURVEYS	We think this particular survey is very important because the questions are ones that people in government want to know answers to, so would really like to have your opinion too.
OBJECTS TO TELEPHONE SURVEYS	We have just recently started doing our surveys by telephone, because this way is so much faster and it costs a lot less, especially when there aren't very many questions like in this survey.

record to provide any other information that would be helpful to another interviewer who places a later call. The abbreviations help accomplish this concisely and help supervisors sort questionnaires easily. The call record in this illustration can be used either with directory sampling or random digit methods. In the former, the interviewer would be provided with a questionnaire with the name already on it. With random digit methods, the interviewer is provided with a list of numbers, and he transfers the number to a blank questionnaire only when a respondent is reached.

Administering the Questionnaire

Administering telephone questionnaires to respondents shares some features with face-to-face interviewing. The perennial problems of reading questions exactly as they are written, making certain respondents understand the questions, and probing neutrally but persistently apply equally to both, and must be addressed in interviewer training. To overcome such problems, a great deal of emphasis is placed on having interviewers participate in several practice interviews.

These practice interviews give them a chance to experience all aspects of a study, from dialing the telephone to answering questions about the study. This also gives the trainer a chance to provide feedback to the interviewer of the myriad of details associated with successful interviewing by telephone. These include adjustment of voice inflection and speed, learning to write an answer while mentally preparing to state the next question, and gaining skill at politely asking respondents to slow down so that there is time to record verbatim answers.

A "rule book" is prepared to help interviewers master the interviewing task (Example 7.8). Consisting of a page or more of instructions, it is designed to acquaint interviewers with pre- and postinterview procedures, as well as with the actual interview schedule. It is posted in front of the interviewers so that it can be consulted for appropriate probes and responses to difficult situations. Provided to the interviewer in the first practice session, it serves as a constant reminder of the most important aspects of interviewing and becomes an important part of the training process.

The process of training interviewers involves four types of practice interviews. The first is one in which the prospective interviewer only observes. The interview is role-played by experienced interviewers, one of whom acts as the respondent and the other as the interviewer. The respondent presents many problems to the interviewer, such as unintelligible answers to open-ended questions and frequent "I don't knows," which require the interviewer to overcome them. The observation of interviewer errors, some of which are

Example 7.7   Example of Cover Page with Call Record

Washington State University
Public Opinion Laboratory
Community Preference Study
(April 1973)

Name _____

Phone # _____ + _____

Street _____

City _____

Hello.   Is this the _____(last name)_____ residence?
         (IF NO. The number I was calling is _____
         and it was for the _____(first and last name)_____
         residence.)
         (IF WRONG NUMBER, TERMINATE WITH, E.G.: I am sorry to
         have bothered you.)

         This is _____(interviewer's name)_____ at Washington
         State University. I am calling from our Public
         Opinion Laboratory in Pullman. We are doing a
         state-wide research study in order to find out how
         people feel about the communities in which they live
         and what can be done to improve them. Your telephone
         number was drawn in a random sample of the entire
         state. (Go to page 2)

COMPUTER CODE
ID #..........1-5
Sex 1 Male   2 Female..6
County.......7-8

Final Status..9
   1 = IC
   2 = PIC
   3 = REF
   4 = DISC
   5 = WN
   6 = NA

Date	Time	Interviewer	Result	Code for Recalls

Abbreviations:

NA = No answer

NH = Not home

WR = Will return (when)

REF = Refused (when, why,
      at what point, M or
      F)

IC = Interview
      completed
      (we like
      this one)

PIC = Partially
      completed

WN = Wrong
      number

DISC = Disconnect

Code for Recalls:

A = Respondent not selected

B = Respondent selected only

C = Have talked with
    respondent (give any
    instructions helpful for
    interview)

Example 7.8   Example of Rule Book Provided to All interviewers

Example 7.8   Example of Rule Book
provided to all interviewers

Washington State University
Public Opinion Laboratory
Community Preference Study
April, 1973

RULE BOOK

A. Before you start, be sure . . .

1. To post this "Rule Book," and "What the Respondent Might Like to Know," in front of you.
2. To put name tag in place above your interviewer station.
3. To look through names on stack of questionnaires; if you know anyone, have even heard of them, or used to live in that community, give that questionnaire back to supervisor.
4. You have three sharpened pencils with erasers.

B. Who to talk to:

Avoid going through enumeration process with person who is not member of the household (e.g., babysitters) or young children. Ask when the family (or parents) will return and tell them you will call back.

C. The interview: Be sure . . .

1. To mark the time the interview starts.
2. To read questions precisely as written.

As you know even a single word can drastically change the meaning of a question for respondents. Attempts to interpret the question in response to a respondent's query frequently does the same thing. Key phrases you might use to respond to the question of "What do you mean?"

I'm sorry, I don't have that information.

Its important that the question be answered as best you can in terms of the way it's stated, maybe I could read it to you again.

I will write down the concern (or qualification) you just mentioned so it will be taken into account in the analysis.

3. The respondent misunderstands the question.

It is very easy for respondents to miss a word or two, that is crucial to the meaning of the question. Sometimes they are embarrassed to admit that they didn't quite understand. If you suspect a question has been misunderstood do not tell the respondent that you think he misunderstood, these responses may be of help.

Could I reread the question and the answer I've written down just to be sure I have everything you wanted to say.

I think I may not have read the question correctly, so, may I read it again to be sure.

Example 7.8   Continued

4. Use neutral probes as needed.

    When you are in doubt about how to interpret the respondent's answer
    or what it means, the coder will be in even greater doubt. Probe,
    until you are sure. But, do it neutrally. A statement like, "Then
    what you really mean is ..." does not convey neutrality.

    Before accepting an answer of "I don't know," be sure to probe.
    Respondents frequently use that phrase in a way that says, "I'm thinking!"

    Some examples of probes you might use:

    > Yes, I see, (or) Uh-huh, stated in an expectant manner and
    > followed by a pause.
    >
    > Could you be a little more specific?
    >
    > I'm not sure I am entirely clear about what you mean. Could
    > you explain it a little more?
    >
    > Could I read back what I have written down to be sure I have
    > exactly what you wanted to say?

5. Write down everything.

    If a respondent qualifies an answer, or if a comment (probe) you offer
    stimulates a new response, write it down. Attempt to get it in verbatim
    form. Remember if your handwriting is poor you may need to rewrite
    answers after interviews. Therefore, don't waste space by writing in
    the answer while on the telephone.

6. If you need help, raise your hand or excuse yourself and get a supervisor.

    Sometimes a respondent wants to know more about a question or reasons for
    the study, etc. than you can tell them. If in your judgment it's
    warranted don't hesitate to ask the supervisor for help.

7. If respondent becomes incensed, uses abusive language, etc., be nice!
    Do not hang up! Keep cool!

    This is not likely to happen. If it does be patient, maybe the person
    had a bad day. Some responses that might help:

    > Yes, I see. Uh-huh.
    >
    > Yes, I understand you do feel quite strongly about this matter.
    > But, we really do need the information.

    If all else fails, call for a supervisor or wait for the opportunity to
    say something to this effect:

    > I think I can understand your feelings, and your not wanting to
    > complete the interview. But, thank you very much anyway.
    > Good bye.

Example 7.8   Continued

D. When you hang up:

    1. Immediately record time and calculate length of interview.

    2. Immediately go over every single answer to make sure it was done correctly. Rewrite answers to open-end questions which you even suspect might be illegible.

    3. Fill out the interview evaluation form.

    4. Hand completed form to supervisor immediately (if available). Or, put on top of stack of "call-backs" in plain view so that supervisor will know its ready to be picked up.

E. When you are done for the night:

    1. Fill out hours on time sheet.

    2. Check out with supervisor, explaining any call-backs that need special attention.

    3. Do not take anything home with you. All questionnaires, codebooks, etc. must remain in the Laboratory.

F. After you have left:

    We have an obligation to respondent's to keep their interviews confidential We feel very strongly that this obligation should be honored. Therefore, please do not tell anyone the substance of any interview or part of an interview, no matter how fascinating or interesting it was. Also, please avoid giving your own summary of findings. Just because 90 percent of your respondents feel a certain way does not mean that 90 percent of everyone else's feel the same way. Confidentiality is essential. Please help us maintain the reputation we have established for protecting the anonymity of respondents, and honestly analyzing and reporting data. If you want a copy of results from this survey, let the supervisor know, and we will be sure you get them just as soon as they are available.

intentional, as well as nicely handled situations, provide a basis for group discussion aimed at identifying the importance of each point in the rule book. Role-playing these example interviews well requires a great deal of effort, and once perfected they can be committed to video tape for use in later training. Their primary purpose is to sensitize new recruits to the problems of interviewing.

The second type of training interview requires one of the interviewers being trained to interview another trainee. Each is given an opportunity to play the role of respondent and the interviewer. This is done for each study, regardless of the previous experience of the interviewer. It helps interviewers learn the flow of questionnaires. More important, it provides a view of the interview from both ends of the telephone. For example, respondents often give a lengthy answer to an open-ended question far more rapidly than an interviewer can write it down. Then they wonder why they are asked to repeat it, or why it takes as much as a minute or more before the interviewer is ready to continue. Interviewers also learn how difficult it is to understand some questions and become aware of those places in the questionnaire; thus they will know to read them slowly and be sensitive to the occasional need to repeat them. Many interviewers have a tendency to underestimate the difficulty of the respondent's task until placed in the respondent role. The person acting as respondent is strongly encouraged to ask questions of the interviewer so that skill is gained in the use of the "what the respondent might like to know," sheet.

The third type of training interview is an extension of the second and provides a crucial test of the interviewer's preparedness for dealing with respondents. In this one, the trainee interviews a supervisor who acts the role of a very difficult to interview respondent. It does not take place until the interviewer is thoroughly acquainted with the nature of the study, the "what the respondent might like to know" sheet, and the "rule book." This interview is designed to be as difficult as any interview the interviewer is likely to encounter. Such training serves as a crucial test of an interviewer's readiness.

No matter how much one practices in situations like those proposed above, a sense of reality is always lacking. Therefore the fourth and final practice interviews are actual pretests of the questionnaire with a sample of persons from the same population as the study sample itself. These interviews help the trainees overcome any last reservations or concerns. Interviewers learn that actual interviews are usually far easier to conduct than most practice ones, because most respondents are genuinely cooperative and ask relatively few difficult questions. Thus these last practice interviews tend to build confidence and increase interviewer enthusiasm for the actual study.

Editing the Completed Questionnaire

Another important aspect of interviewer training is what the interviewer does after concluding a call to a respondent. It is essential that the interviewer go over each completed questionnaire carefully (as stated in the rule book). Occasionally interviewers do not circle answers, or they write comments in a cryptic form that needs elaboration. The best time to edit interviews is while the interview is fresh in one's mind. Waiting until all the evening's interviews are completed and then editing them all at once should be strenuously avoided. We mention this because it may seem quite reasonable to increase the number of calls made in an evening by going straight from one interview to the next until it is too late to call respondents, and only then begin the editing process. However, telephone interviewers have little more than the memory of a voice to refresh them and inevitably find it difficult to distinguish between interviews. The result is frequent confusion of the content of one interview with another.

Interviewers are trained for the postinterview activity first by asking them to examine completed interviews from previous studies in which many errors are present, such as answers not circled for some questions, more than one answer circled for others, and illegible answers to open-ended questions. Finally, after each practice interview, the interviewer is asked to edit his or her own questionnaire, which is then rigorously checked by the trainer.

When the selection and training of interviewers are rigorous, the commencement of the actual interviewing is in many respects anticlimactic. Starting 10−20 interviewers on long distance phone calls is a very unexciting event, with very few problems simultaneously needing a supervisor's or study director's attention. That, of course, is the best indicator that the selection and training process has been successful.

SCHEDULING THE INTERVIEWING SESSIONS

It is important to decide as soon as possible when—days of the week and times of day—the interviewing sessions will be scheduled. The earlier this is done the better, inasmuch as interviewing facilities must be acquired before interviewers can be scheduled. In planning the set of interviewing sessions, several considerations should be taken into account.

The best time period(s) to call respondents depends on the population surveyed. For exampl' people surveyed on a work-related topic are most receptive to being interviewed at their place of work or during the day. Some may be openly resentful of being contacted at home. Thus calls to agency directors, doctors, and store managers are best made only to their places of business during working hours. Certain other populations, such as ministers, have irregular work hours, and it is difficult to know either the best hours or places to contact them. Thus evening as well as daytime hours are used. Still other populations, such as students and homemakers, can be surveyed during the day as well as evening hours, allowing the researcher considerable flexibility.

To increase the efficiency of contacting all respondents, the time periods for calling must be varied, especially for heterogenous populations such as the general public. We have developed a procedure for scheduling interviewing sessions that maximizes interviewer efficiency at telephoning and at the same time minimizes the likelihood of calling respondents at objectionable times. In practice it works like this: surveys are scheduled to start early in the week (Monday or Tuesday) during the evening hours. Weekday evenings are times at which respondents are most likely to be available and therefore provide the best opportunity of obtaining completed interviews. These are also socially acceptable times for asking someone to be interviewed. One result of these first evenings of work will be a number of questionnaires for which successive "no answers" are obtained. These will include households in which occupants are at work during the evening and those in which the calls are answered, but it is discovered that the respondent can only be reached at a certain time. The latter group includes a number of people who are routinely away from home except on weekends. To reach these groups, weekend calls are scheduled for Saturday and Sunday afternoons as well as evenings. During these sessions priority is given to calling those numbers for which no answers were obtained during the week, or for which a weekend call-back was specifically requested. Although of lower priority, uncalled numbers are also tried inasmuch as we have not found weekend calls to result in a higher refusal rate.

Those households for which no answers are received throughout the week and weekend are made the subject of weekday afternoon calls. Finally, as a last resort before declaring a household unreachable, morning calls are tried. Sometimes, when a survey involves a very large sample size and calling is extended over a lengthy period of time, the questionnaire is set aside and tried a week or so later.

Even though households are tried a number of times during different time periods, there still may be no answer. Extended vacations, hospital and recovery stays elsewhere, visits to second homes, and a variety of other situations contribute to this fact. In statewide surveys we have conducted using directory listings as a sampling source, we normally end up with 4–7 percent "no answers," despite our intensive call-back efforts.

Besides the characteristics of the population under study, the geographic locale is an important consideration in planning the time of day at which surveys should begin and how adjustments in calling schedules should be made. In many rural communities those persons working unusual hours are very rare indeed and are limited to essential services, such as hospitals and police. In other locations, primarily large cities, people work "around the clock," or many places of business are open 24 hours a day. Las Vegas, a tourist city, is a good example of how local conditions must be considered. There, a very high proportion of the work force is employed on weekends, primarily during evening hours. Early afternoon calling, particularly during the week, represents a very desirable time in which to reach respondents.

Third, holidays and special events must also be taken into account. For example, many respondents may consider it in extremely bad taste to be called for an interview on Easter Sunday. The afternoon of the "Super Bowl" Sunday seems likely to produce some adamant refusals. Legal holiday weekends and vacation times (e.g., late August) are also likely to result in an increasing number of no answers or even terminations. Further alienation, and often refusals, result when the researcher is unfortunate enough to schedule interviews during a television program that is of interest to a large segment of the population. Such was our experience when a scheduled interview session overlapped with a delayed launch of an Apollo moon shot. The number of refusals and the "call me laters" went up markedly; it was deemed necessary to immediately cancel interviewing for the remainder of the evening. Although researchers cannot let television or the notion that "everyone has a favorite program" be a deterrent to calling, they must consider the timetable with regard to dramatic events that are taking place during the scheduled calling period.

A mistake sometimes made in scheduling interviewers and interviewing sessions is to plan for the same number of interviewers to work each evening. During the first few sessions a full complement of interviewers can keep quite busy, producing a high proportion of complete calls. However, in later sessions, as the number of uncalled households decreases and the proportion of "no answers" rises, interviewers may find themselves recalling unanswered telephones every five minutes or so, a very inefficient use of time. It is possible to make needed adjustments by decreasing the length of interviewing sessions, but this is less desirable than decreasing the number of interviewers.

A final aspect of planning interviewing sessions is to be able to have one or two interviewers on call for conducting interviews at any hour. Respondents frequently request that they be called back at a specific time. We have sometimes been in the position of asking interviewers to conduct an interview after midnight, and at other times before breakfast.

Example 7.9 presents a hypothetical log of interview times and the number of interviewers needed to complete a survey of 1000 names drawn systematically from directories, with interviews lasting an average of 15 minutes. The example is labeled hypothetical inasmuch as it does not represent the exact results from a particular survey, but is based on results from several surveys. The example suggests the "ideal" number of interviewers and "ideal" scheduling of sessions to reach a sample of the general public. It also illustrates several important aspects of interviewing, including the increase in the number of hours per day in which calls are made as the interviewing progresses, the need for fewer and fewer interviewers in later sessions, the need to have interviewers prepared to make calls at times not regularly scheduled, and the gradual decline in interviewing efficiency (completed calls/interviewer hour) because of the increasing portion of time spent in making calls that do not produce completed interviews.

This example is intended only as a general guide to the scheduling of interviewers and interview sessions. A variation of only a few minutes in the average length of the interview could mean substantial changes in the number of days, interviewers, and calling periods needed for a particular study. There is no substitute for a constant monitoring of a study's progress,

Example 7.9   A Hypothetical Log of Interviewing Sessions for a Study with These Characteristics: 1000 State-wide Listing Drawn Systematically From Telephone Directors, Prior Letters Sent, Interviews Lasting an Average of 15 Minutes, Interview Facilities Having 15 Stations Used

Day	Time of Interview Session	Number of Interviewers	Completed Interviews	Interviews Completed per Interview Hour
Monday	6-9 p.m.	15	89	2.0
Tuesday	6-9 p.m.	15	97	2.2
Wednesday	6-9 p.m.	15	101	2.2
Thursday	6-9 p.m.	15	95	2.1
Friday	6-9 p.m.	14	80	1.9
Saturday	1-4 p.m.	12	59	1.6
	6-9 p.m.	10	66	2.2
Sunday	2-5 p.m.	8	40	1.7
	6-9 p.m.	12	72	2.0
Monday	1-5 p.m.	3	12	1.0
	6-9 p.m.	6	28	1.6
Tuesday	9-12 a.m.	2	6	1.0
	1-5 p.m.	2	8	1.0
	6-9 p.m.	3	12	1.3
Wednesday	9-12 a.m.	2	6	1.0
	1-5 p.m.	2	8	1.0
	6-9 p.m.	3	12	1.3
Thursday	9-12 a.m.	2	4	0.7
	1-5 p.m.	2	5	0.6
	6-9 p.m.	3	8	0.9
Called by special appointment during and after above date.*		2	12	

* The remaining 180 households are accounted for by disconnects, no answers, and refusals.

and adjustments in a schedule such as the one shown should be viewed as probable rather than possible.

FINAL PREPARATIONS: A CHECK LIST

The most difficult part of conducting TDM telephone interview surveys is not the skill associated with performing each task. Rather it is the problem of orchestration—performing everything at the right time so as not to interfere with the other tasks. Each act of preparation is oriented to a single critical event, the commencement of interviewing, when everything must come together. Failures to obtain successful results from telephone interviews result as frequently from the failure of organization and coordination as from not giving needed attention to specific tasks.

Tasks left undone, even simple ones, threaten results. For example, we know of one case in which a box of pencils was left in a locked office, and the realization of that just minutes before interviewing was to commence resulted in a hectic scavenger hunt among interviewers and the supervisory staff. Even then, several interviewers had to use ball point pens, increasing the difficulty of interpreting some answers because of smudging and cross-outs. In another case dialing instructions were forgotten in a study that required three different methods of locating respondents. Before hurried individual verbal instructions could be given to the various interviewers, considerable confusion resulted in mismarking several interviews as "disconnected," when a mistake in dialing was the only problem.

A countdown list of activities that must be completed prior to starting the survey is a useful device for preventing oversights and organizational failures. Example 7.10 shows the one we use. As each task is completed, it can be checked off, and the complete list can be used as a constant reference sheet near the start of interviewing. Many items on the list have already been discussed, and further treatment is not needed. However, others appear for the first time and require discussion.

Drawing the Sample

When the sample is drawn from telephone books, the information may be stored in any number of ways including, for example, hand-written file cards or computer tape. We have found it convenient to type the information directly onto gummed labels, which themselves are printed on rolls of perforated 8½ by 11 inch sheets of paper. The labels can then be transferred directly to the cover page of the questionnaire. It is important that all the information from the directory be transferred, including the name of the directory (to facilitate possible future checks for errors), each person's name and complete address (for mailing the advance letter and facilitating the tracing of disconnected telephones), and of course the telephone number itself.

Random digit numbers, on the other hand, are obtained on computer printouts (if derived by a computer program) or regular sized (8½ by 11 inch) sheets of paper (if derived manually from tables of random numbers). In either case, space is provided for "no answers" and "disconnect" information to be recorded. As noted earlier, the number is transferred to the question-

Example 7.10   The Count-Down List of Activities that Must Be Done Prior to the Start of Interviews

DRAW SAMPLE
___Names, street addresses, and telephone numbers drawn from directories typed
      onto gummed labels and attached to cover page of questionnaire
    [or]
___Random numbers generated by computer (or manually from table) and printed on
    lists for distribution to interviewers

FACILITIES AND EQUIPMENT
___Access to telephones arranged
___Telephones checked to be sure they are in working order
___Access to leased lines arranged (if needed)
___Chairs and tables assembled (if needed)
___Labeled boxes for sorting questionnaires into appropriate categories (e.g.,
    refusals, completions, and call-backs)

COMPUTER RELATED NEEDS (If immediate data processing is planned)
___Arrange access to computer
___Arrange access to computer equipment (e.g., keypunch, and sorter reproducer)
___Decide analysis programs to be used and set up format statements for their use.
___Do preliminary computer runs with "Dummy" data to check for errors in analysis
    programs

MATERIALS
___Questionnaires
    ___Duplicated
    ___Assembled
    ___Cover page and selection procedures (if any) added
    ___Directory listing attached to cover page (if applicable)
    ___Randomized for distribution to interviewers
___"What the Respondent Might Like to Know" duplicated
___"Rules Book" duplicated
___Special dialing instructions duplicated (if needed)
___Pencils and notepads, thumbtacks, rubber bands, and other miscellaneous supplies
___All of the above placed at each interviewing station

ADVANCE LETTER
___Printed, personalized, and stuffed into envelopes
___Each letter is mailed three to five days before call is likely to be made

PERSONNEL
___Interviewers
    ___Hired
    ___Trained
    ___Scheduled
___Supervisory personnel schedule
___Persons to check questionnaires for completeness scheduled
___Coders and/or keypunchers
    ___Hired
    ___Trained
    ___Schedule
___Person to "trouble-shoot" disconnected numbers and other problem calls scheduled

OTHER RESOURCES
___Telephone directories that cover study area (to aid in checking possible errors)
___Notify relevant officials that survey is in process

naire only if and when an answer is received. This points to an important difference between the sampling methods in terms of when a sample must be drawn. A sample drawn from a directory must be done very early in the process so that the information can be used for advance letters and placed on the cover pages for questionnaires. In contrast, random digit listings need not be available until just prior to commencement of the actual interviewing.

Facilities and Equipment

Although it seems unlikely that anyone would forget to arrange for the use of telephones, the need to be certain that each phone is in working order is easily overlooked. This is more than a check to see if a phone call can be completed on it. Dial telephones sometimes develop annoying sounds when they are dialed. In other cases the dialing action becomes slow and laborious. These characteristics may not be a problem to the occasional user of a telephone, but they become of much concern under the intensive use necessitated by telephone interviewing.

A procedure is needed for the continuous sorting and resorting of questionnaires so that recalls are made at the appropriate times, and continuous monitoring of the disposition of all types of calls is maintained. For example, a sudden increase in the "stack" of refusals would suggest that the supervisor immediately check the reason to see if it appears to be a random fluctuation or is caused by a common factor (e.g., extremely popular television movie) about which something can be done (e.g., stop interviewing). Likewise, the accumulation of extraordinarily large numbers of disconnects would suggest that errors in dialing are being made. To facilitate checks of this nature, considerable work space is needed (thus the requirement for extra tables). In addition, clearly labeled boxes or some other device for sorting questionnaires is needed.

Computer Needs

Although immediate processing of data by computer is not a part of many surveys, careful preparations must be made when it is. Access must be obtained to all the needed computer equipment. The kind of procedures followed, and even whether this goal is possible, will of course depend on the researcher's local situation.

At our university, rapid coding and analysis are achieved through the use of mark-sense cards. These are computer cards on which 27 columns of information can be coded with the appropriate soft lead pencils. These cards are filled out by coders while the interviewing is in process. Within minutes after the last interview is completed, the coded cards can be run through a specially equipped reproducer that reads the coded information and punches it into the appropriate columns of the same cards. The punched cards are then ready to be entered into the computer.

One of the most important computer planning steps for those wanting immediate analysis is to set up computer programs ahead of time. It is possible that programming errors willl be made in setting up the initial run. Thus it seems important that a pretest run be made, perhaps using data from pretest questionnaires.

Materials

The final preparations are inevitably characterized by a deluge of printed paper. Not only must the questionnaire be duplicated and assembled complete with cover page and selection procedures, but the "rule book," "What the Respondent Might Like to Know," and sheets outlining any special dialing instruction must be reproduced. The earlier this is done the better, inasmuch as these are important parts of interviewer training. The importance of having final questionnaires assembled prior to the start of interviewing stems from the need to randomize the questionnaire. This is done to be sure that any one interviewer does not call a homogeneous subgroup (e.g., all the households in the sample from a single town). To minimize confusion at the start of interviewing, all the materials needed by the interviewers are placed at the work stations before they arrive, and the various instruction sheets are posted.

Advance Letter

Ideally, the advance letter used with directory listing samples is sent 3–5 days before the anticipated date of calling. If a very large survey is being conducted, with more than a week passing before the first calls are made to a household, the sample should be split and the advance letters sent according to the dates on which the first calls to each portion of the sample are anticipated. It is important to remember that if the advance letter is to be sent in phases, this must be very closely coordinated with sample drawing and the distribution of questionnaires to interviewers. The final consideration, which is easy to overlook, is the need to print the letter far enough ahead that it will be possible to personalize each letter before it is mailed.

Personnel

To achieve maximum speed and efficiency, an extensive division of labor is established. Rather than training interviewers to follow up on calls (e.g., call operator for help with disconnects), this task is usually assigned to one person—a person who is experienced in the appropriate questions to ask operators. This helps to ensure a consistent and thorough follow-up of all such calls. One or two people are assigned the task of scrutinizing each completed questionnaire for errors; thus the supervisor is freed from this task and can then watch interviewers more closely. The creation of this role also ensures that feedback to interviewers on any problems is very rapid.

Other Resources

Our experience in several surveys suggests that having telephone directories available for the entire study area is quite useful. Occasionally errors are made in transferring telephone numbers or names from the directories; having the directory readily accessible makes this problem quite easy to solve. Sometimes, in random digit dialing, errors are made on the existence and location of certain exchanges (three-digit prefixes). The information contained in the early pages of most directories can sometimes be used to clarify problems of this nature.

Finally, we believe it is a good idea for the researcher to notify relevant officials in the sponsoring organization that the survey is in progress. In some cases, inquiries about a survey we were conducting were made to a top official of the university, who in turn referred the inquiry down the appropriate lines of authority. The department chairperson or agency director must be in a position to respond easily to any inquiries. The few moments it takes to inform relevant persons can be very effective in avoiding later misunderstandings.

CONDUCTING THE INTERVIEWING SESSIONS

Despite the numerous surveys we have conducted, an air of apprehension always seems to prevail as final preparations are completed and the interviewers begin placing their calls. That feeling seldom subsides until a number of interviews have been completed and checked, and all activities take on the appearance of an uneventful routine.

At this stage it is especially important that the supervisor, the key to orderly implementation, be free from undone chores, such as stapling cover sheets to questionnaires and compiling additional lists of random numbers. The attention of the supervisor must be focused on several routine activities that underscore the need for him or her to be free of such tasks. One is the need to listen to interviewers for the purpose of identifying problems of individual interviewers so that suggestions for improvements can be made. Another is to talk to interviewers between calls in an attempt to identify unanticipated problems or ambiguities that need clarification.

Still another routine task is to see that completed questionnaires are picked up and that they are checked for completeness. Our goal is that no more than one call intervene between the completion of an interview and its being checked; thus clarification from the interviewer or more information from the respondent can be obtained before either has a chance to forget the details of the interview.

The final routine task is to continuously monitor disposition of uncompleted interviews—refusals, disconnects, and no answers. Tentative refusals can be assigned to a "top" interviewer for another try. Requests to call back at a certain time can be organized and assignments made for specific interviewers to call at the appointed time. The supervisor also must be alert to successive "no answers" and organize them in such a way that later calls are made at different times to increase the chance of finding someone at home.

The number of interviewers needed for later sessions and the number of sessions that are needed depend on how fast interviews are completed. An alertness to the length of time it is taking to complete interviews and the proportion of refusals and no answers is essential for making adjustments in the schedule for later interviewing sessions.

Unfortunately, all studies are not uneventful, and unanticipated problems may sometimes require as much time as the routine ones. Sometimes a supervisor may find it necessary to talk directly to a respondent and even complete the interview. A sudden rash of refusals may require an extensive check into what is happening and whether anything can be done about it, such as stop interviewing for the night or equip interviewers with a new argument to help overcome respondent objections.

In one survey we were suddenly faced with line difficulties in which all the telephones would cut off simultaneously and become operational only a few seconds later. This required emergency repair service, in addition to giving instructions on what to say to respondents when they were recalled a minute or so after the cut-off. It is impossible to anticipate all the problems likely to be faced, but the point that should be made clear is that the supervisor must be prepared for the unexpected and should not be so overburdened with other details that he or she does not have time to handle the unanticipated problems.

CONCLUSION

The outward appearance of the TDM telephone survey is that it is substantially different from a TDM mail survey. Much of the apparent difference stems from the introduction of a third party—the interviewer—between the researcher and the respondent, requiring us to devote much of this chapter to this new element. A second difference concerns the basic mode of implementation. Virtually every implementation activity for a telephone survey points toward the critical time at which the interview occurs and all the elements must come together. This is in decided contrast to mail surveys, for which the activities that concern a single respondent are seemingly played out in slow motion, being implemented over a period of several weeks. Add to this the sole dependence on verbal communication during the interview, and it should not be surprising that the reader is more impressed with how the mail and telephone TDMs differ than with how they resemble one another.

However, fundamentally we attempt the same thing in both kinds of surveys. The basis of the telephone (as well as the mail) TDM rests on identifying all aspects that might influence the quality and quantity of response. Thus we found it necessary to focus in depth on controlling the interviewer's behavior and adapting to the limitations of verbal communication. Social exchange theory remains our basic guide. This suggests that an effort be made to allow a social exchange process to operate during the interview by the use, whenever possible, of a carefully worded advance letter. In addition, the interview is conducted in a way that is designed both to reduce the costs of response (such as embarrassment, apprehension and difficulty) and increase the rewards (such as making it interesting and useful). The similarities that underly the TDM mail and telephone surveys is perhaps most evident from the fact that it has been possible to deal with some topics, such as principles of question order and construction of the advance letters, far more briefly in the telephone chapters than in the mail chapters in which they were first discussed.

Our experience has shown that response rates to telephone surveys are less sensitive to individual elements left undone than mail surveys. We should expect this inasmuch as the mail respondent tends to react to one element at a time, any one of which can determine the outcome, whereas the telephone respondent must react to everything within a few short minutes. Further, the telephone interviewer can often compensate for those elements that are left undone. It is for these reasons that the TDM response rates are not greatly different from those obtained by some (but not all) other telephone survey methods now in use.

As with the mail TDM, the telephone TDM cannot be considered complete. Many questions remain unanswered. For example:

The amount of improvement that can be obtained by using random digit methods to improve sampling frames.

What characteristics of interviewers produce the best results.

How response quality is affected for different populations, different topics, and different types of questions.

Although the telephone has finally gained acceptance as a legitimate survey method and its use will continue to increase, the research base on which our use is predicated remains preciously thin. Expanding that research base must therefore be considered a very high priority for those engaged in telephone surveys.

NOTES

1. See Don A. Dillman, W. Williams, and D. Stadelman, Preliminary Report on WSU/UW Tax Surveys, Social Research Center, Washington State University, 1972, for a complete discussion of this study.

1a For a more complete discussion of sampling issues and alternatives, the reader is referred to Seymour Sudman, *Applied Sampling* (New York: Academic Press, 1976).

2. See Earl R. Babbie, *The Practice of Social Research,* (Belmont, Calif.: Wadsworth, 1975), Part Two, for a discussion of this point.

3. The switch from actual number of listings to *column inches* of listings is done as a matter of much needed convenience. In our view, it does not sacrifice overall accuracy.

4. Sanford L. Cooper, "Random Sampling by Telephone—An Improved Method," *Journal of Marketing Research, 1, 1964, pp. 45−48.*

5. U.S. Bureau of the Census, "Mobility of the Population of the United States, March 1970 to March 1974," Current Population Reports, Series P-20, No. 273, December 1974.

6. James A. Brunner and G. Allen Brunner, "Are Voluntarily Unlisted Telephone Subscribers Really Different?" *Journal of Marketing Research, 8,* 1971, pp. 121−124.

7. Seymour Sudman, "The Uses of Telephone Directories for Survey Sampling," *Journal of Marketing Research, 10,* 1973, pp. 204−207. He suggests comparing the telephone directory estimate of telephones in use with the Census estimate of total phones in use.

8. Cooper, *op. cit.*

9. See Cooper, *op. cit.,* and Gerald J. Glasser and Gale O. Metzger, "Random Digit Dialing as a Method of Telephone Sampling," *Journal of Marketing Research, 9,* 1972, pp. 59−64, for a description of two methods for contacting a national sample; Stephen B. Friedman, "People and Places: A Report on a Survey of People's Locational Preferences, 1973," Draft, State Planning Office, Wisconsin Department of Administration (Madison), September 1973, for a less detailed but informative description of how to contact a statewide sample; and Seymour Sudman, *op. cit.,* 1973 for a description of a way to combine the advantages of directory sampling with random digit methods. The most recent treatment of random digit dialing is contained in Seymour Sudman, *op. cit.,* 1976.

10. Glasser and Metzger, *op. cit.*

11 Sudman, *op. cit.,* 1973.

12. *Glasser and Metzger, op. cit.*

13. *Ibid.,* p. 63

14. Sudman, *op. cit.,* 1973, p. 204.

15. Don A. Dillman, Jean Gorton Gallegos, and James H. Frey, "Reducing Refusal Rates for Telephone Interviews," *Public Opinion Quarterly,* 40, 1976, pp. 66−78.

16. *Ibid.*

17. *Ibid.*

18. *Ibid.*

19. *Ibid.*

20. These experiments are reported in greater detail in Dillman, Gallegos, and Frey, *op. cit.*

21. *Ibid.*

22. Christine Larsen Tollefsen, "Occupational Dress of Veterinarians," Unpublished M.A. Thesis, Washington State University, 1973.

23. Dillman, Gallegos, and Frey. *op. cit.*

24. Jean G. Gallegos, "An Experiment in Maximizing Response to Telephone Interviews Through the Use of a Preliminary Letter, Based on Principles of Exchange Theory," Unpublished M.A. Thesis, Washington State University, 1974.

25. Verling C. Troldahl and Roy E. Carter, Jr., "Random Selection of Respondents within Households in Phone Surveys," *Journal of Marketing Research, 1,* 1964, pp. 71–76.

26. See Troldahl and Carter, *op. cit.,* for a more extensive discussion of bias and their procedure.

27. J.O. Eastlack, Jr. and Henry Assael, "Better Telephone Surveys Through Centralized Interviewing," *Journal of Advertising Research, 6,* 1966, p. 2.

28. Dillman, Gallegos, and Frey, *op. cit.*

29. In this study the refusal rate for male interviewers was 13.8 percent and females 14.5 percent, a nonsignificant difference.

Chapter Eight

LOOKING TO THE FUTURE:
....

Prospects and Concerns

Clearly, mail and telephone surveys are coming of age! Interest in using both of these methods is greater than ever before. It is the direct result of the high costs and other problems of doing face-to-face interview surveys and the improvements in procedures for doing surveys by mail and telephone. The TDM procedures described in this book demonstrate that mail and telephone surveys can consistently produce good results, relegating to the past the view that neither could be anything more than a poor substitute for face-to-face interviews.

The increasing acceptance of mail and telephone surveys raises certain questions for which answers are needed if the full potential of such surveys is to be realized. Our purpose in this chapter is to consider three of the most important ones. First, can the methods described here be improved still further? Second, what differences might the TDM (or other similarly effective methods) make in how survey researchers go about their craft? Third, will the widespread availability of methods for conducting mail and telephone surveys lead to new uses (and perhaps misuses) of surveys? Answers to each of these questions are important in answering the even larger question of the eventual worth of the methods. Accordingly, we view this final chapter less as an epilogue to the preceding ones than a prologue to future survey research.

BEYOND THE TOTAL DESIGN METHOD (TDM)

The precise sets of step-by-step procedures for conducting mail and telephone surveys described in this book are destined to become obsolete. This should come as no surprise to the reader, inasmuch as we emphasize throughout that the TDM (for both the mail and telephone) is only a perspective on how to stimulate response and should not be viewed as a finalized, definitive set of specific procedures. It is quite apparent that evidence concerning the specific effects of each element in the TDM does not yet exist; only a few elements have been manipulated experimentally. The TDM recommendations for step-by-step procedures are based primarily on the strength of two important arguments. The first is that the elements comprising the total sets of mail and telephone procedures have demonstrated (in the numerous studies cited in Chapter 1) the capability of producing very satisfactory results. Second, plausible arguments for the effectiveness of individual elements in the TDM are based on two frames of reference—social exchange theory and a belief that attention to administrative details is crucial. The single aspect of the TDM that seems most likely to persist in the future is its basic premise, that to maximize both the quantity and quality of response, all aspects of the survey must be considered. Thus everything likely to affect the quantity and quality of response should be identified and then manipulated in a manner that appears (on the basis of social exchange theory) most likely to produce good response.

We would be surprised if future research does not suggest some, and perhaps many, modifications in the specific procedural details of the TDM. In fact, it seems quite possible that the mail TDM procedures described here, although already achieving good response, are still somewhat below their maximum potential. Only carefully designed research can answer that question. The time has passed, if it every really existed, when our knowledge of how to improve the quantity and quality of response is advanced by the kind of research that dominated the mail survey literature of the past few decades. Such research was generally atheoretical and examined the effects of manipulating one or two aspects of the surveying process (e.g., use of personalized cover letters or real stamps on return envelopes) on response. Further, it was often done on unrealistically small samples without attempting to take into account the numerous uncontrolled aspects of the particular study. The fact that these other aspects could vary to such a large extent from one survey to another implied that drawing conclusions about the probable impact of the experimentally tested elements was essentially impossible.

In contrast, the research approach that holds the most promise for advancing our knowledge of how to maximize response quantity and quality will probably be characterized by several attributes. First, it will be theoretically based, providing interpretations for "why" specific techniques do and do not work. Thus it will help us move beyond situation-specific conclusions and the inevitable reliance on simple conjecture about whether a technique employed in one survey will work in another. A good theoretical framework, such as that provided by social exchange theory, can suggest which element of the survey process should be examined, especially in combination with which other elements.

Second, studies of survey techniques must be designed in a way that will maximize response. Regardless of how good a particular element of a method appears to be, its true worth can never be assessed if its effect is examined in combination with poor questionnaire format, poor timing of the follow-up sequence, or other response-inhibiting factors. Future research must produce knowledge about what a specific element of the survey process can accomplish once we have carefully designed every remaining element of the process.

Third, there is a definite need for experiments on large samples —containing perhaps 1000 respondents or more. Some elaboration on this point should be helpful for substantiating this claim. Let us assume that the difference in response rates between mail TDM surveys and the less systematic efforts often used in the past is 50 percentage points (e.g., 75 percent versus 25 percent). In the neighborhood of half that difference can probably be attributed to the use of three follow-ups in TDM mail surveys. This leaves 25 percent of the response rate that can be attributed to the combined effects of the several dozen specific elements applied under the TDM. Thus we would be quite surprised if the independent effects of some of these elements are as much as a full percentage point. The detection of such small differences requires experiments containing very large sample sizes. The probable result of experiments conducted on small samples will be to reject many, if not most, such elements as "not significant." However, their deletion from the TDM on these grounds may have the *combined* effect of reducing TDM response rates by a considerable amount. Thus data to adequately evaluate the various aspects of the TDM must be produced via large-scale research efforts.

In the past, the two primary sources of articles dealing with response rates have been experiments done on very small samples for the sole purpose of testing certain techniques and tests of individual techniques added to studies conducted for other purposes. We do not believe that either type of study will suffice to advance our current knowledge of the survey process. Experiments to examine the effects of methods on improving response quantity and quality must be as carefully designed and carried out as any substantive studies to which they are applied.

The need for research on improving survey research methods is emphasized by still another concern. It must be recognized that studies using either mail or telephone surveys are necessarily implemented within the cultural context of the society, and that society's culture is constantly undergoing change. What is new and novel today, and thus has a certain effect on people, may soon become old and outdated, and will affect people differently. For example, in past decades people tended to receive few letters; those they did receive had stamps that were characteristically dull in appearance. When brightly colored commemoratives were introduced to the public and used by social researchers, they probably had a positive effect on response rates. However, now that new stamps of varying shapes and colors are available almost every time one goes to the post office, we doubt that they are any more effective than a metered envelope. We would be surprised if the effects of the specific elements in the mail TDM, such as the personalization procedures, pressed ball point pen signature, and the rest, are exactly the same now as they would have been in the past, or as they will be in the future, as technological improvements make full personalization of any mass mailing feasible at little cost. Similarly, we wonder about the effectiveness of the advance letter for telephone surveys and the introduction for telephone interviews in terms of their response-inducing capabilities in the future. In short, it is hazardous to predict exactly in what manner our culture will change. As a result, future research will be required for discovering ways to adapt survey technologies to our changing society.

However, certain changes in the TDM do seem imminent. Because of the passage of the 1974 Privacy Act, it is possible that respondents will regularly have to be advised of their right to refuse to be surveyed. Although some developmental work on the TDM was conducted after passage of the act, procedures for incorporating such notices into the mail or telephone surveys were not attempted. The reason for this is the considerable confusion that has existed, and still exists, as to what is required by the act for survey researchers. Indeed, court decisions and subsequent agency interpretations are still in the offing. Suffice it to say at this time that changes in the TDM to accomodate the effects of this act and any future ones will likely be required. Studying the effects of various techniques of providing such information is thus a high priority for future research.

The possible effects of this act point to a difficulty that must be faced by all researchers employing the TDM—changing one aspect of the TDM will probably require changes in other aspects to achieve consistency. For example, should a formal statement of respondents' rights and perhaps a signed statement of their consent be required, the cover letters for mail surveys and the advance letters for telephone surveys may have to be drastically changed. In fact, the basic thrust may have to be directed toward reducing the threat implied by the statement in the cover or advance letter, which, ironically, is designed specifically to reduce the threat of the survey itself. Although future research can hopefully improve the response to mail and telephone surveys, it is possible that problems on the horizon will cause researchers to run just to stand still to attain this goal—continually devising new procedures for maintaining adequate response rates in the face of new barriers to survey research.

In past methodological research dealing with the mail and telephone surveys, the issue of response quality always took a back seat to work on response rates. At that time such a research emphasis was understandable, inasmuch as low response rates appeared to be the most severe problem of mail and telephone surveys. Thus other concerns pertaining to response quality seemed far less important. However, now that response rates are relatively high, a myriad of response quality issues must be faced. One such issue is the extent to which people who respond to surveys differ from those who do not respond. Even though the number of refusals is fairly small, it cannot be assumed that they have the same characteristics and hold the same views as respondents. Another response quality issue concerns the adequacy of directory sampling as opposed to random digit dialing. Experiments must be done to determine whether the latter effectively elicits interviews from unlisted respondents and the extent to which variable distributions (e.g., percentage holding a particular attitude) are affected. Further, more work must be conducted to determine whether the answers people give for telephone interviews, mail questionnaires, and face-to-face interviews are equivalent. Although the results of past research suggest for the most part that any differences are minor, very few studies have systematically addressed this issue.[1]

The research required to adequately examine these issues of response quality will be even more difficult to conduct than that concerning response rates, because of two factors. First, response quality is a general term that covers a variety of matters, including the characteristics of respondents versus nonrespondents, completeness of answers, inadvertent errors, and item nonresponse. Second, response quality seems likely to vary greatly in relation to the population sampled, the study topic, and the particular type of questions in the survey. Each of these issues may have an independent and substantial effect on the various dimensions of response quality. Thus definitive answers to the various response quality issues cannot be provided by a few studies of, say, the general public on inherently interesting topics (e.g., crime, community development, and environmental protection). Rather, addressing these issues seriously will require distinguishing between homogeneous and heterogeneous populations, interesting and boring study topics, complex and simple questions, and so forth. In short, imaginative and rigorous research must be conducted to assess the quality of response attained by the TDM mail and telephone surveys.

DEVELOPING DATA COLLECTION SYSTEMS

Much of the writing of this book was guided by the goal of providing criteria that researchers can use to select the most satisfactory method for conducting a survey. However, there is some danger that this emphasis on choosing the "best" method will mask what we believe to be the greatest potential for the mail and telephone methods, or, for that matter, the face-to-face method. This potential emanates from the *joint use* of the various methods in a single survey, rather than sole reliance on one method or another for a specific survey. Each method would be incorporated into the survey to complement the other methods. Thus a particular survey might use two, or even all three, survey methods to collect portions of the data. Each would be used to accomplish what it does best and thus compensate for the inadequacies of the others.

Fundamentally, two kinds of system-building efforts can be distinguished. One involves using more than one method to collect *different information* from the *same individuals*. The other involves using more than one method to collect the *same information* from *different individuals*. Attention must be devoted to the development of both types of systems.

There are several approaches that might be followed in developing the first type of system. One procedure is to combine an initial interview by telephone with a follow-up mail questionnaire. In this way, the telephone interview can, for example, be used primarily to elicit answers to the types of questions that are difficult to ask on a mail questionnaire—questions that are open-ended, must be asked in a certain sequence, or require numerous screen questions. The mail follow-up, on the other hand, would be used for those questions which are difficult to handle in a telephone interview—questions that are longer, require items to be ranked, or need diagrams and pictures. Preceding a mail questionnaire with a telephone interview allows researchers to gain rapport with respondents and answer their questions, paving the way for the follow-up mail questionnaire. However, the most persuasive reason for developing such a data collection system is that it provides an opportunity to use each survey method for the things it does best and replace it by another method in areas in which it has known weaknesses.

Another example of such a system pertains to panel studies and involves employing either the mail or telephone survey to follow up respondents who were initially interviewed with the face-to-face method. The cost advantages could be numerous in this case, inasmuch as some respondents would have inevitably moved away from the area in which they were initially interviewed. Using the telephone for such follow-up interviews is already a widespread practice, but the mail questionnaire has seldom been used in this way, even though it offers further cost reductions. In addition, it enables researchers to use the "automatic" tracing procedures of the U.S. Postal Service, which forwards mail anywhere in the United States for up to 1 year to locate people who have moved.

Still another approach for using one method to complement another is to leave a mail questionnaire with respondents at the close of a face-to-face interview, with instructions to mail it back at a later date. There are many possible reasons for using the mail questionnaire in this manner. First, it might be for purposes of shortening a lengthy interview. Second, it might be to allow respondents to answer some potentially objectionable questions in private, rather than in the face-to-face situation in which their answers could be overheard by other members of the family. A third use is as a diary for activities to be engaged in for a period of time following the interview. Finally, it might be used to get the opinions of a second member of the household who does not happen to be at home at the time of the interview, or simply to obtain their consultation on some issues with which the interviewed respondent has little familiarity.

Our enthusiasm for employing various combinations of the three methods to collect different portions of the data for a given study is considerable. In the past, one of the major shortcomings of much social science research was its reliance on cross-sectional studies (i.e., those done at one point in time) to address questions that could better be answered by following the same respondents over time. Almost any study that attempts to analyze change over time and the reasons for such change represents an example of this. Not having to rely on face-to-face interviews for all (or perhaps any) phases of such studies, thereby reducing the cost barrier, increases the probability that many studies will incorporate a much needed longitudinal perspective into their designs.

The second type of data collection system, using different methods to collect the same information from different individuals, can also be done in numerous ways. One possibility is to collect as much data as possible by the relatively inexpensive mail questionnaire and follow up nonrespondents with face-to-face interviews. This strategy was pioneered in relation to the TDM by Goudy, who raised his response rate from 78 percent after full implementation of the TDM mail method to a final 96 percent by using face-to-face interviews for nonrespondents.[2] One could also follow a TDM mail questionnaire with telephone calls, as was done in Texas by St. Louis, who successfully completed interviews with nearly two-thirds of the nonrespondents.[3] These procedures took advantage of the least expensive method to bring in the bulk of the response, saving the more expensive method to the end, achieving good cost effectiveness.

A reverse procedure might also be seriously considered. Inasmuch as call-backs now represent the biggest cost of conducting face-to-face surveys, it seems important to consider ways to eliminate them. For example, a study might be designed in which questionnaires for all three methods are prepared. When not-at-homes occur, the mail-back questionnaire may be left on the doorstep, or it may be possible through inquiries with neighbors (or other means) to determine the name and/or telephone number of that household; thus if the mail questionnaire is not returned, follow-up mailings may be made. Failing that, a telephone interview may be substituted. The goal would be to eliminate the large cost of a call-back to a particular area or neighborhood to pick up one interview, or the even larger and more frustrating costs of repeated call-backs without results.

The simpler possibility of substituting the mail and telephone methods for one another should not be overlooked, even for refusals. Once, when refusals seemed rather high on a telephone interview survey and a mail questionnaire was standing by for use in another phase of the same study, we decided to send the mail questionnaire to all the telephone refusals. It was accompanied by an appropriately worded letter that began by noting our realization that, "some people prefer not to be interviewed over the telephone, perhaps because of not being able to know for sure who was on the other end of the line. . . ." This mailing elicited fully completed questionnaires from 20 percent of those who had previously refused the telephone interview, without the use of any follow-ups.

Whereas one method of surveying may produce an unfavorable reaction from certain people, another may not. People who refuse to let strangers into their households may be more willing to respond to a telephone interview. Other people who are uncomfortable with their ability to write answers to a mail questionnaire may respond enthusiastically if someone else does the writing. Still others may be frustrated by the intensity of concentration required for responding to a telephone interview and find greater comfort with the more relaxed nature of a face-to-face interview or a mail questionnaire that can be completed at their own pace. Further, the persistence suggested by following refusals with attempts by another method effectively emphasizes to respondents the importance of a study; thus no matter how they react to specific methods, response may be improved.

In considering the possibilities for building data collection systems, it is important to identify the shortcomings of each method and consider how other methods might be used to avoid them. For example, many social scientists would suggest that the major drawback of both the telephone and mail procedures, when used for surveys of the general public, is the inevitable bias, albeit less than in the past, of the lists from which samples are drawn. This suggests that when survey organizations conduct face-to-face surveys they might include an effort to prelist names and telephone numbers of other houses in the same block for use in later mail and telephone surveys. Although this is far from a costfree activity, the advantages for later surveys may more than compensate for the added cost.

The development of data collection systems of either of the two types we propose assumes that each method produces equivalent responses. Past research, including our own, suggests that differences in the quality of responses obtained from the mail, telephone, and face-to-face methods are rather minor.[4] For example, based on an experiment comparing the responses produced via face-to-face and telephone interviews, Rogers concluded that, "the quality of data obtained by telephone on complex attitudinal and knowledge items as well as on personal items is comparable to that collected in person."[5] However, as noted earlier in this chapter, there has been an astonishingly low number of studies that have examined differences in information produced by the various methods. In our view, this represents a glaring omission in research concerning the survey methods and should be made a very high priority for future research. In fact, such research is imperative if serious work on the building of data collection systems is to occur.

If future efforts to build data collection systems are successful, two kinds of results can be envisioned. One result is the reduction of the overall cost of conducting surveys, making it possible to do surveys that would not otherwise be done. The other result, and perhaps the most important, is to prevent the compromises that are now accepted as a matter of course. For example, should the building of mail, telephone, and face-to-face interview systems lower the per interview cost substantially, it may be possible to enlarge sample sizes to a level more compatible with survey objectives, to expand the geographic coverage of samples to allow greater generalization of findings, and to overcome the various other frequently made sacrifices discussed in Chapters 1 and 2. Although only time will show the conditions under which efficiency and cost effectiveness can best be achieved, the necessary prerequisite of having viable telephone and mail methods removes the major obstacle that has prevented the data collection system concept from heretofore being widely considered.

NEW USES FOR SURVEY METHODS

Viable mail and telephone methods open the door to conducting surveys that until now have usually been dismissed as not feasible. Used individually or as components of data collection systems, these methods can overcome the technical and cost barriers that once seemed insurmountable and resulted in requests for surveys being met by a pessimistic shrug of the shoulders. Much of the demand for such surveys derives from people in policy-making positions who would like to include survey data as an additional basis for making decisions. This could involve knowledge about people's behavior (e.g., how they spend their vacation time) or their attitudes (e.g., how they would *like* to spend that time), perhaps as a basis for judging the impact of a proposed policy on longer vacations.

There are several reasons why such data, so easily obtainable by survey methods, have not routinely been gathered and brought to bear on policy deliberations.[6] One is that the lag time between issues becoming precisely enough defined to allow meaningful survey questions to be written and the time at which a decision is to be made is usually fairly brief. In fact, it is often the effort to make a decision that clarifies both the issue and the alternatives for resolving it. Thus the time period in which a survey would have to be designed and executed is too short for finding funds and mounting the appropriate effort. The problem is confounded further by the extreme difficulty that always seems to exist for quickly raising the thousands of dollars necessary to finance a face-to-face interview survey. Except for the largest of agencies and businesses, the discretionary funds necessary for doing expensive surveys whenever desired simply do not exist. As a result, policy makers are left with the alternatives of either foregoing any consideration of people's preferences or depending on past surveys done for other purposes. Those who attempt to do the latter usually discover that the questions asked in other surveys are too general or otherwise inadequate to address the specific issues they are attempting to resolve.[7]

Just such a situation existed in the case of the aforementioned statewide tax survey we were asked to do, of which details are given in the beginning of Chapter 7. Several variables contributed to the fact that 2 weeks was all the time that could be allowed for planning, implementing, and reporting the final results. The group that asked for the survey was the State Committee for New Tax Policy, a broadly based citizens' committee appointed by the state's Governor for the explicit purpose of developing a proposed new tax policy and recommending it to a special session of the state legislature. The deliberations of this committee, whose membership included representatives from all sectors of the economy, plus the traditional pro- and antitax forces in the state, were complex and painfully slow. Thus it was not until the eve of the special session that consensus was reached. The leaders of the committee wanted some indication of how the general public might receive the proposal should it be referred by the legislature to the voters in the fall election —information that could be used either to support the proposal or, alternatively, provide a basis for last-minute modifications before the date (2 weeks hence) when legislative action was slated to occur. Thus the time frame for conducting the survey was exceedingly narrow. The only option available to the committee, for reasons of time and cost, was a telephone survey, which they quickly decided to sponsor.

The decision to do the survey by telephone was made with some reluctance by the committee, because of the extreme complexity of the tax issue. They feared that respondents would not adequately comprehend such a complex issue over the telephone, a concern that early pretests tended to support. For this reason, a mail questionnaire was also prepared and subsequently administered to the same sample. Although it was too late for the earliest legislative deliberations, responses to the mail questionnaire were destined for possible later use. Finally, as so often happens, the possibility of making a substantial modification in the bill was proposed during the legislative debate. When this occurred respondents were contacted yet another time for one more assessment of their views. The precise question asked in this third and final survey was quite different from any of those questions proposed for inclusion in the earlier surveys. Only the unique unwinding of this particular legislative process seemed likely to have produced the particular question that suddenly became so overwhelmingly important. Thus three separate surveys were conducted, each seeking specific timely information that could be fed into the policy-making process. The nature of this process meant that none of the individual surveys could have been conducted any earlier and still have been meaningful.

Although the scenario for each use of surveys to provide input to policy makers will differ, the fundamental implication is the same—adequate telephone and mail methods provide a new range of possibilities for producing survey results for utilization by policy makers. The low costs and rapid speed with which they can be mounted (and for the telephone implemented), seem likely to increase their use for crises that develop so easily in our exceedingly complex society. The energy crisis of late 1973 and early 1974 is a case in point. Caught by surprise, policy makers were attempting to arrive at quick decisions about how to cut energy consumption. This required assumptions about what would be least and most acceptable to the American people and the savings that any decision would produce. Should future crises arise, it would seem that an interplay between policy questions and the provision of survey data could be developed using combinations of the three methods. In addition, as some questions are decided and their implementation brings forth new questions, additional surveys could seek information to help solve these new questions.

The potential for developing and implementing new kinds of policy-relevant surveys is also apparent when considering a number of TDM mail surveys that have been conducted in several states, including Kentucky, Michigan, and North Carolina.[8] These surveys focused on various state and local community problems (e.g., crime, pollution, jobs, etc.), by ascertaining people's perceptions about the seriousness of each problem and the priorities that people gave for spending public funds to resolve them. The surveys were unusual in that each involved several thousand respondents, ranging from 5000 to 22,000. The large samples were justified because of the desire to make meaningful comparisons among subregions of the various states, and in some cases to cities and counties. State and local decision makers were often involved in identifying the issues to be addressed by the surveys, and the results were published specifically for their use.[9] In addition, it appears that various public agencies have made considerable use of the survey results in their work.[10] One reason for the great interest of state and local decision makers in these surveys was the ability to compare different localities, something that is normally precluded by the small samples relied on for face-to-face surveys. Indeed, it is safe to suggest that face-to-face interviews with enough people to permit such generalizations would never have been attempted, no matter how salient the issues might have been.

Another application of the TDM for policy purposes occurred in the state of Washington, where an attempt was made to set goals for the state's future.[11] Called Alternatives for Washington, this experience is of particular interest to us here because it aptly illustrates how TDM surveys can be timed to fit into a policy-setting process. Described in *The Futurist* as the most generously funded of more than a dozen state-level efforts at future planning that have occurred across the United States, it attempted to involve the state's citizens to the greatest possible extent.[12] The process of setting state goals centered around a statewide task force, 165 people selected from some 4000 nominees to represent all segments of the population. This group met for several 3-day marathon sessions in which alternative directions for the state were developed, discussed, analyzed in terms of their impacts, and redeveloped. The experience consisted of classroom educational sessions, in-depth exchanges of views among the participants, and "futures creating" sessions, as the delegates sought not only to identify desirable goals, but to understand how accomplishing one desirable goal would affect the chances of achieving another. The goal-setting process was expanded to areawide meetings held in 10 locations throughout the state, involving about 1200 more people. Participants in these sessions went through a similar, but much briefer, experience of exchanging views and articulating alternative futures for the state. The first part of the process ended with the acceptance by the statewide task force of 11 different generalized futures for the state and a very large number of more specific goals. An effort was then made to present and explain these alternatives to the people of the state through television programs developed especially for that purpose. Then statewide surveys were conducted to determine citizens' views toward the various alternatives, the results of which would be used by the task force as an input for deciding what recommendations to make to the governor and legislature.

Thus the stage was set for surveying to be done in a particular time frame, with the results to be provided to the statewide task force for their deliberations. Actually, four surveys were conducted, each for a purpose that would complement the others. The first was a statewide telephone survey of 1000 persons. The reason for its selection was that surveying could not commence until after the final television program had been aired, but survey results were needed in exactly 1 month, when the statewide task force was scheduled to begin work on its final recommendations. Although it would have been desirable (from the point of view of the researcher) to delay their meetings until a later time, that simply was not possible because of the importance of having the results before the legislature when it convened only a short time later.

A statewide mail survey of 5000 people was begun at the same time as the telephone survey. It was a sample stratified by geographic region of the state, with large enough subsamples from each region to allow for the comparison of results from each of them to determine if different goals should be recommended for different regions of the state. This was a question of particular significance, inasmuch as the economies of the state's subregions are quite different.

The third survey was of the participants in the statewide task force. Their collective opinions were deemed particularly significant as an input into any final decisions for several reasons. First, they came from all walks of life, all areas of the state, and represented all demographic strata. Second, many were highly knowledgeable in specialized fields, ranging from agriculture to medical care, and international trade to welfare agencies. Having gone through the intensive seminar discussions and numerous subgroup meetings, they had spent a great deal of time struggling with the issues, digesting presentations, and reading stacks of resource material. Thus they were viewed as a particularly knowledgeable group whose "informed" opinions might be weighed more heavily than those of the general public on certain complex issues in deciding what policies to recommend.

The fourth survey was of those who had participated in the areawide conferences. The explicit purpose of this survey was to allow regional concerns to be aired from groups that had intermediate involvement in the total process. They too seemed likely to have greater knowledge of the issues than the statewide sample of the general public.

The point of conducting four surveys was obviously not that one was better than any other. Rather, it was that each might complement the others, contributing certain information that was otherwise unavailable. The telephone survey had the added purpose of providing the first glimpse of what seemed likely to come out of the public survey, and thus allow final deliberations to commence at an earlier date. When results from the same question in all four surveys were matched, it allowed the statewide task force to ask more than the simple question of what do the people desire. The task force could also ask, Are there differences among regions of the state? Do those who have examined the issues for nearly a year—members of the task force—differ greatly from those who have only recently heard about the issues for the first time? The cross-tabulations made possible because of the large sample size allowed differences between the young and the old, the rich and the poor, and so on, to be examined in great depth. When, as was often the case, the results from all four surveys were quite congruent, it was possible to support a position by saying that not only did the general public support it, but those who have studied the issue in some detail feel the same way; thus a somewhat stronger case for recommending a particular policy could be made.

The Alternatives for Washington program resulted in some 7000 people being surveyed. It suggests the very real possibilities of going well beyond the general survey, so often done on public policy issues. It suggests combining methods and surveying specific groups whose views might be weighted more heavily in deciding what course of action to take. It suggests ways of getting better readings on the extent to which conflict and consensus prevail on particular issues. Most important, it suggests doing such surveys in a time frame amenable to policy deliberations, whether it is a serious effort in "futuring," or, for example, an attempt to assess the consequences of energy shortfalls.

Although we envision many exciting possibilities for the increased use of surveys for policy purposes, it seems prudent to end our discussion of them on a note of caution. Specifically, increased use may also mean increased misuse of surveys for policy purposes. The ease with which TDM surveys can be done augments the probability of surveys being designed and implemented entirely under the control of the policy maker who proposes to use the results produced. Under these conditions, the possibility of survey results being selectively used in a manipulative fashion to support predetermined courses of action seems great. Therefore, we deem it just as important to research the constraints under which policy-relevant surveys get done and the ethical implications of doing them, as it is to develop the methods that made such surveys feasible in the first place.[13]

BOON OR BOONDOGGLE: WHICH WILL IT BE?

The widespread acceptance of mail and telephone survey methods has some rather awesome implications. For very little investment of money, almost any academic institution or agency can establish the capability for conducting credible mail and telephone surveys. Indeed, even now the number of telephone polling laboratories is increasing dramatically. The extension of survey capabilities to researchers throughout the country has implications that appear to be both positive and negative.

One positive implication stems from the fact that good research ideas for surveys have never been the exclusive property of those with access to face-to-face interview surveys, either by virtue of their employment situation or because of their grantsmanship skills. Such people are few in number. In addition, the months and even years it sometimes takes to acquire the very large grants and contracts necessary for conducting large face-to-face interview surveys sometimes result in the most opportune time for doing a survey being well passed before the effort can be mounted. This is particularly unfortunate when inputs into policy decisions are at stake. Further, the research most likely to receive large-scale funding is generally that which is defined as having the greatest national significance (e.g., national surveys of energy consumption, mental health, or crime). This means that surveys focusing on problems faced by states and local jurisdictions are not funded, or, if they are, at a much lower level. In short, the near complete reliance on costly face-to-face interview surveys is often not suitable for meeting research needs that surface in a very dynamic and ever-changing society. Further, our society is one noted more for the heterogeneity of its regions than a homogeneity that would allow national studies to substitute for state and local ones. Mail and telephone methods provide a tremendous potential, and a most welcome one, for addressing problems in a more timely manner.

The increased use also holds some negative implications. For example, a substantial increase in the number of surveys conducted may provide unprecedented credence to the often heard complaint that Americans are being oversurveyed. Thus one defense that social scientists frequently offer for doing surveys—the fact that most Americans have never been surveyed—will no longer be valid. Further, the cries of those segments of the population who are frequently subjected to surveys (e.g., college sophomores and some metropolitan residents) may be augmented by complaints of others (e.g., residents of rural areas and other widely dispersed populations) who were previously protected from surveys by the costs of conducting face-to-face interviews.

Even more worrisome is the possible emergence of "survey mania," the implementation of thousands of ill-advised and poorly constructed surveys that produce results of no use to anyone. We are reminded here of the perceptive comment by the director of one university's survey research center, who noted that he spent far more time convincing people to not conduct poorly conceived or inappropriate surveys than he did helping those who had questions that a well-designed survey could answer. His comment covered a variety of situations, ranging from politically motivated attempts to do a survey as a means of delaying an inevitable policy decision (under the guise of seeking public input from the general public) to occasions when those who wanted to conduct a survey could not specify what questions they hoped the survey would answer.

Add to the above the possibility that surveys can conceivably be conducted by people with little or no training in the theory and practice of surveying, and the likelihood of useless surveys being done is increased even further. When surveys are designed and conducted by those who lack appropriate training, it is likely that mistakes will be made that diminish the accuracy of the survey results.

In addition, there is a considerable chance that the person doing the survey will not detect any such errors. Thus the implementation of seemingly mindless surveys by people with little or no training in survey methods becomes a substantial risk and the fallout from them a grave concern to the entire survey industry.

Still another concern is the ethical implications inherent in the TDM. For example, it is very easy to promise respondents that they will be sent a copy of the survey results as an inducement for them to respond, a procedure called for by the TDM, but never quite get around to sending them out to respondents. It is also relatively effortless to develop the required social utility argument (and even questions that seem to exhibit it) with the promise of presenting the results to relevant policy makers, but have no real intention of keeping that promise. It is also easy, and regrettable, that letters and questions from respondents are ignored because their questionnaires have already been returned. If the TDM—which fundamentally involves an "exchange" between researcher and respondent based on the trust that the former will carry through on their promises—is used deceitfully, the inevitable long-range result will be to detract from the credibility of the survey research enterprise.

Thus our view concerning the coming of age of the mail and telephone survey methods is an ambivalent one. The manner in which they are used is just as important as whether they are used at all. Unless they are used carefully and with ethical concern, what now seems like a boon to social science may in the end be an unfortunate and regrettable boondoggle. It is our hope that the former will prevail, and that the TDM will not only be used for conducting mail and telephone surveys, but that those who use it will do so responsibly.

NOTES

1. See, for example, Theresa F. Rogers, "Interviews by Telephone and in Person: Quality of Responses and Field Performance," *Public Opinion Quarterly, 40,* 1976, pp. 51–65.
2. Willis J. Goudy, "Interim Nonresponse to a Mail Questionnaire: Impacts on Variable Relationships," Journal Paper No. J-8456, Iowa Agriculture and Home Economics Experiment Station, Ames, Iowa, 1976.
3. Alfred St. Louis, *The Texas Crime Trend Survey,* Statistical Analysis Center, Texas Department of Public Safety, 1976.

4. Rogers, *op. cit.;* F. Wiseman, "Methodological Bias in Public Opinion Surveys," *Public Opinion Quarterly, 36,* 1972, pp. 105–108; J. Colombotos, "Personal Versus Telephone Interviews: Effect on Responses," *Public Health Reports, 84,* 1969, pp. 773–782; J. R. Hochstim, "A Critical Comparison of Three Strategies of Collecting Data From Households," *Journal of the American Statistical Association, 62,* 1967, pp. 976–989; Don. A. Dillman, Jean Gorton Gallegos, and Kenneth R. Tremblay, Jr., "Increasing Response Quality in Telephone Interviews," paper presented at the Annual Meeting of the Pacific Sociological Association, San Diego, California, 1976; Ramon Henson, Aleda Roth, and Charles F. Cannell, "Personal Versus Telephone Interviews and the Effects of Telephone Reinterviews on Reporting of Psychiatric Symptamatology," report prepared for U.S. Public Health Service, 1974; John M. Wardwell and Don A. Dillman, *The Alternatives for Washington Surveys: The Final Report,* report prepared for the Washington State Office of Program Planning and Fiscal Management, 1975.

5. Rogers, *Ibid.,* p. 65.

6. Don A. Dillman, "Preference Surveys and Policy Decisions: Our New Tools Need Not Be Used in the Same Old Way," Proceedings of the National Conference on Nonmetropolitan Community Services Research at Columbus, Ohio, United States Department of Agriculture, Washington, D.C., 1977. A shortened version of this paper is forthcoming in the *Journal of the Community Development* 8, 1977, pp. 30—43.

7. *Ibid.*

8. James A. Christenson, *North Carolina Today and Tomorrow,* Miscellaneous Extension Publications, 141–149, North Carolina Agricultural Extension Service, Raleigh, North Carolina, 1975–1976; William Kimball, personal communication, 1976; Paul D. Warner, Rabel J. Burdge, Susan D. Hoffman, and Gary R. Hammonds, *Issues Facing Kentucky,* Department of Sociology, University of Kentucky, 1976.

9. *Ibid.*

10. James A. Christenson, "Public Input for Program Planning and Policy Formation," *Journal of the Community Development Society, 7,* 1976, pp. 33–39.

11. Wardwell and Dillman, *op. cit.*

12. David Baker, "Anticipatory Democracy," *The Futurist, 10,* 1976, pp. 262–271.

13. For further elaboration of this point, see, for example, Don A. Dillman and Kenneth R. Tremblay, Jr., "Research Ethics: Emerging Concerns From the Increased Use of Mail and Telephone Survey Methods," *Humboldt Journal of Social Relations,* Forthcoming.

REFERENCE BIBLIOGRAPHY

....

The preparation of this book involved an extensive literature search for information about how to conduct mail and telephone surveys. Listed below are the located publications judged relevant to conducting such surveys. They are of two types—those that deal explicitly with mail or telephone surveys and the remainder which do not provide a direct treatment of either method, but consider relevant survey issues. Each listed reference is coded:

(M) = An explicit treatment of mail surveys.
(T) = An explicit treatment of telephone surveys.
(G) = Not an explicit treatment of either mail or telephone surveys, but has implications for conducting them.

Our goal was to identify all the available published material relevant to the conduction of mail and telephone surveys. However, the large number of sources in which relevant materials are published probably resulted in our falling short of that goal. Nonetheless, we believe it to be a very comprehensive bibliography of available material relating to the conduct of these surveys.

ARTICLES

Adams, J. Stacy, "An Experiment on Question and Response Bias," *Public Opinion Quarterly, 20,* 1956, pp. 593–598 **(G)**

Adams, S., "Trends in Occupational Origins of Physicians," *American Sociological Review, 18,* 1953, pp. 404–409 **(M)**

Alutto, Joseph A., "A Note on Determining Questionnaire Destination in Survey Research," *Social Forces, 48,* 1969/1970, pp. 252–253 **(M)**

Alutto, Joseph A., "Some Dynamics of Questionnaire Completion and Return Among Professional and Managerial Personnel: The Relative Impacts of Reception at Work Site or Place of Residence," *Journal of Applied Psychology, 54,* 1970, pp. 430–432 **(M)**

American Statistical Association Conference on Surveys of Human Population, 1974 "Report on the ASA Conference on Surveys of Human Populations," *The American Statistician, 28,* 1974, pp. 30–34 **(G)**

Anderson, John F. and Douglas R. Berdie, "Effects on Response Rates of Formal and Informal Questionnaire Follow-up Techniques," *Journal of Applied Psychology, 60,* 1975, pp. 255–257 **(M)**

Andreasen, Alan R., "Personalizing Mail Questionnaire Correspondence," *Public Opinion Quarterly, 34,* 1970/1971, pp. 273–277 **(M)**

Armstrong, J. Scott, "Monetary Incentives in Mail Surveys," *Public Opinion Quarterly, 39,* 1975, pp. 111–116 **(M)**

Arndt, Johan and Edgar Crane, "Response Bias, Yea-saying, and the Double Negative," *Journal of Marketing Research, 12,* 1975, pp. 218–220 **(M)**

Aronson, Sidney., "The Sociology of the Telephone," *International Journal of Comparative Sociology, 12,* 1971, pp. 153–167 **(T)**

Asch, M. J., "Negative Response Bias and Personality Adjustment," *Journal of Counseling Psychology, 5,* 1958, pp. 206–210 **(G)**

Athey, D. R., Joan E. Coleman, Audrey P. Reitman, and Jenny Tang, "Two Experiments Showing the Effect of the Interviewer's Racial Background on Responses to Questionnaires Concerning Racial Issues," *Journal of Applied Psychology, 44,* 1960, pp. 244–246 **(G)**

Backrack, Stanley D. and Harry M. Scoble, "Mail Questionnaire Efficiency: Controlled Reduction of Nonresponse," *Public Opinion Quarterly, 31,* 1967/1968, 265–271 **(M)**

Ball, Donald, W., "Toward a Sociology of Telephones and Telephoners," in Marcello Truzzi (Ed.), *Sociology and Everyday Life* (Englewood Cliffs, N.J.: Prentice-Hall, 1968, pp. 59–75 **(T)**

Ballweg, John A., "Husband-Wife Response Similarities on Evaluative and Non-Evaluative Survey Questions," *Public Opinion Quarterly, 33,* 1969/1970, pp. 249–254 **(G)**

Barlett, Dorothy L., Pamela B. Drew, Eleanor G. Fable, and William A. Watts, "Selective Exposure to a Presidential Campaign Appeal," *Public Opinion Quarterly, 38,* 1974, pp. 264–270 **(M)**

Barnette, W. L., "The Non-Respondent Problem in Questionnaire Research," *Journal of Applied Psychology, 34,* 1950, pp. 397–398 **(M)**

Barnette, W. L., "Report of a Follow-Up of Counseled Veterans," *Journal of Social Psychology, 32,* 1950, pp. 129–142 **(M)**

Bauer, Rainald K. and Frank Meissner, "Structures of Mail Questionnaires: Test of Alternatives," *Public Opinion Quarterly, 27,* 1963, pp. 307–311 **(M)**

Baur, E. Jackson, "Response Bias in a Mail Survey," *Public Opinion Quarterly, 11,* 1947, pp. 594–600 **(M)**

Baxter, R. E., "Use Both Mail-Type Questionnaire and Personal Interviews in Readership Research," *Printers Ink,* May 7, 1943, pp. 24–82 **(M)**

Becker, Boris W. and John G. Myers, "Yeasaying Response Style," *Journal of Advertising Research, 10,* 1970, pp. 31–37 **(G)**

Bender, D. H., "Colored Stationery in Direct-Mail Advertising," *Journal of Applied Psychology, 41,* 1975, pp. 161–164 **(M)**

Benjamin, Kurt, "Combining Responses on Two Forms of a Questionnaire with Options in Inverse Order," *Public Opinion Quarterly, 13,* 1949, pp. 688–690 **(G)**

Bennett, E. M., R. Alpert, and A. C. Goldstein, "Communications Through Limited-Response Questioning," *Public Opinion Quarterly, 18,* 1954, pp. 303–308 **(G)**

Bennett, E. M., E. L. Blomquist, and A. C. Goldstein, "Response Stability in Limited-Response Questioning," *Public Opinion Quarterly, 18,* 1954, pp. 218–223 **(G)**

Benson, Lawrence E., "Mail Surveys Can Be Valuable," *Public Opinion Quarterly, 10,* 1946, 234–241 **(M)**

Berdie, Douglas R. and John F. Anderson, "Mail Questionnaire Response Rates: Updating Outmoded Thinking," *Journal of Marketing, 40,* 1976, pp. 71–73 **(M)**

Berg, E. A. and G. M. Rapaport, "Response Bias in an Unstructured Questionnaire," *Journal of Psychology, 38,* 1954, pp. 475–481 **(G)**

Berger, Philip K. and James E. Sullivan, "Instructional Set, Interview Context, and the Incidents of 'Don't Know' Responses," *Journal of Applied Psychology, 54,* 1970, pp. 414–416 **(T)**

Bevis, Joseph C., "Economical Incentive Used for Mail Questionnaires," *Public Opinion Quarterly, 12,* 1948, pp. 492–495 **(M)**

Biel, Alexander L., "Abuses of Survey Research Techniques: The Phony Interview," *Public Opinion Quarterly, 31,* 1967/1968, p. 298 **(T)**

Birnbaum, Z. W. and M. G. Sirken, "On the Total Error Due to Noninterviews and to Random Sampling," *International Journal of Opinion and Attitude Research, 4,* 1950, pp. 179–191 **(G)**

Birnbaum, Z. W. and M. G. Sirken, "Bias Due to Non-Availability in Sampling Surveys," *Journal of the American Statistical Association, 45,* 1950, pp. 98–111 **(G)**

Blankenship, Albert B., "Does the Question Form Influence Public Opinion Poll Results?" *Journal of Applied Psychology, 24,* 1940, pp. 27–30 **(G)**

Blumberg, Herbert J., Carolyn Fuller, and A. Paul Hare, "Response Rates in Postal Surveys," *Public Opinion Quarterly, 38,* 1974, pp. 113–123 **(M)**

Boek, Walter E. and James H. Lade, "A Test of the Usefulness of the Post-Card Technique in a Mail Questionnaire Study," *Public Opinion Quarterly, 27,* 1963, pp. 303–306 **(M)**

Bogart, Leo, "No Opinion, Don't Know, and Maybe No Answer," *Public Opinion Quarterly, 31,* 1967, pp. 331–345 **(G)**

Bradburn, Norman M. and William M. Mason, "The Order Effect of Question Order on Responses," *Journal of Marketing Research, 1,* 1964, pp. 57–61 **(M)**

Bradt, Kenneth, "The Usefulness of a Post Card Technique in a Mail Questionnaire Study," *Public Opinion Quarterly, 19,* 1955, pp. 218–222 **(M)**

Brennan, R. D., "Trading Stamps as an Incentive in Mail Surveys," *Journal of Marketing, 22,* 1958, pp. 306–307 **(M)**

Britton, J. H. and J. O. Britton, "Factors in the Return of Questionnaires to Older Persons," *Journal of Applied Psychology, 35,* 1951, pp. 57–60 **(M)**

Brooks, V., "Can You Trust Mail Questionnaires?" *Printers Ink,* Sept. 19, 1947, pp. 86–104 **(M)**

Brown, George H., "Randomized Inquiry Vs. Conventional Questionnaire Method in Estimating

Drug Usage Rates Through Mail Surveys," *Technical Report 75-14, Human Resources Research Organization,* June 1975 **(M)**

Brown, Morton L., "Use of a Postcard Query in Mail Surveys," *Public Opinion Quarterly, 29,* 1965/1966, pp. 635–637 **(M)**

Brunner, G. Allen and Stephen J. Carroll, Jr., "The Effect of Prior Telephone Appointments on Completion Rates and Response Content," *Public Opinion Quarterly, 31,* 1967/1968, pp. 652–654 **(T)**

Brunner, G. Allen and Stephen J. Carroll, Jr., "The Effect of Prior Notification on the Refusal Rate in Fixed Address Surveys," *Journal of Advertising Research, 9,* 1969, pp. 42–44 **(MT)**

Brunner, G. Allen and Stephen J. Carroll, Jr., "Weekday Evening Interviews of Employed Persons Are Better," *Public Opinion Quarterly, 33,* 1969/1970, pp. 265–267 **(G)**

Brunner, James A. and G. Allen Brunner, "Are Voluntarily Unlisted Telephone Subscribers Really Different?" *Journal of Marketing Research, 8,* 1971, pp. 121–124 **(T)**

Bunning, Bruce and Don Cahalan, "By-Mail Vs. Field Self-Administered Questionnaires: An Armed Forces Survey," *Public Opinion Quarterly, 37,* 1973/1974, pp. 618–624 **(M)**

Burchinal, Lee G., "Personality Characteristics and Sample Bias," *Journal of Applied Psychology, 44,* 1960, pp. 172–173 **(G)**

Buse, R. C., "Increasing Response Rates in Mailed Questionnaires," *American Journal of Agricultural Economics, 55,* 1973, pp. 503–508 **(M)**

Cahalan, Don, "Measuring Newspaper Readership by Telephone: Two Comparisons with Face to Face Interviews," *Journal of Advertising Research, 1,* 1959, pp. 1–6 **(T)**

Cahalan, Don, "Effectiveness of a Mail Questionnaire Technique in the Army," *Public Opinion Quarterly, 15,* 1951, pp. 575–580 **(M)**

Campbell, Donald T., "Bias in Mail Surveys," (A Letter to the Editor), *Public Opinion Quarterly, 13,* 1949, p. 562 **(M)**

Carpenter, Edwin H., "Personalizing Mail Surveys: A Replication and Reassessment," *Public Opinion Quarterly, 38,* 1974/1975, pp. 614–620 **(M)**

Carter, R. E. and V. C. Trohldahl, "Use of a Recall Criterion in Measuring the Educational Television Audience," *Public Opinion Quarterly, 26,* 1962, pp. 114–121 **(T)**

Carter, Roy E., Jr., "Field Methods in Communication Research," in R. O. Nafziger and D. M. White, *Introduction to Mass Communication Research,* (Baton Rouge: Louisiana State University Press, 1963), Rev. Ed., pp. 78–127 **(T)**

Cartwright, Ann and Wyn Tucker, "An Attempt to Reduce the Number of Calls on an Interview Inquiry," *Public Opinion Quarterly, 31,* 1967/1968, pp. 299–302 **(M)**

Clark, K. E., "A Vocational Interest Test at the Skilled Trades Level," *Journal of Applied Psychology, 33,* 1949, pp. 291–303 **(G)**

Clausen, John A. and Robert N. Ford, "Controlling Bias in Mail Questionnaires," *Journal of the American Statistical Association, 42,* 1947, pp. 497–511 **(M)**

Colley, R. H., "Don't Look Down Your Nose at Mail Questionnaires," *Printers Ink,* March 16, 1945, pp. 21–108 **(M)**

Collins, W. Andrew, "Interviewers' Verbal Idiosyncrasies as a Source of Bias," *Public Opinion Quarterly, 34,* 1970/1971, pp. 416–422 **(G)**

Colombotos, John, "The Effects of Personal vs. Telephone Interviews on Socially Acceptable Responses," *Public Opinion Quarterly, 29,* 1965, pp. 457–458 **(T)**

Colombotos, John, "Personal Versus Telephone Interviews: Effect on Responses," *Public Health Reports, 84,* 1969, pp. 773–782 **(T)**

Conrad, Herbert S., "Clearance of Questionnaires with Respect to Invasion of Privacy," (Public Sensitivities, Ethical Standards, Etc: Principles and Viewpoint—the Bureau of Research, U.S. Office of Education), *Sociology of Education,* Spring 1967, pp. 171–175 **(G)**

Conrad, Herbert S., "Some Principles of Attitude Measurement: A Reply to 'Opinion Attitude Methodology'," *Psychological Bulletin, 43,* 1946, pp. 570–589 **(G)**

Coombs, Clyde H. and Lolagene C. Coombs, " 'Don't Know': Item Ambiguity or Respondent Uncertainty," *Public Opinion Quarterly, 40,* 1976/1977, pp. 497–514 **(G)**

Coombs, Lolagene and Ronald Freeman, "Use of Telephone Interviews in a Longitudinal Fertility Study," *Public Opinion Quarterly, 28,* 1964, pp. 112–117 **(T)**

Cooper, Sanford L., "Random Sampling by Telephone—An Improved Method," *Journal of Marketing Research, 1,* 1964, pp. 45–48 **(T)**

Cornfield, J., "On Certain Biases in Samples of Human Populations," *Journal of American Statistical Association, 37,* 1942, pp. 63–68 **(G)**

Cox, Eli P., W. Thomas Anderson, Jr., and David G. Fulcher, "Reappraising Mail Survey Response Rates," *Journal of Marketing Research, 11,* 1974, pp. 413–417 **(M)**

Cox W. E., Jr., "Response Patterns to Mail Surveys," *Journal of Marketing Research, 3,* 1966, pp. 392–397 **(M)**

Cozan, Lee W., "Type of Mailing and Effectiveness of Direct-Mail Advertising," *Journal of Applied Psychology, 44,* 1960, pp. 175–176 **(M)**

Crespi, L. P., " 'Opinion-Attitude Methodology' and the Polls—a Rejoinder," *Psychological Bulletin, 43,* 1946, pp. 562–569 **(G)**

Crider, Donald M. and Fern K. Willits, "Respondent Retrieval Bias in a Longitudinal Survey," *Sociology and Social Research, 58,* 1973, pp. 56–65 **(G)**

Crossley, H. M. and R. Fink, "Response and Non-Response in a Probability Sample," *International Journal of Opinion and Attitude Research, 5,* 1951, pp. 1–19 **(T)**

Cuber, John F. and John B. Gerberich, "A Note on Consistency in Questionnaire Responses," *American Sociological Review, 11,* 1946, pp. 13–15 **(G)**

Dale, Edgar and Jeanne S. Chall, "A Formula for Predicting Reliability," *Educational Research Bulletin, 27,* 1948, pp. 11–20 **(G)**

Dalenius, Tore, "Treatment of the Non-Response Problem," *Journal of Advertising Research, 1,* 1960/1961, pp. 1–7 **(G)**

Dalenius, Tore, "Time and Survey Design," *Journal of Advertising Research, 5,* 1965, pp. 2–5 **(G)**

Daniel, Wayne W., "Nonresponse in Sociological Surveys: A Review of Some Methods for Handling the Problem," *Sociological Methods and Research, 3,* 1975, pp. 291–307 **(G)**

DeLamater, John and Patricia MacCorquodale, "The Effects of Interview Schedule Variations on Reported Sexual Behavior," *Sociological Methods and Research, 4,* 1975, pp. 215–236 **(M)**

Deming, W. Edwards, "On Errors in Surveys," *American Sociological Review, 9,* 1944, pp. 359–369 **(G)**

Deming, W. Edwards, "Some Criteria for Judging the Quality of Surveys," *Journal of Marketing, 12,* 1947, pp. 145–157 **(G)**

Deming, W. Edwards, "On a Probability Mechanism to Attain an Economic Balance Between the Resultant Error of Response and the Bias of Non-Response," *Journal of American Statistical Association, 48,* 1953, pp. 743–772 **(MT)**

Deming, W. Edwards and F. E. Stephan, "On the Interpretation of Censuses as Samples," *Journal of American Statistical Association, 36,* 1941, pp. 45–59 **(G)**

Deutscher, Irwin, "Physicians' Reactions to a Mailed Questionnaire: A Study in Resistentialism," *Public Opinion Quarterly, 20,* 1956, pp. 599–604 **(M)**

Dillman, Don A., "Increasing Mail Questionnaire Response in Large Samples of the General Public," *Public Opinion Quarterly, 36,* 1972, pp. 254–257 **(M)**

Dillman, Don A., James A. Christenson, Edwin H. Carpenter, and Ralph M. Brooks, "Increasing Mail Questionnaire Response: A Four-State Comparison," *American Sociological Review, 39,* 1974, pp. 744–756 **(M)**

Dillman, Don A. and James H. Frey, "Contribution of Personalization to Mail Questionnaire Response as an Element of a Previously Tested Method," *Journal of Applied Psychology, 59,* 1974, pp. 297–301 **(M)**

Dillman, Don A., Jean Gorton Gallegos, and James H. Frey, "Reducing Refusal Rates for Telephone Interviews," *Public Opinion Quarterly, 40,* 1976, pp. 66–78 **(T)**

Dix, A. H., "Here's What Happens When Starch Scores are Checked by Mail," *Printers Ink,* Nov. 23, 1956, pp. 24–27 **(M)**

Dodd, Robert W. and Thomas W. Wipple, "Item Selection: A Practical Tool in Attitude Research," *Journal of Marketing, 40,* 1976, pp. 87–89 **(G)**

Dohrenwend, Barbara Snell, "Some Effects of Open and Closed Questions on Respondents' Answers," *Human Organization, 24,* 1965, pp. 175–184 **(G)**

Dohrenwend, Barbara Snell, John Colombotos, and Bruce P. Dohrenwend, "Survey Methodology," *Public Opinion Quarterly, 30,* 1966/1967, pp. 452–453 **(G)**

Dohrenwend, Barbara Snell and Bruce P. Dohrenwend, "Sources of Refusals in Surveys," *Public Opinion Quarterly, 32,* 1968, pp. 74–83 **(G)**

Donald, Marjorie N., "Implications of Nonresponse for the Interpretation of Mail Questionnaire Data," *Public Opinion Quarterly, 24,* 1960, pp. 99–114 **(MT)**

Duncanson, J. P., "The Average Telephone Call is Better than the Average Telephone Call," *Public Opinion Quarterly, 33,* 1969/1970, pp. 112–116 **(T)**

Dunkelberg, William C. and George S. Day, "Nonresponse Bias and Callbacks in Sample Surveys," *Journal of Marketing Research, 10,* 1973, pp. 160–168 **(G)**

Dunlap, J. William, "The Effect of Color in Direct Mail Advertising," *Journal of Applied Psychology, 34,* 1950, pp. 280–281 **(M)**

Dunnette, Marvin D., Walter H. Uphoff, and Merriam Aylward, "The Effect of Lack of Information on the Undecided Response in Attitude Surveys," *Journal of Applied Psychology, 40,* 1956, pp. 150–153 **(G)**

Eastlack, J. O., Jr., "Recall of Advertising by Two Telephone Samples," *Journal of Advertising Research, 4,* 1964, pp. 25–29 **(T)**

Eastlack, J. O., Jr. and Henry Assael, "Better Telephone Surveys Through Centralized Interviewing," *Journal of Advertising Research, 6,* 1966, pp. 2–7 **(T)**

Eastman, R. O., "Don'ts About Mail Questionnaires," *Printers Ink,* March 12, 1943, pp. 24–29 **(M)**

Eastman, R. O., "Dangers in Direct-Mail Surveys," *Printers Ink,* Jan. 5, 1945, pp. 36–40 **(M)**

Eckland, Bruce K., "Effects of Prodding to Increase Mail-Back Returns," *Journal of Applied Psychology, 49,* 1965, pp. 165–169 **(M)**

Edgerton, Harold A., Stewart Henderson Britt, and Ralph D. Norman, "Objective Difference Among Various Types of Respondents to a Mailed Questionnaire," *American Sociological Review, 12,* 1947, pp. 435–444 **(M)**

El-Badry, M. A., "Sampling Procedures for Mailed Questionnaires," *Journal of American Statistical Association, 51,* 1956, pp. 209–227 **(M)**

Ellis, Albert, "Questionnaire Versus Interview Methods in the Study of Human Love Relationships," *American Sociological Review, 12,* 1947, pp. 541–553 **(M)**

Erdos, Paul L., "How to Get High Returns From Your Mail Surveys," *Printers Ink,* Feb. 22, 1957, pp. 30–31 **(M)**

Erdos, Paul L., "Successful Mail Surveys: High Returns and How to Get Them," *Printers Ink,* March 1, 1957, pp. 56–60 **(M)**

Etcheverry, B. E., "Want Confidential Purchase Data? It's All in How You Ask," *Sales Management, 72,* March 1, 1954, p. 48ff **(M)**

Farber, Bernard, "Response Falsification and Spurious Correlation in Survey Research," *American Sociological Review, 28,* 1963, pp. 123–130 **(G)**

Fauman, Joseph S. and Harry Sharp, "Presenting the Results of Social Research to the Public," *Public Opinion Quarterly, 22,* 1958, pp. 107–115 **(MT)**

Falthzik, Alfred M., "When to Make Telephone Interviews," *Journal of Marketing Research, 9,* 1972, pp. 451–452 **(T)**

Feild, Hubert S., "Effect of Sex of Investigator on Mail Survey Response Rates and Response Bias," *Journal of Applied Psychology, 60,* 1975, pp. 772–773 **(M)**

Ferber, Robert, "Which—Mail Questionnaires or Personal Interviews?", *Printers Ink,* Feb. 13, 1948, pp. 44–66 **(M)**

Ferber, Robert, "The Problem of Bias in Mail Returns: A Solution," *Public Opinion Quarterly, 12,* 1948, pp. 669–676 **(M)**

Ferber, Robert, A rejoinder to a letter to the editor from Donald T. Campbell, *Public Opinion Quarterly, 13,* 1949, pp. 562–563 **(M)**

Ferber, Robert, A letter to the editor commenting further on bias in mail surveys, *Public Opinion Quarterly, 14,* 1950, pp. 193–196 **(M)**

Ferber, Robert, A follow-up on further comments on bias in mail surveys stated in a letter to the editor, *Public Opinion Quarterly, 14,* 1950, pp. 196–197 **(M)**

Ferber, Robert, "Order Bias in a Mail Survey," *Journal of Marketing Research, 17,* 1952, pp. 171–178 **(M)**

Ferber, Robert, "The Effect of Respondent Ignorance on Survey Results," *Journal of the American Statistical Association, 51,* 1956, p. 576 **(G)**

Ferber, Robert, "Item Nonresponse in a Consumer Survey," *Public Opinion Quarterly, 30,* 1966/1967, pp. 399–415 **(G)**

Ferriss, Abbott L., "A Note on Stimulating Response to Questionnaires," *American Sociological Review, 16,* 1951, pp. 247–249 **(M)**

Field, Donald R., "The Telephone Interview in Leisure Research," *Journal of Leisure Research, 5,* 1973, pp. 51–59 **(T)**

Filion, F. L., "Estimating Bias Due to Nonresponse in Mail Surveys," *Public Opinion Quarterly, 39,* 1975/1976, pp. 482–492 **(M)**

Filion, F. L., "Exploring and Correcting for Nonresponse Bias Using Follow-ups of Nonrespondents," *Pacific Sociological Review, 19,* 1976, pp. 401–408 **(G)**

Filipello, F., H. W. Berg, and A. D. Webb, "A Sampling Method for Household Surveys," *Food Technology, 12,* 1958, pp. 387–390 **(M)**

Flesch, Rudolph, "A New Readability Yardstick," *Journal of Applied Psychology, 32,* 1948, pp. 221–233 **(G)**

Ford, Neil M., "The Advance Letter in Mail Surveys," *Journal of Marketing Research, 4,* 1967, pp. 202–204 **(M)**

Ford, Neil M., "Consistency of Responses in a Mail Survey," *Journal of Advertising Research, 9,* 1969, pp. 31–33 **(M)**

Ford, Neil M., "Questionnaire Appearance and Response Rates in Mail Surveys," *Journal of Advertising Research, 8,* 1968, pp. 43–45 **(M)**

Ford, Robert N. and Hans Zeisel, "Bias in Mail Surveys Cannot be Controlled by One Mailing," *Public Opinion Quarterly, 13,* 1949, pp. 495–501 **(M)**

Ford, Robert N. and Hans Zeisel, A rejoinder to a letter to the editor from Robert Ferber, *Public Opinion Quarterly, 14,* 1950, p. 196 **(M)**

Francel, E. G., "Mail-Administered Questionnaires: A Success Story," *Journal of Marketing Research, 3,* 1966, pp. 89–91 **(M)**

Francis, Joe D. and Lawrence Busch, "What We Now Know About 'I Don't knows'," *Public Opinion Quarterly, 39,* 1975, pp. 207–218 **(G)**

Frankel, Lester R., "How Incentives and Subsamples Affect the Precision of Mail Surveys," *Journal of Advertising Research, 1,* 1960/1961, pp. 1–5 **(M)**

Frankel, Lester R., Rejoinder, *Journal of Advertising Research, 1,* 1960/1961, pp. 23–24 **(M)**

Franzen, R. and P. F. Lazarsfeld, "Mail Questionnaire as a Research Problem," *Journal of Psychology, 20,* 1945, pp. 293–320 **(M)**

Frazier, G. and K. Bird, "Increasing the Response to a Mail Questionnaire," *Journal of Marketing, 23,* 1958, pp. 186–187 **(M)**

Freeman, John and Edgar W. Butler, "Some Sources of Interviewer Variance in Surveys," *Public Opinion Quarterly, 40,* 1976, pp. 79–91 **(G)**

Freitag, Carl B. and John R. Barry, "Interaction and Interviewer Bias in a Survey of the Aged," *Psychological Reports, 36,* 1974, pp. 771–774 **(G)**

Friedman, Hershey H. and Larry Goldstein, "Effect of Ethnicity of Signature on the Rate of Return and Content of a Mail Questionnaire," *Journal of Applied Psychology, 60,* 1975, pp. 770–771 **(M)**

Friedman, Stephen B., "People and Places: A Report on a Survey of People's Locational Preferences," 1973, Draft, State Planning Office, Wisconsin Department of Administration (Madison), September 1973 **(T)**

Fuller, Carol H., "Weighting to Adjust for Survey Nonresponse," *Public Opinion Quarterly, 38,* 1974, pp. 239–246 **(M)**

Funkhouser, Ray G. and Nathan Maccoby, "The Role of a Poll in Resolving a University Crisis," *Public Opinion Quarterly, 33,* 1969/1970, p. 459 **(M)**

Gallup, George, "The Quintamensional Plan of Question Design," *Public Opinion Quarterly, 11,* 1947, pp. 385–393 **(G)**

Gannon, Martin J., Joseph C. Northern, and Stephan Carroll, Jr., "Characteristics of Nonrespondents Among Workers," *Journal of Applied Psychology, 55,* 1971, pp. 586–588 **(M)**

Gelb, Betsy D., "Incentives to Increase Survey Returns: Social Class Considerations," *Journal of Marketing Research, 12,* 1975, pp. 107–109 **(G)**

Gergen, Kenneth J. and Kurt W. Back, "Communication in the Interview and the Disengaged Respondent," *Public Opinion Quarterly, 30,* 1966/1967, pp. 385–398 **(G)**

Gill, Sam, "How Do You Stand On Sin?" *Tide,* March 14, 1947, p. 72 **(G)**

Glasser, Gerald J. and Gale D. Metzger, "Random-Digit Dialing as a Method of Telephone Sampling," *Journal of Marketing Research, 9,* 1972, pp. 59–64 **(T)**

Glasser, Gerald J. and Gale D. Metzger, "National Estimates of Nonlisted Telephone Households and Their Characteristics," *Journal of Marketing Research, 12,* 1975, pp. 359–361 **(G)**

Goldberg, David, Harry Sharp, and Ronald Freedman, "The Stability and Reliability of Expected Family Size Data," *Milbank Memorial Fund Quarterly, 37,* 1959, pp. 369–385 **(MT)**

Goldstein, Hyman and Bernard H. Kroll, "Methods of Increasing Mail Response," *Journal of Marketing, 22,* 1957, pp. 55–57 **(M)**

Goldstein, Larry S. and Hershey H. Friedman, "A Case for Double Postcards in Surveys," *Journal of Advertising Research, 15,* 1975, pp. 43–47 **(M)**

Goudy, Willis J., "Interim Nonresponse to a Mail Questionnaire: Impacts on Variable Relationships," *Public Opinion Quarterly, 40,* 1976, pp. 360–369 **(M)**

Gough, H. G., "A Short Social Status Inventory," *Journal of Educational Psychology, 40,* 1949, pp. 52–56 **(G)**

Gray, P. G., "A Sample Survey with Both a Postal and an Interview Stage," *Applied Statistics, 6,* 1957, pp. 139–153 **(M)**

Greenberg, A. and M. N. Manfield, "On the Reliability of Mail Questionnaires in Product Tests," *Journal of Marketing, 21,* 1957, pp. 342–345 **(M)**

Guest, Lester, "A New Training Method for Opinion Interviewers," *Public Opinion Quarterly, 18,* 1954, pp. 287–299 **(T)**

Guetzkow, Harold, "Unitizing and Categorizing Problems in Coding Qualitative Data," *Journal of Clinical Psychology, 6,* 1950, pp. 47–58 **(G)**

Gullahorn, Jeanne E. and John T. Gullahorn, "Increasing Returns from Non-Respondents," *Public Opinion Quarterly, 23,* 1959, pp. 119–121 **(M)**

Gullahorn, Jeanne E. and John T. Gullahorn, "An Investigation of the Effects of Three Factors on Response to Mail Questionnaires," *Public Opinion Quarterly, 27,* 1963, pp. 294–296 **(M)**

Hackler, James, C. and Patricia Bourgette, "Dollars, Dissonance, and Survey Returns," *Public Opinion Quarterly, 37,* 1973, pp. 276–281 **(M)**

Hagburg, Eugene C., "Validity of Questionnaire Data: Reported and Observed Attendance in an Adult Education Program," *Public Opinion Quarterly, 32,* 1968, pp. 453–456 **(G)**

Hammond, E. C., "Inhalation in Relation to Type and Amount of Smoking," *Journal of the American Statistical Association, 54,* 1959, pp. 35–51 **(M)**

Hancock, J. W., "An Experimental Study of Four Methods of Measuring Unit Costs of Obtaining Attitude Toward the Retail Store," *Journal of Applied Psychology, 24,* 1940, pp. 213–230 **(M)**

Hansen, M. H. and W. N. Hurwitz, "The Problem of Non-Response in Sample Surveys," *Journal of the American Statistical Association, 41,* 1946, pp. 517–529 **(M)**

Haskins, Jack B., Comment on "How Incentives and Subsamples Affect the Precision of Mail Surveys," *Journal of Advertising Research, 1,* 1960/1961, pp. 22–23 **(M)**

Hauck, Mathew and Michael Cox, "Locating a Sample by Random Digit Dialing," *Public Opinion Quarterly, 38,* 1974, pp. 253–260 **(T)**

Hawkins, Darnell F., "Estimation of Nonresponse Bias," *Sociological Methods and Research, 3,* 1975, pp. 461–488 **(T)**

Heath, A. M., "A Demonstration of Bias in a Mail Survey," *Printers Ink,* Sept. 22, 1950, pp. 36–37 **(M)**

Heaton, Eugene E., Jr., "Increasing Mail Questionnaire Returns with a Preliminary Letter," *Journal of Advertising Research, 5,* 1965, pp. 36–39 **(M)**

Hendricks, W. A., "Adjustment for Bias Caused by Non-Response in Mailed Surveys," *Agricultural Economics Research, 5,* 1949, pp. 52–56 **(M)**

Heneman, Herbert G., III, Donald P. Schwab, Dennis L. Huett, and John J. Ford, "Interviewer

Validity as a Function of Interview Structure, Biographical Data, and Interviewee Order," *Journal of Applied Psychology, 60,* 1975, pp. 748–753 **(G)**

Hensley, Wayne E., "Increasing Response Rate by Choice of Postage Stamps," *Public Opinion Quarterly, 38,* 1974, pp. 280–283 **(M)**

Henson, Ramon, Aleda Roth, and Charles F. Cannell, "Personal Vs. Telephone Interviews and the Effects of Telephone Reinterviews on Reporting of Psychiatric Symptomatology," Survey Research Center, Institute for Social Research, 1974 **(T)**

Hertel, Bradley R., "Minimizing Error Variance Introduced by Missing Data Routines in Survey Analysis," *Sociological Methods and Research, 4,* 1976, pp. 459–474 **(G)**

Hill, A. B., "The Doctor's Day and Pay," *Journal of the Royal Statistical Society, 114,* 1951, pp. 1–36 **(G)**

Hinrichs, J. R., "Effects of Sampling, Follow-up Letters, and Commitment to Participation on Mail Attitude Survey Response," *Journal of Applied Psychology, 60,* 1975, pp. 249–251 **(M)**

Hitlin, Robert, "A Research Note on Question Wording and Stability of Response," *Social Science Research, 5,* 1976, pp. 39–42 **(G)**

Hochstim, Joseph R., "Comparison of Three Information-Gathering Strategies in a Population Study of Sociomedical Variables," American Statistical Association, *Proceedings of the Social Statistics Section,* 1962, pp. 154–159 **(TM)**

Hochstim, Joseph R., "Alternatives to Personal Interviewing," *Public Opinion Quarterly, 27,* 1963, pp. 629–630 **(MT)**

Hochstim, Joseph R., "A Critical Comparison of Three Strategies of Collecting Data from Households," *Journal of American Statistical Association, 62,* 1967, pp. 976–989 **(MT)**

Hochstim, Joseph R. and Demetrios A. Athanasopoulos, "Personal Follow-up in a Mail Survey: Its Contribution and Its Cost," *Public Opinion Quarterly, 34,* 1970/1971, pp. 69–81 **(MT)**

House, James S., Wayne Gerber, and Anthony J. McMichael, "Increasing Mail Questionnaire Response: A Controlled Replication and Extension," *Public Opinion Quarterly, 41,* 1977, pp. 95–99 **(M)**

Houseman, Earl E., "Statistical Treatment of the Nonresponse Problem," *Agricultural Economics Research, 5,* 1953, pp. 12–19 **(M)**

Houser, J. David, "Measurement of the Vital Products of Business," *Journal of Marketing, 2,* 1938, pp. 181–189 **(M)**

Houston, Michael J. and Robert W. Jefferson, "The Negative Effects of Personalization on Response Patterns in Mail Surveys," *Journal of Marketing Research, 12,* 1975, pp. 114–117 **(M)**

Ibsen, Charles A. and John A. Ballweg, "Telephone Interviews in Social Research: Some Methodological Considerations," *Quality and Quantity, 8,* 1974, pp. 181–192 **(T)**

Jenkins, J. G., "Validity For What?" *Journal of Consulting Psychology, 10,* 1946, pp. 93–98 **(G)**

Johnson, R. F. Q., "Pitfalls in Research: The Interview as an Illustrative Model," *Psychological Reports, 38,* 1976, pp. 3–17 **(G)**

Johnson, W. Russell, Nicholas A. Sieveking, and Earl S. Clanton, "Effects of Alternative Positioning of Open-Ended Questions in Multiple-Choice Questionnaires," *Journal of Applied Psychology, 59,* Dec, 1974, pp. 776–778 **(M)**

Johnson, Weldon T., "Response Effects in Sex Surveys," *Public Opinion Quarterly, 40,* 1976, pp. 165–181 **(G)**

Judd, Robert C., "Telephone Usage and Survey Research," *Journal of Advertising Research, 6,* 1966, pp. 38–39 **(T)**

Kanuk, Leslie and Conrad Berenson, "Mail Surveys and Response Rates: A Literature Review," *Journal of Marketing Research, 12,* 1975, pp. 440–453 **(M)**

Katz, Daniel, "Do Interviewers Bias Poll Results?" *Public Opinion Quarterly, 6,* 1941, pp. 248–268 **(G)**

Katz, Daniel and Hadley Cantril, "Public Opinion Polls," *Sociometry, 1,* 1937, pp. 155–179 **(G)**

Kawash, Mary B. and Lawrence M. Aleamoni, "Effect of Personal Signature on the Initial Rate of Return of a Mailed Questionnaire," *Journal of Applied Psychology, 55,* 1971, pp. 589–592 **(M)**

Keane, John G., "Low Cost, High Return Mail Surveys," *Journal of Advertising Research, 3,* 1963, pp. 28–30 **(M)**

Kegeles, S. Stephen, Clinton F. Fink, and John P. Kirscht, "Interviewing a National Sample by Long-Distance Telephone," *Public Opinion Quarterly, 33,* 1969/1970, pp. 412–419 **(T)**

Kephart, William M. and Marvin Bressler, "Increasing the Responses to Mail Questionnaires: A Research Study," *Public Opinion Quarterly, 22,* 1958, pp. 123–132 **(M)**

Kildegaard, Ingrid C., "Rejoinder" (to Robert Judd's article, "Telephone Usage and Survey Research), *Journal of Advertising Research, 6,* 1966, pp. 40–41 **(T)**

Kimball, Andrew E., "Increasing the Rate of Return in Mail Surveys," *Journal of Marketing, 25,* 1961, pp. 63–64 **(M)**

Kinard, A. J., "Randomizing Error in Multiple-Choice Questions," *Journal of Advertising Psychology, 47,* 1963, pp. 223–224 **(M)**

Kish, Leslie, "A Procedure for Objective Respondent Selection Within the Household," *Journal of American Statistical Association, 44,* 1949, pp. 380–387 **(M)**

Kivlin, Joseph, "Contributions to the Study of Mail-Back Bias," *Rural Sociology, 30,* 1965, pp. 322–326 **(M)**

Klecka, William R. and Alfred J. Tuchfarber, Jr., "Random Digit Dialing as an Efficient Method for Political Polling," *Georgia Political Science Association Journal, 2,* 1, 1974, pp. 133–151 **(T)**

Knox, John B., "Maximizing Responses to Mail Questionnaires: A New Technique," *Public Opinion Quarterly, 15,* 1951, pp. 366–367 **(M)**

Kraut, Allen I., Alan D. Wolfson, and Alan Rothenberg, "Some Effects of Position on Opinion Survey Items," *Journal of Applied Psychology, 60,* 1975, pp. 774–776 **(M)**

Krotki, Karol J. and Bonnie Fox, "Randomized Response Technique, the Interview, and the Self-Administered Questionnaire: An Empirical Comparison of Fertility Reports," *Proceedings of the Social Statistics Section,* American Statistical Association, 1974, pp. 367–371 **(M)**

Larson, O. N., "The Comparative Validity of Telephone and Face-to-Face Interviews in the Measurement of Message Diffusion from Leaflets," *American Sociological Review, 17,* 1952, pp. 471–476 **(T)**

Laurent, Andre, "Effects on Question Length on Reporting Behavior in the Survey Interview," *Journal of the American Statistical Association, 67,* 1972, pp. 298–305 **(T)**

Lawson, Faith, "Varying Group Responses to Postal Questionnaires," *Public Opinion Quarterly, 13,* 1949, pp. 114–116 **(M)**

Lazarsfeld, P. F., "The Use of Mail Questionnaires to Ascertain the Relative Popularity of Network Stations in Family Listening Surveys," *Journal of Applied Psychology, 24,* 1940, pp. 802–816 **(M)**

Lehman, E. C., Jr., "Tests of Significance and Partial Returns to Mailed Questionnaires," *Rural Sociology, 28,* 1963, pp. 284–289 **(M)**

Le Roux, A. A., "A Method of Detecting Errors of Classification by Respondents to Postal Enquiries," *Journal of Applied Statistics, 17,* 1968, pp. 64–69 **(M)**

Leuthold, David A. and Raymond T. Scheele, "Patterns of Bias in Samples Based on Telephone

Directories," *Public Opinion Quarterly, 35,* 1971, pp. 249–257 **(T)**

Levine, Sol and Gerald Gordon, "Maximizing Returns on Mail Questionnaires," *Public Opinion Quarterly, 22,* 1958, pp. 568–575 **(M)**

Linksy, Arnold, "A Factorial Experiment in Inducing Response to Mail Questionnaires," *Sociology and Social Research, 49,* 1965, pp. 183–189 **(M)**

Linksy, Arnold S., "Stimulating Responses to Mailed Questionnaires: A Review," *Public Opinion Quarterly, 39,* 1975, pp. 82–101 **(M)**

Lipstein, Benjamin, "In Defense of Small Samples," *Journal of Advertising Research, 15,* 1975, pp. 33–40 **(G)**

Locander, William, Seymour Sudman, and Normal Bradburn, "An Investigation of Methods, Threat and the Response Distortion," *Journal of the American Statistical Association, 71,* 1976, pp. 269–275 **(G)**

Locander, William B. and John P. Burton, "The Effect of Question Form on Gathering Income Data by Telephone," *Journal of Marketing Research, 13,* 1976, pp. 189–192 **(T)**

Longworth, Donald S., "Use of a Mail Questionnaire," *American Sociological Review, 18,* 1953, pp. 310–313 **(M)**

Lundberg, George A. and Otto N. Larson, "Characteristics of Hard-to-Reach Individuals in Field Surveys," *Public Opinion Quarterly, 13,* 1949, pp. 487–494 **(G)**

Magid, Franklin, Nicholas G. Fotion, and David Gold, "A Mail Questionnaire Adjunct to the Interview," *Public Opinion Quarterly, 26,* 1962, pp. 111–114 **(M)**

Mandell, Lewis, "When to Weight: Determining Nonresponse Bias in Survey Data," *Public Opinion Quarterly, 38,* 1974, pp. 247–252 **(G)**

Manfield, Manuel L., "A Pattern of Response to Mail Surveys," *Public Opinion Quarterly, 12,* 1948, pp. 493–495 **(M)**

Manfield, Manuel, Letter to the editor commenting on an article by Faith Lawson, *Public Opinion Quarterly, 13,* 1949, pp. 563–564 **(M)**

Marquis, Kent H., Charles F. Cannell and Andre Laurent, "Reporting for Health Events in Household Interviews: Effect of Reinforcement, Question Length, and Reinterviews," *Vital and Health Statistics* (Washington D.C.: U.S. Government Printing Office, 1972), National Center for Health Statistics, DHEW Publication No. 1000, Series 2, No. 45 **(G)**

Mason, Ward S., Robert J. Dressel and Robert K. Bain, "An Experimental Study of Factors Affecting Response to a Mail Survey of Beginning Teachers," *Public Opinion Quarterly, 25,* 1961, pp. 296–299 **(M)**

Matteson, Michael T., "Type of Transmittal Letter and Questionnaire Color as Two Variables Influencing Response Rates in a Mail Survey," *Journal of Applied Psychology, 59,* 1974, pp. 535–536 **(M)**

Mayer, Charles S. and Robert W. Pratt, Jr., "A Note on Nonresponse in a Mail Survey," *Public Opinion Quarterly, 30,* 1966/1967, pp. 637–646 **(M)**

Mayer, Edward N., Jr., "Postage Stamps Do Affect the Results of Your Mailing," *Printers Ink, 17,* 1946, p. 91 **(M)**

McDonagh, Edward C. and A. Leon Rosenblum, "A Comparison of Mailed Questionnaires and Subsequent Structured Interviews," *Public Opinion Quarterly, 29,* 1965, pp. 131–136 **(M)**

McNemar, Quinn, "Opinion-Attitude Methodology," *Psychological Bulletin, 43,* 1946, pp. 289–374 **(M)**

Mercer, Jane R. and Edgar W. Butler, "Disengagement of the Aged Population and Response Differentials in Survey Research," *Social Forces, 46,* 1967/1968, pp. 89–96 **(M)**

Metzner, Helen and Floyd Mann, "Effects of Grouping Related Questions in Questionnaires," *Public Opinion Quarterly, 17,* 1953, pp. 136–141 **(G)**

Miller, Frank B., "Resistentialism in Applied Social Research," *Human Organization, 12,* 1954, pp. 5–8 **(M)**

Miller, J. T., "Better Results from Mail Surveys," *Public Opinion Quarterly, 18,* 1954, p. 439 **(M)**

Mitchell, G. H. and E. M. Rogers, "Telephone Interviewing," *Journal of Farm Economics, 40,* 1958, pp. 743–747 **(T)**

Mitchell, Walter, Jr., "Factors Affecting the Rate of Return on Mailed Questionnaires," *Journal of American Statistical Association, 34,* 1939, pp. 683–692 **(M)**

Mooney, H. William, Beatrice R. Pollack, and Leslie Corsa, Jr., "Use of Telephone Interviewing to Study Human Reproduction," *Public Health Reports, 83,* 1968, pp. 1049–1060 **(T)**

Moore, C. C., "Increasing the Returns from Questionnaires," *Journal of Educational Research, 35,* 1941, pp. 138–141 **(M)**

Morgan, Roy, "A Note on Question Wording," *Public Opinion Quarterly, 12,* 1948, p. 328 **(G)**

Morgan, Roy, "Follow-up Letters Disclose Trends Following Opinion Surveys," *Public Opinion Quarterly, 13,* 1949, pp. 686–688 **(G)**

Murphy, D. R., "Test Proves Short Sentences and Words Get Best Readership," *Printers Ink, 18,* 1947, pp. 61–64 **(G)**

Murphy, D. R., "How Plain Talk Increased Readership 45% to 66%," *Printers Ink, 20,* 1947, pp. 35–37 **(G)**

Myers, James H. and Arne F. Haug, "How a Preliminary Letter Affects Mail Survey Returns and Costs," *Journal of Advertising Research, 9,* 1969, pp. 37–39 **(M)**

Namias, Jean, "Measuring Variation in Interviewer Performance," *Journal of Advertising Research, 6,* 1966, pp. 8–12 **(G)**

National Education Association, "The Questionnaire," *National Education Association Research Bulletin, 8,* 1930, pp. 1–51 **(M)**

Neter, John and Joseph Waksberg, "A Study of Response Errors in Expenditures Data from Household Interviews," *Journal of American Statistical Association, 59,* 1964, pp. 18–55 **(G)** **(G)**

Nevin, John R. and Neil M. Ford, "Effects of a Deadline and a Veiled Threat on Mail Survey Responses," *Journal of Applied Psychology, 61,* 1976, pp. 116–118 **(M)**

Nichols, Robert C. and Mary Alice Meyer, "Timing Postcard Follow-ups in Mail Questionnaire Surveys," *Public Opinion Quarterly, 30,* 1966/1967, pp. 306–307 **(M)**

Nixon, John E., "The Mechanics of Questionnaire Construction," *Journal of Educational Research, 47,* 1953, pp. 481–487 **(G)**

Noelle-Neumann, Elisabeth, "Wanted: Rules for Wording Structured Questionnaires," *Public Opinion Quarterly, 34,* 1970/1971, pp. 191–201 **(G)**

Norman, Ralph D., "A Review of Some Problems Related to the Mail Questionnaire Technique," *Educational and Psychological Measurement, 8,* 1948, pp. 235–247 **(M)**

Nuckols, Robert C., "Personal Interviews Versus Mail Panel Survey," *Journal of Marketing Research, 1,* 1964, pp. 11–16 **(M)**

Nye, F. Ivan and Alan E. Bayer, "Some Recent Trends in Family Research," *Social Forces, 41,* 1962/1963, pp. 290–301 **(G)**

Oakes, Ralph H., "Differences in Responsiveness in Telephone vs. Personal Interviews," *Journal of Marketing, 19,* 1954, p. 169 **(T)**

O'Dell, William F., "Personal Interviews or Mail Panels," *Journal of Marketing, 26,* 1962, pp. 34–39 **(M)**

Ognibene, Peter, "Traits Affecting Questionnaire Response," *Journal of Advertising Research, 10,* 1970, pp. 18–20 **(MT)**

O'Neill, Harry W., "Response Style Influence in Public Opinion Surveys," *Public Opinion Quarterly, 31,* 1967, pp. 95–102 **(MT)**

Orr, David B. and Clinton A. Neyman, Jr., "Considerations, Costs, and Returns in a Large-Scale Follow-up Study," *Journal of Educational Research, 58,* 1965, pp. 373–378 **(M)**

Pace, C. Robert, "Factors Influencing Questionnaire Returns from Former University Students," *Journal of Applied Psychology, 23,* 1939, pp. 388–397 **(M)**

Parry, Hugh J. and Helen M. Crossley, "Validity of Responses to Survey Questions," *Public Opinion Quarterly, 14,* 1950, pp. 61–80 **(G)**

Parten, Mildred, *Surveys, Polls, and Samples,* Chapter 11, "Mail Questionnaire Procedures" (New York, Harper, 1950) pp. 383–402, **(M)**

Payne, Stanley L., "Case Study in Question Complexity," *Public Opinion Quarterly, 13,* 1949, pp. 653–658 **(G)**

Payne, Stanley L., "Respondents or Contestants by Mail," *Public Opinion Quarterly, 14,* 1950, pp. 550–551 **(M)**

Payne, Stanley L., "Thoughts About Meaningless Questions," *Public Opinion Quarterly, 14,* 1950, pp. 687–696 **(G)**

Payne, Stanley L., "Some Advantages of Telephone Surveys," *Journal of Marketing, 20,* 1956, pp. 278–280 **(T)**

Payne, Stanley L., "Combination of Survey Methods," *Journal of Marketing Research, 1,* 1964, pp. 61–62 **(MT)**

Payne, Stanley L., "Are Open-Ended Questions Worth the Effort?" *Journal of Marketing Research, 2,* 1965, pp. 417–418 **(G)**

Pearlin, Leonard I., "The Appeals of Anonymity in Questionnaire Response," *Public Opinion Quarterly, 25,* 1961, pp. 640–647 **(G)**

Permut, Steven E., Allen J. Michel, and Monica Joseph, "The Researcher's Sample: A Review of the Choice of Respondents in Marketing Research," *Journal of Marketing Research, 13,* 1976, pp. 278–283 **(G)**

Perreault, William D., Jr., "Controlling Order-Effect Bias," *Public Opinion Quarterly, 39,* 1975/1976, pp. 544–551 **(G)**

Perrin, E. M., "You're Right, Mr. Eastman: Mail Questionnaires Aren't Worth Their Salt," *Printers Ink, Feb. 1945, pp. 102–106* **(M)**

Perry, Joseph B., "A Note on the Use of Telephone Directories as a Sample Source," *Public Opinion Quarterly, 32,* 1968, pp. 691–695 **(T)**

Phillips, Derek L. and Kevin J. Clancy, "Some Effect of 'Social Desirability' in Survey Studies," *American Journal of Sociology, 77,* 1972, pp. 921–940 **(T)**

Phillips, W. M., "Weaknesses of the Mail Questionnaire," *Sociology and Social Research, 35,* 1951, pp. 260–267 **(M)**

Plog, Stanley C., "Explanations for a High Return Rate on a Mail Questionnaire," *Public Opinion Quarterly, 27,* 1963, pp. 297–298 **(M)**

Politz, A. and W. Simmons, "An Attempt to Get the 'Not at Homes' into the Sample Without Call Backs," *Journal of American Statistical Association, 44,* 1949, pp. 9–31 **(G)**

Price, D. O., "On the Use of Stamped Return Envelopes with Mail Questionnaires," *American*

Sociological Review, 15, 1950 pp. 672–673 **(M)**

Pucel, David J., Howard F. Nelson, and David N. Wheeler, "Questionnaire Follow-up Returns as a Function of Incentives and Responder Characteristics," *Vocational Guidance Quarterly, 19,* 1971, pp. 188–193 **(M)**

Reeder, Leo G., "Mailed Questionnaires in Longitudinal Health Studies: The Problem of Maintaining and Maximizing Response," *Journal of Health and Human Behavior, 1,* 1960, pp. 123–129 **(M)**

Reid, Seerley, "Respondents and Non-Respondents to Mail Questionnaires," *Educational Research Bulletin, 21,* 1942, pp. 87–96 **(MT)**

Reinmuth, James E. and Michael D. Geurts, "The Collection of Sensitive Information Using a Two-Stage, Randomized Response Model," *Journal of Marketing Research, 12,* 1975, pp. 402–407 **(G)**

Reuss, Carl F., "Differences Between Persons Responding and Not Responding to a Mailed Questionnaire," *American Sociological Review, 8,* 1943, pp. 433–438 **(M)**

Robin, Stanley S., "A Procedure for Securing Returns to Mail Questionnaires," *Sociology and Social Research, 50,* 1965, pp. 24–35 **(M)**

Robinson, R. A., "Five Features Helped This Questionnaire Pull From 60% to 70%!" *Printers Ink,* Feb. 22, 1946, pp. 25–26 **(M)**

Robinson, R. A. and Phillip Agisim, "Making Mail Surveys More Reliable," *Journal of Marketing, 15,* 1951, pp. 415–424 **(M)**

Robinson, R. A., "How to Design a Mail Survey," *Printers Ink,* June 6, 1952, pp. 27–29 **(M)**

Robinson R. A., "How to Boost Returns from Mail Surveys," *Printers Ink,* June 6, 1952, pp. 35–37 **(M)**

Roeher, G. Allan, "Effective Techniques in Increasing Response to Mailed Questionnaires," *Public Opinion Quarterly, 27,* 1963, pp. 299–302 **(M)**

Rogers, Theresa F., "Interviews by Telephone and In Person: Quality of Responses and Field Performance," *Public Opinion Quarterly, 40,* 1976, pp. 51–65 **(T)**

Rollins, M., "The Practical Use of Repeated Questionnaire Waves," *Journal of Applied Psychology, 24,* 1940, pp. 770–772 **(M)**

Roper, Elmo, "Sampling Public Opinion," *Journal of American Statistical Association, 35,* 1940, pp. 325–334 **(G)**

Rorer, L. G., "The Great Response-Style Myth," *Psychological Bulletin, 63,* 1965, pp. 129–156 **(MT)**

Roscoe, A. Marvin, Dorothy Lang, and Jagdish N. Sheth, "Follow-up Methods, Questionnaire Length, and Market Differences in Mail Surveys," *Journal of Marketing Research, 39,* 1975, pp. 20–27 **(M)**

Rosen, H. and Ruth Rosen, "The Validity of 'Undecided' Answers in Questionnaire Responses," *Journal of Applied Psychology, 39,* 1955, pp. 178–181 **(M)**

Rosenau, James N., "Meticulousness as a Factor in the Response to Mail Questionnaires," *Public Opinion Quarterly, 28,* 1964 pp. 312–314 **(M)**

Roslow, S., W. H. Wulfeck, and P. G. Corby, "Consumer and Opinion Research: Experimental Studies on the Forms of Questions," *Journal of Applied Psychology, 24,* 1940, pp. 334–346 **(G)**

Ross, H. Lawrence, "The Inaccessible Respondent: A Note on Privacy in City and Country," *Public Opinion Quarterly, 27,* 1963, pp. 269–275 **(G)**

Ruckmick, Christian A., "The Uses and Abuses of the Questionnaire Procedure," *Journal of*

Applied Psychology, 14, 1930, pp. 32–41 **(M)**

Rugg, Donald, "Experiments in Wording Questions: II," *Public Opinion Quarterly, 5,* 1941, pp. 91–92 **(G)**

Salisbury, Philip, "18 Elements of Danger in Making Mail Surveys," *Sales Management, 42,* 1938, pp. 28ff **(M)**

Schiller, Herbert I., "Polls Are Prostitutes for the Establishment," *Psychology Today, 6,* July 1972, p. 20 **(G)**

Schmiedeskamp, Jay W., "Reinterviews by Telephone," *Journal of Marketing, 26,* 1962, pp. 28–34 **(MT)**

Schreider, E. M., "Dirty Data in Britain and the USA: The Reliability of 'Invariant' Characteristics Reported in Surveys," *Public Opinion Quarterly, 39,* 1975/1976, pp. 493–506 **(G)**

Schuman, Howard and Otis Dudley Duncan, "Chapter 9—Questions About Attitude Survey Questions," in Herbert L. Costner (Ed.), *Sociological Methodology,* (San Francisco, Jossey-Bass, 1974), pp. 232–251 **(G)**

Schwirian, Kent P. and Harry R. Blaine, "Questionnaire-Return Bias in the Study of Blue-Collar Workers," *Public Opinion Quarterly, 30,* 1966, pp. 656–663 **(M)**

Scott, Christopher, "Research in Mail Surveys," *Journal of Royal Statistical Society,* Series A, *124,* 1961, pp. 143–205 **(M)**

Scott, F. G., "Mail Questionnaires Used in a Study of Older Women," *Sociology and Social Research, 41,* 1957, pp. 281–284 **(M)**

Seitz, R. M., "How Mail Surveys May be Made to Pay," *Printers Ink,* Dec. 1, 1944, pp. 17–19ff **(M)**

Sergean, R., "The Response of Industrial Firms to an Approach by Letter Questionnaire," *Occupational Psychology, 32,* 1958, pp. 73–85 **(M)**

Sessions, Frank Q., Robert J. Epley, and Edward O. Moe, "The Development, Reliability, and Validity of an All-Purpose Optical Scanner Questionnaire Form," *Public Opinion Quarterly, 30,* 1966/1967, pp. 423–428 **(G)**

Sewell, William H. and Vimal P. Shah, "Socioeconomic Status, Intelligence, and the Attainment of High Education," *Sociology of Education, 40,* 1967, pp. 1–23 **(MT)**

Sharp, Harry, "The Mail Questionnaire as a Supplement to the Personal Interview" (a letter to the editor), *American Sociological Review, 20,* 1955, p. 718 **(M)**

Sheppard D., "Immersion Cleaning: Its Results on Farms," *Dairy Industries, 24,* 1959, pp. 259–261 **(M)**

Sheth, Jagdish N. and A. Marvin Roscoe, Jr., "Impact of Questionnaire Length, Follow-up Methods, and Geographical Location on Response Rate to a Mail Survey," *Journal of Applied Psychology, 60,* 1975, pp. 252–254 **(M)**

Shuttleworth, F. K., "A Study of Questionnaire Technique," *Journal of Educational Psychology, 22,* 1931, pp. 652–658 **(M)**

Shuttleworth, F. K., "Sampling Errors Involved in Incomplete Returns to Mail Questionnaires," *Journal of Applied Psychology, 25,* 1941, pp. 588–591 **(M)**

Simon, Raymond, "Responses to Personal and Form Letters in Mail Surveys," *Journal of Advertising Research, 7,* 1967, pp. 28–30 **(M)**

Sirken M. G., J. W. Pifer, and M. L. Brown, "Survey Procedures for Supplementing Mortality Statistics," *American Journal of Public Health, 50,* 1960, pp. 1753–1764 **(M)**

Sirkin, Monroe G. and Morton L. Brown, "Quality of Data Elicited by Successive Mailings in Mail Surveys," American Statistical Association, *Proceedings of the Social Statistics Section,* 1962, pp. 118–125 **(M)**

Sjoberg, Gideon, "A Questionnaire on Questionnaires," *Public Opinion Quarterly, 18,* 1954, pp. 423–427 **(G)**

Sletto, Raymond F., "Pretesting of Questionnaires," *American Sociological Review, 5,* 1940, pp. 193–200 **(M)**

Slocum, W. L., T. Empey, and H. S. Swanson, "Increasing Response to Questionnaires and Structured Interviews," *American Sociological Review, 21,* 1956, pp. 221–225 **(MT)**

Smith, Edward M. and Wendell Hewett, "The Value of a Preliminary Letter in Postal Survey Response," *Journal of the Market Research Society, 14,* 1972, pp. 141–151 **(M)**

Smith, L. L., W. T. Federer, and D. Raghavara, "A Comparison of Three Techniques for Eliciting Answers to Sensitive Questions," BU-525-M, *Mimeo Series, Biometrics Unit,* Cornell University, Ithaca, N.Y. **(G)**

Stafford, James E., "Influence of Preliminary Contact on Mail Returns," *Journal of Marketing Research, 3,* 1966, p. 410–411 **(MT)**

Stanton, Frank, "Notes on the Validity of Mail Questionnaire Returns," *Journal of Applied Psychology, 23,* 1939, pp. 95–104 **(M)**

Stephen, Frederick F., "Advances in Survey Methods and Measurement Techniques," *Public Opinion Quarterly, 21,* 1957, pp. 79–90 **(G)**

Stevens, Robert E., "Does Precoding Mail Questionnaires Affect Response Rates?" *Public Opinion Quarterly, 38,* 1974/1975, pp. 621–622 **(M)**

Stock, J. Stevens, "How to Improve Samples Based on Telephone Listings," *Journal of Advertising Research, 2,* 1962, pp. 50–51 **(G)**

Suchman, Edward A. and Boyd McCandless, "Who Answers Questionnaires?" *Journal of Applied Psychology, 24,* 1940, pp. 758–769 **(MT)**

Suchman, Edward A., "An Analysis of 'Bias' in Survey Research," *Public Opinion Quarterly, 26,* 1962, pp. 102–111 **(G)**

Sudman, Seymour, Andrew Greeley, and Leonard Pinto, "The Effectiveness of Self-Administered Questionnaires," *Journal of Marketing Research, 2,* 1965, pp. 293–297 **(MT)**

Sudman, Seymour, "New Approaches to Control of Interviewing Costs," *Journal of Marketing Research, 3,* 1966, pp. 56–61 **(G)**

Sudman, Seymour, "New Uses of Telephone Methods in Survey Research," *Journal of Marketing Research, 3,* 1966, pp. 163–167 **(T)**

Sudman, Seymour, "Qualifying Interviewer Quality," *Public Opinion Quarterly, 30,* 1966, pp. 664–667 **(G)**

Sudman, Seymour, "The Uses of Telephone Directories for Survey Sampling," *Journal of Marketing Research, 10,* 1973, pp. 204–207 **(T)**

Sudman, Seymour, "Sample Surveys," in *Annual Review of Sociology,* Vol. 2 (Palo Alto: Annual Reviews, 1976), pp. 107–120 **(MT)**

Szilagyi, Andrew D. and Henry P. Sims, Jr., "Cross-Sample of the Supervisory Behavior Description Questionnaire," *Journal of Applied Psychology, 59,* 1974, pp. 767–770 **(G)**

Tallent, Normal and William J. Reiss, "A Note on an Unusually High Rate of Returns for a Mail Questionnaire," *Public Opinion Quarterly, 23,* 1959, pp. 579–581 **(M)**

Tauber, Edward M., "Predictive Validity in Consumer Research," *Journal of Advertising Research, 15,* 1975, pp. 59–64 **(G)**

Terris, Fay, "Are Poll Questions Too Difficult?" *Public Opinion Quarterly, 13,* 1949, pp. 314–319 **(G)**

Toops, H. A., "The Returns from Follow-Up Letters to Questionnaires," *Journal of Applied Psychology, 10,* 1926, pp. 92–101 **(M)**

Toops, H. A., "The Factor of Mechanical Arrangement and Typography in Questionnaires," *Journal of Applied Psychology, 21,* 1937, pp. 225–229 **(G)**

Toops, H. A., "Coding Questionnaires," in *Encyclopedia of Educational Research* (New York: Macmillan, 1950), pp. 218–220 **(G)**

Troldahl, Verling C. and Roy E. Carter, Jr., "Random Selection of Respondents Within Households in Phone Surveys," *Journal of Marketing Research, 1,* 1964, pp. 71–76 **(T)**

Veiga, John F., "Getting the Mail Questionnaire Returned: Some Practical Research Considerations," *Journal of Applied Psychology, 59,* 1974, pp. 217–218 **(M)**

Vincent, Clark E., "Socioeconomic Status and Familial Variables in Mail Questionnaire Responses," *American Journal of Sociology, 69,* 1964, pp. 647–653 **(M)**

Waisanen, F. B., "A Note on the Response to a Mailed Questionnaire," *Public Opinion Quarterly, 18,* 1954, pp. 210–212 **(MT)**

Wallace, David, "Mail Questionnaires Can Produce Good Samples of Homogeneous Groups," *Journal of Marketing, 12,* 1947, pp. 53–60 **(M)**

Wallace D., "A Case For and Against Mail Questionnaires," *Public Opinion Quarterly, 18,* 1954, pp. 40–52 **(M)**

Watson, John J., "Improving the Response Rate in Mail Research," *Journal of Advertising Research, 5,* 1965, pp. 48–50 **(M)**

Wayne, Ivor, "Nonresponse, Sample Size, and the Allocation of Resources," *Public Opinion Quarterly, 39,* 1975, pp. 557–562 **(G)**

Weaver, Charles N., Sandra L. Holmes, and Norval D. Glenn, "Some Characteristics of Inaccessible Respondents in a Telephone Survey," *Journal of Applied Psychology, 60,* 1975, pp. 260–262 **(T)**

Weilbacher, William M. and Robert H. Walsh, "Mail Questionnaires and the Personalized Letter of Transmittal," *Journal of Marketing, 16,* 1952, pp. 331–336 **(M)**

Weiss, Robert W., "Effect of Social-Desirability Set in Responding to Questionnaires on Ethnic Stereotypes," *Psychological Reports, 36,* 1975, pp. 247–252 **(M)**

Weitz, Joseph, "Verbal and Pictorial Questionnaires in Market Research," *Journal of Applied Psychology, 34,* 1950, pp. 363–366 **(G)**

Welch, Susan, "Sampling by Referral in a Dispersed Population," *Public Opinion Quarterly, 39,* 1975, pp. 237–245 **(G)**

Wells, William D., "The Influence of Yeasaying Response Style," *Journal of Advertising Research, 1,* 1961, pp. 1–12 **(G)**

Wells, W. D., "How Chronic Over-Claimers Distort Survey Findings," *Journal of Advertising Research, 3,* 1963, pp. 8–18 **(G)**

Wheatley, John J., "Self-Administered Written Questionnaires or Telephone Interviews?" *Journal of Marketing Research, 10,* 1973, pp. 94–96 **(MT)**

Whitmore, William J., "Mail Survey Premiums and Response Bias," *Journal of Marketing Research, 13,* 1976, pp. 46–50 **(M)**

Williams, Thomas Rhys, "A Critique of Some Assumptions of Social Survey Research," *Public Opinion Quarterly, 23,* 1959, pp. 55–62 **(G)**

Wiseman, Frederick, "Methodological Bias in Public Opinion Surveys," *Public Opinion Quarterly, 36,* 1972, pp. 105–108 **(MT)**

Wiseman, Frederick, "A Reassessment of the Effects of Personalization on Response Patterns in Mail Surveys," *Journal of Marketing Research, 13,* 1976, pp. 110–111 **(M)**

Wotruba, Thomas R., "Monetary Inducements and Mail Questionnaire Response," *Journal of Marketing Research, 3,* 1966, pp. 398–399 **(M)**

Zimmer, H., "Validity of Extrapolating Nonresponse Bias From Mail Questionnaire Follow-Ups," *Journal of Applied Psychology, 40,* 1956, pp. 117–121 **(M)**

BOOKS

Adams, J. Stacy, *Interviewing Procedures: A Manual for Survey Interviewers,* (Chapel Hill, N.C.: University of North Carolina Press, 1958).

Babbie, Earl R., *The Practice of Social Research* (Belmont, Calif.: Wadsworth, 1975).

Backstrom, Charles H. and Gerald D. Hursh, *Survey Research* (Evanston: Northwestern University Press, 1963).

Berdie, Douglas R. and John F. Anderson, *Questionnaires: Design and Use* (Metuchen, N.J.: Scarecrow, 1974).

Converse, Jean M. and Howard Schuman, *Conversations at Random: Survey Research as Interviewers See It* (New York: John Wiley, 1974).

Davis, James A., "Are Surveys Any Good, and If So, For What?" in H. Wallace Sinaiko and Laurie A. Broedling (Eds.), *Perspectives on Attitude Assessment: Surveys and Their Alternatives* (Champaign, Ill.: Pendilon, 1976).

Erdos, Paul L., *Professional Mail Surveys* (New York: McGraw-Hill, 1970).

Forcese, Dennis P. and Stephen Richer, *Social Research Methods* (Englewood Cliffs, N.J.: Prentice-Hall, 1973).

Green, Paul E. and Donald S. Tull, *Research for Marketing Decisions* (Englewood Cliffs, N.J.: Prentice-Hall, 1966), Chapter 5, "Information from Respondents," pp. 119–148.

Green, Paul E. and Donald S. Tull, *Research for Marketing Decisions* (Englewood Cliffs, N.J.: Prentice-Hall, 1966), Chapter 6, "The Means of Obtaining Information from Respondents," pp. 149–182.

Hyman, Herbert H., *Survey Design and Analysis* (Glencoe, Ill.: Free Press, 1955).

Kerlinger, Fred N., *Foundations of Behavioral Research* (New York: Holt, Rinehart, and Winston, 1965).

Kish, Leslie, *Survey Sampling* (New York: John Wiley, 1965).

Lewis, George H., *Fist-Fights in the Kitchen. Manners and Methods in Social Research,* (Pacific Palisades, Calif.: Goodyear, 1965).

Matarazzo, Joseph D. and Arthur N. Wiens, *The Interview: Research on Its Anatomy and Structure* (Chicago: Aldine-Atherton, 1972).

Miller, Delbert, *Handbook of Research Design and Social Measurement,* 2nd ed. (New York: David McKay, 1970).

Moser, C. A. and G. Kalton, *Survey Methods in Social Investigation* (New York: Basic Books, 1972), pp. 175, 238–240, 256–269, and 303–349.

National Center for Health Services Research, *Advances in Health Survey Research Methods: Proceedings of a National Invitational Conference,* May 1–2, 1975, DHEW Publication No. (HRA) 77-3154.

Oppenheim, A. N., *Questionnaire Design and Attitude Measurement* (New York: Basic Books, 1966).

Parten, Mildren, *Surveys, Polls, and Samples,* (New York: Harper and Row, 1950).

Payne, Stanley, *The Art of Asking Questions* (Princeton, N.J.: Princeton University Press, 1951).

Reichard, Robert S., *Practical Techniques of Sales Forecasting* (New York: McGraw-Hill, 1966), Chapter 14, "Other Techniques—Combination Forecasts," pp. 188–204.

Sackman, Harold, *Delphi Critique: Expert Opinion, Forecasting, and Group Process* (Lexington, Mass.: Lexington Press, 1975).

Sellitz, C., M. Jahoda, M. Deutsch, and S..Cook, *Research Methods in Social Relations* (Chicago: Holt, Rinehart, Winston, 1959), "Data Collection: II," pp. 236–263.

Stewart, Charles J. and William B. Cash, *Interviewing: Principles and Practices* (Dubuque, Iowa: W. C. Brown, 1974).

Sudman, Seymour and Norman M. Bradburn, *Response Effects in Surveys: A Review and Synthesis* (Chicago: Aldine, 1974).

Sudman, Seymour, *Reducing the Costs of Surveys,* (Chicago: Aldine, 1967).

Sudman, Seymour, *Applied Sampling* (New York: Academic, 1976).

Survey Research Center, *Interviewer's Manual: Revised Edition* (Ann Arbor: University of Michigan, Survey Research Center, Institute for Social Research, 1976).

Uhl, Kenneth P. and Bertram Schoner, *Marketing Research: Information Systems and Decision Making* (New York: John Wiley, 1969), Chapter 10, "Securing Information from Respondent," pp. 292–329.

Warwick, Donald P. and Charles A. Lininger, *The Sample Survey: Theory and Practice* (New York: McGraw-Hill, 1975).

Wasson, Chester R., *The Strategy of Marketing Research* (New York: Appleton-Century-Crofts, 1964), Chapter 5, "Descriptive Research: Observational and Survey Methods," pp. 130–164.

AUTHOR INDEX

TOPIC INDEX